Notes of a Witness

Notes of a Witness

Laos and the Second Indochinese War

Marek Thee

Random House   New York

Library of Congress Cataloging in Publication Data

Gdański, Marek.
  Notes of a witness.

  Includes bibliographical references.
  *1. Vietnamese Conflict, 1961– —Laos. 2. Vietnamese Conflict, 1961– —United
States. 3. Laos—Politics and government. I. Title.*
DS557.A64L35 1973   959.704'33594   72-8766
ISBN 0-394-46836-8

Manufactured in the United States of America

98765432

Contents

Preface

This book is a personal fragmentary account of my Indochina experience. It focuses particularly on my tenure with the International Commission for Supervision and Control in Laos during the fateful years of the Kennedy administration. Though the book tries to view the Indochina developments as a coherent whole, it concentrates mainly on Laotian events in 1961–1962, with special attention to great-power interaction and local political dynamics. It is a study of a crucial stage in the conflict, reflecting its general trends and patterns.

In search of better understanding and historical judgment I consulted many published sources: documents, memoirs and reports.* But the bulk of material in this book consists of notes I made on the spot summing up daily events, conversations and discussions. Part of these notes found their way into regular reports to my superiors. Being a historian by education, I had a feeling of historicity and the exceptional nature of occurrences. But then my vantage point and perspective were unique. I found myself almost right on the battle line, with the opportunity to speak to both the local actors and the diplomatic representatives of all the great powers. Of special value were my close contacts with the revolutionary Left in Indochina, and the representatives of the Eastern powers. Hence, to some extent I could see things in the making. As a member of the Control Commission I myself had a role to perform, but little could be done in the actual circumstances. More and more I became preoccupied with the drama as a whole. Well aware of the dangers of keeping notes in such a situation, I could nevertheless not resist the temptation.

My purpose now is to offer through this eyewitness account a

*The Pentagon Papers were released after I delivered the manuscript to the publisher. A note on the Papers appears as Appendix 1.

modest contribution to the understanding of the Indochina conflict. I might as well indulge in the illusion that this account could help advance peace research on the nature of contemporary international relations and local conflicts. But I am conscious of many subjective judgments contained in the book, and also of the fact that we still do not know enough about many essential aspects of the Indochina wars. I would therefore be grateful for any comments and constructive criticism of my presentation, and would at the same time hope that more research on Indochina could bring into relief the lessons needed for peaceful change in contemporary world affairs.

This book was written while I was a research fellow at the International Peace Research Institute, Oslo (PRIO), and the value-loaded atmosphere of this institute in many ways influenced my work. I am indebted to the whole PRIO staff as a collective, and to every one of my colleagues at the Institute. I owe special gratitude to Johan Galtung and Ingrid Eide who generously extended a helping hand to me and my family at exceptional hard moments, and from whom I learned so much. My sincere thanks go also to the Norwegian Council for Conflict and Peace Research, which has financed my stay at PRIO. Needless to say, I alone am responsible for the views expressed.

I received encouragement from many friends. In particular, I am grateful for encouragement and succor to Berenice A. Carroll of the Conference on Peace Research in History; to I. F. Stone, whose personal insistence served as a special inspiration, as well as to Jason Epstein of Random House, who was most helpful in suggesting the framework of the book. My deep gratitude goes to John Cohen, who edited the manuscript with great understanding and expenditure of time and energy; to Susan Høivik who read the manuscript at PRIO; and to Janet Kafka, who prepared the book for publication.

Finally, I am indebted to many friends dispersed in various corners of the world. I feel profound gratitude first of all to my Laotian and Vietnamese friends who received me warmly, offered confidence and gave the primary understanding of Indochinese realities and the nature of their struggle. I recall also with pleasure the numerous friendships entered into while I was staying with the

Control Commission in Indochina—Indians, Canadians, Poles—
who showed good will in their work and cordiality in private
relations.

For nearly two decades I have been living with Indochinese
affairs and my house resounds with Indochinese echoes. The understanding, forbearance and encouragement I received from my
wife, Erna, and my two daughters, Maya and Halina, have been
of invaluable assistance in writing this book.

M.T.
Olso, Spring 1972

Notes of a Witness

Chapter 1

Background on Laos

Laos, ancient Lan Xang, the Kingdom of a Million Elephants, lies in the heart of the Indochina Peninsula, cut off from the sea and surrounded by five countries: Vietnam, Thailand, China, Burma and Cambodia. Its location has cast it both in the role of buffer between contending neighbors and empires and as a battlefield for expansionist schemes. Again and again this location has drawn Laos into the foreground of conflict in Indochina.

Laos has a surface area of 91,425 square miles, more than both North and South Korea. It is an oblong enclave with a spadelike head turned northwards, 60 miles wide at its narrowest point, 300 at its widest, and 650 miles long. It indents deep into China and Vietnam in the north and east, and into Thailand in the west. Its borders extend over 3,186 miles—1,319 miles with Vietnam (1,018 North and 301 South), 1,090 with Thailand, 366 with Cambodia, 264 with China and 147 with Burma. Sloping from high mountains in the north and east (with peaks from 5,000 to 9,000 feet), through vast central plateaus (3,500 to 4,500 feet), it reaches down to the fertile Mekong Valley in the east. The Mekong, Asia's fourth-longest river, flows a thousand miles through Laos, half of it forming the border with Thailand; its majestic waters constitute Laos's main axis. On its banks nestle the country's major cities, including the small, colorful royal capital, Luang Prabang, in the north, and the administrative capital, Vientiane, just across from Thailand.

Temperature and humidity vary considerably according to latitude and altitude, but life is generally regulated by the tropic monsoon cycle. The dry season lasts from November to April, the rainy season from May to October. Even military activity has followed this cycle, the dry season favoring the land operations of the mobile, lightly armed Pathet Lao and Vietnamese forces, the rainy season offering greater advantages to the much better equipped, air-supplied, U.S.-backed government and mercenary troops.

Most of Laos is covered by dense jungle. There is no railway, and the Mekong is only partially navigable. France left only about 1,500 miles of roads, and hardly any of these were uninterruptedly passable in the rainy season. For strategic reasons, this mileage has been doubled in recent years, yet interprovincial communication still has to be maintained largely by air—a very limited and expensive link. In the mid-fifties Laotians joked that there were only three roads which the Royal Government cared about: the King's road, leading from Luang Prabang to Vientiane and the Thai border, which the King used when going to France; the Prime Minister's road, leading from Vientiane to Prince Souvanna Phouma's residence at Nong Thevada; and the road of the Minister of the Interior, leading from Vientiane to Nhouy Abhay's country house on the way to Paksane.

Laos is underpopulated, a rare situation in Asia. Exact population figures do not exist, as an accurate census has never been taken, but there are probably about three million people in Laos. Some Laotians estimate the population at five or six million; they attribute the lower figures to French poll taxes that Laotians tried to avoid paying by claiming small families. Most Laotians live in the river valleys, mainly along the Mekong, but the population is unevenly distributed. This uneven distribution has been exaggerated greatly by the war, especially by the heavy U.S. bombing. Whole areas have been depopulated, and refugees have been forced from the countryside, which is controlled by the Pathet Lao, to the cities (mainly Vientiane), which remain in the hands of the Royal Government.

The Laotian population exhibits great ethnic diversity, but it is possible to distinguish three main groups: the Thai-Lao group, commonly known as the Lao Loum (Valley Lao), the members of which constitute a slight majority; and two minority groups, the Indonesian and Mon Khmer group commonly known as Khas (savages or slaves) or Lao Theung (Highland Lao), and the Sinitic and Tibeto-Burman group commonly called the Lao Soung (Mountaintop Lao).

The Lao Theung are descendants of the oldest inhabitants of the country. In the ancient pre-Christian era they developed a lively culture, to which many iron, bronze and pottery objects, as well as the famous stone containers on the Plain of Jars, still bear witness. During the sixth or seventh century, Lao Loum coming in from the southern provinces of China drove the Lao Theung to the lower parts of the mountains; there the Lao Theung were first called Khas. At present, they are mostly concentrated in middle and lower Laos; the ethnic Lao—the Lao Loum—have occupied the valleys, mainly along the Mekong. The Lao Loum came under the influence of the Khmer and Indian cultures, and in the fourteenth century embraced Theravada Buddhism as a state religion.

The Lao Soung began to migrate to Laos from South China early in the eighteenth century, settling on the mountains and hilltops of northern Laos. The most numerous and best-known Lao Soung tribe are the Meo, a group that came to Laos in the middle of the nineteenth century.

Apart from these three main ethnic groups there are also fairly large foreign colonies in the cities of Laos. Large Vietnamese and Chinese communities deal in trade and crafts;

there are a small number of Indian and Pakistani merchants; a constant flow of Thais serves as a labor force and a source of mercenaries. And finally there is the European colony, several thousand strong—mainly French and American— linked more or less to political and military operations.

Despite their different cultural backgrounds, the main ethnic groups of Laos have achieved a certain rapprochement during recent decades. To be sure, this has been a difficult process, especially considering the *divide et impera* policy pursued by the French and exacerbated by CIA activities among the minorities. But emergence from colonialist oppression, modernization trends, new social mobility and a common striving for freedom have contributed to assimilation and to greater closeness. A basic impulse in this direction came from a conscious policy on the part of the Laotian Left. Relying heavily on minority cadres, and having their main bases in regions inhabited by minorities, the Pathet Lao have devoted considerable effort to harmonizing relations between nationalities. As a rule, there has been more mingling between the ethnic Lao and the Lao Theung than between the Lao Soung and the other two groups. On the whole, Lao culture—representing a higher level of settled peasant economy—has become predominant; the Lao language has become generally accepted as the lingua franca.

Lao culture and values strongly reflect the Lao Buddhist way of life. This is a gentle way of living, preaching moderation in joy and sorrow, asking for humility, self-restraint, kindness, justice and charity. The Lao world is full of spirits and wandering souls *(phi)*. Everyday life is only one among thousands of incarnations in which a person reaps the fruits of his past existences; at the end of this series of rebirths is *nirvana,* the final redemption. Each individual is thus responsible for himself, shaping his own destiny by means of his deeds; salvation depends upon his own behavior. It is a deeply human, just, and conscientious philosophy. It asks to avoid conflict and preaches respect for all life. It invites men to acquire virtue and merit.

The bearers of the Lao Buddhist tradition are the bonzes —the ascetic Buddhist monks. Laos is the land of bonzes. Every young Lao is supposed to join the ranks of novices in the pagodas, shave his head and eyebrows, put on a saffron gown and live on charity, spend time in meditation and learning—a kind of alternative youth service. There are over twenty thousand bonzes in Laos, and they constitute a highly influential spiritual elite with its own organization which parallels that of the state bureaucracy. Village bonzes are subordinated to district councils that in turn are guided by a central state council of bonzes headed by the King of Bonzes, who resides in Luang Prabang. A rival sect of Thai bonzes implanted in Laos in the early forties tried to undermine this organization, and the war has contributed to this process. Yet Buddhism remains one of the chief sources of Lao identity and spiritual strength.

Laos is an underdeveloped agricultural country; the majority of the population used to maintain a subsistence economy producing almost everything they needed, from food to cloth and tools. In prewar times about 90 percent of the population lived off the land, tilling rice fields in the water-rich valleys or growing rice in burnt-out clearings on uplands and hillsides. Although the per capita gross national product was low—far less than one hundred dollars yearly —it was sufficient. War conditions, especially U.S. bombardments, have destroyed this economy. High enlistment into the armed forces, the eradication of whole villages, and the dislocation of a high percentage of the peasantry have so critically cut basic food production that instead of exporting food products, Laos has been obliged to import even rice. The Royal Government's deficit has been covered by the main war entrepreneur—the United States—but in 1968, excluding war materials, imports amounted to $42,000,000 while exports were only $2,800,000.*

Lao agriculture also produced maize, sweet potatoes, cassava, and a large variety of fruit—bananas, tangerines, coconuts, mangoes and others. Industrial crops included cotton, tobacco, cardamom, coffee and tea, grown mainly on the fertile Bolovens Plateau in the south. An important income crop of opium poppies was grown in the uplands and mountains; in the mid-sixties the opium crop was estimated at 1,500 tons yearly. Crops were supplemented by stock-breeding and fishing. Domesticated animals—buffalo, oxen, pigs and chickens—were popular, and pasture land abounded. Almost every village kept a herd of buffalo; sometimes they roamed the forests.

Laos has a high industrial potential. One of its natural treasures is its wood. Two-thirds of the country is covered by forest, much of which—teak, hardwoods, ebony—is of export value. Forests also provide bamboo, rattan and other fiber plants, and various chemicals. Though barely explored and largely unexploited, mineral resources are also said to be rich: tin, iron, coal, lead, copper, gold, silver, sulphur and— some suspect—oil. The French exploited only tin, producing 1,000 tons yearly. Generally France kept Laos as a kind of natural resources reserve. Large-scale exploitation would have necessitated investment and the development of a com-

---

*According to a 1966 report prepared for USAID (U.S. Agency for International Development) Laos had: one of the world's lowest gross national products—$77 per capita yearly; the lowest highway density, 0.1 kilometer per square kilometer; one of the lowest levels of electric power consumption, 2.9 kilowatt-hours per person; one of the highest illiteracy rates, 85 percent; one of the lowest life expectancies in Southeast Asia, thirty years. Out of the entire population, only about 300,000 people actually earned and spent money. Most of the country's economy was on the subsistence level. To this it may be added that, beginning in the mid-fifties, 95 percent of the country's administrative and military budgets were covered by U.S. funds. U.S. military aid to Laos came to the highest per capita American foreign assistance anywhere in the world.

munications network with links to ports in neighboring countries, which was inconceivable as long as Indochina was not fully subdued. Incessant warfare in recent decades has continued to make economic development impossible. While war profiteers have become rich overnight, the vast majority of the Laotian population is more impoverished than ever.

Historical Evolution

The Kingdom of Laos emerged as a united country in the fourteenth century. Its capital was Luang Prabang, and the king's authority stretched far on both sides of the Mekong. For 350 years the kingdom of Lan Xang's influence grew. But in the beginning of the eighteenth century dynastic quarrels undermined the kingdom's cohesion, and Lan Xang split into the kingdoms of Luang Prabang in the north, Vientiane in the middle, and Champassak in the south; meanwhile the principality of Xieng Khouang, in the northeastern part of the country, steered toward autonomy.

Laotian lands came under increasing pressure from Siam (Thailand) in the west and Annam (Vietnam) in the east. In 1778 Vientiane was sacked and plundered by the Siamese, and for a while at the beginning of the nineteenth century Laotian kings and princes paid double tribute—both to Bangkok and to the Emperor of Annam. In 1828 Vientiane was plundered agian by the Siamese; after this the Kingdom of Vientiane ceased to exist, and Siam extended its power to the left bank of the Mekong. Laos was reduced to the relatively autonomous Kingdom of Luang Prabang, which paid homage to Siam. Champassak was annexed by Siam, Xieng Khouang by Annam.

In the last quarter of the nineteenth century Laos came under the influence of the increasing southeast Asian rivalry between Great Britain, expanding eastward through Siam, and France, pushing westward through Vietnam. In 1893

France, having conquered Vietnam and Cambodia, occupied the left bank of the Mekong and forced Siam to recognize the Mekong boundary. This marked a turning point in Franco-British rivalries; in 1904 the Franco-British convention delimited respective zones of influence. Except for two narrow strips of land—the province of Sayaboury in upper Laos and right-bank Champassak in the south—vast Laotian lands on the right bank of the Mekong, with a large Lao population, were incorporated into Thailand.

France's colonial rule of Laos lasted over fifty years, until the end of World War II. During this time Laos stagnated economically and culturally. Except for small numbers of the town population, illiteracy was the rule; during French rule only ten Laotians graduated from high schools in France and Hanoi. Repressive measures provoked continuous unrest. There were several armed uprisings, including the 1901 peasant insurrection of the Savannakhet, Thakhek and Saravane populations, under Pho Ka Duat, against forced labor and heavy taxes; the prolonged revolt of the Lao Theung tribes in the Bolovens and southern Laos (1910–36) under the leadership of Ong Keo and Ong Kommadam; the Meo uprising under Tiao Pha Patchay (1918–22), which spread through the provinces of Xieng Khouang, Sam Neua and Luang Prabang; and the 1934–35 movement protesting economic hardships, which spread through the cities of the Mekong, including Vientiane, and was crushed with a heavy hand by the French.

During World War II the Japanese occupation of Indochina weakened the French grip; in a desperate effort the French themselves called on Laotian nationalism to counter Japanese political infiltration. But Japan finally ousted the French administration in the coup of March 9, 1945; and Japan's surrender the following August gave further impetus to the Laotian independence movement.

The central Laotian personality at that moment was

Prince Phetsarath, hereditary viceroy and premier of the Luang Prabang Kingdom, residing in Vientiane.* He took over leadership of the Lao Issara, the Free Laos movement, prevented the French from regaining power after the Japanese surrender, and declared the unification of the kingdoms of Luang Prabang and Champassak. On October 12, 1945, he formed a Lao Issara government headed by Prince Phaya Khammao, the governor of the province of Vientiane. This government proclaimed the independence of Laos. France, however, refused to recognize the new state. Taking advantage of the preliminary convention signed in Hanoi with the government of Ho Chi Minh on March 6, 1946, France sent an expeditionary force to Laos and brutally crushed Laotian resistance. The Lao Issara government took refuge in Bangkok.

Between 1946 and 1954 developments in Laos paralleled the course of the First Indochina War. In response to nationalist pressures, France was obliged to grant Laos ever greater self-government—internal autonomy in August 1946, and formal independence within the framework of the French Union in July 1949. In October 1953 France and the Royal Government signed a treaty of friendship and association confirming Laos's sovereignty. The 1946 treaty was accompanied by a secret protocol by which the heir to Champassak, Prince Boun Oum (no relation to the royal family in Luang Prabang) renounced his rights to the Kingdom of Champassak, in this way recognizing the unity of Laos under the king of Luang Prabang. Yet the fate of Laos was not decided in Paris, nor in Luang Prabang, nor Vientiane. It was determined by the course of the Indochinese war, and by the

---

*Prince Phetsarath and his two younger brothers, princes Souvanna Phouma and Souphanouvong—who became his close collaborators in the Lao Issara movement—were descendants of the vanguard line of the Luang Prabang royal family. They were cousins of the reigning king of Luang Prabang, Sisavang Vong, and are uncles of the present king of Laos, Savang Vatthana, the son of Sisavang Vong.

emergence of a Laotian liberation movement, the Pathet Lao, headed by Prince Souphanouvong.

The 1954 Geneva agreements, which ended the First Indochina War, assigned the "fighting units of the Pathet Lao" two northern provinces, Sam Neua and Phong Saly, as assembly areas—"pending a political settlement" (Article 14). French rule in Laos ended; but France was replaced by the United States, which was critical of the Geneva agreements. On January 1, 1955, the United States Operation Mission (USOM) opened its offices in Vientiane and, step by step, the Royal Government was reduced to a tame client of Washington. Appearing in Vientiane in February 1955, John Foster Dulles proclaimed the protection of Laos under SEATO and set out to convert the country into "a bastion of the free world" on the borders of China and Vietnam. Internal political pressures compelled Vientiane leaders to revert for a short time to the Geneva accords, to seek a political settlement with the Laotian Left, and to accept neutrality in foreign affairs. But the government of national union formed in 1957 with the participation of the Pathet Lao lasted only a few months. The government was toppled, the Geneva agreements were discarded, Pathet Lao leaders were jailed, and in the process rightist militarists headed by CIA strongman General Phoumi Nosavan took power.

This situation was responsible for a resurgence of Laotian national feelings. Guerrilla activities, which had ceased for the duration of the government of national union, began again, the Pathet Lao leaders broke out of prison, and in August 1960 the rightist regime was overthrown by a neutralist coup d'état led by Kong Le. The coup was greeted with enthusiasm and Prince Souvanna Phouma, Prime Minister in the first government of national union, was once again called upon to head a cabinet under the banner of peace and neutrality. But neutrality was not acceptable to the United States. Enjoying active U.S. support, Nosavan staged an armed rebellion and set off a new, large-scale civil war. By the spring of 1961, the war was in full swing, with the allied Pathet Lao and neutralist forces, in control of two-thirds of the country, on the offensive.

Laos, Spring 1961

By the time John F. Kennedy was inaugurated in January 1961, the Laotian civil war had become one of the major preoccupations of the world's great powers. On March 23, Kennedy devoted an entire press conference to the Laotian crisis, saying that in his "last conversation with General Eisenhower, the day before the inauguration, on January 19, we spent more time on this hard matter than on any other thing. And since then it has been steadily before the Administration as the most immediate of the problems that we found upon taking office."[1]

Eisenhower had considered Laos to be of crucial importance. Summarizing his views at an emergency White House meeting on December 31, 1960, he had said, "We cannot let Laos fall to the Communists even if we have to fight—with our allies or without them"; and he approved the secret use of the U.S. and Thai air forces in the civil war.[2]

Kennedy was no less firm than Eisenhower. While he indicated a willingness to begin "constructive negotiations" ("If in the past there has been any possible ground for misunderstanding of our desire for a truly neutral Laos, there should be none now."), he committed himself "to honor its [America's] obligations to the point that freedom and security of the free world and ourselves may be achieved . . . No one should doubt our resolution . . . The security of all Southeast Asia will be endangered if Laos loses its neutral independence. Its own safety runs with the safety of us all."

Kennedy presented Laos as a testing ground: "This is a critical area, and I think the kind of response that we get to our efforts for peace in this area will tell us something about what kind of a future our world is going to have."[3] Meanwhile he alerted U.S. land, air and naval forces in a wide arc stretching from Japan and Okinawa up to Thailand and Laos, and "preparations were initiated for a seventeen-part plan of increasing military action, moving from military advisers to a token unit to all-out force."[4] Nixon urged Kennedy toward an immediate "commitment of American air power" in Laos,[5] and the use of tactical and strategic nuclear weapons was considered.

Thus, amazingly, events in a tiny, underpopulated, jungle-covered, landlocked, unexplored country on the Indochinese Peninsula suddenly weighed critically on the fate of all mankind. Through some mysterious quid pro quo in the decision-making process, Laos had attained a prominence no student of international affairs otherwise would have dreamed possible. Even taking into account its potential value as a land-bridge from Thailand, Cambodia and South Vietnam to Burma, China and North Vietnam, the importance attributed to Laos seemed grossly exaggerated: events there presented an extreme example of the unconstrained use of the ambiguous notion of "national interest."

Yet just when it seemed that the war might escalate to a much more dangerous level, new developments counseled prudence and restraint. Defiant and cocksure after their conquest of Vientiane, Laos's administrative capital, the U.S.-supported rightist forces suffered a string of defeats. France and Britain, allies in SEATO, remained reluctant to take part in any military intervention. And in mid-April the United States was defeated and exposed at the Bay of Pigs in Cuba. All this continued to turn U.S. policy toward negotiation.

On April 24, 1961, the Soviet Union and Great Britain, Co-chairmen of the 1954 Geneva conference on Indochina, announced the reconvening and reactivation in Laos of the ICSC (the International Commission for Supervision and

Control), suspended *sine die* since July 1958. The ICSC's reactivation, produced through strenuous behind-the-scenes diplomatic negotiations, was part of a framework of international compromise which included 1) an appeal to the parties in Laos to cease hostilities; 2) a note to the government of India, as chairman of the ICSC, to reactivate the commission; and 3) an invitation to fourteen countries—including the five great powers, all the neighbors of Laos, and the three members of the ICSC (India, Canada, Poland)—to a conference on the settlement of the Laotian problem, to be opened on May 12, 1961, in Geneva. This was only the second time that the United States had agreed to participate in a conference that included the People's Republic of China. The first had also been at Geneva, in 1954.

Chapter 2

Moscow, Washington, and Peking

On the evening of April 24, 1961, an advance party of Polish diplomats involved in the reactivation of the International Commission for Supervision and Control (ICSC) in Laos, arrived in Moscow on their way to New Delhi and Indochina. Jerzy Michalowski, director general of the Polish Ministry of Foreign Affairs, led the party. With him were the commissioner-designate to Laos, Ambassador Albert Morski; myself, an alternate delegate with the rank of minister plenipotentiary; military and legal advisers, some administrative staff and other personnel.

Michalowski was only to attend the discussions in Moscow and participate in the inaugural meetings of the ICSC in New Delhi; I was to proceed with Morski to Laos. Although Morski had had peace-keeping experience as head of the Polish delegation to the cease-fire commission in Korea, Indochina was a new field for him. On the other hand this was my third mission to Vietnam and Laos: in 1955 I had stayed nine months in Hanoi and Saigon as counselor of the Polish delegation and head of the Saigon Office, and in 1956–57 I had been assigned to Laos as Polish commissioner to the ICSC.

The morning after our arrival in Moscow, the senior members of our group were invited to the Soviet Ministry of Foreign Affairs for consultations. Soviet Deputy Foreign

Minister Georgi M. Pushkin presided over the meeting. The atmosphere was intense and marked by a sense of urgency. Recognizing the seriousness of the situation, the Soviet Union was bent on avoiding military confrontation with the United States. At the beginning of December 1960, Moscow had begun extending military aid to the government of Prince Souvanna Phouma, then recognized generally by West and East. But the military measures taken by the Eisenhower and Kennedy administrations, together with their contingency plans, frightened Soviet leaders. Their principal desire was for a political settlement, and they were ready to make concessions in favor of middle-of-the-road forces at the expense of the Left. Khrushchev feared that the local conflict might be transformed into a world power struggle.

Soviet leadership had interpreted the November 1960 declaration of the Moscow conference of eighty-one communist and workers' parties as a victory for the Soviet line of peaceful coexistence and international understanding, even though the declaration was full of compromises. But Moscow felt in a position to impose its policy on its Asian allies. As a result, Pushkin offered our delegation a rather simplistic formula for the initial tasks of the Commission: after landing in Laos we were to contact the parties and arrange an effective cease-fire. Lines dividing the hostile groups were to be fixed and controls instituted. In the meantime the Geneva conference would start work on a political settlement; it was estimated that the conference would last no longer than six weeks.

This was pure theory—events turned out very differently and only marginal elements of the Moscow plan could be implemented. The Soviet leadership's notions about the conflict seemed no less distorted than the Americans'. Both focused on power relations and disregarded local forces. The Soviet leadership was concerned mainly with relations with the United States and China, and because its attention was focused in these directions it had insufficient knowledge of actual conditions inside Laos. Significantly, our hosts in Moscow did not invite representatives from Peking, Hanoi or the Pathet Lao/Neo Lao Haksat to our consultations.* Nor had the Soviet government held preliminary discussions about the commission's tasks with the Vietnamese or Laotians; otherwise Moscow could not have held such a mistaken understanding of field realities. Moscow had consulted with an official Laotian delegation headed by Prince Souvanna Phouma during the previous week, when the leader of the Neo Lao Haksat, Prince Souphanouvong, was also in Moscow. But talks then centered on broader issues—the diplomatic scene, the forthcoming Geneva conference, and aid for Laos. Commission activity and local strategy in Laos were left untouched.

In general, this situation reflected the growing mistrust between Moscow and Peking, as well as the Soviet Ministry of Foreign Affairs' mistaken confidence that events could be manipulated according to Moscow's point of view. These delusions must have begun to fade in early May, when a Chinese delegation headed by Deputy Premier and Foreign Minister Chen Yi arrived in Moscow en route to Geneva. Chen Yi was very definite: conditions in Southeast Asia did not yet allow for stabilization and final settlement. The Left in Laos had gained great victories, but those victories were not yet solid, and the United States was not yet reconciled to defeat. Thus it would be necessary to continue the political and military struggle. Vigilance and readiness for action were still required. This had been the lesson of Korea, Vietnam and China. It was necessary to strive for a settlement that would take advantage of the existing situation, enable

*The Pathet Lao (Land of Laos) was created in the second half of the 1940's as a resistance movement against the French. The movement was reconstituted at a national congress in January 1956 as the Neo Lao Haksat (Lao Patriotic Front). However, the popular name Pathet Lao is still widely used.

the forces of the Laotian Left to rally, mobilize the masses, liquidate enemy bands in the rear, and strengthen points of resistance. The ideal solution would include both preservation of the Pathet Lao's territorial autonomy and military independence, and the formation of a coalition government. Neither the full unification of Laos under Souvanna Phouma, nor its division, was acceptable. Both would tie the hands of the Pathet Lao. The main enemy was the United States, bent on aggression: there could be no final solution in Indochina as long as the United States maintained a military presence there.*

Wars of National Liberation

Khrushchev had explained Soviet strategy and general thinking in a speech given on January 6, 1961.† An ardent plea in the dispute with China, the speech dealt with the results of the November 1960 conference, and emphasized that the prime task of the moment was the prevention of a new world war. He devoted special attention to the issue of wars of national liberation, as it was relevant to the main current of the Soviet-Chinese controversy; but, characteristically, he subordinated it to the general problem of war and peace.

Khrushchev explicitly distinguished three categories of war: "world war, local war, and wars of liberation or popular uprising."‡ These distinctions, he said, were necessary "in

*This information was recorded in an internal Soviet summary. In line with the view outlined above, and expecting long and hard bargaining at the conference table, the Chinese brought to Geneva a large delegation and made arrangements for a prolonged stay.

†At a general meeting of the party organizations of the Central Committee of the Higher Party School, the Academy of Social Sciences, and the Institute of Marxism–Leninism of the Central Committee. For an excerpt from this speech see Appendix 4.

‡The version of Khrushchev's speech in *American Foreign Policy—Current Documents* erroneously translates "liberation wars" and "popular

order to work out the proper tactics in regard to each." After such an introduction, Marxists would expect exact definitions of each category, including especially an elaboration of those characteristics which draw the dividing line between local wars and wars of national liberation. But Khrushchev preferred to keep to description. While lacking theoretical precision, this method had the double advantage of justifying his policy and allowing him to appear a fervent revolutionary.

Khrushchev warned against world wars. Communists, he said, were the most resolute opponents of such wars, especially in modern conditions, when war between capitalist countries is not as likely as war between capitalist and socialist countries, particularly the Soviet Union, the most powerful socialist country. One could not exclude the possibility of world war, but "now that there is a mighty socialist camp with powerful armed forces, the peoples can undoubtedly prevent war and thus ensure peaceful coexistence, provided they rally all their forces for an active struggle against the bellicose imperialists." His emphasis was on preventing war and ensuring peaceful coexistence.

Khrushchev linked local wars to the current world situation, characterized by nuclear balance: "Some of the imperialist groups fear that a world war might end in the complete destruction of capitalism, and are laying their stakes on local wars." He implied that the main characteristic of local wars was aggression started locally against a weaker party or defenseless nation. Significantly, Khrushchev referred to local wars only in the past or future tense: his assumption was that at the moment there were no local wars in progress. However, local wars can be very dangerous: "A small-scale imperialist war, no matter which of the imperialists starts it,

uprisings" as separate categories. The translation of the same phrase in the British *Documents on International Affairs* reads "wars of liberation or popular uprisings."

may develop into a world thermonuclear missile war. We must, therefore, fight against world wars and against local wars." Khrushchev cited only one example of a local war: "the aggression of Britain, France and Israel against Egypt." He used this example to show how Soviet diplomacy was decisive in bringing the war to an end.

Finally, Khrushchev developed the theme of wars of national liberation. The main characteristic of such wars is popular uprising linked to a colonial background.

> These uprisings cannot be identified with wars between countries, with local wars, because the insurgent people fight for the right of self-determination, for their social and independent national development; these uprisings are directed against corrupt reactionary regimes, against the colonialists. The Communists support just wars of this kind wholeheartedly and without reservations, and march in the van of the peoples fighting for liberation.

As examples of wars of national liberation he listed the armed struggle of the Vietnamese people against France,* the Algerian war, and the Cuban revolution. Except for the Algerian war, Khrushchev did not qualify any current conflict as a war of national liberation. He did not refer in any context to the Laotian conflict, the most dangerous war at the moment, nor did he mention the expanding uprising in South Vietnam.

Khrushchev carefully omitted conflicts involving the United States, and was reluctant to define the escalating fighting in Indochina as a war of national liberation. He stressed that: "The U.S. imperialists though eager to help the

---

*Khrushchev used the wording "armed struggle waged by the people of Vietnam." The following context made it clear, however, that he referred to only the First Indochinese War, against France. The *American Foreign Policy* documentation series even carries the footnote, "See *American Foreign Policy 1950–1955.*"

French colonialists in every way, did not venture to intervene directly in the war in Vietnam . . . Batista was a puppet of the United States, and the United States helped him actively. However, the U.S.A. did not directly intervene with its armed forces in the Cuban war."

The speech leaves no doubt. Khrushchev persistently tried to avoid confrontation with the United States, in local wars or in wars of national liberation. None of his descriptions fitted the Laotian situation. If anything, the Laotian conflict —with open U.S. military intervention—could be categorized as close to a local war. The November 1960 declaration had explicitly listed it as a local war unleashed by the imperialists. Given all the inherent dangers, Krushchev seemed to imply that the need for a peaceful solution was paramount.

In his conclusions Khrushchev offered a passionate defense of peaceful coexistence. "Mankind has arrived at the stage in history when it is able to solve problems that were too much for previous generations to solve." He envisaged the victory of socialism on a world scale as "inevitable by virtue of the laws of history," and added: "Wars between countries are not needed for this victory." The first to suffer in the event of war, Khrushchev said, would be "the working people and their vanguard—the working class." The only alternative was peaceful coexistence.

Clearly, these statements were part of the ideological debate with China. Contrary to tendencies in Peking, Khrushchev strongly opposed a militant line in Indochina, and he adhered to this policy until the moment of his removal from office. Having in mind the American adversary, he argued strongly against military undertakings in Vietnam and Laos, particularly in South Vietnam, and refused to increase Soviet military aid to Vietnam above the normal supplies. He became so disappointed with developments in Indochina that he considered complete disengagement. In a move toward that end, he threatened in July 1964 that the Soviet Union would withdraw as Co-chairman of the Geneva conference.

The arguments Khrushchev developed in his January speech were in line with his search for a dialogue and an understanding with the United States—or, as he put it, with those ruling circles in the imperialist camp "which understand how dangerous a new war is for capitalism itself." Those circles included both Eisenhower and Kennedy. After the Camp David talks, Khrushchev described Eisenhower as a statesman who "sincerely wants to liquidate the cold war and improve relations between our countries." It was this pursuit of an understanding with the United States which made Khrushchev so suspect in the eyes of the Chinese. Though the U-2 incident briefly interrupted the U.S.-Soviet dialogue, Moscow considered the change of administration from Eisenhower to the liberal-sounding Kennedy a good omen for a new rapprochement.

Underlying the Soviet attitude was a Euro-centered vision of international relations which gave preference to Europe over Asia, to the preservation of the post-World War II status quo over revolutionary change. China naturally feared that a Soviet-American dialogue developing around the European theme would mean a world strategy demanding concessions in Asia in return for the security of Soviet gains in Europe. In fact this strategy had been clearly discernible during the 1954 Geneva conference.

The reasons for Soviet involvement in Laos in the autumn of 1960 can be summed up in three points. First, the Soviet Union sought to control a crisis through which its Asian allies might draw it into a larger conflict; its aim was to stop the war from growing out of proportion or getting out of hand. Second, as in previous instances, the Soviet Union felt obliged to act because of its competitive relations with China; this was particularly important in view of the sharpening political and ideological controversy between the two countries and because of the clash at the conference of the com-

munist parties in Moscow. Soviet involvement was to serve
as evidence of active help to liberation movements and support for the vigorous language used by Khrushchev. Third,
a political-military position in Laos, while checking its own
allies, could well serve as a good bargaining card in negotiations with the United States. Involvement in Laos enhanced
the Soviet Union's international position and was a useful
asset in diplomatic play.

Misreading the Mind of the Adversary

Astoundingly enough, all this escaped detection by American political analysts. In *To Move a Nation,* Roger Hilsman
notes that President Kennedy attached considerable importance to Khrushchev's speech, and directed all members of
his new administration to read it and think about what it
portended.[1] However, the reading and the interpretation
were wrong from the outset. Washington studied the speech
in conjunction with the strategy of Mao Tse-tung, and saw
Khrushchev as reestablishing the monolithic structure of
expanding communism through passionate support of wars
of national liberation. Khrushchev's thinking was equated
with Mao Tse-tung's, and both became established reference
points for new policy studies in the White House. The general interpretation of Khrushchev's speech—as confirmed by
all the memoirs of Kennedy's close associates—was that
Khrushchev, in line with Mao's strategy, was bent upon
promoting world revolution by means of wars of national
liberation, protected by the nuclear umbrella. Although the
speech, as part of the dispute with China, was meant as a plea
for peaceful coexistence, Kennedy's inner circle interpreted
it as a political and military challenge to the United States.
     This then was a classic case of misreading the mind of the
adversary, an outstanding example of a failure of communication between contending powers. Maybe the rift between

the Soviet Union and China was still too new for its true dimensions to be clearly discerned; the fact remains that minds programmed for years in the school of cold-war thinking were beyond the exigencies of a dispassionate political analysis.

The consequences were far-reaching. The misinterpretation of Khrushchev's design set a pattern for Soviet-U.S. relations for years to come, urged the United States deeper than ever into the Indochina conflict, and helped to bring about a fundamental change in U.S. military and political strategy. The Kennedy administration moved toward a build-up of conventional and counterinsurgency forces, with Indochina as the main target. No later clarifications could reverse the trend. Kennedy was so perturbed by his notion that Khrushchev intended to promote wars of national liberation that he opened the June 1961 summit meeting at Vienna with a grim warning that neither side should try to upset the world balance of power by backing such wars. This inopportune beginning provoked Khrushchev into ideological debate; he felt obliged to put forward forcefully the case for communism.

But it seems clear that Khrushchev did not associate his arguments with anything happening in Indochina. When Kennedy raised the question of Laos concretely, agreement for an effective cease-fire was quickly achieved; in fact, this was the only accord reached in Vienna. Describing the Vienna meeting in a television speech on June 15, 1961, Khrushchev stressed the accord on the Laotian problem, and did not refer to local wars or wars of national liberation at all. He simply said that the situation was extremely dangerous for world peace and that a solution must be sought within the framework of peaceful coexistence. A few days before the summit meeting, Kennedy had told De Gaulle that the United States was bent on turning Indochina into an anticommunist bulwark; more and more, Washington was

becoming obsessed with counterinsurgency and Indochina.[2]
As luck would have it, the Kennedy administration was
blessed with a most dynamic Secretary of Defense, and his
success in the implementation of the new strategy intensified
and magnified the blunders of the policy-makers. Describing
Khrushchev's speech as "one of the most important speeches
on Communist strategy of recent decades," McNamara revealed in March 1964 that in order to meet the challenge:
"Within the past three years we have increased the number
of our combat-ready Army divisions by about forty-five percent, tactical air squadrons by thirty percent, airlift capabilities by seventy-five percent, with a hundred-percent increase
in ship construction and conversion." In order to be better
equipped "against what the Communists call 'wars of liberation,' or what is properly called covert aggression or insurgency, we have therefore undertaken and continue to press
a variety of programs to develop skilled specialists, equipment, and techniques to enable us to help our allies counter
the threat of insurgency."[3] Thus, decisions based on ideological confusion were put into practice, and mistakes and mis-
conceptions were multiplied. The road of "creeping engagement" in Vietnam and the Second Indochina War widened.

Peking's Strategy

From its own perspective, Peking developed a different
strategy to deal with the new situation, and U.S. involvement
in Indochina strengthened Peking's convictions. China
shared over two hundred miles of border with Laos, and the
intruder in Laos, as seen from Peking, was the same enemy
China faced all around its eastern and southern borders—the
United States. For China, Laos presented a vital national
security issue—national security, not ideology, provided the
real motive for China's policy.

Due to these considerations Peking was careful not to get

actively involved in the conflict, and to some extent was content to see the Soviet Union confront the United States. China did not want a bigger war, inherited from the Korean War, to develop on its borders; but because of the U.S. military presence in Indochina, Chinese leaders treated any American pronouncements on peace with deep mistrust. At the same time, Peking became more and more suspicious of Soviet intentions. Khrushchev's statements and behavior led the Chinese to wonder if Moscow did not feel that as a superpower it had more in common with the United States than with China. It seemed that Moscow had opted for the status quo and had concluded that more interests united the Soviet Union and the United States than divided them. "We need nothing from the United States, and you require nothing that we have," was Khrushchev's toast at the White House dinner. Was this an allusion to China's territorial claims on the Soviet Union? Perhaps China hoped that Moscow's military engagement in Laos would hinder the Soviet-U.S. rapprochement and thus serve China's interests. Peking was convinced that the conflict would drag on, and protracted struggle was its traditional technique for defense and for progress. Thus the dispute in Indochina became the main testing ground for the Soviet-Chinese cold war. Underlying the dispute were different considerations of national security, stemming in part from geographical location. Events in the war exacerbated the controversy, and ideological semantics served only to conceal that essentially the rift derived from contradictions inherent in traditional concepts of national interest.*

*The West was very slow to perceive the extent of the Sino-Soviet rift; when it finally did, high government circles greeted it as a fortunate outcome of U.S. engagement in Indochina. But if the main U.S. goal in Indochina was to contain China, then from that perspective U.S. engagement had been counterproductive. The Chinese strategy of protracted war was meant to serve political as well as military goals. The longer the war continued, the greater the disagreements between the Soviet Union and its Asian allies. China's interests, naturally, were more convergent with the

This was a period of intermittent retreat in China's revolutionary thrusts—Peking wanted to proceed prudently. The rift with the Soviet Union had not yet fully crystallized, and Chinese strategy for the next historic phase had not yet been formulated. In addition, the failure of the "great leap forward" and agricultural setbacks of the past two years, together with the brusque withdrawal of Soviet technical experts in July 1960, created pressure for a less challenging line. Internal debate was still developing on military and economic problems, and on attitudes toward both the United States and the Soviet Union. Chinese leaders whose answer to the American threat was a speedy modernization of the army were inclined to want to come to terms with the Soviet Union; they pleaded for traditional and tested means of economic progress. Yet Mao Tse-tung did not trust the Soviet Union, and urged independence in military matters and economic self-sufficiency. He linked this with a strategy of people's war, which had proved effective in the past, and with a search for new and unorthodox ways to revolutionize the economy. However, taking into account the setback of the "great leap forward" and the still-dominant position of the Soviet Union in the communist movement, Mao decided to play for time.*

interests of the revolutionary movements on the Indochinese Peninsula than were Moscow's. Sooner or later Peking's influence had to predominate. As a result, Moscow had to become disillusioned, too. As I learned later, neither Moscow nor Peking was able to set the pace of events to their liking; neither could dictate strategy to the Left in Laos. The Indochinese Left always fought vigorously to keep its independence. Beneath their statements of revolutionary brotherhood and ideological relationship with Moscow or Peking, there always ran a strong consciousness of the real national content of the struggle.

*Chinese policy remained in flux until the escalation of the Vietnam War in 1965. This was an unexpected turn of events. Even Mao Tse-tung —as evidenced in his January 1965 interview with Edgar Snow—had not envisaged such a development. The U.S. attack on North Vietnam ignited the "cultural revolution" and led to a radical turn in Chinese policy. Certainly, other issues also stimulated Mao's urge toward social ex-

Apart from such considerations, the state of affairs in Laos also urged Peking to agree to negotiations. The *Peking Review* of March 31, 1961, pointed out that though the "military situation in Laos [was] becoming increasingly unfavorable to the Laotian [Rightist] rebel group," the war was "in danger of being extended," and "the patriotic troops and civilians of Laos still face a difficult and complex struggle in defeating the enemy's military intervention and political intrigues." Time was needed to digest what had been attained through recent victories, to consolidate the ranks, and to muster new forces.

So when the three great powers met in Geneva, they came for different reasons, with different perceptions of the conflict, and without adequate consultation with the local parties. The conference dragged on for more than fourteen months, and its few actual achievements proved totally ineffective, even after the formation of the coalition government and the signing of the agreement on neutralization. The civil war in Laos could not be isolated; it was a function of the protracted war on the entire Indochinese peninsula. Common interests in this war had forged strong alliances between the Viet Minh and the Pathet Lao, between the Neo Lao Haksat and the Democratic Republic of Vietnam. It was impossible to make peace in Laos while continuing war in Vietnam. After the signing of the Geneva agreements, there was a short lull, followed by the integration of the Laotian struggle into the Second Indochina War.

perimentation—including his passionate search for a solution to the age-old problem of the self-perpetuation of the revolutionary elite and their post-revolutionary proclivity to dogmatic recess and bureaucratic fossilization—but the outside threat was the trigger to the movement.

Chapter 3

Lost Opportunities

In 1956–57, while the Royal Government and the Pathet Lao were negotiating the so-called Vientiane agreements, J. Graham Parsons was U.S. ambassador to Laos. During this period, according to Parsons' own testimony before the House of Representatives Committee on Government Operations in 1959, he "struggled for sixteen months to prevent a coalition" government with the participation of the Pathet Lao. This and later experience caused Prince Souvanna Phouma, who was Prime Minister, to call Parsons "the ignominious architect of a disastrous American policy towards Laos." I met Parsons often. To me it seemed clear that he did not have enough power to shape ideas and policies of broad significance; I was sure he merely carried out a policy elaborated in Washington.

In fact, Parsons' assignment to Laos was the personal decision of Secretary Dulles' right-hand man, Far Eastern expert Walter S. Robertson, and as Sir Anthony Eden remarked in his memoirs, Robertson had such "an emotional approach" to questions concerning China and Indochina "as to be impervious to argument or indeed facts."[1] This remark not only makes it clear that Parsons probably had no choice but to unquestioningly carry out Robertson's instructions, but it may also explain more about U.S. involvement in Indochina than many efforts to rationalize the process. Cold-war zeal dominated American policy planning, and once matters had reached the stage of execution, with the military-industrial complex switched in, forces accumulating behind the already chosen policy became so strong that no administration felt capable of changing direction. It is far easier to bring a machine up to full speed than to stop it.

Roots of U.S. Involvement

In the closing years of World War II, the United States extended help to the anti-Japanese independence movement in Vietnam led by Ho Chi Minh, and Ho repaid this confidence by opening the Vietnamese Declaration of Independence with words he remembered from the American Declaration of Independence: "All men are created equal; they are endowed by the Creator with certain unalienable Rights; among these are Life, Liberty and the Pursuit of Happiness."

But by 1947 a visible change had taken place. France was in the second year of the First Indochinese War, and in Washington cooperation with France, a key ally, had high priority. That the war in Indochina was clearly a colonial war had little influence on the political considerations of a western global strategy. These were the first years of the cold war. The revolution in China was still in progress and Washington had put forward the Truman Doctrine to support "free peoples who are resisting attempted subjugation by armed minorities or by outside pressures." Beyond the merits of France's colonial struggle, the tumultuous international situation shaped the U.S.'s thinking on Indochina. This was spelled out by Dean Rusk in his testimony before the Senate Foreign Relations Committee in February 1966:

> Like so many of our problems today, the struggle in South Vietnam stems from the disruption of two world wars. The

Second World War completed a process begun by the First. It ripped apart a structure of power that had existed for a hundred years. It set in train new forces and energies that have remade the map of the world. Not only did it weaken the nations actively engaged in the fighting, but it had far-reaching secondary effects. It undermined the foundations of the colonial structures through which a handful of powers controlled one third of the world's population. And the winds of change and progress that had blown fiercely during the last twenty years have toppled those structures almost completely ... The line of policy we are following involves far more than a defense of the status quo. It seeks rather to insure that degree of security which is necessary if change and progress are to take place through consent and not through coercion.

Rusk hardly veils the United States' alignment against the anticolonial revolution.

In 1947 William C. Bullitt, the first U.S. ambassador to the Soviet Union and ambassador to France from 1936 to 1941, set out to rationalize the "free world's" interest in Indochina. In what can be termed the first blueprint for the new U.S. approach to Indochina—an article on "The Saddest War" published in *Life* in December 1947—Bullitt wrote:

Since Viet Nam is the extension of South China, Communist control of Viet Nam would add another finger to the hand Stalin is closing around China. Few Americans have forgotten that when Japan established control of the Viet Nam railroad from Hanoi to Kunming in China, we had to build the Burmese road and fly supplies "over the Hump" to help the Chinese against the Japanese invaders. We may need the Viet Nam railroad again to help China to resist another invader—the Soviet Union.

Wrong as this now appears against the background of Soviet-Chinese relations, it is still an accurate statement of

U.S. policy. In his April 1965 address at Johns Hopkins University, President Johnson insisted that "over this war— and all Asia—is another reality: the deepening shadow of Communist China." Though clouded in the sixties by the theme of freeing the Vietnamese, the basic U.S. rationalization for involvement in Indochina has always been mainland China—how best to get a foothold in Vietnam, the "railroad" to China. Bullitt had a ready answer to this question, and it too became a recurrent theme in U.S. policy: Vietnamization of the war. In Bullitt's formulation, this meant that the United States would "permit the non-Communist nationalists of Viet Nam to prepare political, economic and military organizations for control of the country." To defeat Ho Chi Minh, Bullitt bet on former emperor Bao Dai. He was, in fact, instrumental in arranging Bao Dai's return to Vietnam from his self-imposed exile in Hong Kong.

Washington's anxiety over China and Indochina in the overall strategy for the Asian mainland increased during the Korean War. As Assistant Secretary for Far Eastern Affairs William P. Bundy said, the Korean War brought "a recognition that a defense line in Asia, stated in terms of an island perimeter, did not adequately define our vital interests—that those vital interests could be affected by action in Asia itself."[2] It was necessary to move from the "island perimeter" to the continent itself, and since it is located in the so-called soft underbelly of South China, Indochina offered the best opportunity for such a move. Thus Bullitt's "railroad" concept was reinforced by new arguments for a forward Asian strategy. By the spring of 1954, the United States was covering nearly 80 percent of France's war expenditures, and it was at this time that the United States turned toward active involvement—just when the Geneva conference offered the first real opportunity for defusing the conflict.

Several factors favored a final, peaceful settlement. France was ready to disengage, the Bao Dai alternative had ended in failure, and above all, the ice of the cold war seemed to be melting. Stalin was dead, the Korean War had ended, and China was showing growing signs of a desire to concentrate on internal development and join the international community. For the first time, the United States actually met with the Chinese People's Republic, at the conference table in Geneva. And the agreements produced by the conference, though not politically precise, offered a framework for a political solution. But, as only a few knew at that time, this Geneva compromise was not to be implemented.

John Foster Dulles' Design

In the spring of 1954, Secretary of State Dulles initiated confidential negotiations between Washington, Paris and London which were aimed at internationalizing the Indochina war, saving the besieged French garrison at Dien Bien Phu, and averting negotiations by a new effort to force a military solution to the conflict. On March 29, 1954, he proposed "united action," despite all the "serious risks" involved. "Those risks," he maintained, "are far less than those that will face us a few years from now if we dare not be resolute today."[3] On April 4, President Eisenhower sent a letter to British Prime Minister Winston Churchill in which he said:

> Our painstaking search for a way out of the impasse has reluctantly forced us to the conclusion that *there is no nego-tiated solution to the Indochina problem* which in its essence would not be either a face-saving device to cover a French surrender or a face-saving device to cover a Communist retirement. The first alternative is too serious in the broad strategic implications for us and for you to be acceptable . . . Somehow we must contrive to bring about the second alternative. The preliminary lines of our thinking were

sketched out by Foster in his speech last Monday night when he said that under the conditions of today the imposition on Southeast Asia of the political system of Communist Russia and its Chinese Communist ally, by whatever means, would be a great threat to the whole free community, and that in our view this possibility should now be met by united action and not passively accepted . . . I believe that the best way to put teeth in this concept and to bring greater moral and material resources to the support of the French effort is through the establishment of a new, *ad hoc* grouping or coalition composed of nations which have a vital concern in the checking of Communist expansion in the area . . . The important thing is that the coalition must be strong and it must be willing to join the fight if necessary. [Italics added][4]

This stand against a "negotiated solution" and for "united action" to force a military solution was passed on to U. S. policy-makers throughout the fifties and sixties.

In the spring of 1954, however, neither Great Britain nor U.S. Congressional leaders—Lyndon Johnson included—were ready for military action, although Vice-President Richard Nixon, in a talk before the American Society of Newspaper Editors on April 16, called for the United States "to take the risk now by putting our boys in." France was ready to accept U.S. military intervention to save Dien Bien Phu, but was hesitant to enter a Southeast Asian military alliance for fear of harming the forthcoming Geneva negotiations. And it seems that President Eisenhower himself had serious doubts about the wisdom of military intervention. At a meeting with the Joint Chiefs of Staff on April 29, he remarked somewhat prophetically that "if the United States were, unilaterally, to permit its forces to be drawn into conflict in Indochina and in a succession of Asian wars, the end result would be to drain off our resources and to weaken our overall defensive position."[5]

Thus U.S. preparations for military action at Dien Bien

Phu—quite well worked out and, some say, including the use of nuclear weapons—were called off, and the United States bowed to the desire of Great Britain and France to try a negotiated settlement.

In Geneva, however, Dulles labored untiringly to convince his British and French colleagues that negotiations would lead nowhere, and he set special conditions for a continued U.S. stay at the conference table. He unveiled his plans on May 1 in a confidential meeting in Geneva between the leaders of the British and U.S. delegations. Dulles was assisted by Walter S. Robertson; with Anthony Eden was Lord Reading. Eden recalls the conversation as follows:

> I said that we must really see where we are going. If the Americans went into the Indo-China war, the Chinese themselves would inevitably step up their participation. The next stage would be that the Americans and the Chinese would be fighting each other and that was in all probability the beginning of the third world war.
>
> Meanwhile Mr. Robertson, whose approach to these questions is so emotional as to be impervious to argument or indeed facts, was keeping up a sort of "theme song" to the effect that there were in Indo-China some three hundred thousand men who were anxious to fight against the Vietminh and were looking to us for support and encouragement. I said that if they were so anxious to fight I could not understand why they did not do so. The Americans had put in nine times more supplies of material than the Chinese, and plenty must be available for their use. I had no faith in this eagerness of the Vietnamese to fight for Bao Dai.
>
> Our American host then introduced the topic of the training of Vietnamese forces to defend their own country. Whatever the attractions of this scheme, they admitted that it would take perhaps two years to finish. The problem was what would happen meanwhile. When Lord Reading asked Mr. Dulles what he thought about this, he replied that they

would have to hold some sort of bridgehead, as had been done in Korea until the Inchon landings could be carried out. Lord Reading commented that this meant that things would remain on the boil for several years to come, and Mr. Dulles replied that this would be a very good thing.

There was then some discursive and divergent discussion as to the resemblance of the Indo-China conflict to that of Korea. This did not advance us very much and I was not sorry when we broke up.[6]

These remarkable and far-reaching disclosures reveal a policy statement of prime purity, devoid of any diplomatic craft. The heart-to-heart talk revealed long-term intent with a precise program for immediate action. The Korean terminology and the tendency to fall back on Korean strategy were indicative of Dulles' state of mind. What he expounded was not a defensive strategy but a strategy of "roll-back" and "liberation," a strategy of keeping bridgeheads, making Inchon landings and going north—slogans so often repeated later by Diem, General Khan and General Ky. This kind of thinking also served as inspiration for efforts in Laos to subdue the Pathet Lao. It assumed that things would be kept "on the boil for several years," until a final military solution. Also, it again offered the *intermediate* policy of Vietnamization.

Dulles offered similar proposals, including the same two-year timing, to the French delegation.* Ambassador Jean Chauvel, a leading member of the French delegation, elaborating on notes he made at that time, recalls that the Secre-

---

*The question of timing became an important issue in Geneva. While Pham Van Dong demanded that the date for elections be set within six months after the execution of the cease-fire clauses, the Western powers insisted on the two-year time limit envisaged by Dulles. Not suspecting any ulterior scheme, and sure about the election results, Pham Van Dong finally yielded. Similarly, he agreed to fix the provisional demarcation line at the seventeenth parallel, and not at the thirteenth, more in accordance with the *de facto* disposition of forces.

tary of State inquired "if the forces of the French Union, by
withdrawing temporarily to the two deltas (of the Mekong
and the Red River), could, under the protection of the
American Air Force, continue for two years to maintain the
[war] machine, so as to allow the United States to relieve
them and drive the Communists back toward the north."[7]

From such proposals policy soon emerged. As revealed by
Lieutenant General James M. Gavin (a veteran of the Inchon
landing who in 1954 and 1955 was the Army's Chief of Plans
at the Pentagon), concrete plans were worked out for an
expedition which would go north in the spring of 1956,
"destroy the armies of Giap, occupy Hanoi and Haiphong,"
and even seize the Chinese island of Hainan. The plan, as
indicated by Gavin, had the approval of Secretary of Defense
Charles E. Wilson and the members of the Joint Chiefs of
Staff, except for General Matthew B. Ridgway, Chief of Staff
of the Army. General Ridgway, mindful of the Korean experience, went directly to President Eisenhower and presented
all the arguments against such an adventure. At this point,
according to Gavin, the plans were dropped.[8] But the strategic premises remained intact. They were embodied in a secret
agreement initiated by the United States and concluded by
the three Western powers on July 14, 1954, in Paris, one
week before the adoption of the Geneva agreements.

The Secret Western Understanding

The way to the Paris understanding led through two
stages. First, a seven-point Anglo-American position paper
was worked out in Washington at the end of June 1954
during a conference attended by Winston Churchill and Anthony Eden. Two weeks later, the final documents of a tripartite Anglo-American-French understanding based on the
seven points, "were put in shape, signed and exchanged after
luncheon at the American Embassy" in Paris.[9] The docu-

ments carried the signatures of John Foster Dulles, Pierre Mendès-France and Anthony Eden. Eisenhower acknowledged the Paris agreement in his memoirs, saying: "Foster succeeded in obtaining agreement to a position paper which was essentially the same as the agreement between the United Kingdom and the United States at the time of the Churchill visit."[10]

Though the full texts of the Paris agreements are still held in diplomatic archives, their general outline, as contained in the seven-point Washington understanding, was made public in 1960 in Eden's memoirs and in Jean Lacouture and Philippe Devillers' *La fin d'une guerre: Indochine 1954*. "This astounding text, which preceded the agreements of July 20," the French authors remark in a footnote, "was held in amazing secrecy: there is no better proof for the existence of a common Western doctrine."[11]

The three key points of the understanding stipulated that any agreement on Indochina should: (a) "preserve at least the southern part of Vietnam, and if possible an enclave in the delta [of the Red River in the north]; in this connection we would be unwilling to see the line of division of responsibility drawn further south than a line running generally west from Dong Hoi" (near the eighteenth parallel); (b) "not impose on Laos, Cambodia, or retained Vietnam any restrictions materially impairing their capacity to maintain stable non-Communist regimes; and especially restrictions impairing their right to maintain adequate forces for their internal security, to import arms and to employ foreign advisers"; and (c) "not contain political provisions which would risk loss of the retained area to Communist control."[12]

Also, an important part of the Washington understanding was that immediately there would be set up, without publicity, a study group which—as Eden put it—"prepared the way for SEATO."[13] Thus, SEATO was initiated while the Geneva conference was in session. On September 6, 1954, seven weeks after the conclusion of the Geneva agreements, it was officially consecrated. It was meant to provide the police force for the imposition of the Paris agreements.

A comparative study of the seven-point Paris agreement and the Geneva agreements reveals two fundamentally contradictory policies. While the Geneva agreements provide for a political solution, mentioning specifically July 1956 as a date for elections in Vietnam, the Paris document stands against any "provisions which would risk loss of the retained area to Communist control." Moreover, the Paris understanding leaves unmentioned the necessity of consulting the will of the Indochinese peoples. Instead, it retains the idea of a bridgehead preserving "at least the southern half of Vietnam, and if possible an enclave in the delta." Finally, unlike the Geneva agreements, which aimed to neutralize Indochina, the Paris agreement was based on the assumption of converting Indochina into anticommunist military bridgeheads with "adequate military forces," a sufficient supply of arms, and free "employment of foreign advisers."

What in fact has been implemented in Indochina is the Paris agreement, not the Geneva agreement. The French withdrew quickly, transferring their agencies to U.S. missions and leaving the general direction of events to the United States. Everybody including Britain as co-chairman of the Geneva conference, denied responsibility for the execution of the political clauses of the Geneva agreements. Nobody listened to Hanoi's complaints.

Foiling the First Coalition in Laos

Geneva 1954 was thus a lost opportunity for peace. As far as Laos was concerned, American determination to maintain a stable, well-armed, noncommunist regime outfitted with foreign advisers, together with the resolution that no political considerations should be allowed to endanger this regime, precluded neutralization of the country and national reconciliation with the Pathet Lao. Graham Parsons adhered to this strategy firmly.

Developments in Laos from 1956 to 1958, including the destruction of the first attempt at a government of national union, constitute a second lost opportunity for a peaceful, political solution—a lost opportunity that carried with it significant implications for the future of all of Indochina. I witnessed this crucial period, and was in Vientiane during the arduous negotiations leading to the conclusion of most of the Vientiane agreements. As I saw matters—and I was under the direct influence of Polish revulsion against Stalinism—an extremely propitious international constellation had come to coincide with real potentialities for a turn in Laos. Hopes were high not only in Laos but also in neighboring countries. The cold war was receding further and further. Ilya Ehrenburg had just published his remarkable book *The Thaw.* The Soviet Union had agreed to the neutralization of Austria and showed a readiness to proceed with far-reaching plans for disarmament. Notwithstanding the Hungarian events, a certain liberalization was being felt in Eastern Europe, particularly in Poland. In the wake of the four-power meeting in Geneva, there was a general relaxation of tension, as expressed in the phrase "Geneva spirit." "Military disengagement" became part of the European political vocabulary. Events seemed hopeful in Asia, too. The Bandung conference seemed to further the trend toward national emancipation and rapprochement. China set out to establish friendly relations with its neighbors, while internally Peking proclaimed the famous policy of "a hundred flowers."

Laos too seemed to be entering a new phase. The policy imposed after Geneva—the inclusion of Laos in the "protective orbit" of SEATO, the initiation in Vientiane of the United States Operation Mission, disregard for the "political settlement" provided for in Article 14 of the Geneva cease-fire agreement, and the efforts to reconquer by armed force the two northern provinces of Sam Neua and Phong Saly— had only exacerbated the internal conflict. When the Katay government conducted elections in December 1955 without the participation of the Pathet Lao, it could not muster a majority in the new National Assembly. But on February 28, 1956, presenting the program for his new government to the National Assembly, Prince Souvanna Phouma proposed as "preoccupation number one, the settlement of the Pathet Lao problem," and added: "This question is in fact the gravest and most urgent one posed to us. Therein lies, I am sure, our unanimous sentiment. Neither stability nor durability will be achieved as long as this mortgage [hangs over] our national life."[14]

On March 21, 1956, Souvanna Phouma formed his new government; between August 1956 and February 1957, in Vientiane, the Royal Government and the Pathet Lao carried on detailed discussions and signed seven agreements as part of a general political settlement. These agreements concerned the effective implementation of the cease-fire, promulgation of a neutral foreign policy, measures to guarantee civil rights and nondiscrimination against former resistance members, revision of the electoral law in order to make it more liberal and democratic, and the formation of a government of national union. Still open to negotiation were means for the reestablishment of the royal administration in the provinces of Sam Neua and Phong Saly, and the distribution of portfolios in the coalition government.*

The Vientiane agreements in essence meant a return to the letter and spirit of Geneva; as such, they created discontent in the United States and met with opposition in right-wing Laotian circles close to Thailand and the United States. Dissatisfaction was also expressed by British Ambassador L. G.

*See Appendix 7.

Holliday. Souvanna Phouma suspected that Parsons was mobilizing certain politicians against the continuation of the talks, and, believing that there might be some discrepancy between the attitudes of the Western powers and their local representatives, he addressed a note to the United States, Great Britain and France, in which the Royal Government expressed concern that the stand taken by Western powers toward the Vientiane agreements tended "to create uneasiness in public opinion, to hamper the delicate task of the Royal Government and, finally, to endanger the desirable settlement of the Pathet Lao problem." The note was sent on February 22, 1957, the day after the signing of the seventh Vientiane accord dealing with the revision of the electoral law.[15]

The reply was worse than might have been expected. On April 16, in a coordinated move, the United States, Great Britain and France addressed to the Royal Laotian Government identical and carefully worded notes which expressed gross disapproval of the agreements with the Pathet Lao. The notes alleged that the Pathet Lao forces "sought to place extraneous conditions upon their acceptance of the authority of the Royal Government and upon their reintegration into the national community," and called on the Royal Government to "continue in its determination that the political future of the Kingdom of Laos shall not be dictated by dissident groups enjoying no constitutional status."[16]

This was as good as demanding an end to negotiations. The exchange of notes was made public on April 25, and on the same day the U.S. embassy in Vientiane issued a communiqué trying to clarify the "extraneous conditions" referred to in the Western notes. The communiqué enumerated three specific instances: (a) The "dissident group" wanted Laos to accept "economic and other kinds of aid from the communist bloc, particularly from Communist China"; (b) "The dissident group wants representation in a coalition government"; and (c) "The Pathet Lao seeks a special kind of neutrality which would give a favored position to the communist bloc in terms of diplomatic relations."[17] Curiously enough, at that time the Royal Government did not have diplomatic relations with any of the socialist countries, nor was it ready to discuss economic aid with these countries. The Western powers objected mainly to the formation of a coalition government; to them genuine neutrality was immoral.

I was distressed by the whole development, and because I felt that the Commission's efforts to encourage a political settlement were in serious danger, I requested that the Commission accept a resolution to clarify the issues and censure the pressures brought on the Laotian government. After a prolonged discussion, such a resolution was unanimously accepted. In this resolution, dated May 16, the Commission "notes with concern and regret from its study of the situation that the Parties had encountered difficulties of various kinds, so that they have not been able to achieve a final settlement as foreseen in the Geneva Agreement." The resolution declared the Commission's conviction "that a political settlement should be achieved as a result of full and free discussions between the Parties and that in these negotiations the International Commission continues to adhere to the policy that the Parties should remain free to discuss and determine between them what is most equitable and acceptable." The Commission "noted with satisfaction" the agreements signed thus far and recommended "that the negotiations now in progress . . . should be continued with the utmost vigor in an atmosphere of existing goodwill and mutual understanding until a final settlement on all outstanding points is reached with the least possible delay."[18]

The publication of the Commission's resolutions provoked an uproar in political circles in Vientiane. Both parties expressed a willingness to adhere to the Commission's recommendations, and on May 29, the National Assembly unanimously ratified the agreements thus far signed. However, the conservative opposition, roused by high bribes and afraid that it might lose such rich income, put up growing resistance.

It occurred to me that in these circumstances it might be worthwhile to talk matters over with Parsons. I thought that somehow I might impress upon him a view more true to Laotian realities, one that might lead to a general resolution of the conflict in Indochina. On May 28 Parsons invited me to his office, a fine, air-conditioned room in the American embassy. I presented my appraisal of the struggle going on in Laos, its relation to the international scene, the possibility of peace, and the danger inherent in the continuation of a divisive policy. I hoped to make clear that a final political settlement, with the Pathet Lao absorbed into the national community and with peace reestablished on the borders of China and Vietnam, would be bound to ease international tension and should be in the long-term interest of the United States, too. Efforts to suppress the Pathet Lao would only provoke stronger resistance, and continuous strife on China's borders, with an uneasy equilibrium in Vietnam, could only have dangerous consequences.

Parsons seemed to listen attentively, but he was not receptive to my arguments. His mind seemed sealed off by deeply rooted preconceptions of world and local affairs and by completely different perceptions of the nature of the Laotian conflict—not unlike some party functionaries in the East who automatically reject any image of the West that is different from what they have been taught.

Two days after my conversation with Parsons the government of Prince Souvanna Phouma was toppled, and negotiations with the Pathet Lao were suspended. The government crisis lasted over two months, from May 31 until August 9. Still, reason prevailed and Souvanna returned to power, finalized talks with the Pathet Lao, and in November formed the first government of national union. This lasted but eight months. U.S. planners became particularly alarmed by the initial success of the Pathet Lao/Neo Lao Haksat in the May 1958 National Assembly by-elections; in alliance with the left-wing Committee for Peace and Neutrality the Neo Lao Haksat had won thirteen out of twenty-one contested seats. Washington mobilized its SEATO allies and its client-politicians in Laos, and brought down the government of national union. It was not difficult for the United States to bring pressures on Vientiane governments, especially as the bulk of the Lao budget—all military pay included—came from the United States. "By merely withholding the monthly payment to the troops," Hilsman remarks, "the United States could create the conditions for toppling any Lao government whose policies it opposed. As it turned out, in fact, the United States used this weapon twice—to bring down the government of one Lao leader and to break the will of another."[19] The subsequent governments of Phoui Sananikone and the military clan led the country straight to a more serious crisis.

Laos and Vietnam form a sort of communicating vessel, in which local conflicts are closely interrelated. By design or through natural processes, the center of gravity moved back and forth from one country to the other, preserving and adding power to the revolutionary momentum. Political wisdom should have used this intercommunication, starting in Laos, to create a chain reaction toward peace, but this unique interrelationship seemed to escape U.S. policy-makers, at least until the acceleration of the Laotian crisis in 1960–61 forced it to their attention.

The Laos–Vietnam Correlation

During decades of French colonial rule a single Indochinese entity was formed, with the Vietnamese at the center of the colonial administration. It was inevitable that the independence movement should grow within the framework of this historical entity, and that the vigorous and resourceful Vietnamese should be a leading force. I was always struck by the closeness and fraternal spirit that prevailed between Laotian and Vietnamese revolutionaries, despite traditional frictions between the two nations. The patriotic and revolutionary movements in both countries had forged an alliance long before there was any American presence in Indochina. It was not by chance that the French High Command decided to turn Dien Bien Phu, on the Vietnamese-Laotian border, into a major stronghold; it was a Vietnamese-Laotian campaign in the spring of 1954 that brought about the French defeat.

In the last half of the fifties, after Geneva, conditions in Vietnam were indeterminate. Although the political provisions of the Geneva agreements were abrogated, there was no significant protest from Moscow, Peking, or even from Hanoi. In fact, in 1958 Hanoi twice approached Diem with offers for normalizing relations between the two Vietnams. Diem's temporary success in Saigon, where he managed to suppress much of his opposition, seemed to encourage the United States to adopt a similar policy in Laos. Hence, U.S. diplomacy worked against a political solution. But the loss of this chance for settlement in Laos had significant repercussions across Indochina. Resistance strengthened rapidly in Laos, culminating in the Kong Le coup in 1960. Stimulated by these events, the revolutionary movement in South Vietnam—which up until then had grown only slowly—was rekindled. New political perspectives became apparent in South Vietnam, and the way was opened for closer links between both parts of the country: through the land-bridge of Laos, the famous Ho Chi Minh trails came into existence.

Still, for the next three years the center of the Indochina conflict remained in Laos. The negotiations in Laos offered attractive and meaningful possibilities for a settlement in South Vietnam as well; while the growing uprising there made it abundantly clear that, like Bao Dai, Diem too had failed. The two themes of the Laotian talks—neutrality and a coalition government—became central to solutions in both Laos and South Vietnam.

These themes were loosely formulated in an original idea incorporated in the December 1960 program of the National Front for the Liberation of South Vietnam, which suggested the creation of a neutral belt composed of South Vietnam, Cambodia and Laos. The Front proposed the idea explicitly in a four-point manifesto issued on July 20, 1962. Significantly, this manifesto marked the anniversary of the 1954 Geneva agreements, and was published on the eve of the signing in Geneva of the new "Declaration of Neutrality of Laos." It called for the adoption of "a foreign policy of peace and neutrality" and proposed that "South Vietnam, together with Cambodia and Laos, will form a neutral area, all three countries retaining full sovereignty." North Vietnam approved the idea, and the call for a neutral zone in Indochina became a recurrent theme in the Front's political campaign.

The Front repeated this theme with special emphasis in the declaration issued on November 8, 1963, after the fall of Ngo Dinh Diem. This was an extraordinary opportunity for peace and political settlement. The moment was ripe and UN Secretary General U Thant tried to mediate a political solution for Vietnam, but his efforts were in vain. President Johnson answered U Thant's proposal in a New Year's message to General Duong Van Minh, Diem's successor: "Neutralization of South Vietnam is unacceptable." The Tonkin Gulf incidents, crowned by the carefully prepared U.S. congressional Tonkin Gulf Resolution, promised a new storm. The center of gravity in the Indochina conflict moved again to South Vietnam. Another chance for peace was lost.

But is it really accurate to speak about "lost" opportunities? Opportunities recurred so often and were so regularly repudiated that this process in itself reveals a strategic line.

These opportunities were not embraced because they were not wanted. With a different strategy, even in more confused situations, opportunities could have been created. But United States policy reveals a continuous line, evolving from Bullitt's "railroad" concept, through Dulles' forward bridgehead strategy, the counterinsurgency fever and the ever-present policy of Vietnamization, to the full-fledged Asian Doctrine. Historical evidence does not support the theory that the United States "stumbled into the quagmire of Indochina." The "stumbling" theory is valid only insofar as it partly explains the short-sightedness of conscious policies envisaged and pursued in the fog of ideological zeal and the arrogance of power.

Chapter 4

Peace-Keeping on the Mekong

Our party left Moscow for New Delhi after midnight on April 25, 1961 in a Soviet TU 104 jet equipped with caviar and vodka. The first formal meeting of the ICSC took place in New Delhi on April 28. Indian Prime Minister Jawaharlal Nehru, who gave the opening address, seemed worried. He started by saying that the Commission should endeavor to reach Laos as soon as possible, as its presence and advice were greatly needed to stabilize the situation. The first imperative, he emphasized, was complete cessation of hostilities. It was unfortunate, he stressed, that the Commission had been adjourned in 1958; otherwise many of the present difficulties might have been avoided. There was an element of self-criticism in this statement, as India itself had voted, with Canada, for suspension of the Commission's activities.

A few days later, still in New Delhi, the Commission drafted its first report to the Co-chairmen, stating that "the situation [has] deteriorated to such an extent that it [has] become a serious threat to the peace and security in South East Asia," that an "effective cease-fire in Laos should be achieved with the minimum of delay," and that it was ready "to do all in [its] power to supervise and control it with the cooperation of all parties in the present hostilities." These were nice, general formulations. In New Delhi, nobody foresaw the difficulties the ICSC would encounter in the field.

It took another week before all preliminary arrangements were made. Then an Indian Air Force plane took us to Indochina. We arrived in Saigon after midnight on May 8; the leaders of the three delegations and a small staff proceeded immediately to Vientiane. Time was now pressing, as a report from the ICSC on the state of the cease-fire was expected to reach Geneva before the opening of the conference, scheduled for May 12. The United States insisted that the inauguration of the conference be conditional on the effective cessation of hostilities in Laos.

Washington had good reason to make this demand: the tide of battle had turned decisively in favor of the Left. In December 1960, after a fierce battle, U.S.-equipped forces led by General Phoumi Nosavan and supported by Thais on the other side of the Mekong had occupied Vientiane and forced the Neutralists, under Captain Kong Le, to withdraw. But Kong Le had kept his units intact, moved north, and joined the Pathet Lao forces. On New Year's Eve, in a perfect encircling maneuver, the combined forces of the Left and the Neutralists had captured the strategic Plain of Jars, astride the crossroads of central Laos, and from that moment on the Pathet Lao and the Neutralists had been almost steadily on the offensive. They had taken the key points of Ta Viang and Tha Thom, north of Paksane, encircling the Vientiane area, and had established control over practically all of eastern and northern Laos, leaving only the towns in the Mekong Valley and their immediate hinterland in the hands of General Phoumi's army.*

*Phoumi Nosavan was born on January 27, 1920, in Savannakhet, son of a civil servant in the French Residency. He was a close relative of former Thai strongman Marshal Sarit Thanarat. Nosavan started his career as secretary at the French Security Police in 1942; in 1945 he participated in Savannakhet in the anti-Japanese resistance movement; later he joined the Lao Issara independence movement. After the reconquest of Laos by the French, Nosavan followed the Lao Issara government into exile to Thailand. He returned to Laos in 1947 as an officer in the resistance, but early in 1949 he joined the French, received the rank of lieutenant, and

The military situation had a direct bearing on political developments. Two rival governments came into existence. Prince Souvanna Phouma's government, with energetic Minister of Information Quinim Pholsena as its main spokesman, moved from Vientiane to Khang Khay, a former French garrison village east of the Plain of Jars. There it was joined by Souvanna himself, who came over from Phnom Penh, where he had sought refuge before the Vientiane battle. In Vientiane, meanwhile, Phoumi Nosavan set up a rival government headed by Prince Boun Oum, once pretender to the throne of Champassak. The Vientiane authorities were promptly recognized by the West, while Souvanna Phouma's government retained the support of the Soviet Union and established links to North Vietnam, China and other socialist countries. The neutralist countries were undecided, maintaining diplomatic representatives in Vientiane but still recognizing the Souvanna Phouma government. The influential *Dépêche du Cambodge* wrote that if the situation of the Boun Oum government was *de jure* legal under the letter of the Laotian constitution, the situation of the government of Souvanna Phouma was *de facto* legal under the spirit of the same constitution.*

in 1950 was put in charge of the Lao National Anti-Guerrilla Command. In 1959 he was appointed brigadier general. Nosavan's ascendance coincided with Marshal Sarit's seizure of power in Thailand. After an abortive coup d'état in January 1965, Nosavan fled to Thailand. This was over a year after the death of Marshal Sarit.

*Prince Boun Oum Na Champassak was born in Champassak in 1910, to a feudal family of big landowners, pretenders to the throne of Champassak. He attended school in Pakse and studied law in France. In 1945 Boun Oum joined the French, first fighting against the Japanese and then the Lao Issara. In the French-Lao *modus vivendi* of 1946, Boun Oum renounced his rights to the defunct Kingdom of Champassak and was granted for life the title of Inspector General of the Kingdom, the second personality after the king. In 1948–50 he served as Prime Minister of the Royal Government, and was known later as titular head of the Lower Laos feudal-comprador pressure group. He reappeared in active politics in 1960 as nominal head of the "Revolutionary Committee" organized by Phoumi

The *De Facto* Cease–Fire

Military operations instigated by both sides were still continuing when the Commission arrived in Laos. Though a cease-fire urged by the Co-chairmen had been declared on May 3, the situation was by no means calm. This was especially the case behind the lines of the Pathet Lao and the Neutralist forces, where the Vientiane authorities and U.S. commandos, relying on armed groups of Meo mountaineers, were trying to hold and enlarge military strongholds. In turn, the Pathet Lao, with North Vietnamese help, instigated actions intended to wipe out these enemy bases.

Commission members were caught in a dilemma: we could tell the blunt truth, and thereby cause difficulties in Geneva, or word our report so as to create the impression that an effective cease-fire was around the corner, and thus clear the way for the opening of the conference. The desire to start negotiations as soon as possible prevailed. On May 11 the ICSC sent to the Co-chairmen a report stating that "the principal parties to the recent hostilities in Laos had ordered their troops to observe cease-fire" and that though "the parties have not yet signed a formal agreement for the cease-fire ... the Commission is satisfied that a general *de facto* cease-fire exists and such breaches as have been informally complained of are either due to misunderstandings or to factors such as the terrain, the nature of disposition of forces, both regular and irregular, of all the parties." This message, in fact, allowed the Geneva conference to open. Its first meeting convened on May 16, 1961.

During the next months, though sporadic fighting continued, the Commission repeatedly confirmed the existence of a cease-fire. In the beginning of June, sharp skirmishes occurred around Ban Padong, a hill position held by a Meo

Nosavan against the neutralist coup d'état of Kong Le and the government of Souvanna Phouma.

detachment in Xieng Khouang Province behind Pathet Lao and Neutralist lines. The Left attacked Ban Padong in force, and on June 6 occupied the stronghold. The incident caused the U.S. delegation in Geneva to interrupt negotiations, and the conference was suspended for five days. The Commission intervened quickly to lessen tension, and then, in a report sent to Geneva on June 12, stated: "The clashes at Ban Padong were the most serious outbreak of local hostilities since the cease-fire was declared on 3rd May. Despite this breach, which it is hoped will not be repeated, the Commission considers from the nature of complaints received since 20th May, from both sides, that the cease-fire continues to be generally effective."

In the same spirit the Commission reported on September 6 that "the military situation in reference to the cease-fire has remained reasonably calm." Certainly, there was no reason to be overly pessimistic. The incidents that occurred had a local character only, and no major engagement aimed at changing the main cease-fire positions was reported. Thus there was hope that a political settlement would stabilize the whole situation. But, taking into consideration the difficulties encountered in the negotiations, in its report of September 6 the Commission also warned that the cease-fire was "tenuous and temporary," and added: "Unless there is a political settlement or a detailed cease-fire agreement in the near future, the situation may rapidly deteriorate."

But in 1961–62 a formal cease-fire agreement was never signed. Both sides were reluctant to tie their hands. Outside observers felt that there was a tacit agreement not to press for a precise document which would clearly define the framework and conditions governing cessation of hostilities. Each side took its position for different reasons, but in essentially the same mood. Vientiane agreed to cease hostilities only under the pressure of military events and, as in the past, **never abandoned** the hope that new circumstances might reopen the way to a military solution. On the other hand, the Pathet Lao, also mindful of past experiences, was suspicious of rightist intentions and was careful to preserve freedom of action for whatever contingency might occur. "While the parties have agreed to cease-fire, they have as usual retained the right to use force when provoked or in self-defense," concluded the Commission's report on May 20, 1961. The Laotians must have had in mind their traditional saying, "One should believe only with one ear, and keep the other in reserve."

International Commission Activities

The Commission found itself in a delicate position—eager to establish effective control and send out teams to investigate complaints, but practically immobilized by the absence of concrete terms, which could only derive from a formal cease-fire agreement or a similar mandate agreed to by both parties. In this instance the Vientiane authorities were perhaps more inclined to empower the ICSC with mobility, so as to check the thrust of the Pathet Lao and the Neutralists, while the Pathet Lao and Neutralists were less receptive to such demands; they recalled that the ICSC had not always been welcomed by the Rightists and the West.

Indeed, love for the Commission had a distinct political flavor. In 1958 the West had pressed for suspension of the Commission; its departure was followed by the dissolution of the government of national unity, the exclusion of the Neo Lao Haksat from the government, and the formation of a right-wing administration which renounced neutrality and jailed the Pathet Lao leadership. In the following years, as long as the Rightists seemed to be strong, the West opposed the reconvening of the Commission. Only when the military situation changed did the West agree to reactivate the ICSC. Now, the Left suspected that the Americans intended to use the Commission to halt their reemergence into the political scene.

This situation reflected the changing role of the ICSC. The Commission was not as "neutral" as the general public thought; it was a political unit set up in the specific circumstances of the 1954 Geneva conference as a compromise solution between East and West, and its effectiveness was dependent on political conditions pertinent to this very compromise. In 1954, the three governments represented on the Commission may have been the best choices: not having direct interests in Indochina and being averse to world tension, they seemed sincerely to favor a peaceful settlement. There were, however, political assumptions which went beyond the independent judgment of the individual governments. It was assumed that Canada and Poland would *de facto* act as representatives of West and East respectively, while India—then on good terms with both China and the spokesmen of the emerging Third World—would hold the neutral balance.

From the start it was tacitly agreed that each delegation to the ICSC would operate according to its own political premises. The three delegations were to be guided more by the political considerations of their own governments or larger bloc units than by neutral evaluations of hard facts or by the spirit of the Geneva agreements. Loyalties were national or ideological rather than international. Within the Commission the roles assigned to each delegation were not secrets, though they were not always openly admitted. The Canadian delegation had to defend the position of the West and its local clients, come what may, while the Polish delegation had to take care of the interests of the East and the local Left. Initially, the Indians were obliged to stick to their nonaligned mandate.

For a while this arrangement worked fairly well, as long as India's position remained neutral and the Commission continued to adhere, if somewhat vaguely, to the letter of the Geneva agreements. Indeed, the Commission performed useful tasks, particularly in the fifties immediately after Geneva, as long as military, not political, problems predominated. The cease-fire was then generally accepted, and differences that lay in the political sphere were expected to be solved in the future, as foreseen in the Geneva agreement. Within this framework, India executed its balancing role in a rather simple way. Judgments of the Commission and reports to the Co-chairmen simply contained equal numbers of charges against each conflicting party; in cases of majority votes in the Commission, India on principle alternated its alignment from one to the other delegation. A vote with Canada against Poland was followed by a vote with Poland against Canada —in essence, an exercise in symmetry! In this early period the Commission was usually able to work out compromise solutions acceptable to all three delegations. Commission unity before the outside world was sometimes valued more highly than straightforward statements.

Then two developments changed the situation considerably: the reassertion of political issues; and a change in international configurations, with the deterioration of Indian-Chinese relations, and the growing split within the socialist world. In fact, these changes rendered the 1954 ICSC arrangements obsolete. When the political configuration in which it was created had ceased to exist, the Commission, which was to reflect that configuration, lost its sense of purpose. At the same time, its cohesion and work were strongly affected by the West's refusal to implement the political clauses of the Geneva agreements.

Consequently, no Commission member could continue to perform the role originally assigned. This was especially true of India, but Poland and Canada were affected as well. The whole Commission began to drift toward the West, and its usefulness decreased markedly.

The reactivation of the ICSC in 1961 occurred when this drift was entering a decisive stage. A basic imbalance became more and more obvious: as the ICSC reflected the compromise sought by the British and Soviet Co-chairmen and in the dialogue between the United States and the Soviet Union, it became increasingly alienated from local conditions. Naturally, this did not ease its task; and China, North Vietnam and the Left in Laos treated the Commission with increased suspicion. However, everything seemed to be in flux, and the Commission tried its best to continue its mission: we still hoped that a lasting political solution could be found.

At this time the Commission bowed to the desires of the local parties, allowing them fluidity and flexibility in military affairs; underlying this development was the reality of guerrilla warfare. As stated in the Commission's report of May 20, 1961, the situation was marked by "the absence of precise limits in which the hostile forces were operating . . . When the forces are mixed together, particularly in the jungle, or are facing each other in close proximity, it is nearly impossible to say who shot first or who gave first provocation." Given such conditions, and in the absence of any political understanding that could infuse trust and good will, an effective cease-fire seemed extremely difficult to achieve. Likewise, control and supervision of the cessation of hostilities, without fixed cease-fire lines and with no precise terms, seemed nearly impossible.

Experiences in 1954 and 1961

It now seems clear why the execution of the cease-fire in Vietnam in 1954 proceeded more or less smoothly while the same problem posed so many difficulties in Laos in 1961: in 1954 cessation of hostilities had been preceded by agreement (reached in Geneva) on the general outlines of a political settlement and on an established, continuous cease-fire line;

neither of these elements was present in Laos in 1961. A cease-fire can, of course, be enforced by military strength if there exists at least a clearly delimited, continuous cease-fire line—this was, for instance, the case in Korea. But an undefeated guerrilla army is unlikely to agree to such a settlement without prior political understandings.

Lacking this understanding and a precise cease-fire agreement, cessation of hostilities in Laos in 1961 meant only a pause, a breathing space, after which either a political settlement or renewed fighting could be expected. Thus the Commission constantly warned against a possible breakdown of the cease-fire, and urged that political negotiations be speeded up. The Commission actually became a strong proponent of "an agreement which would quickly lead to the formation of a coalition government" (report of September 6).

The problems of the cease-fire soon became entirely subordinate to the political negotiations. On May 13, 1961, at the opening of the conference in the village of Ban Namone, north of Vientiane, only lip service was paid to military questions. The parties signed a communiqué promising to repeat cease-fire orders to their troops with instructions "to keep the order very strictly in every battlefield," and all quickly agreed to place on the agenda discussions for a "detailed agreement on the cease-fire." But these were merely formalities. The main interest centered around political issues.

Chapter 5

Xieng Khouang
and Khang Khay

The three commissioners and an advance party of ICSC personnel left Saigon for Vientiane on May 8, 1961, but a second group of Indian, Canadian and Polish officers—myself included—stayed behind to determine how to reach the government of Prince Souvanna Phouma in Xieng Khouang Province, located near the Plain of Jars. The ICSC wanted to be equally represented on both sides of the front, in Vientiane and in Xieng Khouang. As there was no direct air or land connection from Saigon to Xieng Khouang, we hoped to travel via Hanoi, which was linked to Saigon by regular Commission courier flights. From Hanoi, we hoped, the Russians or Vietnamese would help us get to the Plain of Jars. It was no secret that Soviet planes carrying supplies for the Kong Le and Pathet Lao troops had established an air-bridge between Hanoi and the Plain of Jars airfield. However, Hanoi advised us to contact Xieng Khouang directly from Vientiane.

The Xieng Khouang Environment

On May 11 we flew to Vientiane, and the next afternoon, after an hour's flight over mountains and jungles, landed on a primitive airfield on the Plain of Jars. We were greeted by officers of the Kong Le forces and a representative of the Chaokhoueng (the governor of Xieng Khouang Province).

U.S. jeeps were waiting to take us to the town of Xieng Khouang, which was less than twenty miles away. The journey took more than three hours, over roads that were rugged, narrow and unpaved; we could never go more than twenty miles per hour. One of the jeeps broke down, and when we finally arrived, night had fallen. Still, we had been lucky: Meo tribesmen armed by the Vientiane authorities sometimes held the nearby hills and shelled the road or laid ambushes. The Meo, we were told, were paid for every pair of enemy ears they could produce.

In Xieng Khouang we were received warmly by the Chaokhoueng, a former Vientiane police officer. In honor of our arrival, electricity from the small local generator remained on later than usual. The three Commission delegations were provisionally lodged in the governor's residence, previously the home of the French commissioner. Everything was done to make us feel comfortable. The next day, to welcome us and wish us good health and success, we were offered a traditional Laotian *baci*, a colorful ceremony attended by the town elders.

Compared to the relative luxury of Saigon and Vientiane, Xieng Khouang was a different world. Life was full of hardships, and we had to devote much of our attention to the details of daily life. Provisions were scarce. Much of our food had to be airlifted from Vientiane; water was not always available; electricity was rationed and supplied irregularly, and only for a short time after dark. Although we had been given some of the town's best accommodations, roaming rats still had to be kept at a distance. We found some compensation in the beautiful surroundings and the good climate, however. Xieng Khouang is situated about 3,500 feet above sea level in hilly countryside covered with intense subtropical green. The air is less humid than in the Mekong Valley, and temperatures are moderate. On some nights we even had to use a blanket.

Eventually I came to like Xieng Khouang. It was a small

town with about 5,000 inhabitants, one unpaved main street, and side streets which ended in wide rice fields or mountain forests. In the center of town shops owned by Chinese, Indian, Laotian and Vietnamese merchants surrounded a central marketplace. On market day the town filled with Meos who came to deal in opium, which was traded openly in various stages of its processing, but mostly as a black, greasy substance. There were several pagodas inhabited by saffron-robed Buddhist monks, a Catholic church with four French missionaries, a French military mission of six officers attached to the units of Kong Le, and three French teachers looking for a chance to leave.

Communication with the Parties

We soon found that contact with government authorities would not be easy. Though Xieng Khouang was the provincial capital, the seat of Souvanna Phouma's government was located some thirty miles away in the village of Khang Khay. We had been lodged in Xieng Khouang, we were told, because there were no accommodations in Khang Khay. While there was some truth in this, the arrangement also served to make direct links with the government complicated and difficult. Transportation was not always available, nor were the roads always passable—especially in the rainy season—and security considerations frequently caused delays.

My main concern was to establish regular contact with the Souvanna Phouma government, the Neo Lao Haksat/Pathet Lao leadership, Vietnamese representatives, and the diplomatic missions of the Soviet Union and the People's Republic of China. Vientiane was cut off from these contacts (which made the Commission's deliberations somewhat unrealistic). I had to establish friendly and confidential relations with the parties concerned. Only in an atmosphere of reciprocal trust could consultations have any value, and informal, honest consultation was vitally necessary in order to learn the limits of the Commission's possible lines of action. To impose solutions against the will of the parties would have been beyond the Commission's power, and instead of advancing a settlement would only have exacerbated the conflict.

During my Commission assignments I learned several basic lessons. First, the Commission itself had no channels of information about local developments beyond its own sporadic, random investigations. These might have been relevant to particular situations, but they were insufficient for general judgments. Most of our knowledge about the nature of the conflict and of concrete incidents had to come from contacts with the parties. Thus the information gathered by each delegation, though not shared in detail, added to the overall orientation of the Commission.

Second, information alone was not enough. Deep insight was necessary to understand the conflict. Commission members were all strangers to the region, and no matter how great our acquired political and historical knowledge, the parties understood much more about the flow of events and long-term trends. We needed somehow to live with the temper and feelings of the real actors. This was possible only through close personal contacts, long informal discussions, social interaction and frank speech.

Third, we always had to be careful not to appear as an outside instrument invested with powers above those of the parties, trying to dictate solutions. Our real goal was to mitigate the differences between the parties and to convince them to act in a concerted manner in their own interests. We had to create good will and show consideration for the parties' interests and perceptions. On this depended the success of the Commission. Of course, we often had to discuss controversial points, where our opinions differed from the parties', but these discussions had then to serve as guidelines for further action. If successful in our efforts, we could proceed with the execution of a line proposed by us. But it would have been unwise to press issues against the expressed will of the parties or to try to force solutions alien to their perceptions. The parties could follow or sabotage any line of action, as they chose.

Fourth, in the application of the spirit of the Geneva agreements, much depended on flexibility and the art of cooperation with the parties. These agreements were far from precise. The wording of some clauses was general, aiming at compromise solutions, and this opened possibilities for differing interpretations. The legal and political provisions were especially vague. All this demanded careful conduct and procedure, and, above all, good lines of communication.

Communication with the local parties was especially important to the Polish delegation, particularly in the beginning of the sixties. The main reason for this lay in the Indochinese Left's established pattern of decision-making. The prevailing myth of a monolithic communism had led the West to believe that strategy and tactics in Indochina were decided either in Moscow or Peking. The truth was completely different: all decisions and plans pertaining to Vietnam were worked out in Hanoi; plans for Laos were worked out cooperatively by Hanoi and the Pathet Lao/Neo Lao Haksat leadership. Moscow or Peking could try to influence Vietnamese and Laotian thinking on certain questions, but the Indochinese were masters of their own strategy. No instructions from Warsaw, Moscow or Peking could have changed these realities, and in daily Commission activities it was useless for my delegation to wait for such instructions. They would never come. It was understood that guidelines for behavior and action would be created through increased communication with the local Left. Their thinking served as a framework for all our actions within the Commission.

The flexibility and relative autonomy of my delegation's line of action were also made necessary by the political relationships among socialist countries in the early sixties. Although the West had not fully understood this, disarray around the Indochina problem had become so great in the socialist world that full strategy coordination was out of the question. In Geneva, some common denominator had been found for political negotiation, but the situation in Indochina was different. Here the local Left, somehow protected by the Soviet-Chinese rift, followed its own lines to an even greater extent than in the past. More than ever it was called on to shape its own destiny. And more than ever I had to rely on consultation with the main actors on the scene, the Vietnamese and Laotians. Certainly, intimate relations with the Soviet representatives and good contacts with the Chinese were a prerequisite for effective action; these contacts added to my general orientation and supplied additional indications of the possible limits of maneuvering. But it was the local Left that dominated the scene. It was quite a task to remain on good terms with all these different groups; I suspect that I was the last Polish representative in Indochina to stay on good terms with left-wing Laotians, Vietnamese, Russians and Chinese.

Erroneous Western Perceptions

It took the West a long time to understand that this was the pattern of decision-shaping in the Left in Indochina. Because the West misread local realities, subsequent confusions had very serious consequences. I know positively of cases in which my moves, which had no special scheme behind them, were misinterpreted as being undertaken on instructions from either Moscow or Peking, and the reactions were accordingly magnified and dangerously misplaced. This was standard behavior in U.S. decision-making centers almost to the end of the sixties; even later the old perceptions often prevailed. The blunders committed because of this erroneous notion—that in every move could be felt the hand of Peking or Moscow—added, perhaps decisively, to the escalation of the conflict. The West confused the real adversary—the Indochinese national movements, admittedly under Left leadership—with global contestants.

Part of the West's misreading of the Polish delegation's actions resulted from the fact that the Canadian delegation followed an entirely different pattern of action: the relationship between the West and its local allies was different from the relationship between the local Left and socialist countries. Our Canadian colleagues cultivated, of course, close contacts with the rightist groupings, the Thais, the American embassy and its various agencies. However, the centers of decision were not inside but outside Indochina. Decisions were made in Washington or, in Commission matters, through channels in Ottawa. This general pattern remained the same, even if from time to time some powers were delegated to local U.S. representatives or agencies. As a rule, general strategy was dependent strictly on U.S. decisions,* and my Canadian colleagues sometimes complained of having difficulties with their American "clients," or of being obliged to wait for detailed instructions from Ottawa. Wording in all key Commission reports was carefully checked on high outside levels before the Canadian delegation could give its final approval.

Such feudalism was even more conspicuous in the relationships between Washington and its local clients. Of course,

---

*This relationship became public when Canadian Prime Minister John G. Diefenbaker came into posession of a working paper prepared by Walt Rostow for President Kennedy before his May 1961 trip to Ottawa. Rostow advised the President "to push" for increased Canadian action in the ICSC "to impede Communist support reaching South Vietnam through Laos." Diefenbaker took this as proof that the Kennedy administration intended to "push Canada around." See Carroll Kilpatrick's report in the *Washington Post,* April 19, 1961. Though Ottawa was bitter about the incident, it did not change the existing relationship.

there were instances when the harmony seemed to have been disrupted; though dependent for finance, supply and stature completely on the United States (with possibly additional inputs from Thailand), the Rightists in Laos occasionally showed resistance, especially when they thought some of their cherished interests were endangered. They ventured such moves particularly when they felt they could count on support from influential groups in Washington itself—most often U.S. military agencies. Ultimately, however, the U.S. administration remained in command.

As it was, Commission action demanded efforts quite different from the usual diplomatic routine or what one might expect from reading the formal terms of reference in the Geneva agreements. In fact, from its reactivation in 1961 up to the conclusion of the 1962 Geneva agreement, the Commission's greatest achievements did not deal with the problems of the cease-fire, although its presence was certainly instrumental in reducing tensions. Its achievements, and they were substantial, arose rather from its role as a go-between—linking the parties, helping to exchange messages and organize meetings, trying to bridge disparities and to help in the arduous and complex process of forming the tripartite government. The Commission was the only body with representatives on both sides of the front and regular communication with both parts of the country. As a collective body it showed real concern for a peaceful settlement, and offered a tangible contribution to peace. It was not the Commission's fault that the peace did not last.

Khang Khay Headquarters

To begin work, it was necessary to open lines of communication to Khang Khay. From Xieng Khouang this at first looked to be far from simple. The initial difficulties were mainly technical and organizational: jeeps were not fit, drivers were scarce, security arrangements had to be tested. But soon Soviet jeeps—the GAZ—were airlifted in from Hanoi for the Commission's use, formalities were arranged, and I began my frequent trips between Xieng Khouang and Khang Khay, on a road running along the fringe of the Plain of Jars. This road, marked on the map as a beaten track, had not been repaired in years. Maximum speed was about twenty miles an hour, and it usually took two hours to get to Khang Khay. Sometimes we got stuck in mud so deep that it took the efforts of whole Pathet Lao units to extricate us. Such an expedition could take a whole day.

I really did not mind these excursions very much; I looked on them as sport. Though tiring and sometimes risky, they were a kind of treat. I could relax and use the time to reflect and rethink matters. The scenery was magnificent and cast a powerful spell. These were fairyland landscapes: untrodden mountains, jungle, virgin soil. The greens were splendid and multihued, especially at the beginning of the rainy season. Thickets of bamboo and jungle brushwood, glittering rice fields and vast savannahs, conifers and banana trees against a background of irregular hills and massive highlands. A paradise for guerrillas. In this exotic milieu even torrential rainstorms had a touch of magic. I particularly liked the moments immediately before and after these storms—the play of colors on the sky, the moving rainbows, beautiful sunsets and elaborate clouds.

About halfway down from Xieng Khouang to the Plain of Jars the road turned to the right, and after crossing a high savannah, led through the village of Phong Savan up to Khang Khay. There, on a hill to the left of the road, stood an old stone barracks formerly occupied by the French Foreign Legion. In 1961 this served as living quarters for both princes and for visiting ministers, housed some government offices, mainly those of the Prime Minister and the Office of Foreign Affairs, and provided space to receive guests and to hold meetings. I couldn't help laughing when I first saw tacked on one of the dilapidated doors a plain piece of paper with the handwritten inscription *Ministère des Affaires Étrangères.* (Once when I urgently needed an official letter, the colonel in charge of the office offered me the privilege of drafting it myself—and of typing it, too.) Not far from the princes' hill other barracks were scattered over the landscape.

The princes lived in two small cells, each furnished with a bed, a table and a chair. A row of suitcases supported the wall in Souvanna's room. In Souphanouvong's room there was a soldier's bed—when we talked that was what we sat on—and a small table covered with papers, a pile of books, and a highly sensitive transistor radio. A big Laotian knife hung on one wall, and in one corner a shirt had usually been hung up to dry. These primitive conditions did not change until late in 1962, when the Vietnamese, as part of an economic agreement with Laos, erected a dozen residences for members of the government. In no other place in the world, perhaps, did a diplomatic staff work under such primitive conditions. The first Soviet ambassador to Laos, Alexander N. Abramov (formerly ambassador to Israel and later the first Soviet ambassador to Algeria) had to confine himself to a small, austere cubicle with water brought from outside. Later, barracks were added for the Chinese economic and cultural missions and the Soviet embassy, which transferred from the village of Phong Savan. Compared with conditions in Khang Khay, we in Xieng Khouang were rather privileged.

There were two closed and well-guarded areas in Khang Khay: the Neo Lao Haksat/Pathet Lao headquarters, and the barracks of the so-called Vietnamese Aid Committee. Pathet Lao headquarters consisted of a number of huts, almost like a village, scattered through the woods along a small stream. Centrally located in the area were a large wooden conference room, a sizable hut used for seminars, and an open space for exercises and meetings. Soldiers came and went constantly. Nouhak Phoumsavan, a leading figure in the movement, lived in one of the small huts. It was built of rice straw, with a dirt floor and open spaces for the door and windows. I once asked Nouhak how he felt in this "flat"; he answered that he could not remember having lived in such luxurious conditions before. All the inhabitants of the Pathet Lao village spent their free time working on a small farm in the rear. Phoumi Vongvichit, secretary general of the Neo Lao Haksat and later minister of information in the government of national union, proudly showed me around the chicken coop, which he and his wife took care of.

The camp of the Vietnamese Aid Committee, which housed advisers, guards and workers who were building the new Khang Khay town area, was a short distance from the Neo Lao Haksat village. A general directed the work of the Committee; guards stood at the entrance, and discipline inside was military. However, as much as the Committee was expert in military matters, it was also expert in political matters; in their eyes, political and military subjects were inseparable. Was this in fact one of the secrets of Vietnamese revolutionary strategy?

At Xieng Khouang and Khang Khay we breathed the spirit of political resistance and revolutionary war. Kong Le's soldiers let their beards and hair grow, modeling themselves on the Cubans. Laotian students just back from Paris passionately discussed national renaissance and democratic change. Souvanna Phouma and government politicians were busy with political planning and rethinking the strategy for negotiations. The Pathet Lao worked strenuously, under great pressure, to expand ranks and train new cadres. The armies, both the Pathet Lao's and Kong Le's, were constantly struggling to clean out rear areas, or to make the cease-fire line safer. Everyone exuded self-confidence and faith in the final victory.

Chapter 6

Souvanna Phouma's Enigmatic Roles

Souvanna Phouma was born in Luang Prabang on October 7, 1901, to the vanguard line of the royal family (Vang-Na), the younger brother of Vice-King Prince Phetsarath and the elder half-brother of Prince Souphanouvong. Souvanna studied in France, graduating as an architect and electrical engineer, and started his professional life in the thirties as an engineer under the French administration. Soon, however, he turned to politics, and in 1945 became Minister of Public Works in the Lao Issara government. After the fall of that government, together with other Lao Issara leaders, he went into exile in Bangkok. In 1949, reconciled with the French, he returned to Laos and was granted a succession of leading governmental positions. He was Prime Minister from 1951 to 1954 and again from March 1956 to August 1958. In November 1957, with the participation of the Neo Lao Haksat, he formed the first government of national union. After the overthrow of this government in 1958 he became Laotian ambassador to Paris. Following the elections, manipulated by General Nosavan, in April 1960 he became president of the National Assembly. In August 1960, after Kong Le's coup d'état, he was again called to head the government. In 1961 he was the most prominent figure in Laotian politics, the leading proponent of Laotian neutralism, president of the Neutral Party of Laos (Lao Pen Kang).

Souvanna was one of the wealthiest men in Laos. He was co-proprietor of several banks and commercial enterprises, including Société Air Lao and Société Fluviale Malpeuch, and he owned a great deal of land, and tenements in Vientiane, Luang Prabang, and France. He led a comfortable life, often spent vacations in France, and was a connoisseur of French wines, food and cigars. Unlike other Laotians, Souvanna never appeared in public places or in Vientiane night clubs with unfitting company: he seemed never to forget that he was a member of the royal family. He was the perfect representative of the Francophile Laotian aristocracy.

I knew the Prince quite well from 1956–57, when he was Prime Minister and Minister of Foreign Affairs. As Polish commissioner, I had met him often, at a desk or at a dining table, or at his fine, tasteful, half-Laotian and half-French residence at Nong Thevada. Thus I was particularly impressed by the very simple living arrangements he had at Khang Khay in the old French military barracks. His brother Souphanouvong had always led an almost ascetic life, even when he stayed in Vientiane; but never before had I seen Souvanna dress drably. He looked more like a country gentleman than a Frenchified Laotian nobleman.

Souvanna received me cordially, visibly glad to see an old acquaintance in these strange circumstances. He seemed in excellent spirits, militant and transformed in his outlook. Twice forced to relinquish the office of Prime Minister under U.S. and rightist pressures, with the experience of U.S. military and political intervention in 1960 and the spring of 1961 fresh in his memory, Souvanna was not about to give up or to drop the struggle. But he did not hide his government's difficulties. Private hardship, he said, was a minor problem; but the government lacked everything—they had no typewriters, no newspapers, no regular supply of daily commodities. I promised to help as much as I could—to get *Le Monde* and the *Lao Presse,* to bring the most needed things.

Souvanna seemed to attach particular importance to the Commission's presence. He had a much more liberal attitude toward the Commission than did the Pathet Lao, and was more willing to assign the ICSC concrete tasks in supervising and controlling the cease-fire; but he placed his main hope in our role as mediators. Speaking to the Xieng Khouang Commission representatives and their military advisers, he promised every possible help for our work. His government, he said, was interested in establishing an effective cease-fire and a prompt political settlement, which would guarantee the neutrality of the country as provided for in the Geneva agreements. But he stressed that breaches of the cease-fire, stemming particularly from the Vientiane government's activities in the rear of Pathet Lao lines, could not be left unanswered. He strongly censured U.S. interference, which he said had brought civil war to Laos, and spoke vigorously of the need to restore peace as quickly as possible. He seemed confident and firm about political questions resulting from the conflict.

A few weeks later, on June 14, at the plenary session of the Geneva conference, Souvanna reviewed the events of recent years and clearly stated his new attitude:

> Immediately after the conclusion of the [1954] Geneva agreements the Government over which I presided began negotiations with the Pathet Lao in order to reintegrate the combatants of this patriotic movement into the national community; foreign interference in our national problems compelled me to resign . . . The situation remained unstable for the next few years. Then, in accordance with the unanimous aspiration of the Lao people for peace, neutrality and national reconciliation, I returned to power [in 1956] and signed with Prince Souphanouvong a series of agreements, known later as the Vientiane agreements, which in the main reaffirmed and developed the principles of Geneva . . .
>
> The policy followed by my government received full ap-

proval of the Lao people. War had raged in Laos from 1939, and everyone aspired to peace and understanding. However, this policy was opposed by certain members of SEATO, and the government of national unity, which I had formed [in 1957], in which Pathet Lao ministers participated, did not last long. An announcement threatened to cut off aid—such pressures provoked my resignation [1958].

Mr. Phoui Sananikone, who replaced me, clearly deviated from the road of neutrality and adopted a pro-American policy. To begin with, he permitted the United States to install American military advisers and instructors in our country; he authorized Taiwan to open a consulate-general in Vientiane; and he raised the level of Saigon's representation —which had existed from the pre-independence period—to the level of an embassy. What was more grave, he introduced a policy of discrimination towards the Pathet Lao, and placed its leadership in prison, despite the fact that several were members of the National Assembly. All this revived the civil war, which broke out again with the affair of the Second Battalion of the Pathet Lao.*

The situation became more grave. In December 1959 a coup d'état brought to power extreme elements of the army and the Committee for the Defense of the National Interests, headed by General Phoumi [Nosavan], strengthening dissatisfaction in all Laos. The general elections in [April] 1960 provoked popular indignation; the rest of the drama was inevitable. These violations of the elementary rights of the people and other acts of injustice provoked the coup d'état of August 9, 1960 [of Kong Le], which faithfully reflected the aspiration of our people for a life of peace and general concord, with good relations with other countries, especially with all those neighbors with whom we share several thousand kilometers of common borders. Does experience not show that only such a policy can guarantee the survival of Laos?

Conscious that these were the wishes of my people, I agreed

*On May 19, 1959, refused satisfaction in accordance with the provisions of the Vientiane agreements, this battalion broke through its encirclement in the military camp on the Plain of Jars and fled into the jungle.

to return to the presidency of the government, and started immediately to work toward understanding among all the Lao . . . However, again I encountered the resistance of the same SEATO powers. A group of Laotians who had named themselves the "Revolutionary Committee of Savannakhet" launched their troops against our capital of Vientiane . . . After December 1960 the fighting became more and more violent, and foreign aid increased in alarming proportions . . . I hope that such developments are things of the past and will not be repeated, and that a real cease-fire will allow the conference to proceed, in order to achieve the neutrality of Laos which was recommended in this very place seven years ago.

Strategy and Tactics

For Souvanna Phouma to openly accuse the United States, SEATO, and the Rightists, while praising the Pathet Lao as a patriotic movement, seemed to be a real change. But I wondered how deep this change went. Was it irreversible and final, or just temporary? Was it a strategic decision or merely a tactical move?

Many things in the past confirmed the validity of the change, but many spoke against it. The Prince was always a man of the West, emotionally attached to France, representing the highest stratum of Laotian society. When he joined his brothers in the Lao Issara independence movement, it was a family affair, a rivalry between two branches of the royal house: King Sisavang Vong was deposed and for a short while Prince Phetsarath, the Vice-King, became the nation's top personality. Souvanna followed his two brothers into exile after the defeat of the Lao Issara, but he was the only one in the family to reconcile quickly with the French, and in 1953, as Prime Minister, he negotiated and signed a Treaty of Friendship and Association with France. Late in the fifties he joined the Western chorus proclaiming Laos the

"Vanguard of the Free World"—this was the title of an article he published (in *France-Asie,* November–December 1960).

True, Souvanna was one of the first conservatives to recognize—after the unsuccessful attempts in 1955 to suppress the Pathet Lao militarily—that only a policy of reconciliation could bring peace to the country, and that neutrality would best suit Laos's geopolitical location. But when he returned to power in 1956, and even after the formation of the coalition government with the Pathet Lao in 1957, he did not establish diplomatic relations with even one of the socialist countries: not with his northern neighbors, China and North Vietnam, nor with the Soviet Union, which was Co-chairman of the Geneva conference, nor with Poland, member of the ICSC. In January 1957 the Chinese People's Republic offered Laos unconditional aid to counter U.S. pressures against the conclusion of an agreement with the Neo Lao Haksat, but Souvanna rejected the offer.

Though he brought the Neo Lao Haksat into the first government of national union, the Prince seemed careful not to allow them to grow beyond certain limits. Radical thinking must have been basically alien to Souvanna's cast of mind. In May 1958, after the Neo Lao Haksat, in coalition with the Peace and Neutrality Party (Santiphab) headed by Quinim Pholsena, gained thirteen of twenty-one contested mandates in the National Assembly, Souvanna immediately moved to check the trend. He initiated and became chairman of the Rally of the Lao People (Lao Luam Lao), which fused his Nationalist (formerly Progressive) Party with the Independent Party of Phoui Sananikone in an effort to create a united conservative front against the mounting influence of the Left. And it was Prince Souvanna Phouma who, on March 20, 1958, apparently submitting to Western pressures, approached the ICSC with the request that the Commission wind up its activities, under the pretext that the coming supplementary elections of May 4, 1958, would "constitute the last phase of the implementation of the Geneva agreements."

While wondering about Souvanna Phouma's changes, I remembered a lengthy conversation I had had in New Delhi with a high-ranking Indian diplomat who had served in Vientiane for years, and seemed to have an intimate knowledge of the Laotian scene. We had met over a superb Indian dinner, recalled past discussions on Laos and other international problems, and compared old views in the light of new developments. When I said that Souvanna Phouma now seemed to have made common cause with the Laotian Left out of inner conviction and with a long-range perspective, my friend smiled graciously and said: "You Europeans do not understand Asian politics, particularly princely games in backward regions. You do not even grasp the relations between a prince or a rajah and his subjects. Souvanna is, next to the king, the leading representative of the conservative forces in Laos. He has been serving time for years with the distinct aim of reaching the key position in the kingdom. He dreams of becoming the man of destiny of Laos and therefore adapts skillfully, whichever way the wind blows." In 1956–57, Souvanna was anxious to form a coalition government with the participation of the Pathet Lao because he wanted to counterbalance the position of Katay (Don Sasorith), the most influential politician on the right and a formidable adversary in Souvanna's bid for power.* The moment illness rendered Katay harmless, Phouma started to try to get rid of the Pathet Lao. He believed that he would get support not only from France but also from the United States. This is

---

*Katay Don Sasorith (1904–59), a wealthy Laotian from the South, Minister of Finance and National Economy in the Lao Issara government, in exile in Bangkok 1946–49, again Minister of Finance and National Economy 1951–54, and Prime Minister 1954–56. He was trusted by the Thai and U.S. governments.

why he demanded the withdrawal of the International Commission. He resigned as Prime Minister with the intention of forming a new government without the Pathet Lao—convinced that he himself was the only possible choice to head the government. But his maneuvering and haughtiness alienated other politicians, and his own party put up Katay and Phoui Sananikone as candidates for Prime Minister. In the internal voting Katay received one vote more than Phoui, but the King, using as an excuse Katay's absence—he was then on his way back from medical treatment in France—directed Phoui to form the new government.

My Indian friend was positive that in 1958 Souvanna Phouma was not defeated by the Americans, but by his own miscalculations and double-dealing. When I asked if the experience of the past years could have changed Souvanna's attitude, my friend said that it would be difficult to alter the mentality of this "obdurate aristocrat."

My friend then spoke of an episode connected with the widely publicized October 1960 mission to Vientiane of J. Graham Parsons, formerly U.S. ambassador to Laos and by then the Assistant Secretary of State for Far Eastern Affairs. The United States had recently suspended aid to Souvanna's government, and Parsons presented Souvanna with a kind of ultimatum: the U.S. would renew aid if he would a) immediately cease negotiations with the Pathet Lao; b) give General Nosavan a preponderant voice in the government; and c) move the administrative capital from restless Vientiane to the royal seat of Luang Prabang. Souvanna rejected this ultimatum and turned for aid to the Soviet Union; A. N. Abramov, the first U.S.S.R. ambassador to Laos, appeared in Vientiane close on Parsons' heels.

Souvanna rejected Parsons' offer not because of any political reorientation but because of the brutal manner in which the United States applied pressure: Souvanna does not want to serve as a stooge openly, my friend said. The appearances of independence are still dear to him. Three months later, while in exile in Phnom Penh, Souvanna remarked that Parsons "understood nothing about Asia and nothing about Laos. The Assistant Secretary of State is the most reprehensible and nefarious of men. He is the ignominious architect of a disastrous American policy toward Laos. He and others like him are responsible for the recent spilling of Lao blood."[1]

Patriotic and Class Attitudes

Though plausible and consistent, my Indian friend's story did not convince me fully. At that time I was inclined to give Souvanna the benefit of the doubt; I believed that patriotism formed an essential motive for his actions. But I later learned additional details which shed new light on Souvanna's posture in the fateful period of 1960–61, and which showed that I was not right in many assumptions, that the Prince's class attitudes were certainly much stronger than I had suspected.

The Parsons story did not end with the rejection of the U.S. offer; immediately after Parsons' failure, U.S. ambassador to Laos Winthrop G. Brown succeeded in working out a curious compromise with Phouma. As told by Hilsman, "Brown pointed out to Souvanna that while the non-Communist forces quarreled among themselves, Laos might well be lost to the Pathet Lao . . . The United States, Brown went on, would be willing to resume its financial payments to Souvanna if he in turn would not object to a resumption of U.S. deliveries of military equipment to Phoumi. The United States, Brown was able to say, had Phoumi's promise not to use the aid against Kong Le and the neutralist forces in an attempt to bring down Souvanna's government, but only against the Pathet Lao. Souvanna quickly agreed—hoping, for one thing, finally to convince the United States Government that he was not so naïve about Communists as they believed."[2]

However, Phoumi Nosavan step by step undermined Souvanna's government. Phoumi had consistently been bent on
a military solution. On November 11, 1960, he took over the
royal capital, Luang Prabang, and made preparations to
move on Vientiane. Souvanna then tried to save his government through another alliance with the Pathet Lao. On
November 18 he flew to Sam Neua, and two days later he and
Prince Souphanouvong signed a joint declaration proclaiming adherence to strict neutrality and their intention to form
a government of national union. Three weeks later Phoumi's
troops reached the suburbs of Vientiane.

The battle for Vientiane was preceded by a coup organized
by the commander of the Vientiane military region, Colonel
Kouprasith Abhay, in close cooperation with Nosavan. Souvanna met Kouprasith in the morning of December 8, and
after he was assured that the action was directed "against
left-wing influences only," he approved the coup. But soon
Kouprasith received direct reinforcements from Nosavan,
partly by air and partly through the Mekong crossing from
Thailand, and a military clash with the Kong Le units
seemed unavoidable. On December 9, considering the situation too tense and explosive, the Prince left for Cambodia.

Souvanna abandoned not only Vientiane but also his government, but Phoumi's conquest of Vientiane would have
sealed his government's fate anyway. Perhaps at this point
Souvanna had no clear intention of continuing the battle,
although he did declare that the Boun Oum government
which Phoumi installed was illegal. The Prince was no doubt
bitter about the whole situation. But Quinim Pholsena, who
took over the main responsibilities of Souvanna's government in the second half of December, flew to Sam Neua,
reinforced links with the Pathet Lao, and labored to maintain the legality of Souvanna's government. Then a series of
defeats for Nosavan's forces must have seemed to open new
vistas.

When Souvanna decided to renew his bid for power, he saw no other way but to seek the help and cooperation of the Pathet Lao: by then they had become a force to reckon with seriously. But Souvanna still nursed notions of danger from the Left. In late March 1961 he met Averell Harriman, President Kennedy's roving ambassador, in New Delhi, and told him that "the people of Laos did not wish to be communist and that Laos could be saved from communism, but that time was running out."[3] Eight years later, in the October 1969 hearings before the Senate Foreign Relations Subcommittee on U.S. Security Agreements and Commitments Abroad, Senator Fulbright remarked about Souvanna Phouma: "He is not a neutralist. He is an ally . . . We are helping him, we are giving him money, we are giving him assistance, and so on. He is not neutral as between the North Vietnamese and ourselves, is he? He does not profess that?"

Chapter 7

The Red Prince
and His Guard

In Laos, the main adversary of U.S. policy was the Pathet Lao—as of January 1956 renamed Neo Lao Haksat, the Lao Patriotic Front. This was the leading party of the Left, closely allied with the revolutionary Left in Vietnam and oriented toward the socialist world. Its charismatic leader was Prince Souphanouvong, younger half-brother of Prince Souvanna Phouma, member of the royal family, and a fervent revolutionary.

Though active on the Laotian political scene for over a quarter of a century, and a legend in his own time, Prince Souphanouvong remains one of the least-known and most mysterious personalities of the Asian drama. Souphanouvong has spent most of his last twenty-five years in guerrilla hideouts in the jungles, mountains and plains of Laos, and relatively few people, particularly from the West, have become closely acquainted with him or have had an opportunity to see him in political action and daily life. Few have met him for more than a casual conversation or conventional interview. This is also true of most Pathet Lao leaders: they rarely appear in public.

During the First Indochina War, because France presented the Pathet Lao fighting units as a "phantom force," a branch of the Viet Minh, the Pathet Lao was refused recognition and representation at the 1954 Geneva conference. The agreement on cessation of hostilities in Laos thus had to be signed by Ta Quang Buu, Vice-Minister of National Defense of the Democratic Republic of Vietnam "for the Commander-in-Chief of the Fighting Units of Pathet Lao and the Commander-in-Chief of the People's Army of Viet Nam." And no Laotian representing the Royal Government countersigned the agreement; instead it was signed by General Delteil "for the Commander-in-Chief of the Forces of the French Union in Indo-China." This reflected Laos's dependent position.

Slowly, however, the Pathet Lao moved into the news and became identified as a substantial political and military force. Territories controlled by the Pathet Lao, however, were practically inaccessible. Pathet Lao statements were given little publicity, and in the West the predominant image of the Pathet Lao corresponded to the perceptions, prejudices and propaganda needs of their enemies. The West most often perceived Laotian realities through war shock, seldom through political and cultural rapprochement. Thus Western knowledge of the Pathet Lao was generally superficial, distorted and sensational. But in point of fact nothing is as important to an understanding of Laos's post-colonial history than an accurate study of the Laotian Left.

The personal story of Prince Souphanouvong serves as an exemplary case, for Souphanouvong embodies Asia's continuity—or rather its revolutionary discontinuity—from its feudal, downtrodden, backward past into national revival, independence and international importance. Most Laotians consider Souphanouvong a national hero—the prince who left the luxuries of the royal family and descended to his people to fight for freedom and a better future. This feeling is shared by friends and foes alike: the Prince is respected even by his sworn enemies. I was always struck by the affection, homage and fervor with which Laotians greeted Souphavounong whenever he appeared in public. In the 1958 elections, when he first ran for elected office, he was elected by a large majority.

Certainly Souphanouvong is not without weaknesses, nor is any political leader. Not everything a revolutionary leader does in conditions of war can be hailed. I learned, however, to value Souphanouvong's honesty, spirit of sacrifice, and rare idealism very highly. Patriotism in his case is no empty word. He has dedicated his life to his country and his convictions. Even more than by the renunciation of wealth, his humility has been tried and proven by his acceptance of collective political discipline and conscious organizational subordination to his movement. All who have met him agree —Souphanouvong is an extraordinary personality, highly intelligent, ambitious and energetic. In personal contacts he astounds by his brilliance, his command of language, his vision, and he reveals a human warmth matched only by the traditional ideal of Laotian gentleness.

Early Evolution

Among my cherished Laotian souvenirs I guard a *khene,* a bamboo musical instrument, presented to me by Souphanouvong. It has the Prince's birthday branded on it: July 13, 1909. Souphanouvong was born in Luang Prabang, the son of Viceroy Tiao Boun Khong and a simple woman—he was a people's prince. Like most upper-class Laotians of his generation, Souphanouvong completed his secondary education in Hanoi and then proceeded to France, where he graduated as an engineer from the École Nationale des Ponts et Chaussées. He traveled widely in Europe, mixed with workers during his apprenticeship, and was attracted to Marxist thinking. He returned to Indochina in 1938, was appointed engineer with the French administration in central Vietnam, and until 1945 lived in the coastal town of Vinh. Many bridges in this area and in central Laos are of his construction; years later, Pathet Lao guerrilla units were faced with the need to destroy bridges erected by their leader. Often, contrary to military wisdom, they let them stand.

His years of work with the French administration in Vietnam during the Second World War helped to form Souphanouvong's outlook and attitude. Exile to the lower echelons of the French colonial technical apparatus, with the customary national and social discrimination, must have deeply hurt the aspiring young prince's feelings. At the same time the Vietnamese, who had a much higher national consciousness than the Laotians, helped crystallize his ideas about freedom and independence. Experience accumulated while living on the fringes of the royal aristocracy, in the French administration, and in Europe was now supplemented by daily contact with common people and the revolutionary spirit of the Vietnamese. Himself an ardent nationalist, the Prince began to see that Laos's future would parallel the thrust of the Vietnamese battle for independence. And then the defeat of the French by the Japanese, an Asian power, opened new vistas of nationalistic revolt.

Souphanouvong is a man of action, competent, full of vitality and enthusiasm; at the same time he is a keen observer, intelligent and accustomed by his educational background to careful calculation. It was natural for him to respect the strong will, exact reasoning, toughness and effectiveness of the Vietnamese revolutionaries. He was impressed by the way they infused mobility into their nation, and from them he learned self-sufficiency, endurance, and precise political and military planning.

With the proclamation of Vietnamese independence in 1945, Souphanouvong traveled to Hanoi, where he met a group of Laotians—including Kaysone Phomvihan and Nouhak Phoumsavan—engaged in forming a revolutionary Laotian national movement. In the meantime (as General Singapo told me) a group of students, teachers and administrative officials, dispersed throughout the cities of Laos but linked by school ties and friendships, were actively promoting the new independence movement, called Lao Issara. In October, Souphanouvong's elder half-brother, the Viceroy Prince Phetsarath, took over the leadership of the Lao Issara in Vientiane and proclaimed Laos's independence. Singapo acted as *de facto* provincial governor of Thakhek and Savannakhet; and in Luang Prabang, Khamphay Boupha, then a young member of the Lao Issara and now a leading figure in the Neo Lao Haksat, forced the abdication of the King, who resisted the new movement.

In an atmosphere of national elation, the Laotians in Hanoi consulted with Ho Chi Minh and decided that Souphanouvong should return to Laos to join the Lao Issara. Souphanouvong was greeted enthusiastically by the Laotians, and as he traveled through central Laos he organized armed units and national liberation committees. When he arrived in Vientiane in early November, he was given the portfolio of Minister of Defense in the Lao Issara government and was named Commander-in-Chief of the national forces. Later he was also named Minister of Foreign Affairs. Thus all three brothers, with Prince Souvanna Phouma occupying the post of Minister of Public Works, came together in the Lao Issara movement.

The Battle of Thakhek

As Commander in Chief of the Lao liberation forces, Souphanouvong took personal command of the southern front, trying to halt French troops advancing northward along colonial Highways 9 and 13. He directed operations at Donghen and Phalane on Highway 9, and at Naxeng and Phom-xim on Highway 13. The last major resistance the Laotians offered was at Thakhek, on March 21, 1946. The French bombarded Thakhek severely, leaving thousands dead and wounded. The Laotians, badly armed and with very limited resources, fought courageously, but finally had to retreat. The Prince refused Singapo's advice to leave in the early hours of the battle, and stayed in the city until the last minute. When he finally arrived on the banks of the Mekong, the last boat had left. Swimming across the Mekong, Singapo turned one boat back to take the Prince. Twenty-five people climbed into the boat with Souphanouvong, but when it reached the middle of the river, a French plane machine-gunned the fugitives. Seven Laotians were killed and twelve wounded, among them Prince Souphanouvong. A bullet passed through his chest, coming within only a finger's breadth of his heart. But he reached Thai soil and managed to regain his health. Soon he joined the Lao Issara leaders in Bangkok, where they had found refuge in exile.

For the next three years, using Thailand as his base of operations, the Prince continued to organize guerrilla activities in Laos. Growing tendencies toward reconciliation with the French split the Lao Issara movement, and more and more the Prince was forced to rely on the cooperation of the Viet Minh. But gradually, between 1947 and 1949, anti-French guerrilla forces were created in Champassak, the Plain of Bolovens, on the Sebang River in southern Laos, in the region of Vientiane, and in Xieng Khouang, Muong Sing and Sam Neua in the north. Resistance was strongest in eastern Laos, where it was easier to get Vietnamese support. Souphanouvong established common cause with the main minorities in Laos. Sithone Komadam, son of the famous Lao Theung leader who led an anti-French uprising for twenty-six years (1910–36), took over his father's cause on the Plain of Bolovens and in southern Laos. In Xieng Khouang and the north, anti-French guerrillas were strengthened by Meo detachments led by Phay Dang.

In November 1947 two old friends and relatives, Singapo and Phoumi Nosavan, left Thailand to join the resistance in

the east. They arrived in Do Luong, near the Laotian-Viet-
namese border in central Indochina, in January 1948. In
June, according to Singapo, Nosavan demanded that the
guerrilla base be moved to the Mekong Valley in western
Laos. Singapo did not agree, arguing that it was necessary
first to build up the Lao forces in the east, in cooperation
with other Lao groups under the command of Kaysone and
Nouhak, so as to be able to move in the direction of the
Mekong later, in greater strength. Since Phoumi Nosavan
insisted on his plan and gained the support of some of the
guerrillas, Singapo agreed to draw lots. Nosavan was the
winner, and with twenty-five of the hundred and twenty-five
men in Do Luong, he left for the Thai Laotian border.
Shortly afterward he abandoned the guerrillas and went to
Vientiane. Later Nosavan explained that he had been sum-
moned to Vientiane by his cousin Kou Voravong, later the
Minister of Defense; Nosavan asserted that he hoped to be
useful in the struggle for independence. But the Vientiane
government collaborated with France, and he was unable to
do anything. In any case, Nosavan stayed with the Vientiane
camp.

Alliance with the Viet Minh

In 1949 the Lao Issara government disintegrated. All its
leaders except Phetsarath and Souphanouvong returned to
Vientiane. Phetsarath stayed in exile in Bangkok until 1956;
Souphanouvong and his comrades moved to Laos to enlarge
the liberated zones. Souphanouvong's participation in the
Lao Issara government had been a trying experience. As
Minister of Defense and Foreign Affairs he had been open to
suggestions, looking for help from any source ready to support the anti-French independence movement. The Laotian
resistance was too weak and its resources too meager to stand
alone against France; help was badly needed in every sphere

—in arms and training, in political leadership and military strategy. Like Ho Chi Minh, Souphanouvong originally cherished hopes that the United States—which for a time showed sympathy with the national revival in Indochina and had even helped to bring the Prince together with Ho Chi Minh—might help the Lao Issara. He soon discovered he was in error. Nor was Thailand ready to lend a helping hand, especially after the reestablishment of the military dictatorship of Marshal Phibul Songgram in 1947. There was no alternative but to enter into alliance with the Viet Minh, the only force actively and successfully opposing the return of French colonial rule. Disagreement over this course, plus the unwillingness of the aristocratic Laotian elite in Bangkok to continue the struggle, caused Souphanouvong to resign from the Lao Issara government in the spring of 1949.

On January 20, 1949, the first detachment of the Fighting Units of Pathet Lao was formed in northern Laos. It was baptized Battalion Latxavong, after the hero of the last period of Vientiane's independence, in the beginning of the nineteenth century. The organizer of the unit was Kaysone Phonvihan. On August 13, 1950, the first Resistance Congress, held in the north, on the border of the Vietnam's Hoa Vinh province, proclaimed the formation of the Neo Lao Issara (Laotian National Liberation Front) and of a resistance government, both under the chairmanship of Prince Souphanouvong. Other members of the government included Phoumi Vongvichit, acting as Souphanouvong's deputy and holding the Department of the Interior; Kaysone, in charge of Defense; Nouhak, in charge of Economy and Finance, and later also of Foreign Affairs; Tiao Souk Vongsak, in charge of Education; and Sithone Komadam and Phay Dang, members without portfolio. A few months later, on March 11, 1951, a conference of the resistance movements of Vietnam, Laos and Cambodia issued a manifesto proclaiming the creation of a Viet-Khmer-Lao alliance "founded on the principle of free consent, equality and mutual assistance, and respect for each other's rights; with the aim of driving away the French colonialists, the American interventionists, and the traitors to the Fatherland; and the establishment of a true independence of the three peoples."

At the time of the Geneva conference of 1954 the Pathet Lao and their Vietnamese allies controlled the whole eastern part of Laos, from Phong Saly in the north to the Cambodian border in the south, including the entire province of Sam Neua, parts of the provinces of Luang Prabang, Xieng Khouang, Thakhek and Savannakhet, and almost the entire provinces of Saravane and Attopeu.[1] Guerrilla activities spread to all the corners of the country. In recognition of this situation, the agreement on the cessation of hostilities in Laos assigned "twelve provisional assembly areas, one to each province, for the reception of the Fighting Units of Pathet Lao." For the Vietnamese People's Volunteer Forces (Vietnamese fighting with the Pathet Lao) and the French forces only five provisional assembly areas were fixed. Though the Geneva conference did not admit the Pathet Lao to the conference table, it nevertheless had to recognize the *de facto* military and political strength of Laotian resistance. "Pending a political settlement," the Pathet Lao was assigned the two northern provinces of Phong Saly and Sam Neua to regroup their forces. The use of the term "political settlement" clearly meant the recognition of the resistance movement in the political life of Laos.

The years of the First Indochinese War completed for Souphanouvong an evolution which began in the thirties. The intensity of an anticolonial struggle and the unique excitement of a people's war added to his awakened national consciousness. National aspirations blended with social awareness—an explosive mixture. These years taught him military and political strategy and the day-to-day application of military inventiveness and political wisdom. And they offered a rare opportunity to get acquainted with his homeland. On horse and by foot, Souphanouvong traversed the whole country. Building on his knowledge of the townspeople and the upper strata of the population, he expanded his exceptional insight into his nation's life. He met peasants and probed their minds. He acquainted himself thoroughly with the numerous minorities in Laos. He became familiar with his country's rich and manifold nature, soil and air, flora and fauna. He learned to walk through the jungle in the footsteps of the elephants, and he learned to live on rice produced by his own toil. Always keen to continue his studies, he carried books with him, and reading in Asian and European languages, including Russian, he became a linguist unmatched in Laos.

Comrade Prince

Thus it was not by chance that in the governments of national union, in 1957–58 and 1962, he was twice entrusted with the key portfolio of Planning and National Economy. For no one in Laos had his knowledge of the country's national resources, his understanding of technology, and his organizational abilities. In Khang Khay in 1961 and 1962 he often showed me collections of ores and minerals, enthusiastically proving Laos's richness and the possibilities for a quick economic takeoff. He always longed for the moment when he could leave the life of a war leader and turn to creative work where, he felt, he could do much more. He worked out a five-year economic development plan for Laos which was approved by the government in 1958; but when he was excluded from the government, the plan was dropped.

The Prince hoped that negotiations with the Royal Government in 1956 would arrive at the "political settlement" envisaged in the Geneva agreements. At its January 1956 congress, believing that a political settlement was near and aiming to adapt its activities to peaceful conditions, the Pathet Lao transformed itself into a political party, adopting the name of Neo Lao Haksat (Laotian Patriotic Front). Souphanouvong, selected chairman, traveled to Vientiane to attend talks with the Royal Government.

I first met him then. After a short stay in August, when the first two documents of the Vientiane agreements were signed, Souphanouvong returned to Vientiane on November 7 to finalize the negotiations. I had arrived in Vientiane five days earlier. Naturally, I was eager to establish good relations with all the parties concerned, especially with the Pathet Lao delegation. My first meetings with the Prince were rather formal, in accordance with the rules of protocol. But slowly, as we worked together for the success of negotiations, diplomatic formalities dwindled, and our relations became cordial.

I remember when I first had to write his title. It was on November 25, 1956, when I gave a dinner in honor of the Prince and the leaders of the Pathet Lao delegation— Phoumi Vongvichit, Nouhak Phoumsavan, Colonel Singapo, Colonel Phoun Sipraseuth, and Thao Ma. My administrative officer inquired about the seating cards at the table; we had no notion about the Prince's feelings on this, and any faux pas might have disruptive consequences. Nobody knew how to proceed. Should I use the term "comrade" and leave "prince" out? But "Comrade Souphanouvong" sounded odd. Should I stick to the customary "Prince Souphanouvong"? Finally, half in jest and half to meet protocol —a foul diplomatic compromise—I decided to mark his place "Comrade Prince Souphanouvong."

The dinner passed splendidly. Neither the Prince nor any of the other Pathet Lao leaders remarked on Souphanouvong's peculiar title. But two weeks later, during a long evening chat between the two of us, Souphanouvong

smilingly recalled the incident. Inside the Pathet Lao delegation, he told me, he was addressed as "comrade." But at the
table in the Pathet Lao's own residence, during common
meals, they often practiced the courtly manners they had to
use in contacts with the outside world. Souphanouvong
laughed with satisfaction—he had to retrain himself in court
language, which in his long resistance years had begun to slip
from his memory.

The Prince's Dreams

It was during this intimate conversation on December 8,
1957, that I first began to understand Souphanouvong's feelings and thinking. He had arrived unexpectedly at a film
performance organized for the staff of the Polish delegation.
After the performance I invited him for a drink at my residence. He accepted gladly. When we entered the house, he
checked carefully to see that the shutters were well closed.
A few weeks later I discovered that the ceiling of the room
where I worked was dotted by a dense net of microphones,
but I recalled Souphanouvong's reflex even more clearly
years later, in the spring of 1963, when the Foreign Minister
of Laos, Quinim Pholsena, was assassinated in that same
house.

Souphanouvong sat in a corner of the large drawing room,
I put a bottle of French champagne on the table, and our
tête-à-tête began. I added little to the conversation; I listened,
taken by the charm of Souphanouvong's narrative. Political
reflections alternated with personal reminiscences. He traced
the lines of the resistance's unremitting struggle. I was impressed by his sensitivity, his fullness of heart, and his enthusiasm. He stressed how happy he was to have a set of goals
and to have lived according to his ideals. Political reflections
alternated with personal reminiscences, and Souphanouvong
spoke with passion and with pathos. He said that he lived in

constant excitement. In sleep he dreamt about action and battlefields; and he often indulged in daydreams about the future. Though nearly fifty, he looked young, robust and radiant.

Souphanouvong showed me his hands, and told how many duties they had to perform. Because the Pathet Lao lacked qualified cadres, he and the other members of the delegation had to work day and night writing memos, translating documents, and planning things great and small. The Pathet Lao mission formed a close collective, with Nouhak Phoumsavan and Phoumi Vongvichit as the Prince's closest associates. During the day they met people and discussed matters with their adversaries; by night they exchanged information and experiences and planned for the next day. This was a political battle led with precision and purposefulness.

The Pathet Lao residence, on the bank of the Mekong, was famous throughout Vientiane. People came from far off to admire the vegetable garden around the house, the only farming of this kind in the capital, and to express their support. The chief Buddhist monk for the whole of Laos came to personally bless the Prince. A Thai Buddhist monk whom he knew from the resistance, who once had hidden a radio receiver for him behind an altar of Buddha, delivered greetings and good wishes from the head monk on the Thai side of the Mekong. Youth organizations and boy scouts came to pay their respects, and crowds followed him through the city. One day, Souphanouvong told me, his eighty-seven-year-old mother, whom he had not seen for years, came to him. "Never have the people of Vientiane greeted me so warmly," she said, weeping, "as they have since your arrival here." Relatives of the Prince and former resistance companions now in high government positions declared their allegiance to Souphanouvong.

The Prince's narrative, detailed and profound, opened my eyes to many of the realities of Laos. When we parted, it was well after midnight, but hours later I still could not fall asleep.

Neo Lao Haksat Leaders

As I got to know other Neo Lao Haksat leaders, I learned that their characters and personal qualities distinguished them from the ruling elite in Vientiane in a way that made their personal lives tremendous political assets. They were uncorrupted, dedicated, and true to Laotian traditions. They sincerely tried to practice in personal life the vision of a just, free, egalitarian society that they preached. And they received the active support of the population, while the Vientiane authorities could not even extort obedience through the use of force. Perhaps another story, told to me by General Singapo and Phoumi Vongvichit, Secretary-General of the Neo Lao Haksat,* will illustrate the way the Neo Lao Haksat worked.

After the overthrow of the first government of national union in 1958, the Phoui Sananikone government determined to arrest and disperse the two battalions of the Pathet Lao which, according to the Vientiane agreements, were to be integrated into the Royal Army. One battalion was encamped on the Plain of Jars, the other near Luang Prabang. The government's secret plan, according to Sisouk Na Champassak, Minister of Information and Youth in the Sananikone administration, was to "neutralize as quickly as

*Phoumi Vongvichit was born in Xieng Khouang on April 6, 1909, son of the chairman of the provincial tribunal. He later became chairman of this tribunal (1938), then district chief of Xieng Khouang (1940) and Vientiane (1942), then provincial governor of Sam Neua (1945). He joined the anti-French resistance in 1946. He was chosen to lead the Neo Lao Haksat delegation in negotiations with the Royal Government in 1955–57, became Minister of Culture and Arts in the first government of national union in 1957–58, leader of the Neo Lao Haksat delegation to the Geneva Conference in 1961–62, and Minister of Information, Propaganda and Tourism in the second government of national union, formed in 1962.

possible" the Pathet Lao units: "The government decided finally to take them [the Pathet Lao] at their word, grant them *en bloc* all their demands, let them know that all their officers, or so-called officers, would receive their desired ranks in the Royal Army. Once agreement was reached, the arms delivered, and the two battalions dispersed to all corners of the country, one could always nullify their so easily won advantages by asking, for example, that the newly promoted officers pass examinations corresponding to their ranks; this most of them would be totally incapable of doing."[2]

Following this scheme, government forces encircled the two Pathet Lao battalions, which included about 1,500 men and 105 officers, on May 11, 1959, demanding integration or surrender. Colonel Singapo, who led the two battalions, was offered only the rank of lieutenant colonel; he refused to attend the integration ceremony, and on May 13 he was arrested. The first battalion, near Luang Prabang, complied with the government demands of integration; but during the night of May 18, in an extraordinary operation, the second battalion slipped through the government's encirclement and disappeared into nearby mountains and jungle. The whole camp was emptied—the soldiers, their families, arms and supplies—but their escape was not noticed until early the next morning. Later most of the first battalion joined them. The government accused the Pathet Lao of renewing the civil war, and on July 28 the entire leadership of the Neo Lao Haksat present in Vientiane, which had been under surveillance since May, was arrested and was sent to join Singapo in the Phone Kheng prison. Altogether there were sixteen prisoners, including eight members of the National Assembly: Prince Souphanouvong, Phoumi Vongvichit, Nouhak Phoumsavan, Singapo Chounlamani, Sithone Komadam, Phoun Sipraseuth, Khamphay Boupha, and Sisana Sisane.

The Neo Lao Haksat leaders concentrated on upsetting

government plans for a show trial to discredit the Laotian Left. They wrote long political statements intended to awaken the consciousness of the examining magistrates, and they repeatedly read these aloud to the guards. At the same time the inmates' wives and Quinim Pholsena, who took over the legal defense, worked hard to win over the judicial apparatus. This tactic worked perfectly: the civil judges refused to open the case, claiming insufficient evidence.

At this point, the government decided to bring the prisoners before a military court, and ordered General Ouan Ratikon, chief of the armed forces and close associate of Phoumi Nosavan, to work up documentation proving a Pathet Lao conspiracy against the government; then the prisoners decided to arrange an escape.

Various plans were considered—digging a tunnel, cutting the barbed-wire fences, and others—but they finally decided on the "human" variant: to win over the guards and make the escape a political event.

Singapo had begun preparations for such an escape during his ten weeks of solitary confinement. Among the military police who guarded him, Singapo had met some of his former pupils, and he was able to explain events to them in such a way that they helped him set up contact with the outside world. Since the prison guards rotated between the prison and the private residences of such dignitaries as Phoumi Nosavan and Kou Abhay, the elderly head of the Royal Council, the guards' cooperation meant that Singapo received valuable information about comings and goings in the highest levels of government administration. After the other Neo Lao Haksat leaders were jailed, they set out to win over the other guards. Concentrating only on guards below the rank of sergeant major, and leaving out the higher ranks, they preached in a simple way about the meaning of politics, about Laotian realities, and about the needs of the country. An important part of this education dealt with the wisdom of Buddhism, its philosophy of life, its love of peace and its attitude toward people. This was a real course in political and civic thinking, based on national traditions and a social consciousness. As Phoumi Vongvichit put it, the general aim was to raise the "revolutionary morale" of the guards. The lessons were quickly learned, especially after the guards began to think about the daily life and behavior of their superiors. In three months, eighty of the hundred and twenty guards had become friendly toward the prisoners.

In the meantime, regular communication was maintained not only with the inmates' families but with cadres in the city. Buddhist bonzes, who had access to the prison, served as intermediaries. Through them the prisoners sent flowers and vegetables they cultivated in the prison yard to the higher Buddhist hierarchy. All these contacts were maintained for one single goal: the escape. Singapo was in charge of organization, Phoumi Vongvichit supervised the "educational project," and Nouhak served as secretary of the whole group. The exact plan was kept secret up to the evening of May 22, 1960. At nine that night the prisoners received military police uniforms. One hour later everything was ready. They formed into three groups, according to physical fitness, and at five minutes after midnight, together with the regular changing of the guards, they left the camp by the main gate. Nine guards and five Buddhist monks accompanied them. A heavy rain helped to cover their tracks.

Their way led north, toward the guerrilla bases. Though the sympathy of the population was of great help, this was a difficult route. In order to avoid their pursuers, the fugitives marched through the jungle. Sometimes they had to live on what they could find in the forest, and sometimes this was no more than leaves. But by the time of Kong Le's coup d'état in August, the party had reached the region of Muong Kassy, south of Luang Prabang.

News of the escape shocked government circles in Vientiane: it was distinctly political, and it startled the whole nation. To simple Laotians who felt deceived by promises for national reconciliation and yearned for a change, it brought new hope. The Vientiane government's policy of renouncing the Geneva and Vientiane agreements, returning to repression in internal affairs, and aligning with SEATO strategies in foreign policy, suffered a decisive setback. As Sisouk Na Champassak noted, "This spectacular flight added a new impulse to the rebellion in the countryside."[3]

Kong Le's Coup

The escape led directly to the coup d'état which Kong Le executed ten weeks later. Kong Le, a peasant of the Lao Theung minority, was brought up in an atmosphere of national awakening: one of his teachers at school in Savannakhet during World War II was Singapo. Kong Le spent his youth in the army, and went through French and American training, the latter in the Philippines in 1957–58. As commander of the Second Parachute Battalion, he specialized in counterinsurgency. In the course of years of fighting, he acquired a profound abhorrence for the civil war. He became increasingly indignant over the corruption and moral decay in the government elite, and grew especially bitter about U.S. interference in internal Laotian affairs, which the military establishment felt very strongly. When he was twenty-four, after his return from the Philippines, he contacted Singapo in Vientiane. In view of the developing political crisis he proposed straight away to organize a coup d'état. Singapo counseled restraint—the Neo Lao Haksat still hoped for reconciliation—and brought Kong Le into contact with Bong Souvannavong and Quinim Pholsena, leaders of the Santiphab Neutralist Party. After that Kong Le stayed under the political guidance of Quinim Pholsena. He arranged his "search and destroy" anti-guerrilla campaigns to please his superiors, but he was only waiting for the right moment to change fronts.

When news of the coup reached the Neo Lao Haksat leaders at Muong Kassy, they decided that Singapo should return to Vientiane to join Kong Le. In the meantime, radio contact had been established with Kaysone's guerrilla headquarters in the north. The next steps were carefully worked out in common consultations. When Souvanna invited the Neo Lao Haksat to renew negotiations, they decided to send a political delegation including Phoumi Vongvichit, Nouhak Phoumsavan, Phoun Sipraseuth and Sisana Sisane, editor of the Neo Lao Haksat newspaper. These men moved south to the neighborhood of Vang Vieng, where a French Alouette helicopter dispatched by Kong Le picked them up. On October 11, 1960, negotiations were initiated with the Souvanna Phouma government. The government delegation was led by Quinim Pholsena, and the Neo Lao Haksat delegation by Phoumi Vongvichit. A new chapter had opened in postwar Laotian history.

Ideology and National Aspirations

In search of a better understanding of Laotian affairs, I raised the question of the postwar role of the Pathet Lao with the hero of Laotian independence, Prince Phetsarath, a man held in reverence by the whole nation. Phetsarath clearly felt there was more patriotic devotion and independent thinking among the Pathet Lao than among the members of the Vientiane administration, though each group was led by one of his brothers. Speaking with Phetsarath I realized an essential difference between Asian and Western perceptions of the relationship of ideology to nationalism. Phetsarath said: "The return of the Pathet Lao into the national community will not make Laos communist. I believe that the Pathet Lao are first and foremost sincere patriots." Whereas the general feeling in the West—encouraged by scholars and propaganda media alike—was that Asian revolutionary movements used nationalism as a cover for ideological purposes, the Asian understanding was the reverse: ideology was invoked to serve national aspirations. Socialist thinking and Leninist learning about revolution simply provided effective instruments for modernization. Ideology added consciousness to a latent conflict and brought it out. The Pathet Lao adopted Marxism for reasons of exigency; nationalism remained their basic cause.

This is not to say that the struggle in Laos is devoid of class meaning; social issues are not as striking as in other Asian countries. There is no acute agrarian problem, no land scarcity. The peasants' greatest grievance concerned exorbitant colonial taxation. Social problems were of a national character, concerned with the extreme underdevelopment of the nation itself.

The first program of the Neo Lao Issara, adopted in 1950, did not go beyond demands for general national and democratic reforms. The principal points were:

(1) Resistance against the imperialist aggressor. The establishment of a truly independent and united land of Laos (Pathet Lao).
(2) Democratic liberties, including freedom of religion.
(3) Abolition of all the taxations introduced by the French colonialists; adoption of an equitable and reasonable tax system; abolition of corvée.
(4) Development of industry, agriculture and commerce . . . elevation of the standard of living of the people . . .
(5) Eradication of illiteracy; development of education and national culture.
(6) Development of the people's war; formation and development of the Lao Liberation Army.
(7) Equal rights for all national minorities.

(8) Consolidation and development of the United National Front "Neo Lao Issara."

(9) Close unity with the Vietnamese and Khmer peoples in the common struggle against the French colonialists and against any imperialism which intervenes in the affairs of the Land of Laos (Pathet Lao).*[4]

Lines of Division

Lines of division in Laos developed around these general national and social demands, and deepened during the course of a war brought into the country for reasons completely extraneous to Laotian interests.

The Laotian conservative camp consisted mostly of the upper levels of the former colonial administration; the feudal elite; mandarins; young, aggressive comprador merchants; and army officers who enriched themselves through war profits, acquired a vested interest in continued warfare, and established an ever-increasing influence in the government. U.S. military aid pumped hundreds of millions of dollars into the country. This was far beyond the absorptive capacity of the economy, and it became a major cause of demoralization, corruption and rot. "The greatest danger of communist subversion," Prince Phetsarath declared in an interview with the *Lao Presse* in March 1957, "comes from the bad use of foreign aid . . . It serves above all to outrageously enrich a minority, while the mass of the population remains as poor as ever."†

Political differentiation increased as foreign intervention increased, and the conflict more and more came to depend on foreign priorities. Considering the history and composition of Laos, the inherent divisive forces and traditional

*The Extraordinary Congress held by the Neo Lao Haksat eighteen years later, on October 31, 1968, almost replicated the 1950 policies.
†When Nosavan was expelled to Thailand in 1965 it was said that he took sixty-five million dollars with him.

rivalries within its borders, no Laotian could possibly expect any benefit from an alliance with big powers—unless the particular individual aimed to line his own pockets. National interest demanded abstention from the world power contest —what Prince Phetsarath called "integral neutrality." "When buffalos fight," says an old Laotian proverb, "it is the grass that suffers." Dulles' plan to make Laos into a forward base against China and Vietnam could only spell disaster for Laos.

In the struggle for national independence, the Pathet Lao aligned with the Vietnamese revolutionary movement; but events have shown that Ho Chi Minh himself always steered an independent line, with neutrality for the whole region as a goal. Both the Viet Minh and the Pathet Lao acclaimed the 1954 Geneva agreements as presaging independent neutrality for Indochina; the Pathet Lao followed up the Geneva agreements by virtually forcing the Royal Government to include the 1956 understanding on "peace and neutrality" as a key part of the Vientiane agreements. And it was the Neo Lao Haksat, in cooperation with the neutralists' left wing, headed by Quinim Pholsena, which hammered out the main formulation of the policy of Laotian neutrality in the 1962 Geneva agreements.

Pathet Lao leadership truly represented Laos's awakened nationalism and radical anticolonialism. This leadership originated from the same social strata as the Vientiane elite (with perhaps more links to the middle classes), and family ties closely interrelated both groups; but Neo Lao Haksat leaders understood more deeply the changes that had come to Asia in the wake of World War II. They created the only political movement in Laos with a distinct political program of action and a modern organizational framework. Unlike Vientiane parties, which were dominated by family affairs and clan interests, the Neo Lao Haksat brought into Laotian politics a pattern of disciplined activity which unified different strata of the population, Laotians and minorities alike. Social consciousness and the national awakening infused Pathet Lao leaders with a revolutionary romanticism, inventiveness, an ascetic readiness for hardship, and an inner endurance.

By 1960 the Neo Lao Haksat had become such a vital national force that its influence exceeded its organizational capabilities. As no other Laotian party or organization, the Neo Lao Haksat had penetrated all strata of the population. It had active followers first of all among the more conscious and politically sensitive intellectual and youth circles, among students and functionaries embittered by decay, foreign domination and war, longing for national rebirth, independence and peace. This was an influential group, the main reservoir of political, military and administrative cadres. However, most rank-and-file members of the movement—soldiers, guerrillas, local cadres and sympathizers—came from the common people: peasants, minorities and the embryonic working class. They were mobilized by ardous political campaigns and protracted indoctrination. It was not by chance that the main Pathet Lao bases were in the countryside and in minority regions, that political education preceded armed resistance, and that Pathet Lao strategy was to extend its influence from the rural areas into the cities.

In zones controlled by the Pathet Lao, as far as war conditions permitted, social and economic reforms were immediately introduced as part of an effort to win over the population, increase production, reach self-sufficiency and promote the war aims. The chief concern was agriculture. Peasants were freed from feudal burdens and urged to raise productivity through a variety of measures: through water conservation, building small dams, improving irrigation and drainage, better tools, new farming methods and mutual help. Where necessary, land was redistributed to suit the toiling capacity and needs of each family. Many rice fields were brought to yield two instead of one crop yearly. Simultaneously, workshops were erected to provide essential equipment and services called for by the new intermediate technology: foundries to produce simple farm tools, mechanized repair shops, carpenter's shops, and other locally needed workshops. The goal was to build at least one such shop center in each province. These workshops also served war needs, repairing weapons and supplementing equipment. Other projects were increased cotton growing, the establishment of state-owned weaving workshops, the installation of dispensaries and the construction of small pharmaceutical factories, the expansion of handicrafts and the erection of state stores to buy, sell and distribute goods needed by the population. High on the list of priorities was education, from elementary reading courses to political persuasion.

In 1957 I visited such a developing center in Sam Neua. One of the earliest workshops established in Sam Neua was a printing shop, which produced a daily paper in Laotian language, the first in Laos. It was also the first to print truly national Laotian textbooks for elementary schools. The province of Sam Neua then had over two hundred elementary schools; four years earlier it had had only two schools. I was particularly impressed by the locally produced simple agricultural tools. In 1961–62 I witnessed the beginnings of economic, social and cultural change in the Xieng Khouang area. Of course, resources were scarce; many badly needed goods, not available locally, had to be brought from North Vietnam. Though improvement was felt, poverty was general.

It is difficult to say now how much of this effort has survived U.S. saturation bombing. Jacques Decornoy of *Le Monde,* who visited the Sam Neua area in 1968, told about whole villages destroyed and the population hiding in the jungle or in mountain caves—but still economically active. He saw workshops, a small weaving factory, a pharmaceutical shop producing modern and traditional drugs and employing about a hundred women, schools operating in caves, and an effective administration. The Pathet Lao strength, Decornoy remarks, comes less from outside than from the growth of authentically popular social forces.[5]

Chapter 8

The Political–Military Tangle

In 1961 the parties in the Laotian conflict were confronted with a constant tension between the poles of political and military action. At headquarters the military situation was studied in great detail. Military preparedness was emphasized, but political weaknesses on both sides of the front caused constant hesitation. Each new turn, political or military, produced new doubts.

Two days after my arrival in Xieng Khouang, General Singapo turned up at my residence, unannounced and in private. Singapo Chounlamani was part of Pathet Lao history. Born in 1914 to an influential patrician family in Thakhek, a teacher by profession, he was a veteran of the movement from its first days, one of the organizers of the Pathet Lao armed forces. He took an active part in the Lao Issara independence drive and was chosen by Prince Souphanouvong to command the defense of Thakhek; after Thakhek's fall, he took refuge in Thailand. He returned to Laos in 1948, became one of the leaders of the resistance in central Laos, was elected vice-president of the Neo Lao Issara when it was formed in 1950, and became a member of the Central Committee of Neo Lao Haksat when it was formed in 1956. After the Geneva agreement of 1954 Singapo headed the Pathet Lao military delegation to the cease-fire committee. At the time of the formation of the first government of national union in 1957 he commanded the two Pathet Lao battalions that were to be integrated into (and fled from) the Royal Army. When he returned to Vientiane after Kong Le's coup, he became a member of the high command for the defense of the capital, was one of the architects of the masterly withdrawal from Vientiane, and was in command on December 22, 1960, at the decisive battle of Sala Phoukun, which gave the Pathet Lao and Kong Le forces control over the strategic intersection of highways 13 and 7. Continuing the drive along Highway 7, Singapo led the Pathet Lao–Kong Le forces in the operation which culminated in the conquest of the Plain of Jars on New Year's Eve, 1961. Promoted to general, he became a member of the Mixed Military Council set up to coordinate actions with the forces of the Souvanna Phouma government.

The Military Map

I had not seen Singapo since 1957 and was glad to meet him again. Stocky and robust, he had a military bearing, but was in fact good-natured and human. Greeting me with a large smile and an embrace, we exchanged personal news, and then he briefly explained the military situation.

He spoke with great competence, with knowledge of every detail. The areas under control of the Pathet Lao and the Royal Army faithful to Prince Souvanna Phouma, the so-called liberated areas, he said, covered more than two-thirds of the country. This was less than was shown on a map published by the London *Times* on January 6, 1961, and less than Associated Press estimates of August 1961, which gave the Pathet Lao effective control of about 80 percent of Laos. On Singapo's map, the liberated areas included the northern provinces of Phong Saly and Sam Neua which bordered on China and North Vietnam, as well as the whole mountainous eastern part of Laos down to the southern borders of South

Vietnam and Cambodia. In central Laos, north of Vientiane, Pathet Lao and neutralist control extended over Vientiane Province, the whole of Xieng Khouang Province, and nearly reached the royal capital of Luang Prabang. Except for a corridor in the south along Highway 13, the King's seat was encircled. In the western part of the country, liberated areas extended to the Nam Tha River and south to the Mekong, bordering on Sayaboury Province. In the southern panhandle, they covered the hinterland of all major cities on the Mekong, reaching the outskirts of Saravane and Attopeu. A map showing this situation (as of May 2, 1961) was handed to the ICSC Military Committee on August 18, 1961. With minor changes, the above lines of the *de facto* partition of Laos survived until the beginning of the seventies.

Though confident and full of vigor, Singapo showed concern about the situation. There were many difficulties to overcome, he said. Material and human resources were short, and the greatest effort was required to meet all needs. These were mainly difficulties of growth, but problems of supply and command created strains. Singapo did not hide the fact that Vietnamese aid was essential: it helped reestablish the balance destroyed by massive Thai intervention on the side of the Vientiane authorities, most specifically during and after the conquest of Vientiane by Phoumi Nosavan. Vietnamese aid was needed, too, to meet the higher technological level of the war created by U.S. intervention.

Enemy nests still existed in the rear, mainly in Xieng Khouang Province, manned mostly by the Meo hill minority under direct U.S. command. Of especial concern was a concentration around the slopes of Ban Padong, south of the Plain of Jars. U.S. planes and helicopters were flying over the areas controlled by Pathet Lao and neutralist troops, delivering arms and supplies to the Meo detachments. Such interference could not be tolerated, Singapo stressed, and action would have to be taken to suppress brigandage in areas under the administration of the Pathet Lao and the Souvanna Phouma government. General Singapo was visibly concerned about security, most of all in the regions surrounding the seat of the government in Khang Khay and the Plain of Jars.

The issues Singapo raised recurred frequently in discussions during the subsequent weeks. According to Pathet Lao estimates, in June 1961 there were still about fifty decimated mobile enemy companies—about fifty soldiers each—active in Xieng Khouang Province, and ten companies in Sam Neua Province. The enemy was staying in small units and moving from place to place. All in all, there were between 300 and 400 enemy soldiers still in Sam Neua Province, and about 2,500 in Xieng Khouang. Before the cessation of hostilities, there had been only seventeen enemy companies in Xieng Khouang Province, an assertion in fact partly admitted by the Vientiane authorities. Most of these soldiers had been parachuted in after the cease-fire.

American, Thai, Kuomintang, South Vietnamese and even Philippine military personnel mixed in the ranks of Nosavan's troops. U.S. participation was no secret. On instructions from President Kennedy, U.S. military advisers—who had been active in Laos since 1958 under the inconspicuous name of PEO (Program Evaluation Office—a branch of the United States Operation Mission [USOM] in Laos), under the command of General J. A. Heintges—were ordered two weeks before the cease-fire to exchange civilian clothes for military uniforms. They became known as the White Star teams. After the signing of the 1962 Geneva agreements the United States notified the ICSC of the withdrawal of 666 members of these teams. When Commission leaders visited Khang Khay on May 31, 1961, Souvanna Phouma and Souphanouvong complained about the presence of "a number of American officers" at Ban Padong. They considered this an offensive measure.

Acting in direct cooperation with the Americans were Philippine instructors. The Pathet Lao estimated that in the Vientiane region alone there were over two hundred Philippine military personnel. (After the 1962 Geneva agreements 403 Philippine technicians left Laos under ICSC supervision.) Whole units of Kuomintang troops roamed the regions of Houei Sai, on the Laotian-Thai-Burmese border, and of Muong Sing, on the Laotian-Burmese-Chinese border. Two companies of Kuomintang troops were engaged in operations near Luang Prabang. Their presence was never officially admitted, and they stayed in Laos even after the Geneva agreements. South Vietnamese troops often penetrated the border with Laos, and Thai units were mixed with Nosavan's troops. Apart from this, the Vientiane authorities relied heavily on recruitment of Thais of Lao origin in the northern provinces of Thailand. This kind of Thai involvement could hardly be detected.

The Meos, Opium, and the CIA

Of all the problems connected with enemy military activity in the rear of the Pathet Lao areas, greatest attention was given to the question of the Meo tribes. This was seen not only as a military threat but also as an internal political issue. The Pathet Lao, conscious of minority problems, won over a great part of the Meo population, and one Meo tribal leader, Phay Dang, ranked high in the Pathet Lao hierarchy. To a great extent, however, the Meo problem had been reduced to a socioeconomic question linked to the sale of opium.

Opium provided the Meo's main source of income, and the Pathet Lao could not compete with the CIA's lavish allocations. Time and again the Pathet Lao tried to apply alternative political and military pressures, but the material incentives offered by the Americans (through Vientiane channels) proved stronger. While the Pathet Lao tried to awaken social and national consciousness, the Vientiane generals offered their military machinery and air transport for the marketing of opium at the best selling centers in Southeast Asia and the Far East. They also supplied the Meo with whatever they wished—rice, salt, silver and arms.

The CIA, USOM and the Pentagon were willing to make giant investments to build a subsidiary mercenary army in this sensitive section of the world—to the rear of the Pathet Lao, on China's border, and even with the possibility of penetrating North Vietnam through its Meo population. The large uninhabited spaces of northern Laos, away from the main lines of communication and well-suited to secret activities, seemed to serve ideally the U.S. military's newly adopted master plans for counterinsurgency. The Meo chieftain who was in command at Ban Padong, Colonel Vang Pao, secured so much U.S. support that during the sixties he was able to expand his units into a sizable clandestine army which played a significant role not only in Laos but also in the air war against North Vietnam. Though the Pathet Lao and the Vietnamese often claimed to have studied the Meo problem intensely and to be well on the way to finding solutions, they never mastered the situation. Soviet representatives in Laos and Hanoi understood the urgency of the Meo challenge, and offered more practical solutions than those of the Pathet Lao and the Vietnamese: the Russians aimed at taking over the opium marketing. In order to buy up the opium harvest, the Soviet Union sent to Hanoi fifteen tons of silver—the best exchange currency in the Meo regions— and three and a half million feet of black, green and red cloth, much desired by the Meos. However, not only was it impossible to create the machinery for commercial exchange, but even cutting the silver into small bars became a problem. The Soviet commercial attaché in Hanoi expected the Vietnamese to act as intermediaries; the Vietnamese, however, showed little eagerness, and Souvanna's administration also hesitated. Some difficulties were created by a lack of specialists to handle the whole transaction, but the chief stumbling block seemed to be the price of opium. The Vietnamese maintained that Vang Pao had jacked prices up so high as to be commercially unacceptable. But Vientiane and the Americans didn't seem to mind.

CIA–Meo cooperation stimulated opium production and drug consumption in and outside of Indochina. CIA operational mobility and its wide network in Indochina broadened the Meo markets, and subsequent political and military developments in Indochina—the expansion of Vang Pao's clandestine army, the arrival in Indochina of hundreds of thousands of U.S. soldiers, the growth of the local armies, and the demoralization caused by the war—created conditions very favorable for the increase of opium production and marketing. Supply and demand were ideally matched. Laos became one of the world's largest centers of opium cultivation, and the stream of U.S. soldiers moving to and from Indochina brought drug addiction home to the United States. One side issue of the Indochina war thus became a key social problem within the United States.

The Battle of Ban Padong

In May and early June 1961 the major military problem in Laos was the battle developing around the slopes of Ban Padong. I discussed this situation often with Souvanna Phouma and Souphanouvong, with the chargé d'affaires of the Soviet embassy, Vassili Ivanovitch Tchivilev, and with the Economic and Cultural Representative of the Democratic Republic of Vietnam, Pham Van Thuyen.

The mountain ridge of Ban Padong, about twenty miles southwest of Xieng Khouang, is shaped like a semicircle, ten miles wide at the open side. Not only the slopes of Padong but also the high mountains to the south, including the 8,500-foot peak of Phu Bia, were controlled by Meo guerrillas. Vang Pao, acting under the guidance of a White Star team, had at his disposal eight hundred to a thousand men, well-armed and constantly supplied from Vientiane and U.S. bases in Thailand. The camp had two small airfields, but most equipment was parachuted in. Four Dakotas brought in new supplies daily, and two helicopters were constantly busy transporting airdrops to the main base and evacuating the injured. Not sure about the possible response, the Pathet Lao preferred not to ask the Soviet Union to airlift in supplies. Thus it took them fifteen days to transport supplies from the Vietnamese border to Padong. The delivery of one artillery shell on a soldier's shoulders from the rear to front artillery positions took one day; the withdrawal of a wounded soldier took five days. Because artillery was used by both sides and because airplane-launched rockets were used against the Pathet Lao, Kong Le troops, unaccustomed to heavy weapons, were not brought into action.

About five hundred soldiers—Pathet Lao and Vietnamese —participated in the assault. The Vietnamese were mainly in charge of artillery. Fighting began in February, but there was only one approach open—from the front—and this combined with the difficulties of the terrain to transform the battle into a long struggle. By the end of April the Pathet Lao had conquered the ridges. In May the Americans lost two helicopters and about one hundred Padong defenders were killed or wounded; the Pathet Lao and Vietnamese suffered about thirty killed and wounded. Finally, on June 6, Padong was captured. The bulk of the Meo forces withdrew toward Phu Bia. The Pathet Lao hailed the fall of Ban Padong; in the West it was called an American Dien Bien Phu in miniature.

Although it represented a severe defeat for Vientiane and the United States, and great noise was made about it in

Geneva (occurring as it did two days after the Khrushchev–Kennedy meeting in Vienna) Ban Padong did not change the pattern of the struggle around the Plain of Jars. For the next ten years the CIA and the Pentagon continued to attribute special importance to this mountainous area, which continued to serve as headquarters for clandestine Meo army activities, many aimed across North Vietnamese borders. Padong was soon replaced by military strongholds at Sam Thong and Long Chen, which were not discovered by the Western press and did not become famous until the end of the sixties.

But the battle for Ban Padong added urgency to the Laotian political debate. The West was very interested in halting the Pathet Lao advance, in preserving whatever strongholds the Rightists still commanded, and in establishing a strong machinery of control to limit the Left's freedom of action. It put persistent pressures on the ICSC, which was open to such pressures, and in its report of May 20, 1961, the Commission in no uncertain terms defended Vientiane's territorial holdings in the areas generally administered by the Pathet Lao and the Neutralists. The report stated: "The Commission agree that garrisons or groups of soldiers which find themselves in out-of-the-way places or are cut off in areas generally controlled by military hostile party or parties, should have some possibility of obtaining food and other necessities for their *continued* [italics added] existence. This can only be achieved in the present circumstances if the parties concerned agree to such supplies being brought in under the control and supervision of the Commission and with the cooperation of the opposing side or sides."

The next report, dated May 27, was formulated with even greater clarity. It spoke of Commission visits "to more sensitive places," giving first priority to Ban Padong and including Tchepone (on the Highway 9 in the rear of the revolutionary centers of Quang Tri Province in South Vietnam),

Phalane (on the same highway in the rear of Savannakhet), and Kieucacham and Ban Hin Heup (which corresponded to inspection points suggested by the Pathet Lao and Souvanna Phouma government). The report said that "from among these sensitive places the Commission intends to visit immediately one place to be recommended by the delegation of Prince Boun Oum and another place by the delegations of Prince Souvanna Phouma and Prince Souphanouvong."

These recommendations were carried unanimously, with the support of the Polish Delegation. The Polish commissioner, eager to show the Commission's effectiveness, acted in line with the goal initially set up in Moscow; the same goal, effective cease-fire, reappeared in the Kennedy–Khrushchev Vienna communiqué. Local political implications as felt by the Left were disregarded, or perhaps not even understood, since regular line of communication between the local Left and the Polish delegation had not yet been fully established.

The Canadian delegation went even further, demanding that the Commission include in its report of June 5 requirements for ICSC prerogatives which would give to it authority to act as the highest arbiter, standing above the parties to the conflict. The proposed Canadian amendment read, "The Canadian Representative . . . takes the view that the directive from the Co-chairmen empowers the Commission to take whatever steps may be necessary to preserve and maintain the cease-fire, including the dispatch of teams to investigate complaints of breaches, irrespective of whether a formal detailed cease-fire agreement has been negotiated by the parties. While recognizing that cooperation of the parties is desirable and may in fact be essential, he is not prepared to accept that investigations can be carried out only with the consent of all parties." The amendment proposed to invest the Commission with "a clear mandate" to act "without the explicit consent of all parties." This was, of course, all rhetoric; it was clear—in the words of the same Canadian amendment—that "in fact investigations can hardly be carried out without the cooperation of the parties." The Canadian amendment paralleled proposals which were presented by the United States in Geneva and which were rejected by the conference.

Commission Assignments

For the local parties, naturally, all this was not a question of theory. They saw it in purely practical terms. Phoumi Nosavan was delighted to accept a Commission visit to Ban Padong and even to station there a permanent Commission team; by its mere presence it would have preserved the stronghold and added legality to its existence. He rejected only one detail of the plan. Nosavan could not admit the Commission to the supply centers in Thailand; that would disclose the magnitude of U.S.–Thai intervention.

On the other hand, Souvannna Phouma and Souphanouvong had a completely different understanding of the problem. The same report notes that the princes "took the view that the trouble there [at Ban Padong] could and should have been avoided if, at the time of cease-fire declaration and even after it, the opposing side had not airdropped men and supplies, including arms, ammunition, artillery, and considerable amounts of food and money. They stated that these activities prolonged unrest and feelings of insecurity in that part of Xieng Khouang Province and constituted great provocations and serious threats to their main positions on the Plaine des Jarres . . . They concluded in general: 'It stands to reason that we cannot tolerate the interference of these troublemakers in the liberated areas and that we have the duty to repress them and disable them in order to preserve our territory and insure the tranquility and safety of the population.' "

While rejecting the Commission's interference in the affair

of Ban Padong, the princes were ready to concede concrete assignments for the Commission, though no precise cease-fire agreement existed and no principles for the Commission's activities had yet been adopted by the Geneva conference. Their precondition was a preliminary agreement of the three interested parties on concrete functions to be executed by the Commission. The Pathet Lao and the Neutralists proposed Commission visits, not in the rear areas, but at the main meeting points of the opposing forces.

The important feature in these efforts to activate the Commission was the question: Were the moves of the parties conducive to a settlement, or were they intended to delay, to win time, and finally to disrupt perspectives for a political solution? Sadly, the parties were programmed by experience to believe that military resolution was a precondition for political advance. As far as the Left was concerned, this was the lesson of the First Indochina War, particularly of the causal nexus between Dien Bien Phu and the results of the 1954 Geneva conference. This, in general, was also the lesson of events in 1954 through 1956 in Laos preceding the formation of the first government of national union in 1957. And it seemed that this relationship existed in 1961, when the United States agreed to reactivate the ICSC and convene a new Geneva conference.

The stage did not seem to be set for quick and unequivocal progress in political negotiations. In Geneva there was not even agreement about Laotian representation at the conference. Meanwhile, at the Ban Namone conference of Laotian parties, the question of priorities of political and military issues played a central role. The Left and the Neutralists pleaded for straight political negotiations, while the Vientiane representative pressed first of all to freeze the military situation. Even the agreement reached by the parties on May 26—that military problems would be referred to a subcommittee while the main conference concerned itself with political problems—did not break the ice. No one felt ready to enter serious political negotiations.

The Zurich Agreement

But true to the military-political relationship, the fall of Ban Padong hastened negotiations, and the net result was the meeting of the three princes—Souvanna Phouma, Boun Oum and Souphanouvong—in Zurich, and the signing on June 22, 1961, of an agreement of principles to be followed in settling political problems. This basic document outlined general rules for the future internal and external policy of Laos and procedures for the formation of a government of national union.

The Zurich communiqué unequivocally defined the foreign policy of Laos in the spirit of "peace and neutrality in conformity with the Geneva agreements of 1954." Internal policy was to "give full effect to democratic liberties" and "to bring back into force laws on the democratic freedoms of citizens and the electoral law approved by the National Assembly in 1957" (following the so-called Vientiane agreements concluded between the Royal Government and the Pathet Lao). The communiqué announced agreement to form a provisional government of national union which would designate a unified delegation to the Geneva conference, would release all political prisoners and detainees, and would organize general elections to the National Assembly with a view to forming a definitive government. "During the transitional period, the administrative organs set up during the hostilities will be retained provisionally," the communiqué stated. Finally, the three princes agreed that the government of national union should include representatives of the three parties, and that "it will be formed in accordance with a special procedure by direct designation and nomination by His Majesty the King, without reference to the National Assembly." This canceled the mandate of the Vientiane Assembly, set up through the vote of April 1960 rigged by Phoumi Nosavan. This provision was of basic importance, and later moves to disregard it contributed to the breakdown of the 1962 settlement. The Zurich communiqué represented a great step forward in the political negotiations. The Commission report of June 27 called the meeting of the three princes "beneficial, both in improving the general atmosphere and in the proper maintenance of the cease-fire." But words were not followed by deeds.

The first shock came from Bangkok, which Phoumi Nosavan visited in the first days of July after flying to Washington following the Zurich meeting. In Washington Phoumi had talked with high military officials, with Secretary of Defense McNamara, Secretary of State Rusk, and President Kennedy. When Phoumi arrived in Bangkok his uncle, the Prime Minister of Thailand, Field Marshal Sarit Thanarat, made a statement which the *Bangkok Post* of July 5, 1961, carried under the heading, "Premier: Phoumi Does Not Expect Early Settlement." The statement read: "The Royal Laotian Government will take military preparations for any eventuality that may arise, if the talks fail and no agreement on solutions is reached . . . There is little likelihood of agreement in the current negotiations." Six months later, in a surprisingly frank conversation, Nosavan told me somewhat sarcastically, "I am the most suitable candidate for a neutral Prime Minister of Laos."

Polarization Policy

Always abundant, suspicions among the Pathet Lao and in Hanoi increased sharply after the Bangkok declaration. Neither the Pathet Lao nor Hanoi ever had much confidence that they could find a common language and fruitful cooperation with Phoumi Nosavan or other leaders of the Vientiane military clan. But their new alliance with Souvanna Phouma also was far from cemented, and examples were always at hand to recall the Prince's strong links with the West and with conservatives in Laos. When I met Souphanouvong after his return from Europe he observed that Zurich marked U.S. diplomacy's first step toward winning Souvanna over to their position.* Discussing this subject, Bernard B. Fall revealed that in the spring of 1961 U.S. policy, particularly through the CIA in Laos, worked toward polarization— "forcing the middle-of-the-road elements to take sides either with the pro-American faction or the Pathet Lao," which in itself would result in "a salutary process that would swing key Laotian elements in the West's favor."[1] What Fall discovered in Washington was naturally no secret in Laos, especially in circles directly concerned. Souphanouvong was expressing his fear that the polarization policy, by resorting to verbal concessions and greater political flexibility, was trying to get at Souvanna Phouma himself.

In fact, while General Nosavan went from Zurich to Washington, Souvanna Phouma left for Paris, where he had a long conversation with Averell Harriman, President Kennedy's special envoy. No details of the encounter were published, but when he emerged from the meeting Souvanna told reporters: "We are agreed on the whole of the Laotian problem and the solution that must be found for it," adding that Mr. Harriman offered extensive American support and eco-

*In Khang Khay the two princes met often and talked freely. Both were conscious of family ties and family traditions. Yet relations never became cordial. Their paths split politically and socially, and complete confidence could not be established. Souvanna suspected Souphanouvong of not being free to act, dependent on internal Pathet Lao discipline; he strongly disliked Souphanouvong's plebeian and revolutionary associates. And Souphanouvong looked upon Souvanna as Western-oriented, the leading representative of an aristocratic Laotian oligarchy, unable to break with the past. They shared a lack of confidence and perhaps a sense of rivalry. There was more correctness than friendliness in their dealings.

nomic aid for Laos. In the meantime, as confirmed after Nosavan's visit to Washington by State Department spokesman Lincoln White, the United States continued its military and economic aid to the Vientiane authorities.

This subtle diplomatic game, supported by tremendous military and economic resources, worried the Pathet Lao and the Vietnamese, especially when U.S. tactics proved effective. Nouhak Phoumsavan, one of the top leaders of the Neo Lao Haksat, developed for me a complicated theory on what might have been behind Souvanna's Paris visit. The Prince seemed impressed not only by Harriman's promises, Nouhak thought, but also by inducements coming simultaneously from Paris and London. Nouhak was convinced that Souvanna received encouragement to steer away from an alliance with the Pathet Lao. In this respect the Western powers were united. A long-range political strategy seemed to have been worked out in Paris.

I discussed matters with General Thong Dy, deputy of the Vietnamese Aid Mission in Khang Khay. While stressing the political importance of the Zurich agreement, Thong Dy was concerned about its immediate effects upon the Neutralists. He thought that the higher officials of the Souvanna Phouma government felt undue optimism: they were thinking of their social positions; they wanted a quick return to Vientiane in order to regain their lucrative posts. Such a state of mind, in a situation still fraught with political and military difficulties, could only be destructive, Thong Dy emphasized. Taking into consideration past experiences, the Pathet Lao was naturally reluctant to accept hurried solutions which would not be adequately secured by political guarantees. Consequently, tensions appeared, and certain forms of political mobilization were weakened. Thong Dy was optimistic, however: he felt that the Pathet Lao would stand the challenge, since in the overall struggle, the Pathet Lao was certainly politically and militarily superior to its adversaries.

The Soviet Outlook

Soviet diplomats responded differently to Zurich. They were concerned, and aware of the divergent class outlooks of Souvanna Phouma and the Pathet Lao; but their reasoning was guided mainly by international considerations. In foreign policy, they felt, the Pathet Lao and Souvanna Phouma could find a common language by adopting neutrality. Their eagerness to end the conflict took precedence over internal considerations.

Long before the princes met in Zurich, at the end of May 1961, I spoke at length with the somewhat shy but alert chargé d'affaires of the Soviet Embassy, Vassili I. Tchivilev, on the theme of a political solution. I liked meetings with Tchivilev. He was frank and devoid of stand-offishness. In his profile, his figure and his plebeian background, he had much in common with Khrushchev. Problems were open-heartedly aired over a glass of vodka. Tchivilev felt that a political solution was necessary to give the Pathet Lao time to digest their victories. Events had surpassed Pathet Lao capabilities. Used to guerrilla war and jungle conditions, to the countryside and village activities, they found it difficult to cope with the new circumstances. They lacked political cadres and military experts to deal with administrative, political and military problems. Of course, Tchivilev added, the Vietnamese were helpful in this situation, but it was time to move from military to political solutions. In Tchivilev's opinion, hesitations and difficulties in stabilizing the alliance with Souvanna Phouma were only signs of political weakness. Tchivilev's thinking and his sincere worries truly expressed the Soviet line.

In mid-July, with the arrival in Khang Khay of Soviet Ambassador A. N. Abramov, I had a new occasion for a wide review of the situation. Abramov was a shrewd and intelligent diplomat with a high sense of personal involvement. He also believed strongly in the correctness of the Soviet policy. He emphasized first and foremost the international importance of the Zurich agreement. It was generally interpreted, Abramov said, as an American resignation of the use of force, a belief which created panic among the Asian members of SEATO. As an example he cited the fact that for the first time in eight years, the Thai dictator Sarit Thanarat had turned up at a film show in the Soviet embassy in Bangkok, had received the Soviet ambassador, and had expressed in principle agreement to accept Soviet economic aid. Though this was only a typical Thai play to secure greater U.S. aid, Moscow took it at face value.

Abramov dwelled in some detail on Khrushchev's conversation with Souphanouvong after Zurich. He had carefully studied shorthand notes of the meeting, and he recalled that Khrushchev's main concern had been to tighten the alliance between the Pathet Lao and Souvanna Phouma, with the aim of forming a coalition government. To be sure, Khrushchev spoke about the decisive importance of the internal disposition of forces; yet he insisted on the overriding need for a peaceful solution to the Laotian problem.

By that time Moscow had a clearer awareness of its differences with the Pathet Lao and Hanoi, and Abramov was disturbed that this divergent trend persisted. From his conversation with Khrushchev, Abramov said, Souphanouvong seemed to have chosen those points which suited a hard line, while rejecting the guiding principles of the line suggested; this was a reflection of essentially different approaches to the Laotian problem. While the Soviet Union was convinced that of the burning international problems the question of Laos was best suited to an exemplary peaceful solution, the local perspective inside Indochina seemed different. Hanoi, Abramov concluded, was particularly worried about developments in South Vietnam, and rather inclined to ignore the international context.

I shared Abramov's concern. Yet was Hanoi to be blamed? Was it really possible to arrive at a lasting peaceful solution in Laos, if military solutions were sought in South Vietnam? At this time Hanoi was especially disturbed by Vice-President Lyndon Johnson's visit to Saigon and the cold war atmosphere which surrounded it. High significance was attached to the joint communiqué issued by Johnson and Diem in Saigon on May 13, 1961: "The United States recognizes that the President of the Republic of Viet-Nam, Ngo Dinh Diem . . . is in the vanguard of those leaders who stand for freedom on the periphery of the Communist empire in Asia. Free Viet-Nam cannot alone withstand the pressure which the Communist empire is exerting against it. Under these circumstances—the need of free Viet-Nam for increased and accelerated emergency assistance and the will and determination of the United States to provide such assistance to those willing to fight for their liberties—it is natural that a large measure of agreement on the means to accomplish the joint purpose was found in high-level conversations between the two governments."

These developments, linked to the general trend of U.S. policy in Indochina, caused uneasiness among the Neo Lao Haksat, too. They naturally gave a good deal of thought to the continuous aid extended by Washington to Phoumi Nosavan, and drew parallels with U.S. policy in South Vietnam.

A greater storm was brewing. This was the time when, in the wake of the January 1961 Khrushchev speech, Lyndon Johnson began to develop the so-called "Asian Doctrine"— a blend of traditional "manifest destiny" with a new awareness of the crucial importance of Asia in the world balance of power; a mixture of anti-Chinese obsessions developed in the late forties with a holistic view on world communism; a resolution to stem the tide of revolutionary upheavals by converting Indochina into a "bastion of the free world"; a conviction that reversing the trend in Indochina would prove beneficial for U.S. influence in Latin America and other parts of the rebellious Third World. Thus, though the course in Laos was temporarily set for a political solution, U.S. long-range strategy called for a military contest.

Chapter 9

Hanoi's Views

On June 3, 1961, at the climax of the battle of Ban Padong, Morski (the Polish commissioner, residing in Vientiane) and I received invitations to come to Hanoi to exchange views. Since the situation was tense, Morski preferred to stay in the Laotian capital, and asked me to proceed alone. I left for Hanoi on June 9 in a Soviet Ilyushin transport plane, part of the air-bridge established between the Plain of Jars and North Vietnam. At the Gia Lam airfield in Hanoi I was met by old friends, party and government officials. I was received as a guest of the Foreign Ministry and was allotted a comfortable villa in the center of town.

Hanoi was marvelously green and full of spring colors. On the Great Lake white lotus flowers bloomed, and alleys of huge flame trees were drowned in gay red. The Small Lake in the middle of the town, with its old island pagoda, attracted many visitors; parks were full of young couples, and the central market was crammed with food and all sorts of fruit. However, the air was humid and heavy, unpleasantly different from the cool, dry weather of mountainous Xieng Khouang. Breathing was sometimes difficult, and I sweated all day. Though a large ceiling fan revolved all night in my bedroom, sleep did not come easily.

Of the three days I stayed in Hanoi, the first two were fully devoted to conferences and discussions. I learned most at a meeting with the Acting Prime Minister, Pham Hung, a member of the Political Bureau of the Vietnamese Workers Party and an old acquaintance from 1955, when he had served as chief of the North Vietnamese liaison mission in Saigon. We had gone through violent July 1955 anti-Geneva demonstrations together. Pham Hung, a Southerner with an exceptional knowledge of the problems of that region, naturally viewed Laotian events in the light of U.S. activities in South Vietnam. He spoke with strong inner conviction. Basic national interests were involved. Laos and Vietnam were bound by fate. This was not simply a problem of strategical planning. For Pham Hung this was historical inevitability.

Later I had detailed discussions with Deputy Minister of Foreign Affairs Hoang Van Tien, and with a group of Vietnamese specializing in Laotian affairs: the chief of the Laos desk in the Central Committee of the Vietnamese Workers Party, Nguyen Chinh Giao; his close associate, later ambassador to Warsaw, Tran Chi Hien; department chief in the Ministry of Foreign Affairs Dao Viet Dinh, and others. Discussions were conducted mostly in French; only rarely did we need interpreters. Notes were taken and issues debated at length.

I brought back from Hanoi a comprehensive review of the Laotian situation in spring 1961 as seen by the Vietnamese and, by and large, by the Left in Laos. My previous experience in Indochina was corroborated: in no place could I get such precise insight and considered judgment about developments as in Hanoi. Hanoi's documentation on Indochina was like a huge interdisciplinary treasure dealing with political, military, social, economic, legal and other related issues. True, Hanoi provided a partisan view; but it was based on an extensive knowledge of facts, on a wide range of detailed information, and on profound and mature analysis.

Hanoi kept very close contact with the Pathet Lao, and strategical planning was a joint enterprise. Listening to the information presented by my Vietnamese hosts, I realized how much of the brunt of efforts in Laos was being carried by Hanoi. This was so in many fields: military support, economic and technical help, political counsel. In Hanoi an interdepartmental body was in constant touch with Laos. Apart from an economic and cultural representation accredited to Souvanna Phouma's government, on a confidential level Hanoi also maintained in Khang Khay a military aid committee whose main task was to channel supplies and aid to the forces of the government and the Neo Lao Haksat. North Vietnam provided the nucleus for assault units in the main battles. Vietnamese staff officers aided in military planning. Both the battles at Tha Thom and Ban Padong had been won with Vietnamese support. About twenty thousand Vietnamese were employed in cleaning and repairing roads, while about one thousand Vietnamese drivers were in Laotian service. During the four months since February, with the intensification of the fighting caused by increased U.S. intervention, the Vietnamese had lost in Laos some seven hundred dead and wounded soldiers and auxiliary personnel.

During my stay in Hanoi, one thing was particularly striking. All the Vietnamese carefully avoided even touching upon political differences between socialist countries. Though such matters were then in the air and were closely interrelated with Indochinese events, they were never mentioned in official conversations. The Vietnamese clearly took it for granted that their struggle and the struggles of all revolutionary forces in Indochina were serving the cause of socialism well, and consequently expected international solidarity and help. In private conversations they admitted that the Soviet-Chinese rift was detrimental to Indochina's struggle; but at the same time they strongly believed that this was only a passing phenomenon, and hoped for an early reconciliation. Implied in their presentation of Indochinese problems were interests common to all socialist countries. Their language was revolutionary and their spirit international; but their judgments had a solid underpinning of independent thinking. There was an atmosphere of self-confidence and national pride. Never were Russian or Chinese opinions quoted to support a certain point of view: on the contrary, local experience and specific conditions were invoked. I could sense the strong conviction that theirs was the best understanding and judgment of the conflict, no matter what others might say. Self-respect and national elation were marked.

The Protracted Struggle

When assessing events in Laos, the Vietnamese consistently referred to a general anlysis of recent developments in all Indochina, particularly South Vietnam. Indochina formed a unified strategic arena; Laos was but part of it. The rising revolutionary tide in Laos was seen in the larger context of the uprising in South Vietnam, with the U.S. desperately trying to resist change. Two elements were stressed: the fluidity of the situation, and the long-range, protracted character of the struggle.

Time and again the Vietnamese voiced their belief that the situation was constantly changing in favor of the revolutionary forces. "Progressive forces" had emerged as masters of the situation; this should set the course of negotiations in Geneva, define the talks in Ban Namone, and also fix our attitudes toward the International Commission. Conditions were so favorable that even arguments which normally would be rejected by the adversary could now produce desirable effects. Essentially, this reasoning boiled down to one point: terms for a settlement should be formulated mainly by the winning side. This time-honored point of view was also emphasized by the counselor of the Chinese embassy.

On principle the Vietnamese avoided linking the Laotian

problem to the general international situation and the perspectives of East-West negotiations. They seemed determined that considerations other than those directly resulting
from the Indochinese struggle should not interfere with local
strategy. This seemed to be the lesson of the 1954 Geneva
negotiations, when Vietnam had been used as a pawn by the
great powers. They maintained that the Vienna Khrushchev–Kennedy agreement did not change actual priorities or
the long-range appraisal of events. Concretely, it had nothing
to do with the need to wipe out enemy nests in the rear of
the liberated areas—for instance, at Ban Padong. Now I
understood why the Neo Lao Haksat and Hanoi had neither
informed the Russians about the progress of the Ban Padong
battle nor turned to them for help.

The Vietnamese mistrusted U.S. intentions in Laos and
were skeptical about political negotiations. They felt that as
long as the U.S. insisted on military presence in any corner
of the Indochinese Peninsula, no compromise could last
long. Indeed, because the Left was emerging victorious,
Hanoi thought, the United States must really fear a final
political settlement: Washington therefore encouraged its
Laotian clients to sabotage the talks in Geneva and Ban
Namone, in expectation of a new military turn. Thus only
effective military and political assets were of real value.
Again, the situation demanded an orientation toward protracted struggle, both political and military.

These circumstances, the Vietnamese said, required that
the Neo Lao Haksat adopt a far-sighted strategy: (1) to keep
their actual holdings, even in case of the formation of a
coalition government; (2) to preserve the alliance with the
Neutralists and Prince Souvanna Phouma; and (3) to work
continuously for conditions which would further enhance
their influence and popularity.

The Vietnamese briefed me in detail on the military and
political situation in Laos. Vientiane forces under General

Phoumi Nosavan were estimated at thirty-five thousand soldiers, half of them in garrisons, half in eleven mobile groups
active in the field. The forces faithful to Souvanna Phouma
numbered altogether twenty thousand, three-quarters of
them Neo Lao Haksat, about one-fifth soldiers of Kong Le,
and about fifteen hundred under Colonel Khammouane* in
the northern province of Phong Saly. With Souvanna Phouma's approval, Khammouane secured full equipment for his
units from the People's Republic of China. Yet he did not co-
operate with the Neo Lao Haksat as closely as did Kong Le.

Out of twelve provincial capitals, Vientiane controlled
nine, the Neo Lao Haksat and Souvanna Phouma three. The
proportion was, however, different on the level of districts
and villages. Vientiane controlled only thirty-seven out of
eighty-two district capitals, and 4,323 out of 11,464 villages.
But since Vientiane forces occupied the more densely popu-
lated areas, they controlled approximately 1,200,000 out of
a total of 2,500,000 inhabitants in the whole of Laos.

Hanoi put greater stress on quality than on numbers, and
valued audacity, self-reliance and preparedness more highly
than pure technics. Vientiane's units were much better
equipped and had superior military training: but Neo Lao
Haksat units had incomparably higher political consciousness and fighting spirit. Kong Le's units were not quite so
highly politically motivated. They were paid; Neo Lao Hak-

---

*At the time of Kong Le's coup Colonel Khammouane Boupha was
governor of Phong Saly, the most northern province of Laos, on the
Chinese border. He declared loyalty to Souvanna Phouma's government
and joined the Neutralist forces in the civil war. Phong Saly's location
induced him to maintain friendly relations with China, and Souvanna
agreed to the establishment of a Chinese consulate in Phong Saly's capital.
Khammouane's remoteness from the main battle lines gave him much
opportunity for independent action. After the breakup of the government
of national union in 1963–64, Khammouane remained loyal to the alliance
with the Neo Lao Haksat, and became Vice-Chairman of the Alliance of
the Lao Patriotic Neutralist Forces and a member of the Neutralist Armed
Forces command.

sat soldiers were not. In itself this is an important political indicator. Still, taking into consideration the low level of aggressiveness of all Laotian soldiers, the Kong Le units were superior to the Vientiane soldiers. But even they could not stand heavy artillery fire. The Neo Lao Haksat soldier was much more used to it and thus resistant.

U.S. Aims and Tactics

The Vietnamese presented a broad analysis of the aims and tactics of the United States and Vientiane authorities. Historical thinking dominated here. In general, an analogy was drawn to the period of the Vientiane negotiations in 1956–57 and the subsequent formation of the first government of national union: the Vietnamese estimated that the other side again aimed to utilize the cease-fire and an eventual settlement in order to disarm and suppress the Neo Lao Haksat. In the meantime, having conquered Vientiane with undisguised U.S. and Thai aid, Nosavan was feverishly trying to consolidate his own military positions. Should political negotiations not develop to the liking of the United States and the Rightists, they would resort again to military means, this time perhaps on a larger scale. The enemy's strategy rested on simultaneous applications of political and military instruments: consequently, attention must constantly be paid to both forms of the struggle.

The Vietnamese pointed to several military achievements and advantages gained by the U.S. and Nosavan's forces: (1) consolidation of military positions along the axis of the Mekong River and the Thai border; (2) accumulation of arms and of a considerable military potential, with the Thai channel as main supply route; and (3) arrangements for military training for the Vientiane forces in northeast Thailand—similarities between the Thai and Lao languages greatly facilitated this task.

Everything indicated that Nosavan might renew his military offensive at the start of the dry season. Meanwhile he was intensifying sabotage actions in the rear of the Neo Lao Haksat. The Vietnamese seemed especially sensitive about U.S.–Meo efforts to sabotage Highway 7, the main supply route leading from North Vietnam, through the villages of Ban Ban and Khang Khay, to the Plain of Jars. They were concerned, too, about enemy attempts to reconquer Highway 9, connecting Savannakhet, on the Mekong, through Tchepone, with the South Vietnamese province of Quang Tri. Highway 9—just south of the seventeenth parallel—was of particular importance, being closely related to U.S. plans to consolidate the strategic front in the southern part of the Indochinese Peninsula by establishing a land-bridge through Laos, linking the military hinterland in Thailand with South Vietnam. On the other hand, Highway 9 also cut through the north-south axis linking North and South Vietnam. Tchepone, with its small airfield, was later to acquire fame as a junction in the so-called Ho Chi Minh trails.

The aim of the United States, the Vietnamese said, was to manipulate the International Commission to serve its strategy. The Commission's job would be to cramp the movements of the Pathet Lao; to curtail by its presence aid to Neo Lao Haksat troops in the Plain of Jars area; to weaken the Souvanna Phouma government, and to isolate its military positions. Reciprocity—giving the Commission freedom of movement in areas administered by Vientiane—would act more to the detriment of the Souvanna Phouma and Pathet Lao forces. After all, Vientiane was wealthier, better equipped, and had many more direct supply lines from Thai bases over the Mekong.

Some thought was given, too, to U.S. plans to partition Laos. One such scheme often discussed in the Western press provided for a partition along the seventeenth parallel, in continuation of the Vietnamese demarcation line. Saigon authorities had shown special interest in this proposal. Hanoi estimated, however, that U.S. military circles, anxious to keep open the way northward to the Chinese and North Vietnamese borders, did not favor this partition. Nor did Thailand, which historically tended to expand northward. A meridional partition, which would lay open the whole Mekong Valley to Thai expansion, was more to Bangkok's liking. Hanoi considered that any partition would be harmful to the Laotians and to all revolutionary forces in Indochina. It would not only damage Laotian national interests but it would be strategically disadvantageous. The meridional alternative was as bad as the horizontal plan. It would strongly favor the enemy, who had at its disposal a relatively developed road network along the border, linking Laos with Thailand, whereas links with Vietnam were few and easy to control. Thus if a meridional partition were drawn, aid would reach Vientiane much more easily than the liberated areas.

National Democracy and Neutrality

The Vietnamese and the Neo Lao Haksat had worked out and agreed upon a general strategy. Laos had reached the stage of "national and democratic revolution"—the only notion borrowed from the November 1960 Moscow declaration of communist and workers' parties. As I saw it, this was used to prove adherence to international Marxist thinking and its creative application. It was perhaps nearer Moscow's ideas than Peking's; the content, however, was fully adapted to local needs and revolutionary strategy. Recent developments had produced much more revolutionary fervor and maturity than had existed in the period following the 1954 Geneva agreements or during the Vientiane negotiations in 1956–57. The main slogans of the Neo Lao Haksat, intended to meet the requirements of the new stage, were incorporated in demands for a peaceful, neutral, sovereign, united, prosperous Laos. These would mobilize the nation and provide the revolution with democratic content.

With the opening of negotiations in Laos and Geneva, military struggle intertwined with political effort; but the Vietnamese warned against pacifist illusions. Military problems could not be ignored. It was absolutely necessary to maintain constant pressure on enemy positions and to continue to clean out enemy nests in liberated territories.

Hanoi stressed a few basic guiding principles for negotiations in Geneva and Ban Namone. The Laotian problem was to be resolved by the Laotians themselves, relying on their own forces. This was not a question of procedure; it was a formula intrinsically related to the nature of the national liberation struggle. Its importance had to be widely elucidated, especially to the participants at the Geneva conference. The task of the Geneva conference was only to elaborate and formulate an international commitment to respect the independence and neutrality of Laos—neutrality being the bedrock of a general settlement. The Geneva powers need not guarantee the neutrality of Laos—guarantees should be rejected, since they could be misused to interfere in internal affairs. For precisely this reason, Switzerland had refused great-power guarantees for its neutrality. What was needed was a solemn international commitment to recognize and respect Laotian neutrality and independence.

This model for negotiations meant in practice that the center of gravity of the talks would remain in Laos. It focused attention on the discussions between the Laotian parties, and required constant political and military effort at home. Concretely, it demanded that the Neo Lao Haksat work toward consolidating the national front of "progressive and democratic forces," toward welding the alliance with Souvanna Phouma, and toward isolating the Nosavan partisans as much as possible. Military forces would have to be guarded and developed as a guarantee for further political advances. In negotiations the Neo Lao Haksat should try to secure better points of departure, to widen their range of influence, and to employ the enemy's mistakes to their own advantage. The program of the coalition government was not to be limited to discussions at the negotiation table, but was to be widely propagated, serving for the political mobilization of the people on both sides of the front. Its meaning was to permeate the population, the military and civil servants. It was to broaden the national front from the roots while enhancing the ascendancy of the Neo Lao Haksat.

Regarding the composition of the coalition government, the Neo Lao Haksat put forward the following formula: four portfolios to the Neutralists of Souvanna Phouma, three to the Neo Lao Haksat, and three to the faction of Nosavan and the Rightists. The Souvanna Phouma government would serve as a nucleus for the coalition. However, it was of primary importance to secure the key portfolios for the followers of Souvanna Phouma and the Neo Lao Haksat: Foreign Affairs, Defense, Interior, and Economy and Finance were considered most vital. The Neo Lao Haksat fully supported Souvanna Phouma for Prime Minister, and agreed that a six-point declaration which Souvanna had promulgated on May 6, 1961, should serve as a basis for the new government's program. This declaration stipulated the following: execution of a cease-fire; establishment of a large coalition government; the institution of democratic liberties; the unification of the armed forces; the acceptance of economic aid without strings attached; and the adoption of a policy of peace and neutrality in foreign relations.

The idea of a coalition had already been introduced to a certain extent in the territories controlled by the Neo Lao Haksat and the Neutralists. Four coalition administrations had been created on the provincial level in Sam Neua, Xieng Khouang, Phong Saly, and in Vientiane Province, using Vang Vieng as the capital. In certain cases the coalition administration extended also to the district level, though the districts were mostly controlled by the Neo Lao Haksat. In the villages authority was fully in the hands of the Neo Lao Haksat, as it was in the province of Sam Neua.

Some points in the Neo Lao Haksat political program were given particular emphasis, especially the demand for democratic freedoms. The Neo Lao Haksat stood for the restoration of the constitution, including the liberties and the electoral law incorporated in the Vientiane agreements. It demanded cancellation of all antidemocratic laws introduced by the Vientiane administration, and the dissolution of antidemocratic political organizations created in recent years. According to the Neo Lao Haksat, these were indispensable preliminary steps to free elections for a new National Assembly. Equal rights and solidarity with ethnic minorities had to be assured. Hanoi emphasized that half the population of Laos consisted of national minorities, some sixty different groups, of which the various Thai tribes and the Meo were most important. That special attention be given to the problems of minorities was in line with the traditional policy of the Pathet Lao.

The Vietnamese expounded at length on the concept of neutrality, a slogan which they felt needed to be made concrete. Neutrality did not mean passivity or indifference. Laos should strive toward "active neutrality," anticolonial and anti-imperialist. In substance, neutrality should enhance the struggle of the Asian and African peoples for peace, independence and justice. "Active neutrality" would in reality align Laos more closely with the socialist countries. An essential requirement of Laotian neutrality was nonadherence to any military alliance and renunciation of SEATO. To make use of the French–U.S. rivalry, the Neo Lao Haksat was inclined to accept the presence of French personnel at the military base of Seno, and French military instruction on a very reduced scale. However, concrete problems connected with the Seno base would have to be taken up in negotiations with France after the formation of the coalition government. In other matters related to neutrality, new accords negotiated in Geneva should follow the line indicated by the 1954 Geneva agreements. Imports of arms to Laos should be prohibited, except for small quantities needed for defense, and transit of arms through Laos should be forbidden. Laos should be free to establish diplomatic relations on the basis of equality with all states in both ideological camps, and should be allowed to accept economic aid from East and West.

The Neo Lao Haksat assumed that the unification of the armed forces would be postponed until the major political stipulations had been executed. The mode and course of unification would be conditional on the progress of democratization, the strengthening of the Left, and the broadening influence of all progressive forces. As to unification itself, the Neo Lao Haksat was thinking of a general reduction of the army, whose future composition should follow the pattern and proportions accepted in the coalition government. Until the final fusion was achieved, a collective command based on coalition ratios could be established. On a lower level, mixed military command groups could coordinate action at the meeting points of the different forces, so as to avoid incidents.

Cease-Fire Problems

Special consideration was given to the current problems of the cease-fire. Starting from the assumption that the adversary was bent in the long run on renewing fighting, the Neo Lao Haksat was resolved not to sign any agreement which would tend to bind its hands more than the adversary's. This formula, in fact, converted the cease-fire into a test of intent, and exerted pressure to speed up political negotiations.

In the practical reality of Laotian conditions, it would be

extremely difficult to work out and execute a precise agreement on the cessation of hostilities. The front extended for about 1,250 miles through difficult terrain, and behind both lines there were islands of resistance. Handicaps arose in the liberated areas from the shaky cooperation between the forces of the Neo Lao Haksat and Souvanna Phouma. Even more acute were political pressures felt in areas controlled by Vientiane. The most fitting policy in this situation, Hanoi thought, was a standstill of opposing forces on positions occupied by them at the moment, and constant insistence on the formation of a government of national unity. Since the adversary was not ready to accept such a government, fearing that a settlement would give the Left and its allies a preponderant position, the conclusion had to be that the situation was one of protracted instability.

The Vietnamese summarized the main requirements for a *de facto* cease-fire as follows: (1) The Neo Lao Haksat must aim to preserve all its gains, including positions held inside enemy territory, while at the same time striving to clean its own territory of the adversary's military posts. (2) Larger military concentrations should be forbidden by common agreement. (3) A ban should be proclaimed on the appearance in the air of any military planes, especially those armed with rockets and guns. (4) Violation of the parties' air space should be prohibited; special air corridors should be established for planes going to the conference site in Ban Namone and for ICSC planes shuttling between Vientiane and the Plain of Jars. (5) At the main meeting points of the opposing forces, each side should retreat about one and a quarter miles. (6) A mixed military commission on central and local levels, composed of representatives of the three parties, should be set up and authorized to deal with incidents and other matters at issue; in case of disagreement in the mixed commission, the problems would be referred to the International Commission.

Meanwhile, the policy of the Neo Lao Haksat was to air all complaints concerning the cease-fire at the Ban Namone conference, and not to turn to the ICSC or to the Co-chairmen. Only in very serious cases, when agreement in Ban Namone would be difficult to achieve, could the Commission be called in. The intention of this procedure was to show that cease-fire violations at the moment did not require outside interference. The Vietnamese told me that the Indian representative in Geneva, Krishna Menon, had requested that Chinese Foreign Minister Chen Yi intervene with Souvanna Phouma to get permission for the Commission's control in certain militarily sensitive areas in Laos, particularly at Ban Padong. Chen Yi had replied that in his opinion the whole affair was an internal Laotian problem, and that there was no ground for intervention in any case, since Ban Padong was situated within the liberated areas.

The International Commission's Role

Particular attention was devoted to the role and tasks of the International Commission. The Commission's role had changed basically since the 1954 Geneva agreements. At that time the ICSC somehow served to protect the relatively weak forces of the Laotian Left. Now it tended to impede the strengthening of these forces, which were in a state of ascendancy. This change was related to the modification in India's stand. Hanoi suggested two reasons for this shift: first, the strife with China; and second, the growth of the Left in Laos, which was not to New Delhi's liking.

The Vietnamese felt, however, that the new configuration of the ICSC should not produce passivity in the Polish delegation. Tactically, the situation required efforts to win over the Indians, and to establish good relations with the Canadians as well. Yet it would be futile to try to chip away at the class structure. Nor could one compromise on basic issues;

concessions could be made only in secondary matters. Essentially, the Laotian Left would be helped most by limiting the Commission's activity, especially in those cases where Commission action would work to the disadvantage of the Neo Lao Haksat and the Neutralists.

The Commission had to adhere strictly to its terms of reference. Since the terms laid down in 1954 were eroded, the only valid terms were those formulated recently in the letters of the Co-chairmen. The key wording, included in the Co-chairmen's message of April 24, 1961, was "to fix the cease-fire." The West interpreted this to mean that the ICSC had a free hand to act and decide on military questions in Laos. Hanoi's interpretation was that "to fix the cease-fire" meant only to ascertain the state of affairs. The power to make decisions still remained in the hands of the Laotians. The Commission had no political competence, and could not interfere with any problems except the cease-fire, and then only according to limits agreed upon by the parties. The ICSC could act only with the concurrence of the parties and at places indicated by the parties. At present, the Vietnamese emphasized, the Commission's powers applied solely to the main lines of the cease-fire; in no circumstances did they concern rear areas. Only a new agreement from Geneva could define additional powers for the Commission. In the future the ICSC would have to act on the invitation of the coalition government or of the three parties together.

Unlike the 1954 Geneva agreements, new accords negotiated in Geneva would have to drop provisions for stationing fixed teams in certain points of Laos. This clause was obsolete. The Neo Lao Haksat preferred the use of mobile teams that could be sent out after a violation was ascertained. There were good reasons for such an approach. No fixed teams could help if the government responsible for executing the agreements sought to evade the policy of neutrality. Although this was a position of principle, Hanoi did not rule out possible compromises. In accordance with its general thinking on the Commission's activity, Hanoi stipulated that the ICSC be equipped with minimal means of transport. Mobility was to be kept low, and as a rule all transport was to be provided by the parties.

The Vietnamese felt that the relationship between the ICSC and the mixed commission established by the parties should be marked by a spirit of cooperation, and not by any sense of superiority. The International Commission should aid the parties when invited, but could not impose anything on them. The mixed commission was not obligated to report to the ICSC about its internal discussions, although the ICSC ought to provide the parties with its reports and conclusions. All the activities of the ICSC concerned the problems of Laos, whereas not all the topics considered by the mixed commission and the parties were of concern to the ICSC. The correct channel of contact for the parties was through the liaison mission; the International Commission should not approach ministries or heads of governments directly, but should channel most business through the liaison mission. Direct contacts between the ICSC and the three princes should be limited as much as possible.

The task of the Polish delegation, the Vietnamese stipulated, was to defend Neo Lao Haksat interests as a matter of principle. The Neo Lao Haksat represented progress and revolutionary change, and the Laotian revolution would certainly be victorious. In daily work flexibility might well be necessary, but in essential questions there could be no yielding. If necessary, problems of principle should be defended to the point of being left in a minority: voice the right position and represent the revolutionary cause with dignity—calmly, confidently, and on the offensive. Matters would not be decided finally in the Commission—in the last instance they depended on the ratio of forces. In daily life coexistence was necessary; on political questions one must fight to the end. "You may feel yourself at home in Vientiane and Laos," Nguyen Chinh Giao concluded. "You have many friends there."

A Complex Situation

This then was the thinking in Hanoi; this was the strategy of the Left in Laos. It followed revolutionary learning and drew widely from past experience. It encompassed modern knowledge of making war and peace, and was adapted to an unequal contest with a much stronger adversary. It kept to revolutionary ideals but responded cold-bloodedly to the cynicism of colonial warfare. The Neo Lao Haksat viewed the Vientiane government as an agency of foreign interests; Hanoi had become involved because the same foreign interests were aligned against its own national aspirations. The situation seemed complex, remote from any easy solution. Conflict in Laos and Vietnam was not nearing a settlement but rather moving toward protracted strife: peace and compromise in Laos could only be a temporary device. A lasting solution would have to embody the Indochinese entity as a whole.

As I left Hanoi, I pondered Pham Hung's remarks linking Laos to developments in South Vietnam: Hanoi of course suspected that the negotiations in Laos were meant to cover growing U. S. intervention in South Vietnam.

From Hanoi I flew first to Vientiane, where I spoke to Morski. I had cabled from Hanoi to oppose pressures for Commission intervention in Ban Padong, stressing that Hanoi felt that the ICSC should not undertake anything without the expressed agreement of the three Laotian parties. Otherwise, Commission interference might aggravate the situation, and might actually help those who opposed a political settlement and wished to torpedo the Geneva conference. Hanoi felt that the United States feared a political settlement, which could leave the Nosavan group in the minority, and would tend to eliminate U. S. influence in Laos. To fan passions over local military incidents would serve to divert attention from the main problem of a political settlement.

As I presented Hanoi's and the Neo Lao Haksat's views, Morski looked gloomy. He seemed less concerned with the logic of the argument than with the consequences he would have to face in the Commission. Moreover, this strategy differed in many ways from the understanding we had brought from Warsaw and Moscow. But we could not ignore the position of the main actors. A hard political battle lay ahead.

I immediately wrote a detailed report to Warsaw, perhaps one of the longest ciphered messages ever sent from Indochina. It caused a sensation on the highest levels and without delay was forwarded to Moscow. From then on most of my information was routinely transmitted to Moscow. The Polish ambassador to Moscow later told me that in those years often up to one-third of the messages reaching the embassy consisted of my cables from Laos.

Moscow's Reaction

Both Warsaw and Moscow received the information I brought back from Hanoi with stupefaction and dismay. Although consistent with the policies and actions of the Neo Lao Haksat and Hanoi, my report was unexpected, especially as the revelations from Hanoi followed closely on the Khrushchev–Kennedy Vienna communiqué, which had been rather optimistic as far as Laos was concerned. There was immediate suspicion that Peking had had a hand in shaping the position of the Indochinese Left. Soviet-Chinese controversies were so much in everybody's thoughts that the real national interests of the Laotians and Vietnamese seemed to have been forgotten.

Back in Xieng Khouang I discussed the implications of

Hanoi's attitude with the Soviet chargé d'affaires, V. I. Tchivilev. In two long sessions we carefully reviewed every detail, while the embassy's second secretary took notes. Tchivilev was excited and alarmed. Frequently he wondered why Hanoi had chosen to present the problems to me, while keeping the Soviet representatives in the dark. He stressed that much of my information had not been known by him, or by the Soviet embassy in Hanoi, or by Moscow. True, he somehow had sensed the real state of affairs; but never had the problems been exposed in such explicit terms.

Tchivilev was also quick to see Peking's hand in Hanoi's moves. It was amazing to find that both Washington and Moscow were so eager to ascribe Hanoi and Neo Lao Haksat positions and strategies to Chinese influence. Perhaps this fear reinforced Tchivilev's concern about the situation. This problem, of course, concerned more than just Laos: the entire Indochinese strategy was involved, including the rising wave of South Vietnamese insurgency. Such developments, Tchivilev said, were fraught with danger for world peace. Was Peking pressing for a war to be fought with Soviet hands? Referring to South Vietnam, Tchivilev questioned the Vietnamese assumption that the United States would not intervene militarily on a larger scale. Evidently, he added, Khrushchev appraised the situation differently, devoting so much time to Laos in the Vienna talks with Kennedy and sending Gromyko to Geneva for such a prolonged period.

Tchivilev also focused on the concrete situation in Laos. The orientation toward protracted struggle was not in line with Soviet assumptions. Both sides, he said with concern, were apparently preparing for renewed fighting after the rainy season. He was not sure if the Neo Lao Haksat's appraisal of its superiority was correct. He was especially doubtful about the actual potential of the Laotian Left, its fighting capabilities and organizational readiness for decisive battles, both militarily and politically. In every detail, Mos-

cow's strategy seemed to him more fit to tackle the problems
of the moment. He decided to fly to Hanoi for consultations
at the Soviet embassy.

Neither War nor Peace

I maintained close contact with Hanoi and its representatives in Laos. On July 20, 1961, I had a three-hour conversation with the head of the Vietnamese Aid Mission in Khang
Khay, General Thao Chan, alias Phu Thien; he had invited
me for a talk after his return to Khang Khay from a month's
absence. The circumstances were somewhat unusual, as our
meeting took place before Chan even received the Soviet
ambassador, who had come to Khang Khay a few days
earlier. Abramov wondered about the reason for such behavior—did Hanoi want to communicate through me things it
preferred not to raise in direct contacts with Moscow?

This time Chan had an important message: the formation
of a coalition government was not advisable at the moment.
This change in strategy was caused largely by a coup d'état
that had been planned for July 3 by officers of the Souvanna
Phouma administration. The Pathet Lao and left-wingers in
Khang Khay had foiled the plot, and Souphanouvong, who
had me told about it first, seemed confident that any internal
difficulties with the Neutralists could be mastered. The Neutralists, Souphanouvong thought, did not recognize the seriousness of political diversion carried out by Vientiane agents
in their own midst; but political maturity was increasing, and
so was the ability of Neo Lao Haksat cadres to deal with
sabotage. The Prince was hopeful: the internal relation of
forces would be decisive, and the Left, steadily expanding,
was bound to be victorious.

But Chan concluded, as a result of the foiled coup, that:
(1) The alliance of the Neo Lao Haksat and Souvanna Phouma's followers was not yet sufficiently consolidated. (2) Cir-

cumstances, therefore, were not yet ripe to move beyond this partnership. (3) To let the Nosavan people into the coalition now might prove dangerous; they could destroy the still shaky Neutralist–Neo Lao Haksat alliance from within. Hence, it was necessary to play for time and preserve the current situation until the left-centrist alliance strengthened.

Three of the plot's ringleaders had been detained, Chan said, but the main agents were still free and active. They had established a forward position in Vang Vieng, where they could maintain easy contact with Vientiane. The plotters relied on a neutralist terminology demanding emancipation both from U. S. and Vietnamese forces. They aimed to create enmity toward the Vietnamese and discontent with the predominance of the Neo Lao Haksat. Apparently, French and Canadian officers had contributed advice and money.

According to Chan, even in Souvanna Phouma's cabinet there was still no full political understanding or clear distinction between friend and foe. This was also partially true of Kong Le himself, though he seemed to sincerely want cooperation with the Neo Lao Haksat. But Neutralists often accused the Pathet Lao of taking too much aid from Hanoi and the socialist countries. When Souvanna Phouma, then in Paris, was told about the plot, he was not surprised and ascribed responsibility to Pathet Lao policies.

There were three tendencies among the Kong Le troops, Chan said. First, there was a group bent on sabotage; it had U. S. inspiration and received instructions and financial support from Vientiane. This was a relatively small circle, but it included some officers in command positions. Second, there were people who at heart opposed U. S. policies, but who stood against the Vietnamese and the Pathet Lao. This was a much larger group; their posture was marked by indecision and vacillation. Members of the first group exploited this situation to create confusion and disarray among the Neutralists. Third, there was a group convinced of the necessity of close cooperation with the Left, and laboring to make the alliance with the Neo Lao Haksat as efficient as possible. This was a relatively small group, though it included such leading figures as Kong Le and General Heuan Mongkovilay.

General Chan was also explicit about the weaknesses of the Neo Lao Haksat. Whereas the leadership was conscious of the complexity and delicacy of the situation, most of the cadres lacked sufficient flexibility. They simply expected Neutralist standards to equal those of the Pathet Lao. This created a gap between expectation and reality, and an unduly harsh attitude toward comrades in arms—which, as a consequence, nourished discord. Considering the shortage of qualified Neo Lao Haksat cadres, circumstances demanded greater prudence and step-by-step, cautious advance, Chan declared. While continuing political negotiations, attention had to be paid to a better blending of the substructure in order to assure future national unity. The deepening of political consciousness among Neutralists and the Neo Lao Haksat was of primary importance. Much, of course, would depend on Vientiane's attitude; but realistically, one could not expect the formation of a coalition government in the very near future, say within one or two months.

What alternative could one anticipate? General Chan did not exclude the possibility of renewed fighting after the rainy season. However, he doubted that the United States would increase its intervention. This would bring a military response from Vietnam and the Chinese People's Republic which in turn "would mean the involvement of the whole socialist camp." Thus, since political negotiations were still difficult and military escalation was improbable, Chan expected a prolongation of the status quo of neither war nor peace. Preparedness for any eventuality thus was imperative. The outcome of the struggle would depend on improvement of Pathet Lao forces, political mobility and military readiness to counter any enemy blow. With favorable conditions, the Left could leap to power at a decisive moment, General Chan concluded.

The increased caution and the emphasis on checking unnecessary haste fitted with suspicions about the U. S. polarization policy. Foreign intervention was making Laotian conditions more complex and turbulent. As the Neo Lao Haksat leadership and Hanoi became more aware of what would be required for socio-political change in Laos, they decided that time was needed to assure the consummation of change and to make further advance increasingly sound and safe.

On my way home from the Vietnamese Aid Committee's compound I dropped in on Abramov at the Soviet embassy. His comment on Chan's exposition was that the Neo Lao Haksat and the Vietnamese seemed bent on moving straight to a people's democracy, refusing to recognize the historical necessity of passing through the stage of an anticolonial bourgeois democracy. This was the main difference in their political appreciation of the current situation, and one of the sources of disagreement with the Soviet Union.

Back in my jeep on the route to Xieng Khouang I recalled that about three months had passed since we had sat around the conference table in Moscow trying to outline the possible course of events. At that time the Russians had anticipated that by July the Geneva conference would be over, and the Laotian problem would be settled . . .

Chapter 10

Politics in Vientiane

Hanoi was right in assuming that the mainstream of Laotian negotiations would stay in Laos. The diplomats assembled in Geneva were unable to make headway as long as the parties remained on a war footing in Laos: the formation of a unified Laotian government and of a unified Laotian delegation to Geneva was a precondition for settling the international aspects of the conflict. The stalemate in Laos forced the Geneva conference to drag on for over a year, and relegated the delegations, as Gromyko angrily remarked, to "counting swans" on the Lake of Geneva. Only after the formation of the government of national union in June 1962 could the conference frame the final documents on Laotian neutrality and wind up its work.

Though the Neo Lao Haksat and Hanoi were reluctant to surrender their military-political gains in exchange for an unreliable coalition, it was the Vientiane administration that became the real obstacle to any advance in the negotiations. Phoumi Nosavan was an advocate of various state and group interests, local and foreign, which from the first Geneva conference in 1954 had stubbornly opposed the idea of a coalition government with Pathet Lao participation. First of all, he represented the young, power-hungry officers and those leading Laotian families who made fortunes on U. S. aid. The standing and further prospects for profiteering of both groups depended on continuous strife and the uninterrupted flow of U.S. funds. Secondly, Phoumi Nosavan was a faithful servant of Thai political and military interests bent on domination and expansion in Laos. Phoumi was a nephew of Marshal Sarit, and acted as his agent in Vientiane. Third, and most important, he was an exponent of politics pursued by U.S. military circles and the CIA, who had been instrumental in bringing him to power.

Nosavan was of course aware of the nature of U.S. policy in Laos. He must have known about Washington's long-range strategic planning, and the build-up of conventional and counterinsurgency forces to be made operative in Indochina. Hence he took it for granted that the Laotian negotiations were intended only to buy time until new fighting power would be available. In Hilsman's words, Nosavan "understood the box in which the United States found itself," and had every reason to believe that matters were not moving toward settlement but toward growing confrontation. Nosavan was not convinced that the Rightists in Laos ought to pay concessions, even for diplomatic reasons or as a tactical move. The general U.S. political, military and psychological setup in Indochina acted as an invitation to sabotage the Laotian talks. It was precisely this general setup, seen in conjunction with the past record of Nosavan and his supporters, which gave birth to the suspicions, hesitations and wariness of the Neo Lao Haksat and Hanoi: none of Nosavan's schemes could possibly be kept hidden from Neo Lao Haksat intelligence.

Negotiations in Laos thus were marked by stalling tactics, hard bargaining, and Vientiane's efforts to change the existing power ratios or even destroy the chances of an understanding. In his schemes, as Hilsman remarks, Phoumi Nosavan "could count on the support both of the Pentagon and the CIA." Though the June 1961 Zurich agreement between the three princes seemed to have settled most of the major political issues, it actually represented only an opening move in Vientiane's delaying and bargaining strategy. Under the pressure of U.S. diplomacy, Nosavan offered general concessions in Zurich, only to stiffen his stand when it came to details and execution. After Zurich, the three princes had to go through four abortive meetings—in the Laotian village of Ban Hin Heup in October 1961, on the Plain of Jars and in Vientiane in December 1961, and in Geneva in January 1962—before the shaky compromise of the June 1962 meeting on the Plain of Jars was reached. And just as the battle at Ban Padong had paved the way for the Zurich agreement, so another severe military defeat of the Nosavan forces, at Nam Tha in May 1962, preceded Vientiane's final consent to form the government of national union.

It is easier now, in retrospect, with the agonizing experiences of the Vietnam escalation in mind, to form a better judgment about the developments of those days. In 1961, however, matters did not seem so clear. I myself was optimistic, believing in the possibility of a working coalition government in Laos, even with the inclusion of the Rightists. Perhaps the Laos experience has proved this to be an unrealistic approach; a decade later, the National Liberation Front of South Vietnam insisted on the elimination of the most bellicose Saigon militarists as a precondition for the formation of a sound coalition government.

A Country Torn by War

As the post-Zurich impasse dragged on, I decided to visit Vientiane to gain more insight into political developments on the other side. Morski insisted that it was high time that I come over, and I was obliged to visit Laotian friends living in Vientiane. In addition, I had to make the usual protocolar calls on Western diplomatic representatives.

I flew to Vientiane at the beginning of August 1961, as the

sole passenger in a small Beaver aircraft hired by the Commission. Flying low over the central parts of Laos I was fascinated by its exceptional beauty. Below were rugged green mountains and dense forests, wild and uninhabited; peace seemed to be in the nature of the landscape. But from time to time a hill village appeared, equipped, strangely enough, with either an airdrop zone or a small airfield—supply stations for rice and arms: thus, the war reached the most isolated, underdeveloped villages, and Laotians living in a subsistence economy first contacted the outside world and learned of Western civilization through weapons shipments. Around the Plain of Jars war scars were more visible and still more depressing. A huge plain with great potential for farming and development—the place where Souvanna Phouma hoped to raise a new national capital—had been slashed in all directions by zigzag trenches, and dotted with fortified encampments and military posts.

Vientiane itself was the capital of the war. It had grown with the war—with the military establishment and the foreign aid turnover. When I came to Vientiane in 1956–57, it had about 30,000 inhabitants; the village reached almost to the center of the city, and buffalo grazed before the doors of the National Assembly. By 1961 the city had about 100,000 inhabitants, and hundreds of luxurious new villas, offices and shops, but no sign of a productive economy. A glimpse at the list of the new house-owners indicated the source of wealth: cabinet ministers, army officers, upper-class families involved in processing military aid. (When renting the new villas foreigners were usually asked to transmit payment directly to Swiss or French banks.) There were more night clubs and opium dens. Vieng Ratry, the old half-French night club, had changed its atmosphere: it had become Americanized. Dancing girls of different colors and nationalities served American guests, and U.S. army singers and rock bands dominated the podium.

Worried Laotians

In Vientiane I paid official visits during the day and talked late into the night, either in private homes or at outside dinner parties. The first group I met, naturally, were Indian and Canadian Commission people. I renewed an old friendship and dialogue with Samar Sen, the Commission chairman, a most amiable and knowledgeable companion, with whom I had worked closely in the Laos Commission in 1956–57. The second circle, by far more important from the local point of view, were Laotians, active politicians and members of the intelligentsia concerned about their country's fate. Finally, there was the diplomatic corps, including the ambassadors of the United States, Great Britain and India, and the French chargé d'affaires (the head of the mission was then waiting in Paris for the results of the three Western foreign ministers' consultations on Laos). All seemed keen to meet me, a rare visitor from the headquarters of the opposite camp.

I spent most of my time with Laotians. First I paid some courtesy visits, among others to the elderly chairman of the Royal Council, Kou Abhay. Then I had long, informal discussions with leading figures whom I knew well from my former assignment: Nhouy Abhay, a brother of Kou, former Minister of Interior, now Minister of Education in the Boun Oum government; Ngon Sananikone, the traditional representative of the Sananikone family in almost all the governments after the 1954 Geneva agreements, now Minister of National Economy; and Dr. Oudom Souvannavong, the first Laotian physician to act as Minister of Health, at that time member of the Vientiane delegation to the Ban Namone talks. Nhouy Abhay invited me to a Laotian dinner with other important personalities. In unconventional, straightforward terms, he tried to impress upon me the Laotian mishap, developing views he wanted me to communicate to

Khang Khay. A day later Ngon Sananikone, eager not to miss a place in a new coalition government, gave a delicious Chinese dinner, and in simple terms presented the not-too-encouraging realities of the current situation. I was invited to many Laotian homes and took part in traditional *baci* ceremonies; the more I listened to the war stories, the more I was shocked and depressed.

Most Laotians were deeply worried about the *de facto* partition of the country, feared a renewal of fighting, and longed for reconciliation. They groped for a way out of the dilemma. The Nosavan administration, using stick-and-carrot techniques—police terror executed by the so-called Headquarters for National Coordination, under Col. Siho Lamphouthacoul, and economic incentives created by the military boom—was able to keep matters under control. Still, nobody believed that the situation could last. Cabinet ministers and high officials sent their families abroad and located their funds in foreign banks. The Minister of Interior, for instance, had foreign bank accounts in France, Switzerland, Great Britain and the United States. There was a general atmosphere of impermanence. People on the highest levels could not fail to realize the artificiality of the military prosperity. Joining two fingers to indicate zero, Ngon Sananikone admitted that the "sound Laotian economy" was in fact nonexistent. Moral decay, corruption and bribery were spreading. Only a handful of people, headed by Nosavan, felt at home in this war market and knew how to use it for their ends.

The source of the evil was generally seen as U.S. interference, and anti-U.S. feelings, which a year ago had stirred the Kong Le revolt, were again mounting. No Laotian had a word of praise for the United States. On the contrary, the United States was ridiculed, and many Laotians were very bitter about the behavior of some U.S. officials. Commenting on the activity of U.S. diplomats, Nhouy Abhay exclaimed:

"Ils sont idiots." Nhouy, just returned from Geneva, cited one case of utter tactlessness: just before the address of the Vientiane representative at a plenary session of the Geneva conference, the second secretary of the U.S. delegation, a minor official, showed up, demanding changes in the Vientiane representative's speech. The Vientiane delegate was former Prime Minister Phoui Sananikone, a devoted U.S. adherent; even he was enraged. The story reminded me of Souphanouvong's account of U.S. behavior in Zurich, where, without even trying to hide their interference, U.S. diplomats —the name of Stevenson was mentioned—had orchestrated the activities of the Vientiane delegation. Having had direct contact with Americans, Laotians in Vientiane were inclined to blame the United States much more than Phoumi Nosavan for impeding the negotiations.

General Nosavan's Moves

Aware of the political ferment in his own ranks, Phoumi Nosavan played his cards shrewdly. He realized that, as in the period after the 1954 Geneva conference and during the Vientiane negotiations in 1956–57, public opinion strongly favored a political settlement. Thus he maneuvered artfully, conjuring reconciliation in his words but at the same time inventing conditions to block agreement. His political strategy fit the U.S. line of polarization: lure and blackmail Souvanna Phouma.

Phoumi Nosavan's main political move after the three princes' agreement in June at Zurich was to push through the National Congress—composed of the Royal Council and the National Assembly—a constitutional amendment investing the King with special powers to take over the leadership of the government or to appoint a new government without the vote of the National Assembly. The second alternative might have met the provisions agreed on in Zurich, but the first was meant to warn Souvanna Phouma of other possible moves. The amendment was voted in the National Congress on July 30, 1961, and the following day Nosavan, together with Prince Boun Oum, the figurehead of the Vientiane government, set out for Phnom Penh to meet Souvanna Phouma.

At a government meeting before the departure, Ngon Sananikone confided to me, the general had agreed with him on the necessity of coming to terms with Souvanna. Only two ministers, militant representatives of the Committee for the Defense of the National Interests (CDNI—brought to life through U.S. sponsorship during the political crisis in 1958), openly opposed the formation of a coalition government. But pretending moderation, Nosavan convinced the cabinet to frame terms which could not be accepted either by the Neo Lao Haksat or by the Neutralists. The Vientiane proposals included a government formed by the King; enlarging the government of Boun Oum; and a cabinet presided over by Souvanna Phouma but with a clear Vientiane majority. The last alternative was purely a matter of tactics. To the representative of the French Press Agency, Nosavan declared bluntly that Souvanna, not being neutral, could not be accepted as Prime Minister. Naturally, the Phnom Penh meeting, not attended by Souphanouvong, ended without any definite results—except perhaps to increase pressures on Souvanna Phouma.

The joint communiqué issued after the talks on August 4, 1961, stated that both sides "agreed to give up their respective formulas previously proposed for the formation of a cabinet, which shall not be the enlarging of the old cabinet of either the one or of the other." Instead, when the tripartite political conference met at Ban Namone on August 14, 1961, Vientiane came forward with a list of ten names, including Prince Souvanna Phouma, as potential candidates for the post of Prime Minister. Thus, pressure on Souvanna continued.

Laotians in Vientiane could not think of many candidates
to head a coalition government. They admitted that Souvanna Phouma was the only feasible alternative. At the same
time, however, they advanced several reservations. Misgivings were voiced about the Prince's haughtiness and autocra-
tic tendencies. Nouphat Chounramany, Minister of Agriculture in two of Souvanna's cabinets, now a member of the
Vientiane delegation to the Ban Namone conference, said
that he had not recognized the Prince when he met him
recently in Geneva: Souvanna had become excited, threatened a return to war, and spoken from a position of strength.
These were not methods which would lead to understanding,
Nouphat emphasized. Nhouy Abhay also spoke about Souvanna's psychological mistakes and his condescension.
Nhouy underlined the need for reconciliation, and argued
that stress must be laid not on a mechanical division of
portfolios in a new cabinet but on the choice of people with
aptitudes for the new tasks, including the neutralization of
the country. Naturally, all these arguments aimed at increasing Vientiane participation in the future government. Some
of those I met clearly envisaged their own participation in a
new coalition government under Souvanna Phouma. Ngon
spoke of his nine-year cooperation with the Prince in different cabinets; similar overtones were present in Dr. Oudom's
reasoning; and Nhouy Abhay did not hide his eagerness to
be included in the new team. But Nhouy also wanted assurances that the country would not go left. He feared, for
instance, that if difficulties increased, Souvanna would move
to Paris, allowing the Neo Lao Haksat to inherit the government.

Were these points meant to reach Souvanna's ear, to soften
his attitude, to further the shift of alliances? Whatever their
goals, they reflected a disintegration in the Vientiane ruling
circles, and a recognition of the need for change and a political solution.

One particular possibility worried most of the nationalistic Vientiane elite: fear that if the war should continue, the very existence of Laos as an independent state would be threatened. These Laotians strongly resented the use of the Meo minority to fan a fratricidal war, the creation of a separate Meo force under direct U.S. command—primarily to fight the Neo Lao Haksat but also having grudges against Vientiane. Since half the country's population consisted of minorities, such a division of its forces could only weaken its cohesiveness. This was a specific case of the old *divide et impera* methods used by the French; it enhanced the positions of war lords and introduced war schemes that served only foreign interests. Perhaps the Abhay family, which controlled the military region of Vientiane and had ambitions to spread its grasp over other provinces, felt particularly endangered by this development. Perhaps, too, rivalries in the opium trade were involved.*

The King's Role

The King, Savang Vatthana, played a curious role in Vientiane and U.S. diplomacy. Seldom in the forefront of the news himself, he seemed to accede passively to whatever design Vientiane or Washington advanced to him. For family reasons, he may have disliked Prince Souvanna Phouma, and even more so a coalition of Souvanna with Souphanouvong. But the way he bowed to Nosavan's policies was astonishing. Vientiane and the United States used his name freely without even consulting him.

*This exercise in mercenary warfare brought tragedy to the Meos themselves. Ten years later, the staff report of Edward Kennedy's Subcommittee to Investigate Problems Connected with Refugees and Escapees, published in September 1970, estimated that 50 percent of the 400,000 Meos in Laos "have been lost to the tides of war." At the same time about 700,000 Laotians were uprooted and herded into refugee camps, leaving large parts of the country ready to be bombed back to the Stone Age.

This was the case with the February 19, 1961, proposal for a new international control commission for Laos, to be composed of representatives from Cambodia, Burma and Malaysia. The proposal was designed to bar the return of the ICSC to Laos and to torpedo the idea of convening a new Geneva conference to solve the Laotian problem. As revealed the following day by Dana Adams Schmidt in *The New York Times*, the proposal was cooked up behind the scenes in consultations which the U.S. ambassador to Laos had at the White House. The King had not even been aware that such a proposal was being elaborated.

At the same time, the King seemed to be self-willed and inaccessible to alternative counsel. Kou Abhay, head of the Royal Council, complained that matters were generally settled behind his back. When the Indians and some Laotians, like Dr. Oudom, advised that he consent to a compromise political situation, the King answered evasively, pretending that he only fulfilled the will of the National Assembly or of the government, and that he did not wish to mix in the political game. At a moment of grave crisis, in audiences granted them in December 1961 in Vientiane, he told Princes Souvanna Phouma and Souphanouvong that he was powerless and bound by the constitution. Nevertheless, he agreed to a constitutional amendment which provided for his active role in politics. Nhouy Abhay commented excitedly that this amendment was contrary to the Zurich agreement, and said that he would have opposed it had he been present in Vientiane. But when he returned from Geneva on July 29, it was too late.

Most of my Laotian contacts wanted the King to act independently, to play a balancing role. All of them, Khouy Abhay included, warmly backed the idea that the Soviet ambassador should go to Luang Prabang and impress on the King the necessity for Laotian neutrality.

The Political Market

The King's position seemed strongly influenced by U.S. diplomacy. When I spoke with U.S. ambassador Winthrop G. Brown, he bluntly opposed Prince Souvanna Phouma for Prime Minister in a coalition government. Like Nosavan, Brown accused the Prince of not being neutral, and spoke with rancor about the April episode when during his stay in the Soviet Union, Souvanna canceled his scheduled visit to Washington, flying instead from Moscow to Sochi to meet Khrushchev. The United States is a big power, the ambassador emphasized, and the Prince cannot willfully change appointments with the President. But Arthur Schlesinger revealed later that Secretary of State Dean Rusk caused the cancellation by brusquely announcing that he would not be able to receive Souvanna, alleging a speaking engagement in Georgia; no appointment had been fixed with the President.[1] The Prince later told me that at their mid-September meeting in Rangoon, Harriman apologized to him for the April episode. Was Brown not aware of the true state of affairs?

In contrast to the attitude of the United States, both France and Great Britain endorsed Souvanna Phouma. This divergence among the Western powers helped to confuse the Laotians. Dr. Oudom told me he was unable to get any answer from the counselor of the U.S. embassy when he pleaded for a Souvanna Phouma coalition government, if only on a trial basis, in order to overcome the mounting difficulties. But the British and the French did not hesitate. Both John M. Addis, the British ambassador, and Michel Cadol, the French chargé d'affaires, assured me of their countries' full support for the Prince. Both seemed to have a clear vision: their governments wanted to put an end to the war, and seemed to have faith in the establishment of a pro-Western neutrality by a

Souvanna cabinet.* Both Addis and Cadol spoke about a promising evolution in U.S. policies toward Laos, though the change, they felt, was still too weak and sluggish in relation to the need for a quick political resolution. At the same time, both considered it necessary to carefully balance the composition of the future coalition government, in order to guarantee that the cabinet keep on the desired track.

U.S. vacillation toward Laos was a familiar topic in the Vientiane diplomatic community. The general understanding was that policy-making was handicapped by internal controversies between the White House and the State Department on one hand, and the military agencies on the other. Information reaching Vientiane from Washington suggested that while the civil administration accepted the need for a political solution, if only in order to temporarily freeze the drift to the left and gain greater freedom of action in South Vietnam, the Pentagon and the CIA still backed their man, Phoumi Nosavan. Implicit in this discord was the military's view of Laos as an indivisible part of the larger strategical scene including the whole of Indochina. Any retreat in Laos, the military thought, could aggravate the situation in the whole area. The White House, on the other hand, seemed to feel a need for more political flexibility.

Addis remarked that time was of vital importance. He was disturbed by the slowness with which U.S. policy evolved, and seemed particularly concerned with the possibility of renewed fighting after the rainy season. But unlike Addis, Brown calmly pondered the likelihood of a resumption of hostilities in the autumn. He found many reasons why a

*In Cadol's remarks I noted a certain change in attitude toward the United States. The old bitterness of the French representatives in Indochina seemed to have given way to cooperation. Did the French want to regain lost positions through partnership, or did they fear that the United States would interfere with France's struggle in North Africa?

political solution was still far off, but the essential reason was that Souvanna and Khang Khay still did not show readiness to accept the main U.S. preconditions for a settlement. Brown spoke about the need to guarantee pro-Western neutrality, the withdrawal of Vietnamese units, and, most important, a suitably drawn-up coalition government. He had in this respect very concrete demands: not only did he demand a large representation from Vientiane, but he found it natural to reserve for the United States a voice in the choice of Khang Khay candidates, even candidates from the Neo Lao Haksat. "People like Phoumi Vongvichit, Nouhak, or Kaysone could not be accepted," Brown stressed.

Interestingly, the Neo Lao Haksat leadership itself had briefly considered not presenting Nouhak or Kaysone, even not Prince Souphanouvong, as candidates to the coalition government. The idea stemmed from their distrust of Vientiane's intentions, from security considerations, and from the conviction that political activity outside the government might have greater importance in the future of the country than contests within the cabinet. This was, then, one of those strange cases where extreme positions met, and tended to play into the hands of the adversary. Laotian politics abounds with examples of this complementary interplay of extremes. Consciously or not, the United States buoyed up this mechanism. Brown's approach did not contribute to understanding; in effect, it colluded with Nosavan's maneuvers.

The Vientiane diplomatic community may have granted the benefit of the doubt to U.S. policy, but not to Nosavan. No political observer was misled by Nosavan's protestations of good will, and his moves were viewed with mistrust. Nor did Commission members harbor any illusions. The Canadians grew impatient, and the Indians became annoyed. As the rainy season drew to a close, uneasiness mounted in the

Commission. The chairman of the Commission, Samar Sen, tried to convince me that there was an evident divergence between the policies of the United States and the Vientiane administration. His information was, Sen said, that Washington would not give Nosavan a plain assent to renew fighting. If that were the case, Nosavan might aim to create a situation which necessarily would drag the United States into renewed military involvement. Sen thought that the general could not succeed and must himself have known this. Therefore, even Nosavan could not exclude the possibility that he might be obliged to accept a political settlement. He would consent to such a solution, Sen thought, only if assured of controlling positions in the coalition government. Thus the Indian conclusion seemed to be that a coalition could be created only through concessions to Vientiane.

This perspective appeared partly to suit New Delhi's general interests in the area. Both Sen and Ratnam, the Indian ambassador, were promoting a specific kind of compromise solution. Protesting neutrality and Buddhist kinship, India stood by a Souvanna Phouma government balanced in such a way as to reduce the role of the Neo Lao Haksat and enhance Western influences. China seemed to be New Delhi's great concern, and the Neo Lao Haksat was somehow identified with Chinese influence. India's model closely resembled French and British thinking. Sen strongly advocated including in Souvanna Phouma's center group some Vientiane politicians whom Sen rather freely labeled "neutrals." In this context he mentioned Ngon Sananikone and Leuam Insisienmay, the latter a conservative Southerner, Minister of Interior of the Vientiane government, and a relative of Boun Oum. The Indians appeared satisfied to show a neutral stand by supporting Souvanna Phouma on one hand, and favoring a "fair" Vientiane representation in the future coalition on the other.

In Vientiane I felt as if I were plunging into a political

market where great powers and other external interests traded freely in internal Laotian issues. Though the Vientiane politicians doggedly defended their interests and positions, the fate of the government was mainly in the hands of outsiders. Foreign representatives felt qualified to mix into the process of choosing cabinet ministers; some even thought they had the right and power to decide such matters.

Great Power Diplomacy

In this respect there was a noticeable difference in the atmosphere in Khang Khay. There the main current of discussions on policies and action was confined to the Laotians (the Neo Lao Haksat and the Neutralists), though allies were certainly consulted. Nobody knew exactly the extent to which Souvanna Phouma listened to his Western allies' advice; but the mere fact that he stood between East and West gave him power for independent diplomacy. The Neo Lao Haksat coordinated closely with Hanoi, but their relationship was marked by a spirit of revolutionary egalitarianism: this was a pooling of forces by the small and poor against the big and rich. Soviet and Chinese diplomats came closest to great-power diplomacy; but they were highly conscious of the national pride of the Laotians and Vietnamese, and were careful not to interfere directly in internal affairs.

The different patterns established by East and West produced certain difficulties in promoting Soviet-Western cooperation in the Indochina conflict. On September 11, 1961, on the eve of the Rangoon meeting between Souvanna Phouma and Averell Harriman—mainly devoted to the formation of a coalition government—the British ambassador in Vientiane came over to Khang Khay for a preliminary inquiry. He had talks with Souvanna Phouma, and also tried to discuss preconditions for a coalition with the Soviet ambassador. Abramov, however, refused to touch on these issues, saying that it would amount to crude interference in internal Laotian affairs. Addis tried to explain that his aim was only to help overcome the evident difficulties. But Abramov rejected the argument, maintaining that any interference was inappropriate: it made the situation worse. Left alone, Abramov claimed, the Laotians would easily find a solution to their problems. Two months later Abramov responded similarly to the U.S. ambassador when Brown tried to talk with him about the question of the composition of the coalition government.

Abramov seemed to approach things differently in his relations with the Neo Lao Haksat; but he soon found that he could not cross certain limits. In November 1961, as the Soviet Union became impatient with the difficulties in forming the coalition government, Abramov pressed for greater flexibility and concessions. At that point the new head of the Vietnamese Aid Committee in Khang Khay, General Le Chuong, bluntly told the Soviet ambassador that he had no right to interfere in the Laotians' decision-making process. Abramov rejected this charge, saying that the outcome of negotiations was of concern to others also; problems of major international importance of vital interest to the Soviet Union were involved. Abramov stressed that he was acting on instructions from the Soviet government and the Central Committee of the Communist Party of the Soviet Union, and in accordance with the line agreed to by the international communist and workers' movement. But Le Chuong and the Neo Lao Haksat leaders, unimpressed by these arguments, kept to their strategy and to their understanding of the situation. Out of this and similar exchanges of views. Moscow and its Vietnamese and Laotian allies evolved a changed relationship, a new *modus vivendi*.

Although in their daily behavior Chinese diplomats were careful never to appear haughty, there were also instances when they expressed opinions amounting to vetoes of certain actions or strong encouragement for others. Peking's views were very seriously considered, both by the Laotians and Vietnamese; but never were its opinions decisive. Adjustments were sometimes made, but final judgments were always passed locally.

Formula for a Coalition Government

The midpoint of 1961 was thus marked by intense consultations to overcome the deadlock and move ahead toward the formation of a coalition government. In the beginning of August, after my return from Vientiane, when I met Souvanna Phouma in Khang Khay, he was in a good mood. He interpreted my conversations in Vientiane as indications of a rapidly ripening process leading to the formation of a coalition government, and inferred that the West could not fail to see him as the only possible choice for Prime Minister. He had just returned from Phnom Penh, and the mere fact that Boun Oum and Phoumi Nosavan had come there to negotiate with him encouraged him to think that Vientiane, too, would finally be obliged to accept him. Stressing this, Souvanna said he was waiting for the return to Laos of the French ambassador, Pierre Louis Falaize, who would bring with him the results of consultations on Laos held recently by the three Western foreign ministers. The Prince put great faith in the results of these consultations.

But there was also reason for concern. Two days after my return from Vientiane, on August 10, 1961, Meo units assaulted Xieng Khouang. Enemy detachments penetrated the suburbs, and mortar and artillery shells fell in the center of town. Shops closed, supplies to the market stopped, and the town appeared deserted. Throughout the day both sides exchanged fire, and antiaircraft guns tried to reach a single fighter, believed to be a T-37. Five flights of Dakota-type planes were sighted dropping supplies to the Meos. There were some dead and wounded among the defenders of the town, but the attack was repulsed. At the same time, larger operations were noted in other parts of Xieng Khouang Province, especially along vital Highway 7, leading to the Vietnamese border.

Was this a bargaining maneuver, or was the intention to undo the negotiations? In any case, the military operations did not inspire confidence. True to its policy, the Neo Lao Haksat chose not to protest to the Commission but to respond in force and to increase security measures. When I went to Khang Khay two days later, I was accompanied by two armed cars equipped with six machine guns. I then asked Prince Souphanouvong about their attitude toward flights of enemy planes over territory administered by the Neo Lao Haksat and the Khang Khay government. He smiled: since the beginning of the fighting in 1961 the Neo Lao Haksat had brought down fifteen enemy planes, while during the whole Indochinese war only two French planes had been shot down.

In Khang Khay, discussions began on the formula for a coalition government. At a joint meeting of the government and the Neo Lao Haksat leadership, on August 11, 1961, Prince Souphanouvong presented his party's assumptions. They included: (a) assigning the premiership to Prince Souvanna Phouma; (b) endorsing a tripartite model (Neutralists, the Neo Lao Haksat and the Vientiane group) which presupposed a refusal to recognize as separate partners different political shades among the Rightists; (c) allocating half of the portfolios to the Khang Khay Neutralists, without any co-optation of Vientiane personalities to this center group; (d) fixing different attitudes in relation to the Neo Lao Haksat on the one hand and to the Rightists on the other, conceding preferential treatment to the Neo Lao Haksat allied to the Neutralists. This amounted to the rejection of symmetrical models for the composition of the government: Souphanouvong proposed a formula providing for seven portfolios to the Neutralists, four to the Neo Lao Haksat, and three to Vientiane. Implied in this formula was the notion that the neutralist group included both the wings of Souvanna Phouma and of the more leftist Quinim Pholsena. After some discussion, the meeting accepted in principle the Neo Lao Haksat platform as a point of departure. Souvanna Phouma seemed to have some reservations concerning the categorical exclusion of Vientiane personalities from the center group, but he chose not to comment on the subject at the moment.

In the meantime, the French ambassador's arrival in Khang Khay was postponed. According to certain reports, Falaize had to wait for Washington's approval of the results of the ministerial consultations. When the ambassador finally arrived at Khang Khay at the end of August, he brought what he termed an agreed-upon Western position providing for a coalition government under Souvanna Phouma. The formula presumed the formation of a sixteen-member cabinet with the assignment of eight portfolios to the Neutralists, four to the Neo Lao Haksat, and four to the Vientiane authorities. Falaize apparently did not mention a U.S. reservation providing for the division of the eight center posts into two equal parts, with the allocation of four of these portfolios to representatives of Vientiane. Perhaps, since he knew the Prince personally, he himself assumed that Souvanna would choose half of his people from Vientiane.

In reality, then, the Western formula presupposed that the Neutralists and the Neo Lao Haksat together would receive the same number of portfolios as the Vientiane group alone. Left unaware of this clause, the Neo Lao Haksat and the diplomatic community in Khang Khay were inclined to judge the Western proposal favorably; it suggested realism and good will. Searching for an explanation, the Soviet ambassador suggested that the West intended to set right the harm caused by recent Vientiane military actions, which had caused the Souvanna Phouma government to request increased aid from Moscow, Peking and Hanoi. Abramov presumed that the West had gotten wind of the socialist countries' instant approval of the request, and aimed now to recover lost ground.

Falaize had played his cards skillfully; he had infected Khang Khay with optimism. Souvanna Phouma started to make up lists of possible candidates to the neutral center. In his first version there was only one candidate from Vientiane, Khamsing, director of the Electrical National Administration. Abramov expressed satisfaction and encouraged the Prince to proceed vigorously with negotiations. In fact, all the socialist countries gave wholehearted support to efforts to form a coalition government under Prince Souvanna Phouma. On September 9, 1961, I myself had a long conversation with the Prince and assured him of all possible assistance in his endeavors.

Responding to the atmosphere of urgency, the Neo Lao Haksat expressed readiness to re-negotiate the problems of a coalition government, offering concessions beyond their previous stand. In the beginning of September, Souphanouvong and Souvanna Phouma signed a confidential agreement on the composition of the proposed government. The sixteen-portfolio formula was accepted as a general framework, with the proviso that four out of the sixteen cabinet members would have the rank of vice-ministers. The eight portfolios assigned to Khang Khay Neutralists included the ministries of Defense (Souvanna Phouma), Interior (Pheng Phongsavan), Economy (Patchamkvichit, then governor of Xieng Khouang), Information (Quinim Pholsena), Health (Khamsouk Keola), and Education (Sisoumang). Additionally, two Neutralist vice-ministers would be assigned to the departments of Defense and Interior. The Neo Lao Haksat portfolios comprised the ministries of Foreign Affairs (Phoumi Vongvichit), Public Works, and Religious Affairs, while Vientiane would receive the ministries of Finance, Planning, and Justice. To balance matters, a Neo Lao Haksat deputy minister would serve in the Department of Finance, and a Vientiane representative would be appointed deputy minister of Foreign Affairs. Souphanouvong, Kaysone and Nouhak were not to enter the government; but the Neo Lao Haksat revised their position on this a few days later, after the Rangoon meeting between Souvanna Phouma and Averell Harriman.

In the meantime Vientiane showed no willingness to begin real negotiations. At the Ban Namone talks, Boun Oum's representatives held to their previous list of ten possible candidates for Prime Minister, and in general Vientiane behaved as Falaize had suggested when he warned Souvanna Phouma that Nosavan had rejected the Western proposals.

Harriman in Rangoon

While a new crisis was brewing, Harriman invited Souvanna Phouma to Geneva to discuss the situation; but the Prince refused to travel that far to meet the U.S. envoy, and instead proposed a meeting in New Delhi or Rangoon. They finally agreed to meet in Rangoon on September 15, 1961.

These talks brought certain essential clarifications. While confirming in principle U.S. consent to the sixteen-member formula, Harriman revealed that the United States would insist on assigning to Vientiane four of the eight portfolios foreseen for the neutral center. This was the limit of powers entrusted to him by President Kennedy, the envoy declared. But after discussions with the Prince, Harriman took it upon himself to revise this stand so that only three of the eight center portfolios would go to Vientiane. He also agreed that the Vientiane personalities should be chosen by Souvanna Phouma, though informally the Prince was presented with a list of eleven candidates acceptable to the United States.

Neither Souvanna Phouma nor Harriman was able to confirm any agreed position, as both had to refer back to their capitals. Harriman was not even ready to confirm U.S. support of Souvanna Phouma publicly, and he issued a denial when the Prince told the press in Rangoon that he had the backing of all the Western powers. However, although no binding agreement was reached, the Prince left Rangoon convinced that the main obstacles to the quick formation of a coalition government had been removed.

Harriman himself probably had no clear notion of his mandate or of the goals of U.S. policy in Laos. U.S. policy was still in dispute, and Harriman must have been aware of the intense behind-the-scenes disagreements within Kennedy's administration. Long after the Rangoon meeting, the U.S. ambassador in Vientiane kept to Kennedy's original demand for equal division of the center portfolios between Khang Khay and Vientiane. Also, it was not altogether clear if Harriman had military approval of his request, presented in Rangoon, for the unification of Laotian armed forces before elections. Both elections and unification of the army were very touchy subjects in Vientiane. Surely Nosavan would not agree to relinquish control over his troops; neither would he accept impartial elections. And it would have been naïve to think that the Neo Lao Haksat, after their hard experience, would agree to a unification which would leave Nosavan in control of the army. Yet some quarters in Washington seemed to have indulged in daydreams. Speaking in mid-August 1961 at the Geneva conference, Harriman's aide, William Sullivan, demanded no less than the dissolution of the Pathet Lao armed forces. On the other hand, Souphanouvong later told me that he would readily accept an agreement to reduce all Laotian armed forces in the proportion 4:8:4 foreseen for the composition of the government, and to unify them under neutral control. In fact, preliminary agreement to reduce the number of troops in

Laos to 30,000, with equal division among the three parties, was reached in November 1962, after the formation of the coalition government; but Nosavan later refused to discuss details or execute the accord.

Though somewhat inconclusive, the results of the Rangoon meeting were well-received in Khang Khay: they were taken as an indication of U.S. interest in a coalition government under Souvanna Phouma. The idea of such a government seemed to gain weight and move toward realization. Souvanna Phouma and his entourage were encouraged, and the Neo Lao Haksat, attaching greater importance to the possible role of a coalition government, revised their previous decision on the nonparticipation of their main leaders in the cabinet. In addition, they agreed to consent in forthcoming talks to Souvanna Phouma's co-optation of two Vientiane personalities to the center group. A few days later, Souphanouvong told me that he was even inclined to accept three Vientiane candidates—provided they were chosen by Souvanna and did not include Nosavan's people. The Soviet ambassador, also pleased with the Rangoon results, tried his best to push the negotiations forward. The expectation in Khang Khay was that Vientiane would now agree to a meeting of the three princes and would soberly set about finalizing the talks. Such hopes, however, were thwarted. Vientiane diplomacy provoked ever greater disillusionment and hardened traditional suspicions among the Neo Lao Haksat. At the next meeting of the Ban Namone conference, on September 20, the Vientiane representatives again refused to fix a meeting of the three princes. I was then in Vientiane, and at the insistence of the Commission's chairman I met the U.S. ambassador to ask for explanations. Brown seemed surprised by Vientiane's attitude, but he seemed confident that he was in a position to secure a change. He authorized me to communicate to Souvanna Phouma that he had every reason to believe that at the next session of the Ban Namone conference, on September 22, the Vientiane delegation would agree to a new meeting of the three princes. Brown was even able to tell me that Vientiane would propose Ban Hin Heup, a village south of Ban Namone, as the meeting place.

Shortly afterward I met the British ambassador. Addis did not hide his concern about Nosavan's doings, and told me that Nosavan had not committed himself to any concrete line of action when he met Harriman in Vientiane after the Rangoon talks. What's more, Addis admitted that the Harriman line did not have full support inside the U.S. administration. He assured me, however, that Great Britain was trying its best to clarify the situation and to obtain solid backing for a coalition government under Souvanna Phouma. The problem, he said, had been touched on in a recent conversation between Rusk and Home, and he himself had consequently been instructed by the Foreign Office to visit Khang Khay again and reassure the Prince about Western support.

The Hin Heup Agreement

Finally, on October 6 and 8, 1961, the meeting of the three princes took place, in Ban Hin Heup. The joint communiqué issued afterwards stated that agreement had been reached on the need to form a government of national union, which would consist of sixteen members, and on the presentation of Prince Souvanna Phouma to the King for appointment as the Prime Minister of the government. The communiqué also said that Souvanna was entrusted with the right to call and fix the place of the next meeting of the three princes.

Though a step in the right direction, this was a meager result. The very limited nature of the agreement was an indication of the difficulties still ahead. Yet, as in the case of past rapprochements, the Hin Heup agreement produced a gamut of opinions in Khang Khay, from high optimism to dejection. Each actor and observer interpreted and judged the new development according to his predilections, reflecting partly his historical memory, but mostly his future vision and aspirations.

Souvanna Phouma longed for the final agreement and his return to the office of Prime Minister in Vientiane. So he saw things in bright colors, and was convinced that he would be able to form the new government in a matter of days. The Hin Heup talks coincided with the Prince's sixtieth birthday, which was celebrated modestly on October 7 in the lavishly green village of Vang Vieng, fabulously placed at the foot of steep mountains on the banks of a rushing river north of Ban Namone. A familiar Laotian *baci* was organized in the house of the district chief, and a lunch was offered for members of the government, Neo Lao Haksat leaders, and the heads of the Eastern and socialist diplomatic community. Souvanna was in high spirits. When I congratulated him over a glass of champagne (brought from Vientiane by the Polish delegation to the ICSC), and wished him prompt success in the formation of the government of national union, he thanked me cordially, saying that he now believed himself very near that desired goal. When I met him two days later in Khang Khay, he was waiting impatiently for an answer from Boun Oum concerning his prospective visit to Luang Prabang to get the King's mandate for the formation of the government. He expected to fly to Luang Prabang in a day or two, and fancied that the Vientiane government would then resign, and he would be designated by the King as the new Prime Minister. In reality, bewildered by Nosavan's cunning behavior, the Prince saw in the Hin Heup communiqué much more than there actually was. The general, Souvanna told me, behaved toward him with the utmost respect: "Nosavan feels like a little boy in my presence," he said with satisfaction.

Souphanouvong's reaction was different. Hin Heup was a victory for the alliance of the Neo Lao Haksat and the Neutralists, he noted: Vientiane had to bow to the choice of Souvanna as the future Prime Minister, and had to accept neutrality as the only possible policy for Laos. However, the major problems of the formation of the government were still left open. Nothing had been decided about the distribution of portfolios. Vientiane was still demanding four portfolios from the center pool, even hinting that it should have a say in the choice of the Khang Khay Neutralists. Still more, Nosavan was pretending to the post of Minister of Defense —this seemed to be the real meaning of Harriman's request for the unification of the army: the United States was trying to achieve through negotiations what it was unable to win in war. Souphanouvong suspected that Vientiane would try to increase pressure on Souvanna through the King. In fact, he said, Nosavan aimed to void the Zurich agreement by bringing in parliamentary procedures at a time when the Vientiane National Assembly was left in a key position. Suspicions concerning parliamentary loopholes were also voiced by Pheng Phongsavan, a former president of the National Assembly who had acted as Souvanna's deputy in the Hin Heup negotiations.

Nouhak, expressing the attitudes of the Neo Lao Haksat leadership, was even more skeptical. He had represented the Neo Lao Haksat at the meetings of the deputy leaders, and he told me that the Vientiane delegate had pleaded lack of powers on most important issues; on some questions he had even claimed that he would have to consult certain embassies in Vientiane; and he had refused to dissolve the National Assembly or even discuss the question of new elections. This was of major concern to the Neo Lao Haksat—Nouhak had demanded elections four months after the formation of the coalition government though he was ready to postpone the deadline up to a year. During the princes' talks, Nouhak said, Nosavan had offered Souvanna Phouma carte blanche for further action. Nouhak considered this an artful attempt to buy the Prince and eliminate the Neo Lao Haksat—given special powers, Souvanna could act without even consulting his allies—and therefore Nouhak had intervened immediately, saying that in all concrete decisions all three parties must be consulted and their agreement sought. (Perhaps it was this gesture which had impressed Prince Souvanna Phouma with Nosavan's respect for him.) In sum, Nouhak stressed, fundamental issues had been left undecided. The composition of the government was not fixed, nor was a concrete program for the initial actions of the government worked out. This latter, according to Nouhak, was the most important issue. Taking all this into consideration, the Neo Lao Haksat decided that Souphanouvong would not accompany Souvanna to Luang Prabang for the prospective audience with the King.

Abramov sharply criticized the Neo Lao Haksat position. He seemed to listen more to Souvanna's visions than to reports by Souphanouvong and Nouhak. He was especially impressed by Souvanna's statement that Boun Oum and Nosavan had given him carte blanche for further action. Much could be said for the Neo Lao Haksat's misgivings, Abramov said to Souphanouvong, but their analysis was deficient: it relied on internal realities only and overlooked the international scene, whereas the international disposition of forces was of greatest importance. A comprehensive appreciation of events had to take into consideration the socialist countries' support of the Neo Lao Haksat, the expectations of the Geneva conference participants, and contradictions in the enemy's camp. Seen in this framework, the situation inspired optimism. Abramov dismissed Souphanouvong's anxiety about Nosavan's schemes to exert further pressure on Souvanna Phouma, and considered apprehensions about parliamentary procedures unfounded. He even repeated this opinion during an exchange of views in the presence of both princes and Pheng Phongsavan. Any delaying maneuvers by Nosavan, at a time when the whole world, and the Geneva conference in particular, expected positive action, would only further isolate Nosavan and the United States.

Abramov felt that the army was a key issue. To counter Harriman's pressures for submitting the defense portfolio to Nosavan, Abramov proposed that Nosavan be offered the Ministry of Foreign Affairs and the position of Deputy Prime Minister. In order not to lose control over foreign relations, a deputy belonging to a different party could be appointed to the Ministry of Foreign Affairs. To neutralize Nosavan further, he could be sent abroad—charging him with leadership of the Laotian delegation to the United Nations, for example. Some circles in Vientiane eagerly applauded such a solution —one who showed such interest was the French ambassador. But Abramov's proposal was as naïve as Harriman's.

Such unrealistic thinking was alien to the Neo Lao Haksat. They knew their opponents well, and did not delude themselves by staking all on easy tricks. Laotians and outsiders perceived Laotian realities differently. The Laotians' vision of the past and the future naturally penetrated deeper than an outsider's. Abramov was right to reproach the Neo Lao Haksat for thinking predominantly in national or regional terms, rather than in broad international terms. There may even have been a gap in basic outlooks: the Soviet Union was concerned with peaceful coexistence translated concretely into the Soviet-U.S. dialogue; but the Laotians and Vietnamese were faced with the bread-and-butter problems of national development.

In repeated discussions Abramov repudiated almost every Neo Lao Haksat argument for caution. He interpreted Neo Lao Haksat decisions as a continuation of the militant line. The Neo Lao Haksat, he told me, still did not trust Souvanna Phouma, and thus were pushing him ever more to the right. Abramov felt that greater flexibility was needed, even in the question of elections, which could be left to be decided by the new government. He was especially angry when the Neo Lao

Haksat, against his advice, chose not to delegate Souphanouvong to accompany Souvanna Phouma to Luang Prabang. The whole approach of the Neo Lao Haksat, Abramov
concluded, reflected heavy Vietnamese and Chinese influence.

Interplay in Luang Prabang

Subsequent events, however, confirmed Neo Lao Haksat
anxieties. Notwithstanding Souvanna Phouma's eagerness to
reach Luang Prabang, arrangements were not ready until
October 18. The day before, a Vientiane delegation arrived
at the Plain of Jars to discuss transportation and security.
Heading the delegation was Bounthong Voravong, and at his
side were Nouphat Chounramany and Dr. Oudom Souvannavong. Bounthong was reserved, but Nouphat and Oudom,
professing confidence, readily told me some details of the
Luang Prabang scenario. The King would only listen to
Souvanna, not more, Nouphat said. The King still had no
powers to designate the Prince as Prime Minister; for this the
King would have to receive from the National Congress new
prerogatives in accordance with the recent constitutional
amendment. At the same time, said Nouphat, Boun Oum
had no intention whatever of resigning before the dissolution
of Souvanna Phouma's government. Nouphat asked me to
tell Souvanna Phouma that it would be best for him to submit to the Vientiane National Assembly and solicit it for
investiture; the Prince would no doubt get a high majority.
To this Oudom added a warning that circles much more
extreme than Nosavan's were only waiting to destroy what
had been achieved thus far. He was hinting at the young
CDNI politicians who had no hope of entering a new coalition government, and some high police and military officers
connected with specific CIA services, who were ready to
subvert any chances of a political settlement.

Next day, together with the other Xieng Khouang Commission representatives, I accompanied Souvanna Phouma to Luang Prabang. It was a depressing spectacle. The Prince was subjected to humiliating treatment. When he arrived, he was greeted at the airfield by Nosavan; when he left he was seen off by Oudom Souvannavong, not even by the chairman of the Vientiane delegation to Ban Namone. Both of his visits to the King were preceded by audiences granted to Phoumi Nosavan, and in his free time he was exposed to attempts at brainwashing by a stream of Vientiane visitors. Polarization was the goal. Though no regular political negotiations were initiated, Nosavan again demanded the Ministry of Defense. During the whole procedure the Vientiane authorities labored to glorify their constitutional position: they claimed the King's formal blessing of legality, and they systematically tried to move authority and attention to Vientiane.

This, in fact, was another stage in Vientiane's stalling tactics. Formally, the King agreed that Souvanna should continue his efforts to form a coalition government; in this way he approved the Hin Heup decisions. But he failed to designate the Prince as Prime Minister, and he left intact the Vientiane government structure. Thus he did not basically change the existing political situation. No date or place was fixed for another meeting of the three princes, though Souvanna offered to return soon to Luang Prabang or to meet in a day or two on the Plain of Jars. Despite the explicit wording of the Hin Heup communiqué, Vientiane would not respond to the Prince's call.

Souvanna returned from Luang Prabang depressed, and asked the Soviet ambassador for political support on the international scene, to counter U.S. interference in the formation of the coalition government. Abramov considered this a turning point in Souvanna's orientation, and immediately cabled Moscow endorsing the Prince's request.

The turning point, however, occurred elsewhere. Not only

Laos but all of Indochina was preoccupied at that moment
with General Taylor's mission to South Vietnam. As Special
Military Representative of President Kennedy, Taylor was
accompanied by a team of high-ranking specialists from the
different agencies and departments. It was no secret that
decisions of crucial importance were being made. When I
spoke with Souvanna in Khang Khay after his visit to Luang
Prabang, he was worried, and said that the situation would
clear up only after Taylor returned to the States. He repeated
this to me two days later, expressing confidence that the
United States would not extend its military involvement in
Indochina too far. The United States certainly would not
send troops to Vietnam. There was therefore no reason to
lose optimism. Nevertheless, the Prince seemed nervous
about the Taylor mission, and asked the French and British
ambassadors in Vientiane for more definite information.

The Neo Lao Haksat, the Vietnamese, the Chinese and the
Soviet embassy were no less concerned about the mission,
especially as it was accompanied by a sharp flare-up of military activity. Returning from Luang Prabang to Xieng
Khouang, I learned that a U.S. jet fighter had again flown
over the city; Souvanna's French pilot said it was an F84
fighter. According to Souphanouvong, the plane had made
a survey of the whole area, paying particular attention to
Highway 7, which leads to North Vietnam.

Souvanna Phouma's visit to Luang Prabang caused the
Neo Lao Haksat to become more concerned than before.
Souphanouvong told me that in his judgment the negotiations had arrived at a crossroads: either a breakthrough must
be made to form a coalition government, or renewed fighting
was imminent. Since Nosavan and his advisers would think
twice before initiating a new war, it was necessary to keep the
political initiative and press for a new meeting of the three
princes. Souphanouvong was also disturbed by news from
Luang Prabang that in confidential conversations there Sou-

vanna had promised that even before reaching agreement on the coalition government he would form a unified delegation to Geneva, to be led by Phoui Sananikone. At a joint meeting of the government and the Neo Lao Haksat on October 20, Souphanouvong protested strongly against such a move, recalling that he and other Neo Lao Haksat leaders had been arrested by the Phoui Sananikone government; he stressed that Phoui in fact bore a great responsibility for events of recent years. Even the French, Souphanouvong reminded his brother, had refused to accept Phoui as ambassador to Paris when Souvanna wanted to get him out of Vientiane in the autumn of 1960.

Souvanna Phouma was forced to go back on his promise; when Prince Boun Oum asked Souvanna to execute his "formal agreement" to place the delegation under Phoui Sananikone, Souvanna sent the following reply (on October 29): "Constitution of a single delegation was only a suggestion on my part and not a formal agreement because I had no power to speak in the name of the Neo Lao Haksat. On my return from Luang Prabang, while rereading the joint communiqué of Zurich, I noticed that this suggestion was at variance with that communiqué, which stipulates that the formation of a governmental delegation to participate at the international conference for the settlement of Laotian problems was part of the immediate task of the coalition government. This is why I request you to come to Plain of Jars for a meeting of the three princes in order to discuss our national problems, especially as regards speedy formation of a coalition government . . ."[2]

But Vientiane, while eager to take over leadership in Geneva, was not ready to concede the leadership of the government to Souvanna Phouma. Week after week it refused to heed Souvanna's calls for a meeting. A lively exchange of messages passed through the channels of the Commission, but in its report to the Co-chairmen dated December 15,

1961, the Commission noted that "the course of correspondence shows that two months have been lost since the meeting at Ban Hin Heup in trying to find a place for the meeting
of the three princes." Until the end of the year negotiations
in Laos concerned only secondary problems: the place for a
meeting, security arrangements for the meeting, etcetera.
Such substantial matters as the composition of a coalition
government and the questions of the army and administration were not even mentioned.

In the back of everyone's mind was the Taylor mission,
though in retrospect I tend to believe that the mission's real
importance was still only vaguely comprehended. A few days
after Souvanna Phouma's visit to Luang Prabang I met Hanoi's Deputy Minister of Foreign Affairs, Hoang Van Tien,
who came to Khang Khay as a special envoy of Prime Minister Pham Van Dong to discuss questions of aid with Souvanna. Tien did not hide his concern over the turn of events,
but he did not despair. Hanoi's orientation was toward a
political settlement, he stressed; it might take a long time, but
we have to show patience. Like the Neo Lao Haksat leaders,
Tien did not expect large-scale military operations at that
time.

A day later the new leader of the Vietnamese Aid Committee, General Le Chuong, confirmed this judgment. The general was worried by Taylor's mission, but argued that the
very fact that negotiations proceeded in Laos and Geneva
made renewed fighting unlikely. Le Chuong made a particular impression on me—he was an unusual general, seeming
much better versed and more interested in politics than in
military affairs. He came to Khang Khay from Geneva,
where he had served as counselor to the Hanoi delegation,
and where he had been listed as a professor of political
science. His arrival in Khang Khay at that moment was
significant in itself, I reported to Warsaw: it could be taken
as an indication of Hanoi's state of mind.

Chapter 11

General Taylor's Presidential Review

General Maxwell Taylor's mission to South Vietnam played a paramount role in framing U.S. policy in Indochina. Labeled as "preparatory to a major Presidential review,"[1] the mission set to work with assumptions which of themselves necessitated an escalation of the U.S. engagement. Taylor's mission was based on Vice-President Johnson's May 1961 recommendations for "large-scale American commitments": the mission was to take up the case "for trying the Johnson approach . . . to see if this could be done."[2] The very composition of the mission, Schlesinger remarks, "expressed a conscious decision by the Secretary of State to turn the Vietnam problem over to the Secretary of Defense."[3] Headed by the "Military and Intelligence Adviser and Representative" of the President (Taylor's official title), the mission included Walter Rostow, the hawkish White House aide, as deputy, and Ngo Dinh Diem's friend General Edward Lansdale, the famous CIA counterinsurgency mastermind, as leading expert. Lansdale "was put to work estimating the costs and numbers of men required to 'seal-off' the 250-mile borders of jungle and mountains through which the infiltrators came— a question that he thought itself revealed a misunderstanding of the guerrilla warfare."[4] Lansdale's task consisted of military calculations; it was a quest for military recipes to deal with the conflict. Even Rostow, on whom "the main burden of making the political assessment fell, was preoccupied with the problem of infiltration routes."[5]

Taylor's mission reflected Washington's lack of faith in political expedients. Implicit in the "Presidential review" was a rejection of the idea of neutralization. Before the Taylor mission set about its task, the Kennedy administration was presented with the alternative "of enlarging the concept of a 'neutral and independent Laos' " to include also South Vietnam, Cambodia, and such other Southeast Asian countries as Thailand, Burma and Malaya—all states repeatedly mentioned in connection with the domino theory as endangered by Vietnam-type insurrections.[6] The proposal, which both Schlesinger and Hilsman described as imaginative, had been worked out by Undersecretary of State Chester Bowles, but was nipped in the bud without even a Presidential comment, defeated by the dominant "Johnson approach."

Thus, the Laotian problem was reduced more and more to the military problem of "sealing off" through various technomilitary and counterinsurgency methods. In the question of neutralization diplomacy was subordinated to general military strategy. Instead of transforming the Geneva negotiations into a stepping stone for a regional political settlement, the talks were overshadowed by regional military planning. The Laotian tangle was to provide a recurrent pretext for growing U.S. commitments. "Infiltration" through Laos became a prominent justification for wider warfare. This had in fact been foreseen by President Kennedy when he told Hilsman, "No matter what goes wrong or whose fault it really is, the argument will be that the Communists have stepped up their infiltration and we can't win unless we hit the North. Those trails are a built-in excuse for failure, and a built-in argument for escalation." This remark turned out to be painfully prophetic for both Kennedy and his successor.[7] In fact, the prophecy was self-fulfilling: mounting military operations converted the infiltration trails into highways of warfare.

As expected, Taylor's mission approved the Johnson approach and recommended "increased American intervention."[8] Taylor requested that a U.S. military task force of about ten thousand men be sent immediately to South Vietnam to take over key battle operations. In addition, Rostow brought back a sophisticated theory advocating "a contingency policy of retaliation"—the forerunner of massive bombardments all over Indochina.[9]

Placing great confidence in Taylor and his team, Kennedy approved the mission's conclusions. He introduced only tactical changes in implementation, to make the increased involvement less conspicuous. He endorsed "the step-up in military and economic aid and in the increase of American advisors, technicians, and helicopter pilots," and though "he did not approve the commitment of American ground troops," "he avoided a direct 'no' to the proposal for introducing troops in Vietnam . . . at the same time ordering the government to set in motion all preparatory steps for introducing troops."[10] By the time President Johnson took office, the U.S. task force in Vietnam officially totaled sixteen thousand, most of them highly trained officers.

As American intervention increased, so did Taylor's personal role. In 1962 he became Chairman of the Joint Chiefs of Staff, and just before the crucial Tonkin Gulf probes in August 1964 he arrived in Saigon as U.S. "ambassador." The nomination of a four-star general to an ambassadorial post was remarkable in itself, unprecedented in diplomatic history. Yet no less unexpected was Taylor's resignation a year later, when it turned out that the massive bombardments of North Vietnam initiated in February 1965 had failed. Taylor's famous theory of "flexible response" ended in thorny escalation. Appearing on February 17, 1966, before the Senate Committee on Foreign Relations, the general, embarrassingly enough, cited in his defense—Khrushchev's speech on wars of national liberation. Nikita Khrushchev by then was long out of office; one of the reasons for his fall had been his opposition to a Vietnam commitment.

A New Scent of War

Though largely unaware of the precise import of Taylor's Presidential review, Laotian leaders quite quickly linked events in their country to this mission and the new warlike wind blowing from Washington. At the beginning of the Hin Heup talks, Souvanna Phouma and Souphanouvong published a protest against growing enemy military activities, which they interpreted as proving that the United States and Vientiane "do not wish the peaceful settlement of the Laotian problem." Their statement said:

> While the preparations were on for this meeting, some aggressive American circles and their dummies tried to intensify the "cleaning-up" and advancing operations in several sectors. They are now preparing for a large-scale attack on our liberated territories in the area of national Highway 9 in central and southern Laos. Several companies of South Vietnamese troops stationed at Khe Sanh and Lao Bao attacked our sectors of Muong Nong and Houei Sane. On October 1, 1961, Admiral Felt, commanding officer of the Seventh Fleet in the Pacific, openly declared in Vientiane that American troops and those of SEATO are ready to intervene in Laos in case the three princes' meeting does not produce results anticipated by them, and Phoumi Nosavan impudently declared that his troops had very high morale and were ready for action.[11]

During the last days of October Vientiane forces unrolled a countrywide military offensive, and I myself got to sniff the new smell of war. In the afternoon of October 27, 1961, when

Meo units attacked Xieng Khouang, a mortar fired from the surrounding hills landed right in my living room, wrecking the whole interior. Fortunately, I had left for Khang Khay half an hour earlier and was not taking a siesta at home, as I usually did at this time of the day. I still keep a piece of the shell as a souvenir. The shelling of the seat of the Polish delegation was especially disquieting because the flag of the International Commission fluttered on a thirty-six-foot pole in front of the bungalow, easily visible from the hills from which the fire came. Five additional shells fell in the neighborhood, killing six children in a French missionary school.

Souphanouvong told me that the countrywide offensive started on October 25. It had been preceded on October 12 by a clash on Highway 9, in which Pathet Lao troops encountered an enemy battalion formed in Thailand. Two weeks later, the Neo Lao Haksat High Command counted seventeen enemy battalions involved in operations across the country. The strongest attacks were launched in the south, east of Attopeu, bordering the Pleiku-Kontum area of South Vietnam. The offensive there was supported by two fighter squadrons probably based in South Vietnam. This was the first time that fighters were used to drop incendiary bombs and machine-gun Pathet Lao positions. Simultaneous attacks were directed against Nhommarat, at the junction of highways 8 and 12. Later, General Tong Dy told me that the offensive in the region of Highway 9 had been aimed mainly to cut the new road built from Sa Ang on Highway 12 to Tchepone on Highway 9. A glance at the map reveals a meridional line of attacks covering suspected infiltration routes. Was this then the first large-scale operation to explore the sensitivity of the north-south routes in Laos, and the first exercise in the use of air power in counterinsurgency strategy?

The local implications were grave. Meeting the three Xieng Khouang ICSC representatives on October 28, Souphanouvong declared, as noted in an internal Commission report, "That the other side had started military action in order to prevent the formation of the government of national union. He thought that it was a reversal of policy following General Taylor's visit. He said he knew exactly about the secret meeting which took place between representatives of the Vientiane side and General Taylor four or five days back. He thought that perhaps General Taylor had given encouragement to the bellicose faction of the Savannakhet group. He said that fighting was going on on a countrywide scale."

Souvanna Phouma also appeared worried. Reports of Taylor's contacts with Vientiane and rumors that Taylor himself intended to visit the Laotian capital alarmed Khang Khay leaders, who assumed that there was some connection between Taylor's mission, the outbreak of hostilities, and efforts to undermine the negotiations. Souvanna offered the Commission many details of enemy activities—numbers of troops involved, cases of enemy airlifts and arms drops, mining of roads, etc.—and emphasized that at the very moment in which he was trying to bring about general reconciliation, the other side had attacked Xieng Khouang for the second time. He said, the Commission's report goes on, "that the main objective of those attacks was to put pressure on him to make concessions." In reality, the Prince concluded, "Such acts meant a refusal to negotiate accompanied by military pressures." Privately the Prince was more emphatic, and showed signs of desperation. He told me, "If they want war, they will have it."

The Taylor mission also became a main topic of discussion in the Vientiane diplomatic community. Did the mission augur a retreat to war? Reflecting the dominant mood, the final paragraph of the November 11 ICSC message to the Co-chairmen stated: "The Commission considers that it would be a tragedy if general hostilities were to be resumed when the parties had succeeded in coming so near a solution in their meetings outside and inside Laos, and when agreement at the Geneva conference appeared to be within reach."

Gradually, the Laotian problem was pushed back into its original role as a function of the Vietnamese conflict. One effect of the warlike mood accompanying the "Presidential review" was that Khang Khay's requests for aid from Hanoi increased. Following Taylor's mission, information reached Khang Khay that Saigon and Vientiane had agreed to permit South Vietnam to carry out "hot pursuit" operations several miles into Laos. Consequently, in the framework of "seal-off" efforts, Laotian territory adjoining South Vietnam came under constant military pressure. On December 9, 1961, near Nhommarat, four AT-6 planes bombarded Kong Le units and killed twenty-two persons. Upset by events and resolved to break the stalemate in negotiations, Souvanna Phouma again demanded direct military aid from North Vietnam. At the same time he asked the other socialist countries to help repair the four main roads leading from North Vietnam to Laos. Agreement was reached, too, for the Chinese People's Republic to build a new road leading from the Chinese province of Yünnan to Phong Saly.

The Soviet–Chinese Rift

The expansion of U.S. military involvement in Indochina had one unexpected effect: it deepened the rift between Peking and Moscow. While China's attitudes toughened, the Soviet Union showed a tendency toward appeasement. Peking saw danger moving nearer to its borders and was not ready to surrender; Moscow took the resolution and tenacity of the U.S. military very seriously, and offered concessions. Though China was careful to steer clear of an open military clash with the United States, it thought that the greatest support must be given to Vietnamese and Laotians holding foreground positions on its borders. Peking's reaction to military pressures was not resignation but preparedness for protracted struggle. The Soviet Union, however, considered the risks too great. Moscow wanted to avoid confrontation with the United States, especially in faraway Indochina. Its main policy was "peaceful coexistence," and the objective seemed worth any price paid by the Indochinese.

The Soviet stand was in fact well known in Washington, and this no doubt encouraged the United States to proceed along the military line. In the long run, however, the Soviet stand misled U.S. policy. It emboldened the United States to move deeper into Indochina, but it did not ease U.S. military tasks or help Washington disengage when the situation became critical. Although the international setup following U.S. escalation compelled the Soviet Union to extend aid to Hanoi, this did not allow Moscow to dominate decisions in North Vietnam; but Washington believed for a long time that Soviet diplomacy would be able to exert pressure on Hanoi and help the United States extricate itself victoriously from the Indochinese morass.

The greater the U.S. commitment in Southeast Asia, the sharper were controversies in Khang Khay on strategy and tactics for Laos. These controversies increased as suspicions about Washington's and Vientiane's intentions increased, and paralleled Peking's mounting conviction that the Soviet Union valued dialogue with the United States more than the national interests of its Asian allies. This course of events contributed to the open clash at the XXII Congress of the Communist Party of the Soviet Union in October 1961.

In the beginning of September 1961, the Central Committee of the Communist Party of the Soviet Union transmitted to the Chinese and Vietnamese parties a detailed memorandum on the Laotian problem. It stressed that political errors had been committed, especially in the alliance between the Neo Lao Haksat and the Neutralists; charged that Souvanna Phouma and the Neutralists had received inadequate support, causing a weakening of the alliance; and urged a reversal of current trends, pleading for long-range commitments of cooperation with Souvanna Phouma. (Commenting on the memorandum, Abramov told me that Moscow felt that the Neo Lao Haksat's interest in a coalition government was too vague and was surrounded by too many reservations. Abramov was critical of the Neo Lao Haksat's decision not to present its main leaders as candidates for government positions, and interpreted this as a sign of reticence, or even of opposition to a coalition government: such a reserved attitude was basically wrong, and might assist U.S.-Vietnamese stalling tactics.) Additionally, the Soviet memorandum expressed dissatisfaction with Hanoi's handling of Soviet aid to Laos. One of the examples mentioned to me in the Soviet embassy was that out of 23,000 tons of gasoline delivered to Hanoi for Laos, only 990 tons so far had reached Laos, even though the gasoline shortage was severe.

Following the Soviet memorandum, representatives of the Soviet Union, the People's Republic of China, the Democratic Republic of Vietnam, and the Neo Lao Haksat held a consultative conference in Hanoi. The meeting recorded shortcomings in the management of aid by Hanoi, including delay in delivery and at times alteration in assignment. The Vietnamese representatives ascribed the "errors" to transport difficulties and technical deficiencies, and promised improvement. The conference decided that all aid would continue to go through Hanoi. Quotas were established for the government of Prince Souvanna Phouma and the Neo Lao Haksat: out of the official supply to the government the Neo Lao Haksat would receive two-fifths of the total. To compensate for the reduction in official aid, the Neo Lao Haksat would get additional supplies outside of its governmental quotas. But agreement on the flow of aid did not erase mistrust. Shortly after the conference the counselor of the Soviet embassy remarked that "errors" had been admitted in words only, while old methods still prevailed. Nevertheless, by October a considerable improvement in supply was noted, especially concerning gasoline.

The Hanoi conference also dealt with political issues, and its general recommendations supported efforts to form a government of national union based on the Neo Lao Haksat–Neutralist alliance. Yet Moscow did not seem happy with the outcome. It felt that adherence to the recommendations was weak and formal. Following up the Hanoi decisions, Soviet diplomacy pressed for more initiative, greater political flexibility, readiness for compromise, and substantial concessions. In mid-October Abramov met Nouhak, the Neo Lao Haksat representative at the Hanoi conference, and candidly reproached the Neo Lao Haksat for a faulty line. He said that the Neo Lao Haksat had accepted the decisions of the September consultation in form only, while in reality continuing the old line. The Neo Lao Haksat apparently feared that it would not be able to cope with the exigencies of a leading role in a sustained alliance with the Neutralists. It therefore did not act to strengthen this alliance and hesitated to leave Souvanna Phouma sufficient initiative, as evident in the objection in Ban Hin Heup to the carte blanche offered Souvanna Phouma by Nosavan. The Neo Lao Haksat, Abramov maintained, was also too suspicious about the role of the National Assembly and the position of the King; a correct approach would demand greater efforts to gain the sympathy of the King and less intransigency toward the National Assembly.

Nouhak did not argue with Abramov, but the subsequent Neo Lao Haksat decision not to delegate Souphanouvong to accompany Souvanna Phouma to Luang Prabang proved that the Soviet criticism had not been accepted. Abramov suspected that Hanoi's influence toughened the Neo Lao Haksat's stand—out of all the socialist countries only Albania and the Democratic Republic of Vietnam had passed in silence over the new program of the Communist Party of the Soviet Union presented to the XXII Congress. To win over the Neo Lao Haksat leadership, Abramov proposed to Nouhak that doubts and controversies could be aired directly with Moscow, without Hanoi as an intermediary. In fact, Kaysone was at that moment in Moscow attending the XXII Congress.*

The task for Soviet diplomacy was not easy. No great result could be expected from counseling moderation and retreat while the United States and Vientiane embarked on military adventures and Nosavan openly stalled negotiations. Time and again Abramov had to voice sharp condemnation of U.S. policy. He showed concern about Taylor's mission and related it to the unsatisfactory results of Souvanna's journey to Luang Prabang. Nevertheless, he did not lose hope. He told Souvanna Phouma, "If the Americans do not

---

*Kaysone represented the Laotian People's Party, the inner core of the Neo Lao Haksat.

Leaders of the Neo Lao Haksat never openly admitted the existence of the Laotian People's Party. The nearest they came was in a booklet by Phoumi Vongvichit, *Laos and the Victorious Struggle of the Lao People Against U.S. Neo-Colonialism* (Neo Lao Haksat Publications, 1969), and in an article by Kaysone Phomvihan in the brochure *Un quart siècle de lutte opiniâtre et victorieuse* (Neo Lao Haksat, 1970), published on the twenty-fifth anniversary of the proclamation of Laotian independence (October 12, 1970). The article was reprinted in the March–April 1971 issue of *Tricontinental.* Vongvichit refers to the "revolutionary Party" and Kaysone to the "authentic revolutionary Party" as the leading body of the Laotian revolution. Kaysone traces the roots of the party to the Communist Party of Indochina, and defines its general line as closely combining the tasks of the national revolution with those of the democratic revolution. He goes on to say: "The democratic national revolution in Laos is essentially a revolution for the liberation of the peasantry. The key to the success of this revolution is the construction and consolidation of the worker-peasant alliance under the leadership of the Party." The Laotian revolution is characterized by the use of revolutionary violence against "endless armed counterrevolutionary violence" by aggressor imperialism and its lackeys. To unite the people in its struggle the party built the Neo Lao Haksat, based on a broad national program.

lose their senses, they will not intervene militarily." A peaceful solution in Laos would also calm the conflict in South Vietnam; he thus was inclined to believe U.S. protestations about their desire for a political settlement in Laos.

Six weeks later, with negotiations still stalemated, Abramov told me that he had become convinced that the United States was playing a double game in Laos, speaking one way but acting differently. He suspected that U.S. military circles had won the day in Washington. But even so, he felt that the collision course was being charted by extreme tendencies on both sides.

Chinese Diplomacy

With the deadlock in negotiations under constant review in Khang Khay, the divergence of attitudes between Moscow and its Asian allies became a source of continuous internal tension; finally, a clash occurred over the choice of a location for the new meeting of the three princes. Despite the Hin Heup agreement, Vientiane stubbornly refused to heed Souvanna's repeated calls for another meeting on the Plain of Jars. Occasionally Vientiane mentioned Luang Prabang and Vientiane as possible alternatives, but partly for security reasons and partly out of political considerations, these cities were not acceptable to the Neo Lao Haksat. As a compromise solution Ban Hin Heup was again being considered.

In the midst of arguments around this question, on November 11, Souphanouvong suddenly declared that in order to counter Nosavan's attempts to destroy the Zurich and Hin Heup agreements, the Neo Lao Haksat had decided to accept Vientiane—Nosavan's headquarters—as the meeting place. At the same time the Neo Lao Haksat proposed to initiate a large-scale campaign in Laos and in the international arena to gain wider support for the idea of a coalition government. Their formula for the coalition was widened to an eighteen-member cabinet, allotting the two additional posts to Vientiane. According to this scheme, Vientiane would receive seven portfolios, the Khang Khay Neutralists seven, and the Neo Lao Haksat four. (Formally, three of the Vientiane portfolios would come from the neutral center, thus presenting the cabinet in proportions of 4 : 7+3 : 4.)

This move seemed to reflect a conscious effort not to allow the situation to slip into military confrontation. The Neo Lao Haksat appeared willing to try anything to overcome Vientiane's resistance to a coalition government. Indeed, Nouhak, responding to rumors from Vientiane about differences between Nosavan and the Sananikone family, authorized me to inform the Sananikones, through our delegation in Vientiane, that the Neo Lao Haksat did not nurse feelings of revenge toward them; in fact, in case the Sananikones should support the formation of a neutral coalition government under Souvanna Phouma, they could count on receiving a seat in the cabinet.

Hanoi and the Soviet diplomats warmly welcomed the Neo Lao Haksat initiative, and Prince Souvanna Phouma immediately transmitted the proposal to Vientiane; but opposition suddenly came from the Chinese representatives. The Chinese People's Republic was at that time establishing an Economic and Cultural Mission accredited to the Souvanna Phouma government, and in connection with this mission the Chinese ambassador to Hanoi, Ho Wei, paid a short visit to Khang Khay. While there he voiced many objections to the Neo Lao Haksat gambit. He considered the move a concession which tended to undermine gains achieved so far in the negotiations. It conceded a leading position to Vientiane, and any meeting in Vientiane would involve considerable security risks. But Ho Wei's main argument was that, irrespective of concessions by Khang Khay, the other side was bent on a new military probe, and without another military defeat, Vientiane would not return to the negotiating table. Moreover, broader U.S. intentions should be taken into account. According to Ho Wei, the United States aimed to partition Laos so as to transform the southern part of the country into a strategic bridge linking South Vietnam and Thailand. Security considerations and U.S. activities in South Vietnam and Thailand dominated Peking's thinking. This concern for security was reflected in its representation in Khang Khay: the chargé d'affaires of the new Economic and Cultural Mission to Laos, Liu Chun, was a former general with experience in the Korean War.

Ho Wei left for Hanoi on November 17. Shortly afterward, the Neo Lao Haksat seemed to reverse their position. Although they did not withdraw their proposal for a meeting in Vientiane, they stiffened conditions for security arrangements; at the same time they suggested that the time was not yet ripe for the formation of the coalition government. These arguments were strengthened when Vientiane rejected even minimal security arrangements similar to Souvanna's Luang Prabang precedent, and when on November 20 Nouphat Chounramany and Oudom Souvannavong said quite frankly, on the Plain of Jars, that Nosavan was not interested in any meeting. The idea of a meeting in Vientiane seemed to die out.

Between Moscow and Its Asian Allies

On November 21 I had an intimate conversation with Souphanouvong. He listed several reasons for a new approach to the situation. First, the Laotian population was not yet ready to actively support the idea of a coalition government; more education was necessary to prepare the ground. Second, the enemy was not ready to accept a political solution. One or two military defeats were still needed to bring him to reason—perhaps a defeat in the Dien Bien Phu style would do. Third, new political as well as military accomplishments would have to be exploited on the international scene in order to force a settlement. The Prince even reflected on the advisability of rethinking the very concept of the coalition government—perhaps a more decisive representation of revolutionary forces was called for, so as to forejudge the problems of power once and for all.

We were sitting side by side on Souphanouvong's bed in his small room in Khang Khay. I felt that he was deeply moved by events—he spoke with a sense of historical responsibility, and seemed to believe events had reached a fateful crossroads. He seemed very irritated by Vientiane's obduracy and spiteful responses to Souvanna Phouma's repeated invitations for a new meeting of the three parties. I tried to argue with him, suggesting the possibility of strengthening security arrangements in Vientiane through direct Commission participation. With fire in his eyes he retorted, "Ten thousand United Nations soldiers were unable to protect Lumumba; should I have the same fate?" It was difficult to counter this argument. There certainly was reason for anxiety. Still, I believed that more daring political moves were necessary to break down Vientiane's resistance —the idea of calling the next meeting in Vientiane had been a step in the right direction.

Later, the counselor of the Soviet embassy told Souphanouvong that Moscow felt that to break the stalemate talks should be transferred to neutral ground abroad. Souphanouvong again refused. Negotiations, he said, must be conducted in Laos, under the eyes of the whole nation. Even Geneva would not do.

The Vietnamese also changed tone. The chief of Hanoi's Economic and Cultural Mission, Pham Van Thuyen, put it bluntly: the situation was characterized by a balance of forces which obviously did not favor the conclusion of the negotiations. Only a demonstration of military supremacy could break the deadlock. This was clearly a new turn of

events, and in many Neo Lao Haksat arguments I recognized
Ho Wei's line of thinking. Tchivilev also felt that the turn
could be traced back to Chinese influence. I thought that this
change stemmed from divergencies in the socialist camp
manifested during and after the XXII Soviet Party Congress.
The open dissent between the Soviet Union and the Chinese
People's Republic, I felt, encouraged U.S. military circles to
take a tougher line. In response, the Chinese were resolved
not to make concessions, and to follow an independent line
in Indochina without heeding Soviet policy demands. Tchivilev repeated this appraisal in a message to Moscow, adding
that an evident discrepancy existed between the Neo Lao
Haksat's and Hanoi's declarations of willingness to form a
coalition government, and their deeds, which did not favor
such a policy.

However, matters were not quite that simple. A few days
later, after a series of prolonged conversations in Khang
Khay, I recognized that Peking, Hanoi and the Neo Lao
Haksat had quite distinct approaches. I wrote to Morski on
November 25, 1961, that Hanoi's orientation was definitely
not in line with Peking's. While the Chinese might tend to
think that a new military contest was unavoidable and perhaps desirable, the Vietnamese rather thought in terms of
maintaining the status quo: neither coalition government nor
larger military operations. This best suited Hanoi's prime
concern, to maintain lines of communication with South
Vietnam. Hanoi's line suited the Neo Lao Haksat for quite
different reasons. They reasoned that postponement of a coalition government could well serve to strengthen military and
political gains achieved during the past year.

Characteristically, it was Souvanna Phouma who at this
juncture became convinced of the need to use military pressure to bring Vientiane to its senses. On November 20, after
the failure of conversations on the Plain of Jars concerning
a new meeting of the three princes, Souvanna turned to the

Vietnamese Aid Committee in Khang Khay, requesting military support to deal a decisive blow to Vientiane forces on the central and southern fronts, the scene of the most intense military activity.

At that time the Vietnamese were working to develop new meridional tracks leading through Laos southward to Tchepone on Highway 9. Soviet diplomats suspected that Hanoi was using building machines intended to improve supply lines to the Plain of Jars for its own ends, without consideration for Laotian requirements. Not only Soviet representatives but also Souvanna Phouma constantly pressed Hanoi to reverse priorities and improve the flow of supplies to the Plain of Jars. Aiming for greater efficiency and independence, Souvanna turned to the Soviet Union for direct aid to build an all-weather road linking the Plain of Jars with the North Vietnamese port of Vinh, on the Tonkin Gulf.

Clearly, Hanoi did not let the Russians in on its strategy, and resented Soviet pressures in Laos, where the Russians were seen as demanding settlement at almost any price. At a lunch I gave on November 30 for the leadership of the Vietnamese Aid Committee, I heard some of Hanoi's complaints. General Le Chuong presented a list of "misunderstandings" with the Soviet ambassador. He mentioned one instance when Abramov, speaking to Souvanna Phouma in the presence of Souphanouvong, argued against a Neo Lao Haksat proposal for a new three princes' meeting at Ban Hin Heup. Abramov's intervention was especially improper, Le Chuong stressed, as the proposal had previously been approved by Souvanna Phouma. Moreover, Abramov had insisted that subjecting a prospective Vientiane meeting to complicated security arrangements tended to undermine the very idea of such a meeting. This had been too much for Souphanouvong, who challenged Abramov's views, and remarked that though problems of security might not seem essential to Souvanna, they certainly were to him. Abramov's intervention, Le Chuong said, provoked open divergencies between Souvanna Phouma and the Neo Lao Haksat. Instead of clearing things up with the Neo Lao Haksat, the Soviet ambassador had chosen to sow discord between Souvanna Phouma and Souphanouvong.

The Vietnamese seemed perturbed by the widening rift in the socialist camp; apparently they feared they would be caught between the hammer and the anvil. In the long run, however, the rift actually served to strengthen Hanoi's and the Neo Lao Haksat's independence. But because Hanoi wanted to work out a common approach, Le Chuong proposed a consultation of the local representatives of the socialist countries and the Neo Lao Haksat.

When this proposal was conveyed to the Chinese chargé d'affaires, Liu Chun, he declined to participate. He was not yet well enough acquainted with local problems, he said. This of course was an evasion, as his readiness to offer opinions and advice proved.

Testing Vientiane's Intentions

On December 1, just two weeks after Ho Wei had argued against a meeting in Vientiane, Peking suddenly and unexpectedly reversed itself and consented to Vientiane as a meeting place. I had the impression that in direct discussions between Hanoi and Peking the Chinese had bowed to the strategy chosen by the Neo Lao Haksat and the Democratic Republic of Vietnam. The entire move was perhaps a tactical exercise to push the United States and Nosavan to the wall, to upset their military plans, and to force a return to political negotiations.

When I arrived in Khang Khay on December 1, I found a changed atmosphere: Laotians, Vietnamese and Chinese agreed to transform the proposal for a meeting in Vientiane to a test of U.S.-Vientiane intentions. Discussions moved to technical preparations and the concrete problems of security arrangements. I had a long talk with Nouhak, General Khamtay (commander in chief of the Neo Lao Haksat forces) and General Phoun Sipraseuth (chief of the political department of the Neo Lao Haksat forces) concerning Commission cooperation in assuring the princes' security. Importance was attached especially to the participation of the Polish delegation. I assured the Neo Lao Haksat leaders, and later the Vietnamese and Chinese representatives, that we were ready to extend maximum aid assuring communication links with Khang Khay, active supervision of Vientiane security arrangements, and regular personal contacts with the Neo Lao Haksat delegation. At Souphanouvong's request, the Soviet ambassador promised to leave earlier for Vientiane to prepare the ground for talks, and I promised to accompany the princes in their journey.

It took nearly another month, however, to obtain final agreement from the Vientiane authorities and to make the necessary security preparations. Annoyed with Vientiane's stalling tactics, on December 6, Souvanna Phouma sent a strongly worded message to Boun Oum, saying: "I ask you to tell me whether your group sincerely wants to form the government of coalition for settling the Lao problem by peaceful means or if it wants to continue allowing this tense situation to drag on and at last resume war and once again involve our Motherland in fratricidal carnage."[12]

When he received another evasive answer from Vientiane, Souvanna told me that he was depressed and tired, and that he intended to leave for Paris to be with his family. There he could also mobilize Western opinion for firm action against Vientiane's delaying tactics. On December 13, however, Boun Oum offered to come to the Plain of Jars for an interim exchange of views. The meeting took place the next day. The communiqué published afterwards stated briefly: "As far as the formation of the provisional government of national union is concerned, the three princes have reaffirmed the necessity of enforcing together the Joint Communiqué of Zurich and Hin Heup, in accordance with the intention of His Majesty the King, who has kindly entrusted Prince Souvanna Phouma with the mission of forming this government."[13] The only concrete result of the exchange was a decision to meet shortly in Vientiane. The date was later fixed for December 27.

Hanoi's Apprehensions

In the meantime, anticipating basic decisions, the socialist countries continued their discussions on future strategy in Laos. Opinions still differed. The subject came up at a lunch I gave in Xieng Khouang on December 9 for Nguyen Chinh Giao, Hanoi's expert in Laotian affairs. He did not hide the fact that Hanoi's view was close to the stand taken by Peking, and he felt that some sort of rethinking of the situation was necessary. The points in dispute concerned short- and long-term policies. First, Giao said, Peking insisted that in any coalition government the Neo Lao Haksat and their Neutralist allies should retain two-thirds of the portfolios; the Soviet Union pressed for much larger concessions. Second, and more essential, there were basic discrepancies concerning military forces. Like Hanoi, Peking considered that, because of Vientiane-Thai schemes to preserve Vientiane's armed strength even after the formation of a coalition government, the Neo Lao Haksat had to adopt a similar strategy. The Soviet Union, without heeding the experiences of the 1957–58 government of national union, advocated immediate unification of the armed forces. Third, Hanoi was apprehensive that Souvanna Phouma would swing to the right after the formation of a coalition government; the Soviets stressed the need for trust in him. Finally, touching on the problem of aid to Laos, Giao complained about transport difficulties created by a partial withdrawal of Soviet airplanes.

These were very serious problems. Hanoi seemed particularly worried by the reduction of Soviet aid. The dispute apparently went beyond Laos and touched on the insurrection in South Vietnam. The Soviet Union had ceased air deliveries to Tchepone; it suspected that these were not used to serve Laotian units in southern Laos but to strengthen communication lines with South Vietnam. This was a clear warning from Moscow, objecting to support for the South Vietnamese uprising. On this point a wide gap separated Moscow from its Asian allies.

Speaking at the World Peace Council in Stockholm a few days later, Chinese representatives strongly condemned efforts to disarm oppressed nations for whom "the most important issue is definitely not the disarming of whatever small armed forces they have, but the building and strengthening of their armed forces to defend themselves against imperialism and colonialism." Clearly pointing to the Soviet-U.S. dialogue, the Chinese delegate said, "The idea of a few big countries straightening out international problems without respecting the opinion of small countries is also wrong and can never be realized." Indochina was clearly a key problem at issue.

The Laotian problem had recently been discussed in the Political Bureau of the Vietnamese Workers Party; one result of this was that both Morski and I were invited to Hanoi for an exchange of views. We accepted this invitation and on Saturday, December 16, we spent a whole day in talks in Hanoi. The setting was familiar: experts gathered at a large conference table, discussions interrupted for only a short break after lunch. Morski spoke first. Our understanding was in line with the Soviet point of view, pleading for wider political initiative and stressing that international conditions and the internal situation in Laos were ripe for a political settlement. Negotiations in Geneva had been almost concluded, and Nosavan would either be obliged to accept a political solution or face the danger of complete isolation. Though Nosavan had the support of the CIA, Marshal Sarit and Diem, an expansion of the conflict or its internationalization was inconceivable. The dominant international trend was toward a peaceful solution. The Vientiane administration was therefore constrained to agree to the Plain of Jars meeting on December 14 and to consent to the joint communiqué reaffirming the Zurich and Hin Heup agreements. Despite Vientiane's real intentions, Boun Oum had to pay lip service to the international community's demand for the formation of a coalition government.

Morski stressed that further negotiations would certainly be difficult, as the point at issue was control of state power. But power, he argued, could only be won step by step. A more flexible policy was needed. It might be advisable to enlarge the coalition concept to embrace most of the groupings opposed to Nosavan, including representatives of the three leading Vientiane families—the Abhays, the Sananikones and the Souvannavongs—who were competing with Nosavan for power. Most important, correct strategy demanded commitment to a long-range alliance with Souvanna Phouma and the Neutralists. In negotiations, the Neo Lao Haksat had always been superior to the conservative factions, and though the shortage of political cadres could create difficulties immediately after the formation of a coalition government, we could be confident that cadres would grow simultaneously with the political struggle.

Our hosts responded first with a review of the military and political situation. According to General Chan, Vientiane's forces had grown quickly during recent months, from 30,000 at the cessation of hostilities to 40,000 regular and 13,000 irregular troops. Vang Pao's Armée Clandestine, after the defeat at Ban Padong, had received special CIA attention and had expanded rapidly. Vientiane had replaced much of its French equipment with new U.S. arms, and U.S. advisers had been introduced at battalion and company levels. Military training had been intensified, especially in training camps in Thailand, and five or six batalions from Thailand had recently been transferred to the front along Highway 9. Chan gave details of recent enemy operations, stressing especially combined undertakings including regular Thai and South Vietnamese units in central Laos and around Highways 9 and 12. The main weakness of the enemy, Chan remarked, was his low morale.

The Neo Lao Haksat and the Neutralists also had strengthened their military potential. Their combined regular forces totaled 23,000. Over half were Neo Lao Haksat; 6,000 to 7,000 were under Kong Le; and about 5,000 were under Khammouane in Phong Saly. In addition, all over the country the Neo Lao Haksat had at their disposal guerrilla units numbering 10,000 to 15,000 soldiers. The weak point of these forces was supply. Units in the field sometimes had to endure serious strains. There was no shortage of arms or artillery, but difficulties of transport interfered with regular supply, even of food. This had an impact on fighting capabilities, and there were some cases of desertion. The shortages were reflected politically, in the alliance between the Neo Lao Haksat and the Neutralists. Misunderstandings recurred especially over the availability and distribution of foreign aid—the Neutralists claimed that the Neo Lao Haksat got most of the aid. Aware of this, the enemy constantly tried to use it to increase polarization. But with recent improvements in supply the situation seemed to remain under control.

Giao presented the political perspectives. His initial assumption was that a link existed between the foe's strategy of polarization and its readiness to form a coalition government. Vientiane and its Thai and U.S. protectors would agree to a unified government only if certain of gaining control. The key figure in this strategy was Souvanna Phouma, and the foe was incessantly seeking his cooperation. In the main, the enemy would like to repeat the post-Geneva strategy of the fifties: to use the agreements in order to eliminate the Neo Lao Haksat.* As a possible alternative, the United States was considering the partition of Laos.

However, Hanoi was inclined to believe that U.S. strategy would not succeed. Of the two most likely alternative developments—the formation of a coalition government or the renewal of fighting—Giao saw greater chances for the first, simply because the Neo Lao Haksat and the Neutralists together represented a stronger force than the Rightists. Moreover, the international situation favored a political settlement. A coalition government thus seemed inevitable, and Hanoi's main strategy was oriented toward the formation of such a government and its consolidation. It felt that the growth of revolutionary forces all over Indochina favored this strategy, and its real goal in following this line was stability and peace in the whole area of Southeast Asia. Clearly, there was a link between a Laotian settlement and a political solution in South Vietnam. And a neutral coalition government in Laos would serve world peace as well.

Giao stressed the need for a proper distribution of portfolios in the coalition. Only a truly neutral administration would be able to undertake the internal and external changes needed for a peaceful and democratic Laos. The Neo Lao Haksat had not yet taken a final stand in this matter, though it was generally assumed that the Neo Lao Haksat together with the Neutralists should receive the key government posi-

---

*As told by Walter S. Robertson in the 1959 hearings before the Subcommittee on Foreign Operations of the House of Representatives: "The reason we are encouraged by what has happened, is that they did unify the country. They started off with the coalition but it lasted only a few months. They have gotten rid of the coalition and now we have a government in which no communists are represented."

tions. Equally important were decisions concerning elections, the unification of the army, and administration. Giao repeated apprehensions voiced earlier by Nouhak and Souphanouvong: without elections and a solution to the problem of the National Assembly, the Neo Lao Haksat could not deprive itself of armed forces. Greater flexibility could be shown in administrative matters, but here too there were complications, and vigilance would be necessary. After all, Nosavan was not eager to relinquish control over territories administered by Vientiane, nor was he ready to dissolve his army. Pressed to the extreme he might try to transfer some of his units to Thailand.

Hanoi's position was summed up by Foreign Minister Ung Van Khiem. Our point of departure, he said, lies in the appraisal of U.S. intentions. U.S. policy opposed a compromise solution and aimed at regaining dominance over Laos. Hanoi agreed that the international situation favored a settlement, that the United States and Vientiane had encountered difficulties in trying to implement their strategy, and that they had become more and more isolated. But the balance of forces in Laos was still uncertain, and had not tipped decisively in favor of the Neo Lao Haksat and their allies. This encouraged the enemy, who might try to change the balance through another military strike. Seen from this perspective, the formation of a unified government posed highly complex problems—especially as Souvanna Phouma and his entourage seemed sensitive to U.S. and Vientiane pressures. Khiem concluded by stressing the need for a united stand by the socialist countries. Because there was an evident difference of emphasis, matters would have to be studied and adjusted in broader consultations; in the meantime, Khiem assured us, our views would be taken into consideration.

Shortly afterward I received additional clarification from Hanoi. A matter-of-fact attitude would be adopted in the forthcoming negotiations, and the Neo Lao Haksat would fix the limits of concession, the touchy problems still being composition of the government, elections, unification of the army, and administration. There was still grave doubt as to the possibility of achieving any solution at the Vientiane meeting.

The Neo Lao Haksat Line

On December 20, 1961, a week before moving to Vientiane, I had an intense conversation with Nouhak. He thought that for the moment the chances of forming a coalition government were minimal. In questions of portfolio distribution, the Neo Lao Haksat and Souvanna Phouma kept to the formula of 4:7+3:4. The Neo Lao Haksat were ready to offer Nosavan the post of Vice-Premier and Minister of Finance, on the condition that Souphanouvong would become Vice-Premier and Minister of Information. Nouhak did not worry about the army's unification. If Souvanna Phouma took up the problem, the Neo Lao Haksat would immediately agree in principle to discuss it, aware that Nosavan would oppose any real move in this direction. Nouhak thought that Nosavan would never consent to reduce the number of his troops or to relinquish his commanding position. Nosavan's attitude demanded caution in questions about the army. Long-term cooperation would be required to solve this problem. For the moment, Nouhak thought, the princes could agree to a coalition command presided over by a neutral officer.

Nouhak showed some flexibility about elections. These would have to be held no later than one year after the formation of the coalition government. However, to overcome the deadlock, the Neo Lao Haksat was ready for the time being to leave the fifty-nine-member National Assembly in session, with the proviso that twenty-one members would be co-opted to represent the Neo Lao Haksat. The Neo Lao Haksat was even ready to concede five of these seats to the left

Neutralists represented by Quinim Pholsena.

Realizing Nouhak's doubts about the prospects of forming a coalition government, I inquired about other possible developments. He had a ready answer: renewed fighting was unavoidable. When I said that Vientiane seemed to have larger and better-equipped military forces, Nouhak did not show much anxiety. His oval, tawny face darkened briefly, but then relaxed. He said, "In revolutionary wars it is quality and higher morale that count."

The Vientiane Setback

Khang Khay approached the Vientiane summit with mixed feelings. The Neo Lao Haksat and its Asian allies were suspicious and cautious, but well prepared for discussions. The Neutralists and the Russians, on the other hand, had more faith and even expected considerable progress. Hardly anybody anticipated the immediate constitution of a government of national union, but trust was expressed, as in the December 15 ICSC message to the Co-chairmen, "that serious and sustained efforts" would be made to form such a government.* The security arrangements themselves, which provided for a military escort of one hundred and ten soldiers

*In Geneva expectations were much higher than in Laos. On December 18, the two Co-chairmen, the Foreign Ministers of the Soviet Union and Great Britain, A. Gromyko and Lord Home, addressed to the three princes an urgent appeal to form a government of national union as soon as possible. The message stated that the international conference for the settlement of the Laotian question had largely completed its work, and "if there were now in Geneva a united Laotian delegation . . . then the Declaration on the Neutrality of Laos and the protocol of that declaration could probably be finally completed and signed within a few days." The message went on: "The Conference has taken note of the intention of the three princes to meet within a few days, and urges them to agree during this meeting on the constitution of the Government of National Unity, in accordance with the Zurich and Ban Hin Heup agreements. The Conference intends to convene its next plenary session on Janaury 3, 1962, at which time it hopes to be able to welcome in Geneva a united delegation from Laos."

and thirty advisers and staff for each of the princes, were seen as part of a serious attempt to break the deadlock in negotiations.

However, the actual course of events caused a sensation and shocked all observers. Immediately after their arrival in Vientiane, on December 27, during a courtesy call, Souvanna Phouma and Souphanouvong were told by Boun Oum—as quoted in the ICSC message to the Co-chairmen dated January 1, 1962—that: "(1) The tripartite meeting is unnecessary, and (2) The agreements of Zurich and Hin Heup are out of date." Boun Oum presented the original Kennedy formula for a coalition government with a sixteen-member cabinet, demanding half of the seats for Vientiane, including the portfolios of Defense and Interior. Since Boun Oum was not prepared to alter his position or have a joint tripartite discussion, Souphanouvong returned to Khang Khay on December 29. Souvanna Phouma stayed one day longer, hoping for a change, but he also had to leave Vientiane empty-handed.

On December 30 I cabled Warsaw: "Embarrassment and confusion prevail in Laotian political circle, the highest governmental level not excepted. Responsible officials in the Vientiane ministries openly express their dismay. Nosavan's isolation in the diplomatic corps seems complete. Even Brown did not dare defend him in public. Foreign diplomats suspect that rumors about instructions from Washington to foil Nosavan's stand simply not true."

At the King's New Year's reception on December 31, Nosavan tried to explain his position to me. He was self-confident and aggressive. Twice he repeated that the demand for the portfolios of Defense and Interior were his last word. He refused categorically ever to return to tripartite negotiations with the participation of the Neo Lao Haksat. "Souvanna Phouma only temporarily represents neutralism," he declared. He went on to say that it would in fact be proper for him to replace Souvanna; perhaps then he would be able to find a common language with the Neo Lao Haksat. Finally, Nosavan said that he was under U.S. pressure, but "faithful to national interests" he would not submit.

I spent New Year's Day in three consecutive meetings with the Indian and Canadian commissioners, drafting a new message to the Co-chairmen. There was complete agreement among us: "The Commission is gravely concerned lest this most recent failure of the Laotian parties to reach agreement on the formation of a unified government should accelerate the deterioration in the situation with respect to the cease-fire, signs of which are already noticeable and have been reported in this and preceding messages." As a last resort the Commission proposed to call a meeting of the three princes in Geneva.

One of Nosavan's main interests in staging the Vientiane performance was to humiliate Souvanna Phouma and upset whatever had been achieved during the 1961 negotiations. In his December 27 declaration, read in Souvanna Phouma's presence, Boun Oum told Souvanna: "I think my own group has as much right to claim neutrality as yours . . . Some of your supporters and sometimes you yourself reproach our Government that it receives aid from a Western country. Do you remember, Highness, it was you yourself who solicited that support in order to defeat all those individuals and nations who wanted to prevent Laos from living in peace, unity, sovereignty and neutrality? Your signature is still legible at the bottom of those revealing documents. If today you have changed, it is not the same with us . . . As regards the distribution of portfolios, I think it is essential that National Defense and Interior should be allotted to my group. In fact, Highness, till we have proof to the contrary, nothing guarantees us your true neutrality . . ."[13]

In Vientiane consternation was general. The evening of December 27 Boun Oum had held a press conference and repeated to the astonished reporters much of what he had told the princes. After this conference Reuters cabled: "Western diplomats who had thought they had persuaded and convinced Vientiane government the urgency of three princes meeting and its necessity found their month's hard work completely shattered with hopes for peaceful solution to Laotian problems no nearer." The Associated Press added: "The much heralded Laotian three princes meeting fizzled in such ludicrous manner that it left concerned diplomats and observers tearing out their hair . . . While the situation verged on comedy, it was feared that it could have grave repercussions for the future of the country." United Press International cabled: "Long-awaited conference of Laos' three feuding princes was torpedoed by U.S.-backed Royal Government today before it . . . formally convened . . . To most observers, only U.S. pressure remained as possible check on government policy which threatened today to be leading toward civil war* . . . 'He can stay here as long as he wants,' Boun Oum said, in claiming Souvanna had come for selection of cabinet members rather than a princely conference. 'He has food, drink and security. He can go to Vieng Ratry, Vientiane's flossiest night club. What more does he want?' "

Leaving Vientiane on December 29, 1961, Souphanouvong told the press that Boun Oum's declarations "show his intention not to solve the Laotian problem peacefully, which means renewed war." Not only was there a flare-up of fighting, culminating in the Nam Tha battle of May 1962, but, more significant, the United States further stepped up commitments in the area. An outgrowth of General Taylor's "Presidential review," the Vientiane episode paved the way for the "Thai spring"—the U.S. strategical build-up in Thailand starting in the spring of 1962.

*"As late as November, when Harriman was trying to organize the coalition, some of our people actually urged Phoumi to hold out for both key ministries of Defense and Interior. This only reinforced Phoumi's stubbornness. In December negotiations broke down." (Schlesinger, *A Thousand Days*, p. 451)

Chapter 12

The
Enlistment of Thailand

The way the December summit was wrecked clearly indicated a well-planned design. Strategic objectives overshadowed the local scene. The Vientiane scenario fitted into
Washington's new political-strategic perspectives aimed at
accelerating U.S. military involvement in Southeast Asia.
Hard-liners in Washington and local U.S. clients saw contradictions between new U.S. commitments and the idea of a
coalition government in Laos, and pressed for more consistent and speedier action.

Though the West unanimously accused Nosavan of being
the villain behind the Vientiane performance, it could not
possibly have been the work of one man. The main actors
were easily recognized. Apart from the Royal Army officers
clan, the local aristocracy and politicians who had much to
lose by a political settlement, the Thai military dictatorship
and U.S. military agencies headed by the CIA stood
staunchly behind Nosavan. The Vientiane events were inspired especially by Thai interests competing for profits from
the U.S. "Presidential review." In fact, during subsequent
months the U.S. build-up in Southeast Asia was focused in
Thailand.

The political and strategic U.S.-Thai rapprochement can
be traced back to the First Indochinese War: it closely followed growing U.S. involvement in Vietnam and Laos. Start-

ing with U.S. military assistance in the beginning of the fifties, it reached a turning point just after the 1954 Geneva agreements with the formation of SEATO and the choice of Bangkok as its headquarters. U.S. military objectives in Thailand suited well the ruling elite's expansionist ambitions toward Laos, a country seen as a traditional Thai zone of influence. Thailand had taken advantage of the French defeat in World War II to grab two Laotian provinces on the western bank of the Mekong, Sayaboury and Champassak. Generals in Bangkok who resented that they had been obliged to return these spoils after the war hungered for new opportunities to expand northward and to achieve dominance over Laos.

The Prime Minister of Thailand, Marshal Sarit Thanarat, quickly made common cause with the CIA in order to crown his nephew Phoumi Nosavan strong man of Laos. This triangular alliance persistently struggled to retain power despite strong popular resistance. Toppled by Kong Le in 1959, Nosavan reestablished headquarters in the border town of Savannakhet, reinforcing his troops with extensive Thai and U.S. assistance. Air America planes "began a steady shuttle to Phoumi's base."[1] Thailand became a rear base for U.S.-Thai military intervention in Laos, and Nosavan's troops moved freely through Thai territory in order to land in back of Kong Le's units. Since it controlled the main supply lines, Thailand imposed an effective unofficial blockade on Vientiane, and Thai forces shelled the city from the Thai bank of the Mekong during Nosavan's December 1960 assault. Following the deterioration of rightist positions in the spring of 1961, the Kennedy administration directed a 500-man helicopter-equipped Marine detachment to the Thai-Lao border to shield the Vientiane regime.

In the course of events, the Thai establishment developed a tremendous eagerness—sometimes exceeding U.S. readiness—to build up a U.S. military base in Thailand. The

Taylor mission helped. Famous for its agility—Thailand was the only mainland Asian country which avoided colonial domination—Thai diplomacy attempted to overcome whatever resistance still existed in Washington to what President Kennedy termed an "over-commitment of U.S. policy in Southeast Asia." Thai interests were manifold: more military and economic aid, help in case of political and military trouble, personal wealth through the management of U.S. funds. By the time of his death in 1962, Sarit Thanarat had put aside $140 million.

There was also real anxiety underlying the official Thai posture—fear of a social and national upsurge prompted by the Lao political awakening. Both Souvanna Phouma and Souphanouvong used to tell me about Laos's historical involvement with Thailand. Two centuries earlier Laos had extended far to the west of the Mekong, covering the small kingdom of Chiengmai in the north and reaching to Korat in the south. To this day northeast Thailand is inhabited by an ethnic Lao population speaking the Lao language and keeping to Lao culture. Souvanna Phouma estimated the Lao population in Thailand at about ten million, nearly one-third of the country's inhabitants and several times the number of Laotians in Laos itself. The Prince said that Lao borders in Thailand could easily be marked: wherever people play the bamboo *khene,* they are of Lao origin. The first village where the *khene* is absent marks the limit of Thai stock. Many Laotians, in fact, have not abandoned the dream of again gathering all their kinsmen into one Laotian state, and have not forgotten that the Emerald Buddha (Pra Keo), their most revered religious artifact and the symbol of their own sovereignty, had been carried to Bangkok after the Thai conquest of Vientiane in 1778.

In the eighteenth and nineteenth centuries Laotian lands became battlegrounds for Thai-Vietnamese rivalries. This was interrupted by the French conquest of Indochina, but when France was forced out, it left behind a Laotian national resistance allied with the Vietnamese, full of vitality, and capable of exerting a powerful influence on Thailand itself, especially on the large Lao minority in the northeastern provinces. This caused alarm in the ruling circles of Bangkok.

Saykang (Neutral Voice), the Khang Khay organ of Souvanna Phouma's Neutralist Party (edited by Pheng Phongsavan and Khamchan Pradit), carried in its December 23, 1961, issue an article entitled "A Separatist Movement in Thailand in Favor of a Neutral Laos." Quoting the *Bangkok Post* and the *Bangkok World* of December 18 and 19 respectively, it noted the arrest in Thailand of ninety-six members of a pan-Lao movement headed by intellectuals, members of parliament, and army officers. The movement covered the three northeastern provinces of Thailand: Oudon, Nakhon Phnom and Sakon Nakhon. Thai authorities alleged that the separatists had received arms and support from "Red Lao" coming from the Mahaxay area in central Laos. *Saykang* commented that this was "clear evidence that Lao of any origin are fond of the policy of strict neutrality of H. H. Prince Souvanna Phouma . . . History does not go back. The patriotism that Lao on both banks of the Mekong are starting to feel toward their Motherland stems from ancestors like Khoun Lo, Chao Fangoum and Chao Anou, who fought for the greatness and prosperity of Great Lan Xang [Kingdom of the Million Elephants]."

The Pathet Lao had long-standing contacts with the revolutionary movement in Thailand. General Phoun Sipraseuth told me that in 1952 he himself had led training courses for revolutionaries from the other side of the Mekong. While the Pathet Lao provided instruction and facilities, the Thais covered all the expenses. In mid-1962 Souphanouvong gave me further details. He felt that the liberation movement in Thailand was growing and would have a deep impact on Thai internal developments. Harassed by the authorities, the Thai revolutionaries were experiencing enormous hardships. During the past year, the Prince said, the Neo Lao Haksat had begun receiving wounded guerrillas for treatment in its hospitals, and had established close links with the movement on the other side of the Mekong. Those links, Souphanouvong stressed, were not with Lao separatists but with a nationwide movement that aimed for democratic change and neutralization of the country.

The arrest and execution of some of the leaders of the Lao national movement in Thailand did not suppress resistance against the Bangkok military dictatorship. In November 1964, the Pathet Lao radio broadcast a manifesto of a Thai independence movement calling "for a policy of neutrality, peace, democracy, prosperity and the people's well-being." A year later this movement joined the Patriotic Front of Thailand, whose program demanded national independence, democratic rights, the adoption of a policy of peace and neutrality, economic development, land reform and social justice, and cultural development. The movement was far from Vietnamese or Laotian dimensions, but it was serious enough to make Bangkok worry. At the same time, however, Thai authorities knew how to exploit the situation to produce additional aid.

In addition to their fears of the socio-political influences of revolutionary movements across the Mekong, Bangkok authorities also feared encirclement by a "neutral belt" of states from northeast Burma to southwest Cambodia. In Bangkok neutrality carried the old Dulles overtones of immorality and subversion, and was further tainted with unwelcome democratic trends.

Thus, for a variety of reasons the military dictatorship in Bangkok was interested in creating greater and faster U.S. commitments to Thailand. To achieve its goals Thai diplomacy went to work on the whole gamut of U.S. foreign policy anxieties and perceptions: China obsessions, Indo-chinese engagements and the delusive domino theory. In many instances these efforts were actively supported by U.S. military and intelligence agencies.

The Rusk–Thanat Proviso

During his spring 1961 mission to Indochina, Vice-President Johnson stopped in Thailand after visits to South Vietnam, the Philippines and Taiwan, and issued a joint statement with Marshal Sarit in which "The U.S. government expressed its determination to honor its treaty commitments to support Thailand . . . against subversion and Communist aggression . . . Both Governments reiterated their determination to fulfill the SEATO commitments and to go forward in steadfast partnership. Both Governments examined possible ways to strengthen Thai defense capabilities and agreed to explore ways in which this might be achieved through greater joint efforts and mutual sacrifices and the military assistance program involving the armed forces."

During his "Presidential review," Taylor spent two days in Bangkok assessing possible Thai roles in the new Indochinese strategy. Thailand offered ideal terrain for a military build-up. From the South Vietnamese perspective, the Laotian problem had to be tackled in a defensive way, as a "seal-off" issue; but from Thai territory, Laos and North Vietnam were both open to offensive strategy. Thailand was well suited as a forward base for both air and ground action. Separated by Laos from North Vietnam, and by Laos and Burma from China, Thailand offered a good sanctuary for any military contingency build-up. Naturally, Sarit was aware of his assets and decided to play for high stakes. One of the main goals of Phoumi's December Vientiane performance was to manipulate the U.S. administration into a larger commitment to Thailand.

On January 4, 1962, with excitement about the breakdown of the Vientiane negotiations still in the air, Marshal Sarit announced that a Thai goodwill mission might be sent to Moscow to promote trade with the Soviet Union. In Khang Khay this was seen as a move to soften U.S. diplomacy. Nevertheless, Washington threatened to suspend part of its financial aid to the Boun Oum government if it failed to continue the negotiations on a coalition government under Souvanna Phouma. Thus, on January 24 Thai Deputy Prime Minister Prince Wan Waithayakon declared at a press conference in Bangkok that if the U.S. stopped aid to Vientiane there would be "immense trouble." Waithayakon expressed doubts about the neutralism of Souvanna Phouma and stipulated that the controversial portfolios of Defense and Interior should be in "really impartial hands." "If the Interior Ministry is in the hands of the Souvanna party," the Prince added, "facilities might be given to the Communists to infiltrate Thailand."

In response, U.S. diplomacy took a double track. It continued to pressure Vientiane but started to buy up the Thais. In mid-February, leaving military assistance intact, the United States provisionally suspended a three-million-dollar monthly budgetary subsidy to the Boun Oum government. Simultaneously, in an interview published on February 18 in the *Bangkok World,* U.S. ambassador Kenneth T. Young declared that U.S. military assistance to Thailand in 1962 would be double the 1961 allocation. Official figures were secret; unofficially it was estimated that Thailand had received, up to 1961, a total of three hundred million dollars in military aid.* On February 19 Attorney General Robert Kennedy, stopping in Bangkok on a world tour, told the press that the United States was seriously committed to defending Thailand against any form of communist aggression

*Thailand later acquired fame as "the best ally money can buy." During the escalation of the Vietnam war, U.S. spending in Thailand was estimated at over five hundred million dollars yearly.

"partly through SEATO and partly through affection for a people ready to fight to defend their freedom." In an informal talk to university students he added that he had reaffirmed U.S. commitments to Thailand to the Prime Minister.

On February 28 President Kennedy held a White House consultation with his chief foreign policy advisers and congressional leaders of both parties. Among those present were General Taylor, Admiral Felt, Robert McNamara and Averell Harriman. The new U.S. Southeast Asian policy was discussed and bipartisan approval assured. While Admiral Felt left for Bangkok to evaluate the use of the increased aid to Thailand, Thai Foreign Minister Thanat Khoman arrived in Washington to define with Dean Rusk the range of new U.S. commitments. From their meeting came the famous Rusk–Thanat joint statement, issued on March 6, a document of rare precedent in diplomatic history, containing a unilateral U.S. defense guarantee for Thailand.

The statement went much further than previous SEATO commitments. Freely defining Thailand's "independence and integrity" as falling within the United States' "vital national interest," the Rusk–Thanat proviso—a simple ministerial communiqué—resembled the subsequent Tonkin Gulf resolution and similar commitments in Taiwan, Cuba and the Middle East. It declared that "The Secretary of State reaffirmed that the United States regards the preservation of the independence and integrity of Thailand as vital to the national interests of the United States and to world peace. He expressed the firm intention of the United States to aid Thailand, its ally and historic friend, in resisting Communist aggression and subversion." Recalling that SEATO "provides the basis for the signatories collectively to assist Thailand in case of Communist armed attack against that country," the Secretary of State assured the Foreign Minister that the United States intended to give full effect to this obligation under the treaty, and added: "The Secretary of State reaffirmed that this obligation of the United States does not depend upon the prior agreement of all the parties to the Treaty, since the Treaty obligation is individual as well as collective. In reviewing measures to meet indirect aggression, the Secretary of State stated that the United States regards its commitments to Thailand under the Southeast Asia Collective Defense Treaty and under its bilateral economic and military assistance agreements with Thailand as providing an important basis for United States actions to help Thailand meet indirect aggression." The statement then noted that the two sides reviewed U.S. actions "to meet the threat of indirect aggression" in South Vietnam, and reached full agreement on the situation in Laos. Finally, touching on efforts "to increase the capabilities and readiness of the Thai armed forces," the statement stressed that "the United States intends to accelerate future deliveries to the greatest extent possible" in order to make a "significant contribution to this effort."

These then were far-reaching commitments.* Only four

*Commenting on the statement soon after U.S. troop landings in Thailand in May 1962, Thanat Khoman said:

The significance of the joint communiqué between Mr. Rusk and myself lies in the interpretation of the decision or decisions to be taken within the framework of SEATO. According to the present charter, all decisions must be taken by unanimity. That joint communiqué says that even if the decision is not endorsed by all, any individual country or countries may agree to take action even though there is no consensus, no demand for unanimity within SEATO. That is exactly the understanding between the U.S. and Thailand. This is one point.

The second point is that the SEATO charter talks about open aggression by conventional means, though we know for a fact that the other side, our opponents, have been resorting and will think of resorting to other methods of warfare rather than simple open warfare . . . They have been resorting to what I call a composite warfare system or what the Communists themselves call revolutionary wars or wars of national liberation, and the understanding put forward by the joint communiqué was that if aggression would take the years later Rusk invoked them when he tried to justify the quarter of a million U.S. soldiers engaged in a costly undeclared war on South Vietnamese soil. Appearing on February 18, 1966, before the Senate Committee on Foreign Relations, Dean Rusk declared that "this fundamental SEATO treaty obligation . . . has from the outset guided our action in South Vietnam . . . If the United States determines that an armed attack has occurred against any nation to whom the protection of the treaty applies, then it is obligated to 'act to meet the common danger' without regard to the views or action of any of the other treaty members."

Unlike the Rusk–Thanat proviso, Rusk's 1966 statement caused an uproar in the U.S. International lawyers, politicians and the press pointed out that Rusk's interpretation of SEATO commitments contradicted the very spirit of a multilateral agreement, and was in fact inconsistent with Foster Dulles' understanding of the SEATO commitment as expressed in his 1954 Senate statement, "That is an obligation for consultations. It is not an obligation for action."

Rusk's unilateral commitments, however, were accompanied by a silent bilateral understanding. U.S. "unilaterality" was repaid by Thai "unilaterality." A UPI message from Bangkok on June 15, 1966, quoted Thanat Khoman as saying: "Unilaterally, we allow the United States to make use of military facilities. Unilaterally, I insist upon that. It is not a treaty obligation. It is not a bilateral accord."

Thailand became an indispensable link in the Indochinese war. Three months after the establishment in Saigon in February 1962 of the U.S. Military Assistance Command, Vietnam, the Military Assistance Command for Thailand (MACTHAI) was established in Bangkok. Coordination was assured by placing both commands under four-star general Paul D. Harkins. Huge air and sea bases were built through-

form of composite warfare both sides would consider action under SEATO.

out Thailand. The build-up went on in extraordinary secrecy; Thai diplomacy long refused to admit the real facts. Nonetheless, Harrison E. Salisbury reported in the *New York Times* on September 5, 1966: "In reality, the United States has now close to 35,000 men in Thailand. Most of the 13th Air Force is stationed there. The United States operates— under the Thai flag—a chain of half a dozen major air bases, including the recently inaugurated Sattahip base, one of the largest, best-equipped B-52 super-bomber bases in the world. The United States is constructing a major naval and port facility at Sattahip Bay. It has built a multi-million dollar strategic 'friendship highway,' which links Thailand's northeast provinces with Bangkok. It has installed enormous supply bases, pipelines, and other facilities." Salisbury commented: "Some observers, noting the very large bases which the United States is constructing, have postulated that they might actually be designed for some future eventuality against Communist China . . ."

Simultaneously the Thai establishment increased its intervention in the Laos war. Thai officers, pilots and artillerymen wearing Laotian uniforms manned key rightist positions. Thai units and recruits reinforced the CIA-Meo mercenary army. U.S. and Thai strategy had met in perfect accord.

Stalemate in Laos

Meanwhile there was no progress in Laotian negotiations. In early January 1962 the two Co-chairmen, acting in the name of the Geneva conference, invited the three princes to Geneva "to discuss the situation" and complete their talks on the formation of a government of national union. The Geneva meeting took place on January 19, 1962. Though Boun Oum objected to signing any common declaration, he finally yielded to U.S. pressure and a joint communiqué was issued confirming the Zurich and Hin Heup agreements and announcing further efforts to constitute a coalition government. This was no great achievement. Vientiane still demanded the portfolios of Defense and Interior, and the stalemate continued.

In the meantime, as the Commission's March report noted, "there were serious breaches of the cease-fire at the end of December and during the whole month of January." The places mentioned included Mahaxay and Nhommarath in central Laos, Tha Thom on the southern approaches to the Plain of Jars, and Muong Sai and Nam Tha in the north, near the Chinese border. As the military situation deteriorated, the International Commission was unable to act: "As for exercising supervision and control over the cease-fire . . . the Commission has not found itself in a position to carry out such activity since the consent of all the parties has not been forthcoming."[2]

On February 3 the commissioners conferred with Souvanna Phouma and Souphanouvong in Khang Khay. The princes indicated "that this time they would not be satisfied with a verbal declaration of cease-fire, as on May 3, 1961, but would insist on a written cease-fire agreement fixing a cease-fire line which should not be violated either on land or in the air. They visualized a role for the Commission in observing the cease-fire along such lines." The ICSC report then continues: "When the commissioners explained these views to General Phoumi Nosavan on 4 February, he said . . . that no continuous cease-fire line could be fixed in a country like Laos," indicating, however, his readiness to fix cease-fire lines along the main segments of the front.[3] This debate persisted even after Nosavan's defeat at Nam Tha. On May 16 Souvanna Phouma and Souphanouvong repeated "their former statements that they had proposed several times, *inter alia* at Ban Namone, that the parties should arrive at a written cease-fire agreement which would fix a continuous cease-fire line not to be violated either on land or in the air and on which basis the Commission could supervise the cessation of hostilities." But Vientiane, the report adds, had not accepted this proposal.[4]

Despite Vientiane's defiant stand, Souvanna Phouma continued his efforts to reach a political understanding. On February 16, accompanied by the ambassadors of the Soviet Union and Great Britain, he went to Luang Prabang to report to the King and contact Vientiane leaders. The Prince stayed in the royal capital two days, and met General Nosavan. He then spent five days in Vientiane, from February 21 to 26, discussing issues with local politicians and members of the diplomatic corps. The effort again proved useless. Souvanna returned to Khang Khay with a new Vientiane proposal which was far from anything previously discussed. This proposal reverted to the July 1961 design of entrusting the leadership of the government to the King. As executive chief the King would preside over six committees headed by top Laotian personalities: the three princes and three representatives of the leading Vientiane families, i.e. Phoui Sananikone, Nhouy Abhay, and Outhong Souvannavong (the ambassador to Tokyo). The Committee for Interior would fall to Boun Oum, Defense would be allotted to Souvanna Phouma but with Nosavan as executive deputy, Foreign Affairs would go to Phoui Sananikone, Culture to Nhouy Abhay, Social Problems to Souvannavong, and Economy to Souphanouvong. Complete Vientiane domination of the government. Naturally, the proposal was immediately rejected by the Neo Lao Haksat, and the Neutralists followed suit.

In the ensuing deadlock Vientiane continued to behave provocatively. Addressing the National Assembly on March 10, Boun Oum declared: "We are convinced that a government of national union presided over by Prince Souvanna Phouma, with the ministries of Interior and Defense in the hands of the 'Xieng Khouang Neutralists,' would undoubtedly deliver our country to the domination and cruelties of the communists. For we know that the 'neutralist group' of Prince Souvanna Phouma has no power and no authority. He serves only as screen for the Neo Lao Haksat and agents of international communism." Boun Oum questioned the cut in U.S. financial aid to Vientiane, because "it was generally recognized that our National Army constitutes the defense vanguard of the Free World." In the minds of Vientiane leaders and their advisers nothing seemed to have changed since Dulles brought to Laos the concept of transforming the country into a forward bastion against world communism.

Souvanna Phouma felt deeply hurt by Boun Oum's remarks and the subsequent debate in the National Assembly. But most of all he took offense at the fact that the King in his opening address did not even mention the mandate he had conferred on the Prince to form a government of national union. The King called for full support for the Boun Oum government and blamed "misguided" persons for the existing crisis. There was no mention of seeking understanding between Laotians.

Growing Polarization

More important than Souvanna's discussions with Laotian adversaries during his February travels were his prolonged dinner meetings with the U.S., British, and French ambassadors. Impressed by repeated reassurances of Western support and arguments appealing to his inner convictions, Souvanna became convinced that he had to show himself worthy of the confidence offered. It was at this stage that he made essential commitments to the United States. To prove his independence from the Neo Lao Haksat he promised, among other things, to take over control of areas under exclusive Neo Lao Haksat administration. The United States was particularly interested in central Laos, which included the vital communication trail between the divided parts of Vietnam.

This had major consequences. Drawing nearer to the West and local conservative forces, Souvanna weakened the delicate tripartite balance needed for the success of the coalition experiment. Relations between the Neutralists and the Neo Lao Haksat became strained, and suspicions as to the Prince's real intentions intensified the polarization.

I spent February in Warsaw, and on my return to Laos in mid-March Souphanouvong had much to tell me about this new development: while U.S. diplomacy publicly protested its pressures on Vientiane, it acted in every possible way to soften Souvanna Phouma and to reassure itself about the posture of the future coalition government. The widely publicized partial suspension of financial aid to Vientiane was only a tactical move; U.S. military deliveries increased, enabling Nosavan's extraordinary build-up in the region of Nam Tha. On the other hand, pressures on Souvanna Phouma made him much more susceptible to Western counsels. Reflecting on his brother's past, Souphanouvong added, "The trouble with Souvanna lies in his dual nature—patriotic and reactionary."

According to information received from Vientiane, Souphanouvong continued, Souvanna Phouma had promised to seize control of the area bordering on South Vietnam, including the administration of the adjoining Laotian provinces. After his return from Vientiane to Xieng Khouang, he had sent fifty of his men, some of them known for their enmity to the Pathet Lao, to central Laos. The group, equipped with enough arms for several hundred people, had instructions to join the local administration. However, the Neo Lao Haksat, not consulted beforehand, refused to receive them, and they turned back.

Discord disrupted internal discussions. The Neo Lao Haksat disapproved of Souvanna's "Vientiane diplomacy," and personal relations with the Prince became difficult. During a joint meeting of the Government and the Neo Lao Haksat leadership, when Souphanouvong criticized activities of "some Neutralist personalities," Souvanna Phouma stood up to leave; he was persuaded to stay and the incident was settled, but further discussions were downgraded to the committee level.

Other repercussions were felt. For the first time, Souphanouvong mentioned difficulties in relations with Kong Le. The young captain—since promoted to general—was not consistent in his thinking. He had a low level of political education, and was easily influenced by conservative elements. As head of the Mixed Allied Command at the Plain of Jars, Kong Le particularly resented the exigencies of discipline and advice from more experienced Neo Lao Haksat or Vietnamese officers. Furthermore, his inflated personal ambitions contributed to corrupt his personality.

Souvanna Phouma tried to fulfill his Vientiane commitments in many ways. One sophisticated attempt involved remodeling the alliance. The Neutralists came up with a proposal to proclaim, immediately, without waiting for Vientiane's consent, a coalition government composed of the Neutralists and the Neo Lao Haksat with some seats reserved for the Rightists. The Neo Lao Haksat considered the proposal very seriously; they thought it could help maintain the political initiative and close ranks with the Neutralists. But they had apprehensions concerning their independence and control of areas under their administration; they were reluctant even to admit certain Neutralists to these areas. They inquired about alliance experiences in Poland after World War II, and Phoumi Vongvichit even visited Prague for several days to learn from the experience of the Czechs.

This proposal went against basic Neo Lao Haksat strategy. It clashed with their resolution to maintain their holdings

and strengthen their positions in the field, at least until well
assured that they would not be deceived as they had been in
the fifties.* The proposal was finally dropped when it turned
out that the Neutralists' main interest centered on taking
control of administration away from the Neo Lao Haksat.
Fundamental discord also developed around the coalition's
main tenets. As Phoumi Vongvichit later told me, negotiations deadlocked when it came to appraising U.S. imperialism. In line with Hanoi and Peking, the Neo Lao Haksat
viewed U.S. policy as colonial in nature, aimed at containing
the revolutionary wave in Asia. They proposed to define the
coalition's essential objectives in anti-imperialist terms, with
the United States seen as the foe of all the Indochinese peoples. This Souvanna Phouma categorically rejected.

On March 30 and 31 William Sullivan, Harriman's aide
and later ambassador to Laos, visited Khang Khay and
transmitted to Souvanna President Kennedy's personal invitation to come to Washington. Though he declined for the
moment, excusing himself on family grounds, Souvanna put
great trust in U.S. diplomacy. He told the Vietnamese representatives in Khang Khay that he would visit President
Kennedy as Prime Minister of the coalition government, and
he ordered broadcasting personnel not to assail U.S. policy
any more, but to refer to the United States as a friendly

*The Neo Lao Haksat Program of Action in this regard read as follows:

> In areas liberated by the Pathet Lao, the Royal Government would
> be asked to recognize the representatives appointed by the Pathet
> Lao as province chiefs, district chiefs and functionaries. In areas
> liberated by Government forces where we have no base, the gover-
> nors and officials would be appointed by the Royal Government. In
> areas liberated jointly by the Pathet Lao and Government forces, the
> chiefs of provinces and districts would be appointed by the Royal
> Government, and we propose to designate Neo Lao Haksat repre-
> sentatives as deputy-chiefs of those provinces and districts . . . Re-
> gional power should be in hands of the nationality living in this
> region.

power. Souvanna also tried to convince Souphanouvong to stop attacking U.S. policies, and even went so far as to threaten cessation of government aid to the Neo Lao Haksat. He called Souphanouvong inflexible, and told him that he had no understanding of diplomacy. Such discussions clearly augured hard times for the Neo Lao Haksat–Neutralist alliance.

Harriman's Failure

In the meantime, U.S. diplomacy tried to clear up matters in Vientiane. The partial suspension of U.S. aid to the Boun Oum government did not seem to worry General Nosavan particularly; it was no secret that the loss was covered by Thai funds and CIA subsidies.* Pointing directly to CIA activities in Laos, the London *Times* stated on May 23 that it was "officially believed that the heavy pressure brought upon Prince Boun Oum and General Phoumi to accept the political solution of neutrality, including the suspension since February of the monthly subsidy of $3,000,000, failed because the agency [the CIA] provided them with some funds from its own capacious budget."

Eventually, to strike a deal with Nosavan, U.S. diplomacy decided to enlist Thai mediation. Softened by the Rusk–Thanat statement, Washington felt, Thailand would help the United States. With this in mind, Harriman set out on another mission. He arrived in Bangkok on March 21, and "spent a couple of days here in an attempt to win Thai government backing for what appeared to be a last-ditch attempt to get the Lao government to accept the so-called

---

*Secret Thai military assistance to Nosavan was estimated to have reached about three hundred million dollars during Sarit's rule. In 1962 some Thai aid was given in rice grants; to recover the expenses Bangkok raised the price of paid rice deliveries from nine to eleven dollars per ton. Nhouy Abhay disclosed this to me on May 20, adding some bitter comments on the situation.

neutralist leader Prince Souvanna Phouma as head of a coalition government with control of the key ministries of Defense and Interior."[5] As Phoumi Nosavan refused to meet Harriman in Bangkok, Harriman "persuaded Marshal Sarit, Phoumi's relative and mentor, to come with him to Nong Khai just across the river from Vientiane, to talk to Phoumi."[6]

The Nong Khai meeting took place on March 24. Thai Foreign Minister Thanat Khoman was also present. According to Hilsman, "Sarit urged Phoumi to co-operate in forming a government of national union."[7] But William Sullivan, who accompanied Harriman and later came over to Khang Khay, told Souvanna Phouma and the Soviet ambassador a somewhat different version. The Siamese leaders, he said, responded to Harriman's proposals with silence, which the U.S. diplomats interpreted as agreement. Yet Phoumi Nosavan was still defiant. The United States, Sullivan said, faced the difficult task of killing a fly on a windowpane without damaging the glass. This demanded time and patience. Sullivan counseled Souvanna to make concessions: in order to win Nosavan guarantees concerning his future position would have to be given.

Souvanna Phouma showed readiness to accept Sullivan's advice, but Harriman failed to convince Nosavan and his mentors. The *Bangkok World* stated: "Prime Minister Sarit Thanarat revealed that the Thai government had not given all-out support to the American diplomat . . . Despite Harriman's mission, some basic differences between the American and the Southeast Asian viewpoints seemed to remain . . . In short, when the dust settled, we found things back to just where they were before."[8]

Souvanna was depressed by Harriman's failure, but he did not lose hope, and after his talks with Sullivan his self-confidence seemed restored. For real results, he told me, we would have to wait some time; perhaps three months would be necessary to soften Vientiane's position. Meanwhile, Souvanna planned a two-month stay in Paris. On April 2, before his departure, the Prince issued a statement urging the United States to act decisively to bring Vientiane back to the negotiating table: "I have confidence that the United States will make the Savannakhet group understand the necessity of forming the government of national union in accordance with the joint communiqués of the three princes . . . To show to the world a sincere desire for a peaceful settlement of the Laotian problem, the American government will have to withdraw its military assistance from the Phoumi–Boun Oum group . . . In expectation that the United States will bring the Savannakhet group to respect the concluded agreements, I am going to France to repair my health and to see my family . . ."⁹

But matters were not moving toward negotiations; they were heading toward a new military-political crisis. Well aware of the military preparations, Souvanna chose to be far from the fighting. In early May events climaxed in the battle of Nam Tha and the subsequent landing of U.S. forces in Thailand. This was a new landmark in the Southeast Asian drama; although one of the results was a coalition government, more basically the adversaries were hardened in their collision courses.

The Nam Tha episode is revealing. Both sides, having different objectives in mind, planned well. Both succeeded partially, and had cause for satisfaction. But the general aftereffects must have caused second thoughts in all the great power capitals. Through a chain reaction, short-range strategy hardened into long-term commitments, and thereafter there was no return to the conflict's earlier dimensions. Nam Tha should serve as a classic example of clients manipulating great-power policies, and of the dangers threatening contemporary international relations as a result of wartime great power–client dealings.

Nam Tha–The Western Story

The Thai-Vientiane scenario, worked out in connivance with the CIA, was rather simple. Apart from the general aim of undermining the Laotian negotiations, Thai ruling circles were anxious to cash in as quickly as possible on the benefits of the Rusk–Thanat statement. They aimed for a crisis to test U.S. guarantees for Thailand and to hasten the U.S. strategical build-up on Thai soil. If such a crisis centered on the Laotian border it would at the same time strengthen the hand of the hard-liners opposing a political settlement in Laos. Nosavan seemed to believe that the crisis might even trigger direct U.S. intervention.

Thai-Lao preparations were well known on the highest levels in Washington, and U.S. military advisers actively cooperated in executing plans. A twelve-member White Star team helped to reinforce the Nam Tha garrison, and remained there until the fall of Nam Tha in the early hours of May 6, 1962. A government communiqué published in Bangkok on February 13 announced the dispatch of Thai troops to Nan Province, bordering the Nam Tha area. President Kennedy, speaking at a press conference on February 15, said that the cease-fire in Laos had become "increasingly frayed," and because of communist moves "the government forces reinforced their people at the town of Nam Tha."

Hilsman, however, sees events in a different light: "Against American advice, Phoumi flew in more and more of his troops to reinforce the Nam Tha garrison. By the end of January five thousand of Phoumi's army, which by then totaled fifty thousand, were at Nam Tha, including important elements of his available artillery." At the end of April, at the last moment before the crucial battle, Hilsman adds, "still another attempt was made to persuade Phoumi to withdraw from the trap, but without success."[10] It seems that the same argument went on between the political and military wings of the U.S. administration. In any case, Washington was fully aware of developments and participated in the Nam Tha build-up.

On March 31, during Sullivan's talks with Souvanna Phouma and Souphanouvong, matters were discussed with substantial openness. Sullivan admitted that Nosavan was trying to trigger U.S. military intervention and advised, strangely enough, that Khang Khay try to avoid military operations. He said that U.S. advisers accompanied Nosavan's forces in order to control his moves, citing as an example the checking of Nosavan's attempted offensive on the Muong Sai front, forty miles southeast of Nam Tha. Sullivan got a clear answer from Souphanouvong: if unprovoked, the Neo Lao Haksat would not violate the cease-fire lines. To Sullivan's remark that these lines were not recognized by Vientiane, Souphanouvong replied that the lines had been drawn by force of arms and he did not intend to give them up. Washington thus was given a plain warning.

The time and scene of the battle were well chosen. Nam Tha lies about six miles from the Chinese border and eighty miles from Thailand—an ideal place to develop U.S. anxiety. The scenario suited the aftermath of the "Presidential review" and also fitted CIA eagerness to go ahead with anti-China master strokes. This was the Year of the Tiger on the Chinese calendar, and the Chinese nationalists thought this "a good omen for the long-awaited return to the mainland." The CIA strongly favored these plans and came up with support "for a 'covert' but large-scale landing on the mainland—a sort of even greater Bay of Pigs."[11] In these schemes Nam Tha could serve as a good diversion. On May 23 the Washington correspondent of the London *Times* stated bluntly that CIA agents in Laos were "believed to have encouraged General Phoumi Nosavan in the concentration of troops that brought about a swift and disastrous response of the Pathet Lao." State Department spokesman Lincoln

White denied the *Times* report, but in a further dispatch on May 30 the *Times* upheld its allegations, citing British and French embassy sources in Vientiane.

Skirmishes around Nam Tha continued for weeks, intensifying at the end of April. On May 3, without encountering substantial resistance, Neo Lao Haksat forces occupied the outpost of Muong Sing, twenty-five miles northwest of Nam Tha and only three miles from the Chinese border. Three days later, in the morning hours of May 6, following an artillery barrage, the Nam Tha garrison fled in panic toward Thailand. Survivors reached the small town of Ban Houei Sai on the Mekong, and together with the local garrison crossed the river on May 11 and surrendered to the authorities. The flight was dramatic—heading the fugitives was General Bounleuth Sanichan, commander in chief of Vientiane's forces, and General La Pathammavong, commander of Nam Tha. Two days later Thailand returned the troops by airlift to Laos.

Nam Tha developments were accentuated by highly exaggerated reports emanating from Vientiane and Bangkok. Sarit did his best to amplify events before McNamara and Lyman L. Lemnitzer (Chairman of the Joint Chiefs of Staff), who at the moment were visiting the Thai capital. Repeatedly, Vientiane charged Soviet and Chinese intervention. On May 12, evidently reacting to these reports, President Kennedy put U.S. Pacific troops on action readiness and ordered units of the Seventh Fleet to proceed to the Gulf of Siam. On May 14, Vientiane military authorities published two communiqués stating that enemy forces had captured Ban Houei Sai on the Thai border. On May 15 Kennedy announced the dispatch to Thailand of 4,000 U.S. ground and air troops to join the 1,000 U.S. Marines already on Thai soil as part of current SEATO exercises.* "On the basis of

*All official accounts in 1962 spoke about the dispatch to Thailand of 5,000 U.S. ground and air troops. The same figure was repeated by Harri-

a decision quickly made and quickly executed," Sorensen
notes, "barely going through the formality of asking the
Thais to 'request' our help under the SEATO Treaty, U.S.
Naval forces and two air squadrons were moved to the area.
More than 5,000 marines and Army combat personnel were
put ashore in Thailand and moved up to the Lao border."[12]
A Thai Foreign Affairs spokesman confirmed on May 18 that
Thailand had not asked the United States to send troops, but
had agreed when Washington suggested it.

On May 16 the official Vientiane daily *Lao Presse* carried
the following correction: "In communiqués 93 and 94 of the
Ministry of National Security, published on May 14, 1962,
it was announced by error that on May 10, 1962, communist
troops attacked Ban Houei Sai at about 2300 hours, simultaneously from three sides, and occupied the locality at noon
on May 11. Ban Houei Sai has all the time remained in our
hands and was not attacked by the enemy after the fall of
Nam Tha." By that time foreign correspondents had reached
Ban Houei Sai and could tell the true story of recent events.
Vientiane thus had to deny its allegations but the dispatch of
U.S. troops to Thailand was an accomplished fact. In an
attempt to rationalize events, U.S. ambassador to Bangkok
Leonard Unger stated years later, "The Rusk–Thanat communiqué had reassured the Thais that action under the
SEATO Treaty could be taken by some number of members
less than the total SEATO membership. The U.S. troop deployment later in 1962 convinced them that we were willing
to show our readiness to act to deter the kind of threat that
confronted Thailand."[13]

Harriman was furious. On May 18 he called in the Lao
ambassador in Washington, Prince Khampan, and conveyed

man in his memoirs. But during November 1969 Senate Foreign Relations
hearings both U.S. ambassadors to Bangkok, Graham H. Martin and
Leonard Unger, repeatedly refer to the deployment of 10,000 U.S. ground
and air troops.

to him "his great disappointment" over the developments. The secret message relating Harriman's declaration sent by Prince Khampan to the Vientiane Foreign Ministry chanced to reach my hands, and I was able to make exact notes of it. First, Harriman informed Khampan that Soviet ambassador Anatoly Dobrynin had called on Rusk, and on instructions from Khrushchev told him that the Soviet Union still wanted the constitution of a coalition government in Laos in the spirit of the Khrushchev–Kennedy Vienna communiqué. Dobrynin stressed that as General Nosavan was the author of the Nam Tha provocation, responsibility for the breach and reinforcement of the cease-fire fell on the United States. Harriman strongly accused Nosavan because: (1) "The debacle up until Thailand was carried out in a deliberate manner by Royal troops who did not show any resistance," and (2) "General Phoumi did not accept recommendations by American military experts who demanded that he take up more adequate positions at Nam Tha."

Harriman stressed that the dispatch of U.S. troops to Laos was not foreseen "as Chinese troops would never be so foolish as to invade Laos." He said that "the idea of the partition of Laos was not the object of negotiations." He added: "General Phoumi cannot cause the outbreak of a world war. By his irresponsible deeds he will only destroy his own country. It is not he who dictates the policy of the United States."

Harriman's statement to Khampan brought together all the complexities and inner contradictions of U.S. policy. Washington knew well the intentions of the Nam Tha scenario, but nevertheless played along with the game by sending troops to Thailand. Washington was also well aware of the inherent dangers to world peace, and knew that all Nosavan's inventions about Chinese intervention were lies; but nonetheless it moved onto the brink. The Nam Tha episode serves as an indication of how easily a great power–client relationship, tangled by the involvement of the military-industrial complex, can lead toward disaster.

But to what extent was Harriman himself informed when he spoke to the Laotian ambassador? Was he fully aware of the designs of the CIA and the other military agencies? Or was he partly in the dark, as he was in Rangoon when he and Souvanna Phouma discussed the composition of a coalition government? Such reflections only underline the complexity of the U.S. involvement and the difficulties of remaining in control of events.

Nam Tha—The Eastern Story

SOVIET DISENGAGEMENT

Part of the background to Nam Tha, as far as the East was concerned, lay in the process of differentiation in the socialist camp. After the autumn 1961 rift with China and the Indochinese allies, perceiving that it could not direct events, the Soviet Union decided to leave planning to its Asian allies and to begin a gradual disengagement in Laos. This policy continued, in fact, until Khrushchev's fall, and was reversed only partly in the spring of 1965, when the U.S. escalated the war.

The situation in Laos after the collapse of negotiations in December 1961 was subject to many reviews and discussions among socialist representatives in Hanoi and Khang Khay. Early in March a week-long four-party conference took place in Hanoi; Ung Van Kheim, Ho Wei, Kaysone and Tovmassyan (the Soviet ambassador in Hanoi) headed the delegations of the Vietnamese, Chinese, Laotian and Soviet parties. The conference decided that the situation was not yet ripe for the formation of a coalition government and that efforts must be made to overcome the difficulties. The most important tasks for the Neo Lao Haksat, it was stressed, were to strengthen the alliance with the Neutralists and to expand its military and political forces. The Chinese delegation especially emphasized the need to develop military strength and to solidify positions in the countryside. The conference discussed aid to Laos, and decided to increase unofficial supplies to the Neo Lao Haksat.

In the meantime the Soviet ambassador to Laos spent some weeks in Moscow. When he returned in mid-March he carried letters on the Laotian problem from the Communist Party of the Soviet Union to the parties of China, Vietnam and Laos. On March 21 Abramov, accompanied by the Soviet ambassador to Hanoi, was received by Ho Chi Minh and Pham Van Dong. Returning to Khang Khay, Abramov showed me the text of the letter addressed to the Vietnamese party.

The letter consisted of a short introduction followed by five points. The introduction expressed satisfaction with the common appreciation by the socialist countries of the political line followed hitherto in the Laotian question. Point one stated that internal Laotian problems were now coming to the fore. It had become clear that the Boun Oum–Nosavan clique did not want a coalition government; responsibility for this development fell on the United States.

Point two affirmed that the line of the socialist countries regarding the coalition government was right, and that such a government could be formed only on the basis of the Zurich, Hin Heup and Geneva agreements. The socialist countries could not be indifferent to developments in the Laotian situation, as Laos lies on the borders of the socialist world. Larger concessions therefore could not be made.

Point three stated that as a result of American pressure aimed at destroying his alliance with the Neo Lao Haksat, Souvanna had finally leaned toward reactionary forces, whom he had always favored. The alliance with Souvanna Phouma was desirable only as long as it strengthened national-democratic forces. Such was the nature of the alliance hitherto; the Neo Lao Haksat knew how to draw advantages from it. The Neo Lao Haksat now controlled about half of Laos. This alone, should the enemies not agree to a settlement, was in itself a great achievement. One should now pay great attention to strengthening Neo Lao Haksat positions. According to the Laotian comrades, Souvanna Phouma was now acting to harm the democratic forces, but all possibilities of cooperation with Phouma had not yet been exhausted, especially as Souvanna himself was well aware that without the Neo Lao Haksat he could get no results.

Point four noted that both the Chinese and the Laotian comrades had concluded that conditions were not yet ripe for the formation of a coalition government; that because of the two-faced position of the United States "conditions in Laos would long remain unsettled, and this situation could prolong itself further . . . In this there is nothing unfavorable for us, [but] one has to be morally prepared." The Vietnamese comrades, the letter went on, consider it right to undertake military actions in defense of the liberated areas and to force the adversary to negotiations aimed at the constitution of a coalition government favorable for the national-patriotic forces.

Point four then stated that the Russians accepted the conclusions of the Chinese, Vietnamese and Laotian comrades, and treated them with due understanding: they were nearer to Laos and knew local conditions better. Therefore, they could judge better what practical steps should be taken in Laos in the near future.

Finally, point five said that concerning the Geneva conference the Soviet Union agreed with the Chinese, Vietnamese and Laotian comrades, to leave in Geneva part of the delegations and to keep frequent contact among them.

This was a clear statement of disengagement as far as internal Laotian developments were concerned. The Asian allies were given a free hand to plan and shape events to their understanding; this part of the message was received with satisfaction. But at the same time the letter drew a line of division in the socialist world. Resentment grew in Peking, Hanoi and Khang Khay against the unwillingness of the Soviet Union to join with its allies in an active Indochinese policy to defend their most basic national interests.

CHINESE CONCERNS

Shortly after the delivery of the letter, I was invited to a conversation with the chargé d'affaires of the Chinese mission in Khang Khay, Liu Chun. Offering his comments on the Soviet message, he stressed that it was necessary to separate two sets of problems: those in which the Soviet comrades accepted the point of view of the Chinese, Vietnamese and Laotian parties; and those where they only took cognizance of the Asian point of view without taking a position. The second set of problems concerned statements that conditions were not yet ripe for a coalition government; that the situation would remain unsettled for a long time, which was not seen as unfavorable; that it would be right to try to influence the course of events by military operations. This means, Liu Chun stated, that the Communist Party of the Soviet Union was holding itself aloof, that uniformity of views had not been reached. Moreover, a number of questions raised in the Chinese letter to the Soviet Communist Party remained unanswered. These concerned the Chinese proposals that one should try to introduce in the future coalition government a veto system which would require the unanimity of all three parties on vital decisions; and that at the ministries of Defense, Interior and Foreign Affairs, committees representing the three parties would confirm, on the basis of unanimity, the actions of the ministries.*

*It was amazing to find that a week later Sullivan came up with an almost identical proposal to allot the ministries of Defense and Interior to committees representing the three parties to the conflict. Chinese thinking

Although the exchange of letters between the Soviet Union and its Asian allies did not eradicate dissent, it did result in a procedural understanding applicable to further undertakings: Hanoi, Peking, and the Neo Lao Haksat felt free to proceed with their strategy. As political negotiations were completely blocked, subsequent planning concentrated on military moves. Keeping to the rules of people's war, it was assumed that any military strategy had to be guided by political thinking.

PEOPLE'S WAR STRATEGY

The Nam Tha battle scene was chosen by Phoumi Nosavan and his advisers in the same way as Dien Bien Phu was chosen by the French: both places had to serve as forward strategical strongholds against local revolutionary armies. The revolutionaries simply responded to the challenge. Interestingly enough, the environment of Nam Tha was similar to that of Dien Bien Phu, situated some one hundred miles to the west on about the same parallel. In a sense, Nosavan's choice of remote Nam Tha suited the Neo Lao Haksat: the dispersion of Vientiane's forces eased pressures on more vital fronts.

Active preparations to respond in force to Nosavan's military provocations started elsewhere in March. Two days after Harriman's Vientiane visit, Souphanouvong told me that action had been initiated to strike a severe blow at the enemy. The strategy had a basis in classic people's war strategy: the operation had to take the foe by surprise; had

went along exactly the same lines as Washington's. It might be strange, Sullivan remarked to Abramov, that the United States should come up with a troika proposal; the reason lay in local conditions. Having failed to assure its clients dominance over the Laotian army and administration in a coalition government, the United States was now striving to equip them with a controlling veto. Recalling past Laotian experience, Peking was eager to secure the same guarantees for the Neo Lao Haksat.

to aim at a vital and politically sensitive section of the front; had to destroy as much of enemy forces and material as possible; had to retain a local character; and had to be a short engagement followed by a quick withdrawal. The hope was to execute the final blow in the last days of the dry season, as in the Ban Padong operation, so as to render counteraction impossible. The Prince stressed that the Neo Lao Haksat wanted to avoid a larger military confrontation and would try not to amplify the conflict. The main objective, he said, was to force the adversary to return to negotiations on conditions favorable to the Neo Lao Haksat.

The same day I was invited for lunch by Liu Chun; here also the conversation turned to military action. Liu Chun spoke of the need to strike a *tactical* blow. The general orientation was for a long period of no war and no peace. He assumed that the United States, concentrating its attention on South Vietnam, would not engage in large operations in Laos. At the same time the Neo Lao Haksat had to avoid actions which could aggravate the military conflict. They should hold to dual revolutionary tactics: "Proceed on both feet—keep the initiative in *local* military operations and continue political negotiations."*

Vietnamese thinking developed on similar lines. Its essentials were explained to me on April 5 by generals Le Chuong

---

*One concrete case clarified the Chinese orientation and their concern not to escalate the conflict and not to get involved in it. In one of his angry reactions to Nosavan's war moves, Souvanna Phouma, without even consulting the Neo Lao Haksat, had requested Chinese jet pilots to defend Laotian air space; he hoped to receive the planes from the Soviet Union and asked China for pilots. Liu Chun explained to me in great detail that the Chinese People's Republic had refused because it did not want to be accused of intervention, and did not want to create a pretext for an escalation of the conflict. Transactions involving military personnel must be considered with great prudence, Liu Chun emphasized. Souvanna Phouma was rash in military moves and rashly he had tried to involve China in the conflict; yet he had not agreed to sign a general economic treaty with China.

and Tong Dy: Assuming that recent political developments made imminent settlement improbable, one had to expect a certain period of neither peace nor larger war. To keep the initiative, it was therefore necessary to intensify the small war in order to exert military-political pressure on the foe, yet avoid causing any inflammation of the conflict.

In the beginning of January, Nosavan initiated a concerted military offensive on several fronts under the code name "Seisana" (Victory). The strongest attacks were launched on the central front, east of Thakhek, in the direction of Mahaxay and Nhommarath, and pushed toward the Vietnamese border in order to isolate Neo Lao Haksat-controlled areas and cut north-south communication. Vientiane initiated simultaneous operations at Tha Thom, on the southern approaches to the Plain of Jars, and at Muong Sai, north of Luang Prabang and on the southern border of Phong Saly. Included in Seisana were Meo commando activities in the rear of the Neo Lao Haksat and Kong Le forces, and pacification moves to "clean out" territories under Vientiane administration. Seisana ended in humiliating defeat on January 20, when a well-aimed Neo Lao Haksat counterattack routed Vientiane battalions on the Thakhek front. In a dress rehearsal for Nam Tha, Vientiane troops fled across the Mekong to Thailand.

Central Laos attracted all the parties' attention. Souphanouvong told me that the Neo Lao Haksat had been working toward self-sufficiency in central and southern Laos, and that by the end of March this had been attained in four provinces in the south. The Neo Lao Haksat had been trying to organize an uprising in the southern town of Saravane, which would have severed the whole of southern Laos from Vientiane. However, the plan was discovered and Colonel Sam Li, a former military attaché in Paris who was to have led the coup, brought two of his companies over to the Neo Lao Haksat. Low-level military operations also continued in central and southern Laos. In the last week of March the Neo Lao Haksat annihilated a strongly defended enemy position at Lavi, thirty miles southeast of Saravane, which Nosavan had hoped could be used, in cooperation with South Vietnamese forces, to cut the narrow meridional road on the Lao-South Vietnamese border.

But in March military planning focused on Nam Tha, where Nosavan had built up a large concentration of troops. According to intelligence reports reaching Khang Khay, by the end of March the Nam Tha garrison had grown to fifty-one companies totaling 4,000 soldiers. Together with adjoining posts the concentration reached 6,000 soldiers—10 or 15 percent of Vientiane's total strength. The liquidation of this stronghold would be a harsh blow to the enemy. Le Chuong told me that the operation was intended as both a defensive and an offensive move: it aimed to reduce provocation on the Chinese border, and to destroy a base for aggression against Phong Saly, Sam Neua, and the liberated areas in Luang Prabang Province.

Le Chuong described strategy and tactics for Nam Tha. The standard tactic was to harass and demoralize enemy troops by repeated local skirmishes, and step by step to reduce the effectiveness of his defenses. Though Vientiane forces were far superior in numbers, the Neo Lao Haksat seized the initiative. They dictated the time and place of each action, and were careful to engage in skirmishes only when assured of quantitative and qualitative superiority. In one such attack, on March 23, the Neo Lao Haksat decimated two enemy companies. At the same time the Neo Lao Haksat coordinated operations across the country in order to draw enemy attention away from Nam Tha and to scatter enemy forces.

Le Chuong and Tong Dy were confident that with Vietnamese technical help the Neo Lao Haksat would be able to control the pace of operations; in fact, they said, Vientiane's

forces had already lost the ability to carry out any large-scale
.. offensive. Le Chuong stressed that the aim was not to con-
quer Nam Tha by a large frontal attack, both because of a
lack of troops and supply, and, more important, because of
the need to avoid U.S. retaliation. This was crucial to the
Neo Lao Haksat-Hanoi scenario; but it did not sufficiently
account for the enemy's planning. The Neo Lao Haksat
softened the Nam Tha defenses and demoralized its garrison,
but, as Harriman told the Laotian ambassador, the disord-
ered flight to Thailand was deliberately created by Vientiane's generals. Thus the final stages of the Nam Tha battle
combined the scenarios developed by both sides.

THE DOMINO THEORY OF NEUTRALIZATION

The Soviet Union was aware of planning for Nam Tha, but
did not interfere, neither supporting nor condeming the
move; the Soviet ambassador, however, accepted the view
that a military blow might push Vientiane back to the negotiating table. But more and more the Soviet Union and its
Asian allies began to link the Laotian scene with South Vietnamese developments. Discussing Nam Tha operations in
the beginning of April, Abramov told me that he felt that
Hanoi's main objective was to divert the enemy's attention
from central Laos and drag his forces away from that region.
In a sense, he said, starting with the Taylor mission recent
developments had completely subordinated the Laotian
scene to events in South Vietnam. Increasingly, the resolution of Laotian problems demanded a settlement of the South
Vietnamese conflict. Abramov thought that it might be useful to force the United States to accept negotiations on South
Vietnam within the framework of the Geneva conference;
perhaps a call for volunteers in China and North Vietnam,
as a response to increased U.S. intervention in South Vietnam, would do the trick.

Much the same thinking was developed in Peking. Liu Chun told me that Chinese Foreign Minister Marshal Chen Yi, in conversation with Andrei Gromyko, envisioned a situation in which the Soviet Foreign Minister would remain a permanent Co-chairman of the Geneva conference: after Laos would come South Vietnam, and after South Vietnam would come Thailand. The objective would be to neutralize all of Southeast Asia. Chester Bowles had been right to expect a favorable response to the idea of neutralizing this region; Peking had even developed its own concept of a domino theory of neutralization.

At the same time the struggle in South Vietnam was being reevaluated. Pointing to growing U.S. intervention, Vietnamese representatives in Khang Khay spoke of a change in the character of the war: the uprising had reached the stage of a war of national liberation against U.S. colonialism. This reevaluation became part of Neo Lao Haksat thinking, and was reflected in their proposal that U.S. imperialism be marked as the main enemy of all Indochinese peoples; Laotian problems could no longer be separated from events elsewhere. This new appreciation brought the Neo Lao Haksat nearer to Hanoi and Peking, and at the same time the strong antagonism to the United States deepened the division between the Soviet Union and its Asian allies (although this was not publicly admitted).

Moscow naturally was disturbed by developments. Vientiane clearly opposed a compromise solution; and Souvanna Phouma was turning to the West. Soviet diplomats were instructed to find out the United States' real intentions. Was the partial suspension of financial aid to Vientiane a true indication that Washington still adhered to a political settlement? Or was it only a tactical move? Anyhow, the Soviet Union became reticent. At the end of March, Liu Chun told Abramov that after three years of natural calamities and bad harvests China was in a difficult economic position, and asked about further Soviet aid to Laos. Of course, Abramov said, the Soviet Union would not shirk its duties; however, because of the need to extend aid to many countries, the Soviet Union's abilities were not unlimited. Although it mistrusted U.S. motives, the Soviet Union refused to accept a militant line against the United States, and instead chose progressive disengagement.

THE FALL OF NAM THA

The final stages in the Nam Tha operation, up to the fall of the stronghold, went strictly according to the Neo Lao Haksat-Hanoi scenario. In the early hours of May 3 the Neo Lao Haksat captured Muong Sing, Nam Tha's supply base. Forty-six enemy soldiers were taken prisoner; one Dakota was seized when, unaware that the position had changed hands, it landed on the airstrip; one U.S. military adviser was killed; and large stocks were seized. The operation was so swift that it enabled the Neo Lao Haksat to claim that Muong Sing had been occupied through an uprising of its garrison. On May 5 Neo Lao Haksat forces occupied Muong Lang, twenty-five miles southwest of Muong Sing, and at 10:00 A.M. the next day, after a night of shelling, they entered Nam Tha. They took nearly eight hundred prisoners, and eight battalions of elite enemy troops were either completely routed or dispersed. Following the fleeing Vientiane troops, Neo Lao Haksat units on May 7 reached Vien Phou Kha, twenty-five miles southwest of Nam Tha, and came up to Ta Fa, twenty-five miles northeast of Ban Houei Sai. They could have entered Ban Houei Sai, which had been evacuated by the Vientiane forces, but the political decision was not to proceed to the Thai border, and not to give any pretense for Thai or U.S. intervention.

Three weeks later, on May 29, Nhouy Abhay confirmed to me that Vientiane had purposely claimed that Neo Lao

Haksat forces had occupied Ban Houei Sai in order to trigger U.S. military retaliation. After the landing of U.S. troops in Thailand, Nhouy Abhay added, the U.S. ambassador in Vientiane had charged Nosavan with lying, stressing that U.S. troops had arrived only to defend Thailand and had no intention of intervening in Laos.

Shortly after the fall of Nam Tha, the British and U.S. ambassadors to Moscow called on Gromyko, accusing the Neo Lao Haksat of a breach of the cease-fire and demanding the activation of the International Commission to achieve a return to the status quo ante. Gromyko replied that the incident was an internal Laotian affair and that the Soviet Union would not support steps which would favor the Nosavan group, which was in fact responsible for the developments. The Soviet Union adhered to the Khrushchev–Kennedy declaration, which aimed to form a coalition government in Laos; but the United States and Great Britain did not meet their obligations. Experience had shown, Gromyko said, that words from the United States and Great Britain on their desire to settle the Laotian problem peacefully had not been matched by Nosavan's deeds. And Nosavan was acting in strict coordination with the United States.

Nam Tha initiated a prolonged discussion in the International Commission on steps to be taken and on a new message to the Co-chairmen. Delegation positions differed according to their government's inclinations. The Canadian commissioner pressed for inspections, and showed interest mainly in military problems. Opposing this, I requested a largely political appreciation, indicating that the Commission lacked power to deal with cease-fire problems. The Indian delegation favored the Canadian stand. After some clarification of facts, the delegations reached the joint conclusion that the central issues of the cease-fire depended on a political understanding, and we unanimously drafted the June 2, 1962, message to the Co-chairmen.

The message reported the facts relating to the cease-fire, recalling that Vientiane had again rejected the Khang Khay proposal for a written cease-fire along a continuous line of separation not to be violated either on land or in the air. Concerning Nam Tha, the message extensively cited statements made before the Commission, by Souvanna Phouma and Souphanouvong, stressing that they acted on provocation. "Prince Souvanna Phouma," the report states, "briefly showed the Commission photostated copies of alleged orders by a Vientiane general to his troops in Nam Tha for an attack on positions taken up by the Khang Khay forces in the vicinity of Nam Tha, to take place early on May 6. Prince Souvanna Phouma said that this was a proof of the real sequence of events at Nam Tha."

The message noted that "fairly successful" attempts to bring about a resumption of negotiations had entered a new phase after Souvanna Phouma's return to Laos on May 25, 1962, and concluded by saying, "The Commission continues to hold the opinion that unless a political settlement is reached, the cease-fire cannot be maintained indefinitely."[14]

The Nam Tha episode played a major role in the escalation of the Indochinese struggle. The West no doubt was worried by the course of events: at Nam Tha it had suffered another humiliating defeat modeled on Dien Bien Phu. The circumstances of great power–client relations must have contributed to a feeling of shame. Once again Indochinese revolutionaries had shown the superiority of their people's war strategy. But neither Peking nor Hanoi was happy: the landing of U.S. troops in Thailand was a grim augury for the future. As on many later occasions during the escalation process, events exceeded any planner's calculations, even the most sober political-military assessments.

The only real winners were those who had bet on the collision course. Nam Tha was a result of the Rusk–Thanat statement; it consummated Thailand's enlistment into the

Indochinese struggle. It might have appeared as if the battle had a positive effect, paving the way to the formation of the coalition government in Laos; but more important than the short-lived coalition that was formed six weeks later, the new alignment of forces hardened into new commitments and long-term planning which aggravated the conflict still further.

Chapter 13

The Geneva Pattern

Contrary to Nosavan-Thai-CIA expectations, the United States did not extend troop movements into Laos after the Nam Tha crisis. However, the Nam Tha debate at the White House led to far more serious decisions.

Hilsman states that the "military" argument, supported by McNamara, stipulated as a first step "a large-scale movement of troops to occupy the whole of the panhandle of Laos, right on over to North Vietnam," to be followed by an all-out attack on North Vietnam itself—land, sea and air. In case of Chinese response, "the general impression was that the recommendation would be to retaliate on the mainland with nuclear weapons." Against this line, the "political" argument was "that for the United States the strategic objective was to *deny* the Mekong lowlands and the north-south road to the Communists," and that the "least costly" way to achieve this was through the neutralization of Laos.[1]

Neutralization thus was conceived not as a way to peace but as the cheapest way to deprive the Neo Lao Haksat of its possessions and to effect the "seal-off" strategy in South Vietnam. The "political" solution amounted to advocacy of a limited strategy. The military establishment, Hilsman claims, strongly resisted such strategy: "What the advocates of the 'military' approach really objected to was any course of action that might lead them to a limited war or a defensive position—no matter how good it was."²

From the beginning this debate transcended the Laotian problem: "The real issue is whether there is to be an accommodation, however painfully and slowly arrived at, between the Communist and especially the Chinese world and the non-Communist world or a final showdown in which only one emerges dominant." The generally shared assessment seems to have been "that the Korean War, Dienbienphu, the two Laos crises, and Vietnam are only the opening guns of what might well be a century-long struggle for Asia."* Consequently, "the choice of an over-all strategy [was] fundamental." The "military" and "political" wings in the White House Nam Tha debate merely offered alternative "over-all strategies" for the expected "century-long struggle for Asia."³

Thus, by-passing the Laotian problem, the White House Nam Tha discussions ended in long-range global strategy. "The result of this was that the logistical planning papers slid by the intermediate phase of occupying the Mekong lowlands and defending at the line of the hills, and concentrated on bombing North Vietnam and the other phases near the top of the ladder of escalation favored by the military approach."⁴ The phases of limited engagement advocated by the political approach were

*This basic outlook was common to the whole establishment, Democratic and Republican. Years later, looking beyond Vietnam ("Asia After Viet Nam," *Foreign Affairs,* October 1967), Richard Nixon wrote that the "common danger" for "non-communist Asian governments" and the West had "its source in Peking," and added: "During the final third of the twentieth century, Asia, not Europe or Latin America, will pose the greatest danger of a confrontation which could escalate into World War III . . . The United States is a Pacific power. Europe has been withdrawing from the remnants of empire, but the United States, with its coast reaching in an arch from Mexico to Bering Straits, is one anchor of a vast Pacific community. Both our interests and our ideals propel us westward across the Pacific . . ."

skipped—or built in as intermediate tactics to cover preparations for higher phases of escalation.

Consequently, in a parallel to the circumstances of the 1954 Geneva negotiations, the July 1962 Geneva agreements on Laos were foredoomed: long-range military designs elaborated secretly in Washington before the agreements were signed prescribed failure. The framework for subsequent developments was set not by the Geneva talks but by Taylor's Presidential review and by the White House Nam Tha decisions. More than ever, Washington approached the Indochina conflict—Laos included—in terms of a fateful contest for Asia; a military solution became the beacon of its strategy. Overconfident of U.S. material and military superiority, the military in Washington seemed not even to have bothered to analyze the adversary's possible reponses or war potentialities.

Return to Negotiations

While Washington was planning for "phases near the top of the ladder of escalation," the stage in Laos was set for renewed negotiations. U.S. diplomacy artfully assimilated the Chinese tactics of military and political engagement, aiming to complement long-range military schemes with intermediate political ploys. Washington needed time. In May 1954, J. F. Dulles said he required two years to complete preparations for Inchon-type landings in North Vietnam; in May 1962 approximately the same timing seemed to be in the minds of the military in Washington. Laotian negotiations and the near-fiction of a coalition government were meant to occupy time until McNamara was ready with what he termed "a variety of programs" for the military contest.

Compared to 1954, however, there was one marked difference. By 1962 the other side at the negotiating table had much less trust in the honesty of the negotiators, and less confidence that the letter or spirit of any agreement would be followed. Besides, the test of U.S. intentions lay in South Vietnam: until proof arrived that a Laotian settlement would be followed by a Vietnamese solution in the spirit of the 1954 Geneva agreements, neither the Neo Lao Haksat nor Hanoi or Peking were ready to take U.S. protestations about peace at face value. Contingency planning was not monopolized by the United States alone.

Taking into consideration the distrust among the parties following Nam Tha, it was astonishing that agreement to form a coalition government was reached so quickly. This in itself indicated that appearances were far from reality. On the other hand, Nam Tha did produce internal political conditions which eased the way toward coalition. To a certain extent, the rapid course of events surprised the parties and cornered them into the long-debated government of national union.

This was true not only of the Rightists but also of the Neo Lao Haksat. Two days before the fall of Nam Tha, Nouhak elatedly told me that Laos presented a unique revolutionary experience. Though not a real member of the Khang Khay government, the Neo Lao Haksat was in fact its leading force. The Laotian revolution had evolved from military struggle to negotiations, only to return again to a military contest and reach the next stage of negotiations. He approached new negotiations anticipating a lengthy process, with a coalition government still out of sight.

For a short while in the Nam Tha period, Neo Lao Haksat headquarters nurtured hopes that Nosavan's defeat might trigger a political upheaval in Vientiane resulting in a coup similar to Kong Le's. Tension in Vientiane had long been noticeable. Early in April, the Neo Lao Haksat was contacted by two clandestine groups, one military and one civil, which later joined forces in planning to overthrow the Nosavan regime. Politically, the plotters aimed to eradicate graft and corruption, and were demanding strict neutrality in international affairs. Even Souvanna Phouma was suspect in their eyes. They requested aid from the Neo Lao Haksat, but were mainly interested in support and coordinated action at the moment of the strike. Following Nam Tha, planning advanced so far that the Neo Lao Haksat alerted the Soviet embassy in case air supplies to Vientiane should be needed, and secretly dispatched their military commander in chief, General Khamtay, to Vientiane to take up direct contact with the revolutionary group.

However, a parallel military conspiracy, connected with Phoui Sananikone and enjoying U.S. backing, also developed. According to information reaching Khang Khay, the other group was headed by General Sounthone Pathammavong, General Bountieng Venevongsos, and the King's adjutant, Colonel Ratana Kindavong. The Neo Lao Haksat began to worry that issues might become confused, creating a new pretext for U.S. intervention. But then the Vientiane government, apparently as a result of State Department noises on the need to punish Nosavan for his Nam Tha performance, increased security precautions, including surveillance of leading Lao personalities. This upset all coup preparations. Souvanna Phouma's return to Laos and the renewal of negotiations put an end to the plotters' activities.

The Rightists' military defeat weakened Vientiane's resistance to coalition, while at the same time U.S. landings in Thailand, countering the effects of the Neo Lao Haksat victory, made Neo Lao Haksat and Hanoi more receptive to a provisional political accord. Such an accord was preferable to a larger U.S. intervention. This strengthened the position of Souvanna Phouma, the actor most interested in a quick understanding. A new equilibrium evolved, favoring formal union.

Western Diplomacy

Initiative for resumption of talks came mainly from the West. Though the idea of a coalition government had originated with the Neo Lao Haksat and its allies, this time U.S. diplomacy took the lead. With long-range planning set, and aided by Nosavan's enfeeblement, Washington persuaded Vientiane to accept an interim political solution. The veto device assured Nosavan that he would remain in control of his fiefs and gain time to achieve by polarization results he was unable to achieve by force. Nosavan finally accepted Harriman's strategy: "If Souvanna's government of national union breaks up," Harriman frequently said, "we must be sure the break comes between the Communists and the Neutralists, rather than having the two of them teamed up as they were before."[5] Harriman had every reason to believe that in a new crisis Souvanna Phouma would side with conservative forces rather than the Left, and there was sufficient evidence to make Nosavan act on this line. In any case the troika arrangement, including the indefinite postponement of administration and army unification, gave ample assurance against any unforeseen loss.

The political offensive to form the coalition began even before the fall of Nam Tha. On May 3, the day Neo Lao Haksat forces entered Muong Sing, Khang Khay's Acting Prime Minister, Khamsouk Keola, received a message from Souvanna Phouma saying that U.S. Ambassador in Paris James M. Gavin had informed him of Nosavan's readiness to renew negotiations, assigning the ministries of Defense and Interior to Souvanna Phouma. Concrete conditions were not mentioned, but it was understood that they had to do with the veto arrangement previously sought by Sullivan. The Prince had replied that negotiations could be renewed only on the basis of the Zurich, Hin Heup and Geneva three princes' agreements, and that Vientiane should contact Khang Khay. Commenting on Souvanna's message, Khamsouk Keola told me that if Khang Khay were approached with similar statements by U.S. or British diplomats, it would respond that mediation was not needed and that Khang Khay would wait for direct proposals from Vientiane. However, vague promises would not be accepted any more; Vientiane would have to agree unequivocally to a coalition as outlined by Khang Khay in previous negotiations. Nouhak commented that U.S. diplomacy apparently was trying to induce Souvanna to return to Laos quickly in order to halt the victorious Neo Lao Haksat military operations. The Neo Lao Haksat was ready to renew negotiations, but thought it might be better to postpone their reopening until after a clear military defeat of the foe. This view was generally approved. General Phoun remarked, "When we return to the negotiating table, let it be, again, as victors."

The West, however, left no time for respite. U.S. pressures coordinated with British diplomacy. The British ambassador in Vientiane, John M. Addis (one of the first Western envoys to contact Khang Khay), showed eagerness to establish good relations with Souvanna Phouma and early in April suggested to Khang Khay that he act as liaison with Vientiane. He also proposed to establish a British consulate general in Khang Khay. The offer was not accepted; Khamsouk Keola replied that he did not expect renewed negotiations in Souvanna Phouma's absence, especially as Vientiane was still obstinately holding to old positions. Concerning a consulate general, Keola said, there could only be a transfer of diplomatic recognition from Vientiane to Khang Khay, and in that case Great Britain would have to establish in Khang Khay not a consulate general but an embassy. Installing diplomatic posts on both sides would only sanction the partition of the country.

In early May London dispatched to Laos its chief Geneva negotiator, British High Commissioner for Southeast Asia Malcolm MacDonald. Following discussions in Vientiane, MacDonald visited Khang Khay and had a long talk with Keola and Nouhak. His visit came three days after the fall of Nam Tha, and his first concern was to stop the fighting, reestablish the status quo ante, and send out a Commission team for investigation. The political situation seemed to favor the renewal of negotiations, he said, but military operations obviously frustrated any efforts in this direction. MacDonald then repeated Gavin's assertion that Nosavan seemed ready to return to the negotiating table, no longer insisting on the Defense and Interior portfolios. Moreover, MacDonald added, the United States had promised to increase pressure on Bangkok and Vientiane to ease the way for a peaceful solution.

Nouhak replied with a sort of political-historical exposé which certainly could not have pleased MacDonald: The Neo Lao Haksat was always ready for negotiations, but Vientiane created obstacles. Nouhak wondered why the British were now attempting to extricate Nosavan from the predicament created by his own provocations. There was no return to the status quo ante, he stressed. Vientiane must be branded for its aggression; and should it not stop military operations, it would meet with a proper rebuff. But if Nosavan showed good will, talks could be renewed. Nouhak's arguments were endorsed by Keola, who charged Vientiane with the responsibility for recent fighting.

Souvanna Takes Over

In the meantime, Souvanna Phouma showed increasing determination to act independently and reopen negotiations quickly. On May 9, Keola received a new message from the Prince expressing dissatisfaction with the capture of Nam

Tha and requesting its evacuation while retaining Muong Sing only. Keola replied by giving details of the battle and stressing that the fifty-six Vientiane companies smashed in Nam Tha posed a serious threat to Phong Saly and the neighboring areas. The Prince still did not seem convinced, and decided to return home.

Khang Khay insisted that Souvanna should stay in Paris until Vientiane publicly renounced its hostility toward the idea of a coalition and accepted Khang Khay's principal demands on the new government's composition. Even though he was contradicting his own previous request that Vientiane should first approach Khang Khay directly, Souvanna did not change his decision. He flew to London, where he met Foreign Secretary Lord Home on May 19, and then he took a plane straight through Rangoon to Khang Khay.

On May 21, I had talked with the British ambassador and we had tried to assess the prospects for negotiations. Both Great Britain and the United States, Addis said, were now eager to initiate talks without delay. They therefore did not think it wise to demand the restitution of Nam Tha to Vientiane, though reestablishment of the status quo ante remained an open question and should somehow be dealt with by the International Commission. Nothing, however, should disturb efforts to reopen talks. There was reason for optimism: Nosavan, following Sarit's advice, was trying to regain U.S. confidence. This did not mean that Nosavan had changed deeply: this was a change of tactics rather than a change of mind.

Five days later, with the two other commissioners and the British ambassador, I went to Khang Khay to meet Souvanna Phouma upon his return from Paris, and to exchange views with Khang Khay authorities on further developments. Souvanna was in an excellent mood, full of vigor and self-confidence. To force the issue, he decided to use Mendès-France's 1954 tactics of setting a deadline for the conclusion of negotiations. He did not intend, he told us, to enter into prolonged bargaining. Should the coalition government not be formed by June 15, he would return to Paris and withdraw from politics. He did not cherish great hopes: he still had no confidence in Vientiane's sincerity, and the stationing of U.S. troops in Thailand only reduced prospects for an agreement. There was a one-in-ten chance of success. Souvanna spoke with a marked resolution, and was supported in this stance by Souphanouvong. He also was firm on the question of Nam Tha. Reminded by Addis that Nam Tha constituted a violation of the cease-fire, he responded by presenting photocopies of military orders captured at Nam Tha proving that events had clearly been provoked by Vientiane generals.

The Prince's firmness, when applied to Vientiane, pleased the Neo Lao Haksat; but at the same time Souvanna showed resoluteness toward the Neo Lao Haksat. In private conversation, the Prince told me that he intended to give Vientiane larger concessions than those foreseen by the Neo Lao Haksat. Referring to rumors of U.S. pressures to limit Nosavan's power, the Prince said that Lord Home also had touched on these issues, inquiring about the possibility of forming a coalition without Nosavan. But Souvanna thought it unwise to speculate on such perspectives: if the government were to last, he said, Nosavan had to be included. Souvanna seemed to have a clear vision of negotiation tactics and future government strategies.

A few days later Souphanouvong and Phoumi Vongvichit mentioned that talks with Souvanna on a common line for the approaching negotiations were encountering substantial difficulties. Souvanna tried to retain a free hand and was refusing fixed commitments before the tripartite meetings. He seemed to have particular reservations about the awarding of veto rights to all parties in key ministries, and about unrestricted retention of control by the parties in areas currently administered by them. It is possible that these reservations were only tactical, meant to exert pressure on the Neo Lao Haksat; in any case, the Prince finally bowed to the parties' demands in these matters.

Vientiane's Act of Canossa

Early in May Morski left Laos, and Warsaw asked me to take over the Polish delegation to the International Commission. On May 12, exactly one month before the agreement to form the government of national union, I moved from Xieng Khouang to Vientiane. This was a leap from the primitive into relative comfort. The Polish delegation (about thirty officers and a civilian staff) occupied three new villas on the Mekong. One of these was reserved for the commissioner, his office, and political and military advisers. But even air conditioning in my office and bedroom could not compensate for the loss of Xieng Khouang's fresh mountain breezes.

The move meant a change in working routine. Vientiane demanded more social contacts, more functions in the diversified diplomatic community, and almost daily discussions inside the Commission; but at the same time a strenuous effort had to be made to maintain communication with Khang Khay.*

On May 15, as one of my first functions in Vientiane, I visited the Ministry of Foreign Affairs, where I had an hour-

---

*This became somewhat easier when some Neo Lao Haksat leaders came to Vientiane after the formation of the government of national union. But immediately after the formation of the government, our delegation assumed special duties connected with its links to the socialist world. As the first of the socialist countries to be permanently represented in Vientiane, we had to extend whatever technical help might be needed while other missions were being installed. We had space, staff, a fleet of cars, and wireless communication with the outside world. Our delegation became a meeting place for socialist representatives, and political developments worked out so that we continued in this role for a long time: we offered a relatively neutral ground for the increasingly divided socialist community.

long talk with Sisouk Na Champassak, Acting Foreign Minister of the Boun Oum government. Sisouk, descendant of an influential family in Pakse, was a leading member of the extreme right-wing Committee for the Defense of the National Interest. He was an ambitious statesman of the younger generation, militantly nationalistic and pro-American. I was astonished to find him in a conciliatory mood. Concerning renewed negotiations, he spoke with a certain resignation, mostly concerned with saving face after the Nam Tha defeat and the obvious need to reverse his position. He was bitter about Western pressures, but he assured me that Vientiane was ready to revise its position, and was searching for compromise formulas concerning the composition of the future government. Sisouk seemed more concerned with the setting than the substance of negotiations. To be obliged to meet Souvanna Phouma and Souphanouvong at the Plain of Jars, he said, would amount to an act of Canossa by Vientiane. He pleaded for understanding and time.

Two days later I had a long conversation with Nhouy Abhay, the well-informed Minister of Education, who pretended to represent a "third force" among conservatives. A day before, Nhouy told me, the U.S. ambassador had come to his home to enlist his help in persuading Nosavan to be more flexible; the French ambassador had just attempted to win Nhouy over to an effort to bring Souvanna Phouma back to Laos quickly. The Western diplomats' feverish doings annoyed Nhouy slightly—after all, the West was responsible for the whole mess. Nhouy felt that the formation of a coalition government was now inevitable; this view was largely accepted by a majority of the Boun Oum government. Nosavan had made a last effort to mobilize outside support by going with Boun Oum on a tour of Thailand, South Vietnam, South Korea, Japan, Taiwan, Malaya and the Philippines; but these visits brought no great results. After Nam Tha, the tour had continued only through inertia, because it had been planned beforehand.* Some significance, Nhouy thought, could perhaps be ascribed to the meeting in Rangoon with General Ne Win, who had counseled Nosavan to neutralize Laos. Speaking about a coalition government, Nhouy was naturally concerned to balance its composition with a proper representation of Vientiane "third force" candidates—including, of course, his own family.

General interest concentrated now on the next formal contact with Souvanna Phouma—his visit to the King. Souvanna used the Commission's visit to Khang Khay on May 26 to transmit a message to Vientiane asking, as a preliminary to renewed negotiations, for a royal audience. Yet Vientiane showed no eagerness to act quickly. On May 29, I asked Sisouk Na Champassak about the delay. He assured me that Vientiane sincerely desired an understanding—the delay was caused by unrelated coincidences. First, Vientiane had to wait for the return of Boun Oum and Nosavan from their trip; and second, for astrological-religious reasons, the King wanted to avoid certain inauspicious days, particularly Saturdays and Sundays. Therefore the royal audience had been postponed until June 4. This was a curious explanation. But Sisouk had given a similar response to the U.S. ambassador, who had intervened on this matter just before I did. Mentioning this, Sisouk hinted that the State Department was not only pressing for renewal of negotiations but also wanted to debase Nosavan's position.† He was visibly angry

*In one of the confidential messages from the United States received in those days by the Vientiane Foreign Office, the Laotian embassy in Washington reported that the U.S. government, in Harriman's words, "was shocked that General Phoumi, after the complete defeat of his forces and after declaration of a state of emergency, left the country on a mission to Taipeh. This clearly shows General Phoumi does not take his responsibilities seriously."
†A confidential message from the Laotian Embassy in Washington cited Harriman as saying that "the Nam Tha events have completely destroyed the U.S. government's confidence in the personality of General Phoumi. The United States cannot extend to him its aid, neither militarily nor

about this. Without Nosavan, he stressed, any understanding would be meaningless, for he was the leading representative of Laotian "nationalist conservative" opinion.

I related Sisouk's explanation of the delay in Souvanna's audience with the King to Nhouy Abhay and Ngon Sananikone, whom I met a few hours later. Both were amazed and suspected new tactics. But they confirmed U.S. pressure to downgrade Nosavan's position, and they agreed with Sisouk, and with Souvanna Phouma, that without Nosavan any coalition would be a mere fiction. Nosavan's grip on the Vientiane elite apparently transcended bare police force.

The Quinim Pholsena Issue

With all the parties resigned to renewed negotiations, discussion turned toward the composition of the coalition. The Neo Lao Haksat renewed the autumn 1961 and January 1962 Geneva formula of an eighteen-member cabinet in which the Rightists and the Neo Lao Haksat would hold four portfolios each, with the remaining ten allotted to the neutral center, in the proportion of seven to Khang Khay and three to Vientiane representatives (4:7+3:4). As Nouhak told me on the eve of Souvanna's return from Paris, the Neo Lao Haksat had added three other conditions: (1) that apart from Defense and Interior, the portfolio of Foreign Affairs should also go to Khang Khay Neutralists, the candidate for this post being Quinim Pholsena; (2) that the choice of neutral center candidates should be left to Souvanna, who was expected to consult the Neo Lao Haksat; and (3) that the

financially, or otherwise. The United States cannot support a government in which General Phoumi is the most important personality. General Phoumi ought better to attend to his army, rendering in this way better service to his country than as a political leader." Referring to a possible reshuffling of the Vientiane government, Harriman added: "Such a reshuffling should not give General Phoumi the post of Prime Minister or a portfolio commanding a backing of force."

interim period before the unification of administration and
army and the holding of elections should not exceed fifteen
months. Souvanna Phouma told me that his only reservation
about this formula concerned the composition of the neutral
center: he was ready to add a fourth representative from
Vientiane. The proportion in the center would then be 7:4,
making the total number of representatives nineteen.

U.S. conditions for the coalition were related to me on
June 4 by Winthrop G. Brown, the U.S. ambassador in Vientiane. The first concerned the neutral center: Washington
demanded a proportion of 6:4, which went even further than
Souvanna in favoring Vientiane, and requested a reduction
of Souvanna's own Khang Khay representation. Secondly,
the United States requested that the portfolios of Defense
and Interior be allotted personally to Souvanna Phouma,
with a built-in veto right for all parties in these ministries.
Thirdly, Washington insisted on a preservation of administrative powers according to the existing status quo—an
elaboration of Sullivan's troika. Unable to force an "integration" of the Neo Lao Haksat in 1957 style (subordinating it
to a U.S.-dominated government), Washington was in fact
proposing a veiled partition along the cease-fire lines under
the formal umbrella of a coalition. It now feared that integration might undermine the position of the Rightists, giving the
Left a further lead in the government.

Though Washington apparently did not fully understand
this, its last demand *exactly* matched Neo Lao Haksat
desires. Both parties considered the compromise a temporary
device open to challenge in the future; both wanted to reassure themselves. Matters were clearly moving closer to a
provisional agreement. Bargaining, I thought, would thus
concentrate on final proportions and personal issues in the
composition of the new government.

When I next met Brown, on June 8, after the first round
of the three princes' meeting, he insisted chiefly on two

points concerning personalities: the United States, he said, would not agree to assign the Foreign Ministry to Quinim Pholsena, and also urged that the coalition include a representative of the Sananikone family. Additionally, Brown stipulated that all Vientiane representatives joining the "neutral" center be allotted full ministerial posts, not the rank of secretaries of state—a position equivalent to a deputy minister. I saw some possibility of compromise in the Sananikone issue, but knowing Khang Khay's determination in the case of Pholsena, I hastened to tell Brown that objection to Quinim's candidature might create serious complications, and even lead to failure of the talks.

Since the Kong Le coup in 1960, Quinim Pholsena had become a key figure. Born in 1911 into a merchant family in Pakse, of a Chinese father and a Laotian mother, he had grown up in Souvanna Phouma's home as the Prince's adopted son, and had a long career behind him as civil servant, lawyer and politician. After completing the Collège Pavie in Vientiane, he had served as secretary at the French Residency, district officer of Pakse (1949), governor of Sam Neua (1952), National Assembly deputy from Attopeu (1955), attorney at the Vientiane Court of Appeal, Vice-President of the National Assembly (1956), and Minister of Information, Propaganda and Tourism in the government Souvanna Phouma formed after the Kong Le coup in 1960. Quinim Pholsena participated actively in the December 1960 defense of Vientiane and in the subsequent conquest of the Plain of Jars by the Neo Lao Haksat and Kong Le troops.

In private life, before 1960, Pholsena dealt in trade and commerce. He was a member of the Bank Lao-Vieng and of Air Lao, and owned a bookshop and two houses in Vientiane. In the mid-fifties he moved into political activity, and was one of the founders of the Peace and Neutrality Party (Santiphab), which allied with the Neo Lao Haksat in the May 1958 elections to the National Assembly. In 1959, he defended the arrested Neo Lao Haksat leaders, showing ever greater engagement as a leftist Neutralist. He was a dynamic figure, with deep inner convictions, national and militant. Antagonizing Pholsena was certainly a bad way to begin dealings with the government of national union; U.S. enmity to Pholsena was later to play a central role in destroying the coalition.* It was his assassination in April 1963 which marked a return to open conflict.

Final Negotiations

Negotiations really reopened on June 4, when Souvanna Phouma visited Luang Prabang. During the audience accorded to him that day by the King, Savang Vatthana reaffirmed the mission he had previously conferred on the Prince, that he should form a coalition government. He expressed the hope that Souvanna might succeed quickly, but he demanded that the government be set up in accordance with the constitution. This contradicted the Zurich agreement, which provided for the formation of the government of national union without reference to the National Assembly. Constitutional procedures would require a vote of confidence by the Assembly, which was fully controlled by Vientiane.

Souvanna nevertheless was optimistic, hoping that the National Congress (composed of the National Assembly and the Royal Council) would adopt a constitutional amendment meeting the requirements of the Zurich agreement before the conclusion of talks. Souvanna continued to show resolution,

*Shortly after the June 1962 agreement on the formation of a coalition government, Brown personally told Pholsena that the U.S. government would prefer to see Souvanna Phouma lead the unified Laotian delegation to Geneva, not him, even though he was Foreign Minister. Pholsena mentioned this incident to me on June 14. He was offended and bitter about U.S. interference, especially since Souvanna had taken Brown's advice. Diplomatically, this was a bad start.

again declaring that he would return to Paris if the government was not constituted before June 15. "This is the last chance," he said to a high Vientiane representative; "You may choose peace or war." Even more than such warnings, a widely announced family event made the Prince's threat convincing: the end of June was the date set for his daughter's wedding in Paris.

The Luang Prabang visit intensified informal talks and discussions. On the evening after the royal audience, the French ambassador gave a dinner in honor of Souvanna Phouma, inviting also Quinim Pholsena and the U.S. and British ambassadors. Brown, supported by Falaize, again suggested that the return of Nam Tha was vital for the success of the negotiations. Addis did not seem to share this view, and he later agreed with me that any such demand would cause the Neo Lao Haksat to insist on the withdrawal of U.S. troops from Thailand, at which point the talks might reach a new deadlock. In reality, the U.S. overture concerning Nam Tha was only an initial bargaining stance. Brown seemed much more concerned with the composition of the future government; he insisted on introducing Phoui Sananikone into the coalition. But Souvanna remembered his discussion with the Neo Lao Haksat concerning Phoui's candidacy for leadership of the Lao delegation to Geneva, and rejected Brown's suggestion. If necessary, he would prefer Phoui's brother Ngon Sananikone. But his main theme was that the outcome of talks would depend on the sincerity of the Vientiane authorities.

On June 7 the three princes, accompanied by their deputies—Nosavan, Vongvichit and Pholsena—met on the Plain of Jars for their first exchange of views. Nosavan, Vientiane's main speaker, repeated almost exactly the conditions confided to me three days earlier by the U.S. ambassador. He agreed to cede the portfolios of Defense and Interior personally to Souvanna Phouma, stipulating that in each of these ministries tripartite committees be set up to decide main issues by unanimity. After a short discussion, Nosavan also agreed to cede to the Neutralists the Ministry of Foreign Affairs. There was no opposition to the principles propounded by Vientiane, although Souphanouvong reserved final agreement on the composition of the cabinet.

The discussion then turned to the constitution of the neutral center. As was foreseen, each party asked for different proportions. Souphanouvong requested the assignment of seven portfolios to Khang Khay Neutralists and only three to Vientiane; Nosavan insisted on a ratio of 6:4; and Souvanna Phouma kept to a compromise solution of 7:4. Nosavan also presented a list of prospective Vientiane candidates for the center grouping including three Sananikones. No decision was made, however, and the meeting adjourned until the next day. The very sober atmosphere of discussions seemed to indicate that agreement was within reach.

On the following day progress was considerable. The parties quickly agreed on a 7:4 ratio in the center, and consented to a proposal from Nosavan to postpone any decision on the army, administration, and elections until an unspecified time *after* the formation of the government. This was a tacit agreement to preserve a partitioned administrative status quo and separate armed forces even after the constitution of the government of national union.

Bargaining started on the distribution of portfolios and the selection of candidates. Again, the center group was the subject of the main controversies. Nosavan agreed immediately that Souvanna Phouma, besides being Prime Minister, should keep the Ministry of Defense while allotting Interior to Pheng Phongsavan. But Nosavan opposed two other Khang Khay candidates: he did not agree to Quinim Pholsena for Foreign Affairs, and he categorically rejected Souvanna Phouma's proposal to make General Amkha Soukhavong Secretary of State in the Ministry of Defense, dealing with former combatants. General Amkha, the only Christian general in the Laotian army, though staunchly anticommunist, was known for his pro-French leanings and was at the moment imprisoned by the Vientiane authorities. On formal grounds, arguing that according to the Zurich agreement the prisoners' problem should be settled after the formation of the government, Nosavan refused to accept Amkha's candidacy. And instead of Pholsena he proposed a Vientiane "neutralist," Outhong Souvannavong, Vientiane's ambassador to Tokyo. Additionally, Nosavan demanded that Ngon Sananikone be included in the list of so-called Vientiane neutralists, and insisted that all candidates from the Vientiane neutralist list be allotted full ministerial posts. Here the discussion ended; the meeting was to reconvene on the Plain of Jars on June 11.

Assessing the results of the two meetings, I felt that prospects for the coalition were good, but that difficulties were by no means past. On the question of Amkha Soukhavong, Souvanna Phouma was ready to compromise, substituting for him General Heuan Mongkovilay, a leader of the Kong Le army and a candidate much more to the Neo Lao Haksat's liking. The two most important open issues, as far as the composition of the cabinet was concerned, were the candidacies of Quinim Pholsena and Ngon Sananikone.

Returning to Vientiane from the Plain of Jars I was invited for exchanges of views with the U.S. ambassador and Ngon Sananikone. Next morning, June 9, I met Brown, and later Ngon.

Brown still insisted that the United States could not agree to allot Foreign Affairs to Quinim Pholsena; he was ready instead to offer him the portfolio of Justice. U.S. public opinion, the ambassador said, rated Quinim a communist, and the U.S. government had to take this into account. The argument was not convincing. How many Americans knew anything at all of the existence of Quinim Pholsena? And

why then offer him the post of Justice? But at the moment
more important than arguing about U.S. public opinion was
the need not to endanger the negotiations. I told Brown that
Khang Khay would not yield on this issue, and that the fate
of the talks might be at stake. I insisted he rethink the
problem so as not to block a final agreement.

However, I felt that a compromise could be reached in the
case of Ngon, and that it was the Neo Lao Haksat's turn to
make concessions. When I arrived at Ngon's home, he assured me of his support for Souvanna Phouma. He spoke of
his impartiality and recalled his own role in the 1956–57
Vientiane negotiations. Ngon was the least aggressive of the
Sananikone family, and had taken a reasonable stand during
negotiations with Phoumi Vongvichit in those Vientiane
talks. He now resented the fact that he had been left out. He
said that he was ready to intervene with Nosavan on the
candidacy of Quinim Pholsena. I became more convinced
that it would be right to include Ngon in the cabinet, provided the other side would accede to Quinim. Later I transmitted my views to the Neo Lao Haksat and Hanoi.

On the morning of June 11, before departing from the
Vientiane military airport to the Plain of Jars, Brown came
over to me, saying that agreement on the outstanding issues
was possible. This meant that the United States accepted
Pholsena as Minister of Foreign Affairs, expecting the Neo
Lao Haksat to cede in the case of Ngon. I was encouraged,
and landing at the Plain of Jars I immediately contacted Neo
Lao Haksat representatives and Vietnamese observers, urging flexibility and compromise.

Early in the afternoon, final agreement on the formation
of a government of national union was announced. Shaking
hands, the three princes appeared on the narrow balcony of
the old military barracks and were greeted with jubilation by
a crowd of Laotians, journalists and International Commission personnel. Despite the circumstances, I believed that the

accord would last and that it marked a turn toward peace in Indochina.

It took another day to style the French and Lao texts of the agreement and prepare the necessary documents. These were signed solemnly at 2:30 P.M. on June 12, 1962, on a shaky table in a bare wooden room decorated only with the Laotian flag and the King's portrait on the Plain of Jars.

The Plain of Jars Agreement

The June 12 agreement was based on a nineteen-member cabinet—four representatives each for the Neo Lao Haksat and the Rightists, and eleven in the center divided 7:4 between Khang Khay and Vientiane (4:7 + 4:4). Vientiane thus received eight portfolios while the left-neutral Khang Khay coalition got eleven. This was the largest cabinet Laos had ever had. In an exercise of symmetry, the two leaders of the left and right factions received, in addition to their ministerial posts, the rank of Deputy Prime Minister: Souphanouvong headed the Ministry of Economy and Planning, Phoumi Nosavan the Ministry of Finance (administration of U.S. funds). Seven of the nineteen cabinet members were given the rank of secretary of state (vice-minister): two each from the left and right factions, two from the Khang Khay Neutralists and one from the Vientiane center group. The last of the seven was Keo Viphakone, who was given the portfolio of Social Security in the Ministry of the Interior. (This ministry was used later to channel U.S. supplies to the clandestine Meo army behind the backs of the government.)

At first glance the Neo Lao Haksat and its neutral allies had every reason to express satisfaction. Three key ministries —Defense, Interior and Foreign Affairs—had gone to the Khang Khay Neutralists, two of whom—Quinim Pholsena and Pheng Phongsavan—then cooperated closely with the Neo Lao Haksat. Out of the twelve ministerial portfolios, five had fallen to the Khang Khay Neutralists, two each to the Neo Lao Haksat and the Rightists, and three to the Vientiane center grouping, two of which (Justice and Religious Affairs) were proposed by Souvanna Phouma. The third "Vientiane neutralist" was Ngon Sananikone, who had received the portfolio of Public Works and Transport.

Pure arithmetic, however, was misleading. Playing heavily against the Left was the fact that the government had to move to Vientiane, thus submitting to the existing Rightist governmental bureaucracy and surveillance machinery. In the new environment and under forceful socioeconomic pressures, the U.S. polarization policy met with unexpected success. Contributing to this was the virtual paralysis of the government which the built-in veto arrangements and the postponement of effective unification of the country created. On the other hand, the veto clauses and the preservation of separate powers allowed the Neo Lao Haksat to maintain its holdings when the coalition was disrupted.

The key formulations in the June 12 agreement read: "The three princes agreed to entrust the important departments of National Defense, Interior and External Affairs to the personalities belonging to the party of Prince Souvanna Phouma. All decisions concerning these three departments have to be sanctioned by unanimous agreement of the three group leaders." Another clause went even further: "All the decisions of the provisional government of national union will be taken according to the principle of unanimity."

The agreement stated that "the princes agreed that the provisional government of national union will adhere strictly to all provisions stipulated by the joint communiqué of Zurich." Except for this reference to the general formulations of the Zurich accord there was no word in the Plain of Jars agreement about unification of army and administration, or general elections. The Zurich communiqué contained the following formulations on these issues: (1) it agreed "to preserve the unity, neutrality, independence and sovereignty of the armed forces of the three parties in a single National Army in accordance with a program agreed between the parties," and (2) it stipulated the "holding of general elections to the National Assembly for the formation of the definitive Government," and provided that "during the transitional period, the administrative organs set up during the hostilities will provisionally be left in existence."

The conscious omission of a more precise timetable and program attested to the mood of the parties: the agreement seemed to serve as a device to temporize. At best, it was a contingent experiment whose success depended on the adherence to the spirit of the main Zurich provisions, namely "to build a peaceful, neutral, independent, democratic, unified and prosperous Laos," by giving "full effect to democratic freedoms," following "the path of peace and neutrality" and "resolutely applying the five principles of peaceful coexistence." In Neo Lao Haksat semantics, this was a program tightly linked to the letter and spirit of the 1954 Geneva agreements providing for an end to foreign domination and interference and for the neutralization of Indochina. In 1962, the likelihood of such developments seemed very small.

Nonetheless, expectations were high after the signing of the agreement. This was the most difficult cabinet in Laotian history, said the Neutralist *Saykang* in an editorial on June 13; so many tasks lay ahead—the withdrawal of foreign troops, unification of the army and administration, demobilizing large numbers of soldiers and bringing them into productive life, and the holding of general elections "this time honest and not at the point of bayonets." The editorial went on: "There are so many things to do after peace is established: the roads are mined, bridges have been blown up, rice fields are deserted, graves have been shattered . . . The economy on both sides has been reduced to nothing, the value of money is very low, imports grow and exports are

nill. Unemployment, fatigue and hunger have to be overcome, love of the Lao fatherland reinstated, hate forgotten,
and neutrality, the object of this unnecessary war, has to be
taken out of pawn."

Despairing Ambassadors

Though signed and sealed, the agreement still encountered
resistance. The final clauses of the agreement provided for
the submission "of the formula of the provisional government of national union to His Majesty the King," in accordance with the Zurich accord, and further stipulated that the
first meeting of the coalition government be held no later
than ten days after the signing of the agreement. Playing on
these clauses, Nosavan made a last-minute attempt to foil
enforcement of the accord.

Again, the Vientiane authorities started to play with the
constitution. The Zurich communiqué stipulated that the
government "will be formed in accordance with a special
procedure by direct designation and nomination by his
Majesty the King, without reference to the National Assembly." In contradiction to this provision Nosavan presented
the Plain of Jars agreement to the Vientiane National Assembly. The Assembly approved the accord, but made no arrangements to pass the constitutional amendment necessary
to empower the King to designate the new government without further reference to the National Assembly. The Neo
Lao Haksat naturally stood firm in demanding that the
Royal Decree not mention the National Assembly and in this
way make the new government dependent on a select rightist
body. In the meantime the Vientiane authorities made further procedures formally conditional on the will of the King,
and, to close the vicious circle, the King kept repeating that
the government had to be formed according to the constitution.

As the ten-day deadline approached, the crisis deepened. Day after day Nosavan made contradictory declarations. On June 19 he loosely agreed to omit from the Royal Decree any reference to the National Assembly, but the following day he went back on this declaration. An atmosphere of gloom spread in Vientiane. Souvanna Phouma made it known that independent of further developments he would leave for Paris on June 22. Commission members felt deceived and angry. Hope for peaceful change seemed to be fading.

Some action had to be taken to save the Plain of Jars agreement. On June 20, in a last-ditch effort, I gave a lunch in honor of Souvanna Phouma, inviting my Indian and Canadian colleagues from the ICSC, commissioners Avtar Singh and Paul Bridle, together with the ambassadors of the United States, Great Britain and France, and the Soviet chargé d'affaires. Foreign Minister-designate Quinim Pholsena was also present. This working lunch lasted three hours.

In response to my brief toast expressing the hope that the Prince would finally succeed in his mission, and thanking him and all present for having accepted my invitation at such a short notice, Souvanna said that he was grateful for the opportunity to meet all the ambassadors in an ultimate attempt to rescue the agreement. He then gave a short résumé of the situation: From the beginning of the negotiations, he had felt insincerity on Vientiane's part. He was ready to do anything possible to reach understanding; but should the talks break down, it would not be his fault. He appealed to the ambassadors for one last try to bring Vientiane to reason. All present turned their eyes to Brown: he was the one who could bring pressure to bear on Vientiane leaders. Just before lunch Souvanna had asked Brown why the United States had so hurriedly (on June 14) announced the immediate resumption of financial aid to Nosavan. Brown replied that though the funds were unblocked, they still had not reached Vientiane.

During lunch the main speaker was Falaize, the French ambassador. He emphasized again and again that Vientiane's new demand to refer to the National Assembly was a clear sign of ill will. Pointing to the ten-day deadline, Falaize warned that unless the government was constituted before June 22, the whole understanding would lose legal validity. He then described an audience which the King had granted him the day before. The King had advanced two conditions: that the parties agree among themselves on all matters concerning the new government, and that the parties try as much as possible to keep to the letter of the constitution. The King had asked Falaize his opinion of Chinese intentions. Falaize had replied that although China's general thinking was based on communist expansion, there existed at the moment specific circumstances urging Peking toward a peaceful orientation in Southeast Asia: the general international situation was exerting a moderating influence on China's policy; Peking was encountering internal economic difficulties; and Soviet policy aiming for a peaceful settlement of conflicts in Indochina was having a restraining effect.

I had the impression that in recounting his discussion with the King, Falaize was arguing with Brown. Those who sabotaged the negotiations, Falaize had said to the King, were taking upon themselves a heavy responsibility, not only in relation to the Laotian people but in relation to peace in Indochina and in the world. In long reasonings unmistakably directed at Brown, Falaize said that he had become convinced that Phoumi Nosavan's maneuvers were not simply tactical moves but a cover for sinister intentions.

The lunch had become a kind of court hearing on U.S. policy in Laos. There was no enmity toward the United States, but the diplomats were anxious to make their apprehensions felt in Washington. Nor did anyone mean to attack Brown personally; it was known that during the last weeks he had worked hard to make the coalition a reality. But he certainly must have felt uneasy, and he was the first to leave. Before leaving he assured the Prince that he would do his best to induce Nosavan to abide by the agreement.

After Brown's departure the discussion turned directly to U.S. political behavior. The consensus was that behind U.S. vacillation in Laos was a backstage clash between military and political strategies for Indochina; the hope was that the die was not yet cast, that options were still open.

Eventually, Brown's intervention eased the situation. On June 21 Souvanna Phouma and Phoumi Vongvichit met with Nosavan, and agreement was reached. The government would finally be formed and the Zurich accord heeded. The following day the parties agreed on the wording of the Royal Decree, and on June 23 Souphanouvong arrived in Vientiane, the Boun Oum government resigned, and at 3:30 P.M. the King administered the oath of the government of national union.

In Laos the installation of the government was greeted with relief and jubilation. For a moment threatening circumstances, power plays, maneuvers, temporizing tactics and long-range strategies were forgotten in a strong desire to believe that the government would last and Laotian unity would pave the way for peace in Indochina.

Neo Lao Haksat Expectations

The first meeting of the government took place on June 24; discussion mainly concerned the composition of a unified delegation to the Geneva conference. Vientiane proposed that representatives of the three parties be led by Prince Boun Oum. After this proposal was defeated, Nosavan demanded that the three princes go, led by Souvanna Phouma. This proposal won the support of Souvanna himself. But after some discussion the Neo Lao Haksat view—that like the other delegations to Geneva the Laotian team should be led by the Foreign Minister—was accepted. As other members of the delegation the cabinet designated Phoumi Vongvichit, the Neo Lao Haksat Minister of Information, Propaganda and Tourism; Ngon Sananikone; and Nosavan's brother-in-law Bounthong Voravong, Secretary of State for Fine Arts, Sports and Youth in the Ministry of Education. It was understood that Souvanna Phouma would go to Geneva to attend the winding-up ceremony. As Souvanna was to depart for Paris the next day, the cabinet assigned Souphanouvong as interim Prime Minister, while Nosavan became interim Minister of Defense.

After the government meeting, together with Soviet chargé d'affaires Tchivilev, I gave a lunch for the Neo Lao Haksat members of the government. Before lunch Souphanouvong handed me a personal letter in reply to congratulations I had sent him the day after the Plain of Jars agreement. It said:

> In the name of all my comrades from the Central Committee and in my own name I would like to convey to you our most sincere thanks and gratitude for your precious personal contribution—and for the contribution of all our Polish comrades—to this great common victory of the Lao people, the Lao revolutionary and patriotic forces, and our invincible socialist camp. The formation of the Provisional Coalition Government substantiates "our dominant position" on the Laotian political scene . . . As you pertinently said, "We enter into a difficult period of political struggle . . . noble, difficult and complex," but also "into a new and decisive period" for the Lao Revolution. We agree with you that the progress and development of the Lao Revolution depends largely on organizing and mobilizing our cadres and the large masses of the people and on the consolidation and extension of the national united front with the Neutralist center . . .

Spirits and hopes were high.

Laos and South Vietnam

Yet the crucial questions of the Laos agreement dealt with its wider regional application. Both sides viewed Indochina as a strategic entity, so conflict and accord required regional consummation. In this respect nothing had changed since the First Indochina War, when times of struggle and negotiations for peace encompassed all of Indochina, from the borders of China in the north to the Mekong in the west and Ca Mau Peninsula in the deep south. The fate of Laos hinged on the extension of the understanding to South Vietnam, where the popular uprising throughout the country was reaching the stage of national revolution. At the solemn lunch offered by Souvanna Phouma following the Plain of Jars signing ceremony, the Prince said that now, after reaching an understanding in Laos, the Geneva conference should take up the question of South Vietnam.

In the days following the Plain of Jars agreement Souvanna availed himself of every possible opportunity to draw attention to the urgent need for a solution in South Vietnam. At a gala lunch in Luang Prabang on June 14, after he had reported to the King on the successful conclusion of the talks, Souvanna underlined the indispensability of taking up the question of South Vietnam. He made similar statements on several other occasions, and on June 16 he traveled to Hanoi for a private talk with Prime Minister Pham Van Dong.

No agenda was fixed for this conversation. Souvanna raised three problems: the withdrawal of Vietnamese military personnel from Laos, the question of trails through Laos linking North and South Vietnam, and the problem of finding a peaceful solution in South Vietnam. Concerning the withdrawal problem, Pham Van Dong stated that the Democratic Republic of Vietnam was interested in easing Souvanna Phouma's tasks and would comply with any demands by the Laotian government. Turning to the second point, Pham Van Dong said that it was only natural that the war unleashed by the United States in South Vietnam and southern Laos should flow across the Lao-Vietnamese border. He pointed out that the path through Laos served only for contacts and movement of cadres, not military units. The Democratic Republic of Vietnam did not wish to create unnecessary difficulties for Laos; it was the United States which was responsible for the development. The United States had to return to a settlement as foreseen in the 1954 Geneva agreements. Pham Van Dong made it clear that the Democratic Republic of Vietnam considered that it was its paramount national duty to help its struggling brothers in the South. This was a very frank exchange. For the first time, Hanoi admitted to Souvanna the existence of routes through Laos linking the divided parts of Vietnam.

Saying that peace in Laos demanded peace in the entire region, Souvanna Phouma described his plans for a neutral South Vietnam. He intended first of all to induce the West to cut its support for the Ngo Dinh Diem regime and to pay more attention to exiled South Vietnamese politicians in Paris. This was an alternative force which could assure the neutralization of South Vietnam. Souvanna Phouma inquired especially about Pham Van Dong's views on former emperor Bao Dai and South Vietnamese separatist leader Nguyen Van Tam. Pham Van Dong excluded the return of the first but did not object to Tam's activization. In general, Pham Van Dong welcomed the idea of creating a large neutral zone on the Indochinese Peninsula.

After his return to Laos on June 17, Souvanna invited Tchivilev and me to lunch, where he described his discussions in Hanoi. He was eager to assure us that his interest in the problem of South Vietnam was not inspired by Paris or any other Western capital. He said that he would like to use his trip to Geneva to awaken interest in negotiations on

South Vietnam. On his way to Europe he wanted to stop for two days in Phnom Penh to discuss matters with Sihanouk. Then he intended to speak to De Gaulle, and subsequently solicit support in London. After Geneva he planned to go to Washington, where he hoped to get a hearing in high U.S. political circles. The difficulty, he said, was overcoming resistance from the U.S. military.

The Prince spoke with visible confidence. He had always toyed with the idea of emerging as Laos's man of destiny; now he aspired to enlarge this role to include all of Indochina. Convinced that without a settlement in South Vietnam the Laotian resolution would fail, he hoped to become a mediator between East and West.

Hanoi's Hopes

Hanoi also hoped that the Laotian settlement would set off a peaceful chain reaction. Souvanna's keen interest in the problem was taken as a Western probe, and this encouraged Vietnamese leaders. Would an understanding in Laos induce Washington to talk about Vietnam? Could Souvanna's initiative be helpful in this respect? Though always inclined to judge events with the utmost realism, the Vietnamese seemed ready to yield to wishful thinking; and they dreamed of a quick peace. When I arrived in Hanoi at the beginning of July I could feel excitement over developments in Laos and the open options in South Vietnam. There was a contradiction in speaking about peace in Laos, and U.S. intensification of the war in South Vietnam. Which direction would the United States choose?

On July 4 Pham Van Dong gave a dinner for the Polish commissioner in Vietnam and me. Pham Van Dong told me that in his meeting with Souvanna Phouma he had tried to rouse the Prince's optimism and had prompted him to discuss the South Vietnamese problem in the international forum. The Democratic Republic of Vietnam was interested in convening a conference which would ratify the idea of a neutral zone in Indochina, including South Vietnam. The fact that Souvanna Phouma had linked a final solution of the Laotian problem with a peaceful settlement in South Vietnam, Pham Van Dong added, was evidence of Souvanna's intelligence and understanding. For such a relationship existed organically, intrinsic in the state of affairs.

This idea was later developed by Colonel Ha Van Lau, untiring Vietnamese negotiator at the 1954 and 1962 Geneva conferences and at the Paris talks, and long-time liaison officer on the International Commission. The interdependence between Laos and Vietnam is sustained both by the foe and by us, he stressed. This interaction had existed since the First Indochina War, prompting the French to establish a high command for the whole of Indochina, and similarly shaping U.S. strategy. Ha Van Lau made a sharp distinction between the U.S. war-oriented design, and the potential for peace nevertheless inherent in the Laotian settlement. Forced by political upheaval and military defeat in Laos to pass from offensive to defensive, he said, the United States was now trying to isolate Laos from socialist support, was pressing for Vietnamese withdrawal, and was aiming to cut aid from North to South Vietnam. To achieve these goals Washington was trying to win over Souvanna Phouma. The United States wanted to use the settlement in Laos to weaken revolutionary forces in Laos and suppress revolutionary forces in South Vietnam. However, the United States was wrong in hoping for military success. The victory in Laos by the revolutionary forces would raise spirits in South Vietnam and contribute to the advance of the South Vietnamese revolution.

Despite the war design, other prospects could be envisaged, Ha Van Lau continued. The real solution for Indochina could be found in the neutralization of South Vietnam following the neutralization of Laos. Although the Democratic Republic of Vietnam and Souvanna Phouma were thinking of different types of neutralization—Eastern and Western oriented—there existed at the moment a convergence of interests. South Vietnamese neutrality would in any case be defined by revolutionary forces in the South. In the National Liberation Front declaration published on March 3, 1962, after the conclusion of its first Congress, it called "for an active struggle to form a zone of peace and neutrality comprising Cambodia, Laos and South Vietnam."

Ha Van Lau detailed a new initiative contemplated by Hanoi in the wake of the Laotian settlement. Relying on Point 13 of the final declaration of the 1954 Geneva agreement, which called for consultations between the conference members "in order to study measures that may prove necessary to ensure that the agreements on the cessation of hostilities in Cambodia, Laos and Vietnam are respected," Hanoi considered proposing a reconvening of the conference—enlarged possibly by the three ICSC members—to take up the problem of South Vietnam. Cambodia wanted guarantees of its neutrality, and the international situation also seemed to favor such an initiative. France might support such a move, and Britain, though hesitant as long as there seemed to be prospects of military victory in the South, might finally agree to join such talks. But everything depended on Washington, where belief in a military solution still seemed dominant. Hanoi was waiting for a sign of change, and planned to make its proposal public at the Geneva conference only if it received some proof of such a change. Hanoi ardently desired a settlement, but was resolved to continue the struggle if necessary.

All this was no secret. It became gossip in Geneva, where most of the delegates hoped that South Vietnam would be taken up immediately after a final agreement on Laos. "All the negotiators at the conference fully realized that the implementation of the Laos agreement was intimately bound up with the South Vietnamese situation, that, indeed, a settlement of that situation was a necessary concomitant to the Laos settlement."[6] Souvanna Phouma mentioned the problem directly to President Kennedy at the end of July, and told Kennedy of his conversation with Pham Van Dong. "We are all neighbors," the Prince said, "but I fear that even if it is extinguished in my country, the fire will spring up elsewhere." Kennedy did not answer.[7]

Chapter 14

The Screen of Neutrality

There was marked contradiction in the U.S. policy of professing support for neutrality in Laos but rejecting the neutralization of South Vietnam. Washington's intense opposition to the neutralization of Indochina, persisting from the days of Dulles and the 1954 Geneva conference, caused the Neo Lao Haksat and Hanoi to doubt the sincerity of the U.S. commitment to Laos's neutrality: was this commitment only a temporary move in a long-range strategy of political and military contest?

Roger Hilsman was near the truth when he wrote: "The neutralization of Laos and the Geneva Agreement of 1962 were, in my view, a triumph of statecraft—precisely because Laos was such an unholy mess, such an impossible combination of rival factions, difficult terrain and inadequate power."[1] Neutralization was only a device to by-pass the "mess." The political and military defeat in Laos, strenuous efforts to cope with the situation in South Vietnam, and planning for a general reversal of the current trend in the Indochina struggle dictated the new U.S. Geneva diplomacy.

The formation of the government of national union permitted the conclusion of the Geneva negotiations. As the main texts of the accords—the Declaration of the Neutrality of Laos and the Protocol to the Declaration—had already been drawn up in December 1961, the conference was only

waiting for a united Laotian delegation to put the final touch
on the documents.

On June 26, the Co-chairmen of the Geneva Conference
sent a note to Minister of Foreign Affairs Pholsena asking the
Laotian government to send its delegation to Geneva to participate in the final stages of the conference, and the next day
the Laotian delegation left for Geneva.

The Geneva Conference

The 1961–62 Geneva conference was the most representative international political gathering since the Second World
War. Participating in it, as in the 1954 Geneva conference,
were the five great powers, including the United States and
the People's Republic of China. This time U.S. diplomacy
was much more active in open debate, establishing in fact a
dialogue with China. Unlike 1954, representatives of the
neutral Asian countries—India, Burma and Cambodia—
were among the fourteen participants. This meeting truly
mirrored the balance of power: East, West, the Third World.

With international relations in flux, the conference served
to some extent as a forum where, through the Laotian prism,
larger issues of peace and war and international understanding could be viewed. Laos could have been seen as a test case
for negotiations, reducing tensions, and leading the world
away from cold war and ideological contest toward a reasonable policy of peaceful coexistence. Considering the attitudes
of the Soviet Union and China, it was within the reach of
U.S. diplomacy to tip the balance toward a more permanent
settlement. The Soviet Union, ready to disengage, was bent
on a continued dialogue with the United States; the People's
Republic of China, suspicious of both U.S. and Soviet intentions, was interested in neutralizing the vunerable area south
of its borders; and the local adversaries, Hanoi and the Neo
Lao Haksat, were eager to reach a solution on the lines of

neutralization and self-determination. It was left to the United States to take advantage of this constellation. The opportunity was not grasped. Though the outcome of the conference was hailed as a great achievement of patient negotiation and compromise, in reality it turned out to be a failure. The accords were not wrong; but they were all violated. They never even entered fully into force. As in 1954, the accords produced a short cease-fire; but the political provisions were never implemented. Thus, instead of creating confidence in negotiations, the conference deepened the conviction—especially strong in Indochina—that the most solemn treaty commitments were disregarded by superpowers. As, together with the Soviet Union, the United States used partial disarmament agreements not to halt but rather to impel the strategic arms race, so it used the Geneva agreements to screen its drive to "the other phases near the top of the ladder of escalation."

True, the United States was not the only one responsible for this escalation. Implicit in "escalation" is a constant interaction of venture and response. In Indochina, however, the United States was the intruding force. Lacking a real grasp of local realities, and unable to take the field politically, it tried instead techno-chemical military gadgetry and hazardous escalation. While U.S. contingency planning was in essence aggressive, Vietnamese and Neo Lao Haksat planning was basically defensive.

The United States agreed to the neutralization of Laos as a minor evil in the specific circumstances of a military-political ebb in its Indochina strategy. Southeast Asian neutrality still being taboo in Washington, the Kennedy administration concurred with Laotian neutrality only as an exercise in political flexibility, as a temporizing device in an overall strategy aimed at regaining lost positions. Laotian neutrality became part of the administration's "new look," the essence of which was merely an indulgence in new semantics. In debates within the administration the aim was clear: to support renewed U.S. military efforts in South Vietnam and reverse the political-military balance in Laos itself. The very meaning of neutrality—to cease interference and political-military pressures, and to leave the local actors to shape their own destiny—was discarded entirely.

It was politically unwise, doubtful and deceptive strategy; and it grossly underrated the adversary and his proven local political and military superiority. This supremacy was clearly reflected in the discussion and final documents of the Geneva conference. Just as the Vietnamese had told me in June 1961, in all main issues debated at the conference the decisive voice was with the Indochinese Left, speaking more or less through the formally united Eastern delegations. The arguments and proposals of the United States and the West indicated their confusion, unreality and lack of comprehension of the Indochinese situation. A comparison of the initial draft proposals from East and West with the final wording of the Geneva agreements shows how predominant in political purpose and logic the Indochinese Left really was. Both in relation to the concept of neutrality, and the terms of reference for the International Commission—the two central issues at the conference—the Indochinese Left emerged victorious.

The Declaration on the Neutrality of Laos

The initial Soviet draft "Declaration on the Neutrality of Laos," submitted to the conference on May 17, 1961, and supported by the other socialist participants, stated that the governments participating at the conference:

> Solemnly declare that they recognize and will respect and observe the independence and neutrality of Laos, will abstain from interfering in the internal affairs of Laos, and will not

allow any act that might directly or indirectly impair the
sovereignty, independence, neutrality and territorial integrity
of that State. They undertake not to impose any political
conditions or any assistance that may be given to Laos. They
undertake not to allow the establishment in Laos of any foreign military strong point, not to resort to force or threat of
force, and not to do any other act that might result in the
violation of peace in that country.

All foreign troops and military personnel now present in
Laos shall be withdrawn within a specified period.

The countries participating in this conference agree that all
provisions of treaties and agreements relating to Laos and
conflicting with the independence and neutral status of Laos,
including the provisions of the Treaty on the Collective Defense of South-East Asia (SEATO) and the Protocol thereto,
cease hereby to have effect."[2]

This was part of a larger document recalling the 1954 Geneva agreement and its pledges to observe neutrality in the
Kingdom of Laos; expressing hope for a "peaceful democratic development of Laos"; and proposing—like Point 13
of the 1954 Geneva Final Declaration—to hold consultations in case of violation or threat of violation of the independence and neutrality of Laos, for the purpose of taking
measures to remove that threat.

Against this proposal, the French draft declaration, submitted to the conference on May 23, 1961, and supported by
the Western powers, was a very meager document. It contained three sentences. It proposed: (1) that the governments
participating in the conference "take note of the Declaration
by the Government of Laos," which was worded similarly to
the 1954 Geneva general statement of the Laotian government concerning the cease-fire and withdrawal of foreign
forces; and (2) that the said governments "subscribe to the
principles and conditions set forth in that Declaration, [and]
undertake to do nothing contrary thereto and in particular

to refrain from all direct or indirect interference in the internal affairs of Laos."[3]

Except for the Laotian government declaration that "it would voluntarily proclaim its neutrality," the Western draft did not mention neutrality at all, not even in the title of the proposed declaration—"Draft Declaration in Reply to the Declaration by the Government of Laos." The Western statement followed the example of the 1954 Geneva agreements, which avoided in all its documents the "immoral" (according to Dulles) notion of neutrality.

In the ensuing discussions the West was obliged to accede step by step, and finally to accept the general framework of the Declaration proposed by the socialist countries, together with its heading, especially as the neutral countries leaned toward this position.[4] Of decisive importance was the fact that the Laotians themselves, prompted by the Neo Lao Haksat and the Neutralists, defined neutrality in the Zurich communiqué in terms resembling the socialist draft, laying particular stress on sovereignty, nonalignment and exclusion of foreign interference.

Until July 18 the United States refused to incorporate into the Declaration on the Neutrality of Laos a direct rejection of SEATO, and on the insistence of Phoumi Nosavan, Souvanna Phouma omitted the repudiation of SEATO contained in the prepared draft from his programatic speech presenting the government of national union to the King on June 23, 1962. But both the Neo Lao Haksat and the left-wing Neutralists made rejection of SEATO a condition for drafting the Laotian government statement to be included in the Geneva Declaration. Nosavan had to give in, and then the West had to bow to the expressed will of the government of national union.

The main document of the Geneva Agreement, signed on July 23, was thus named "The Declaration on the Neutrality of Laos." Apart from a specific statement of the Royal Government of Laos patterned after the November 2, 1956, Vientiane agreement "on the Question of Peace and Neutrality" and the June 1961 Zurich communiqué, it stated that the governments participating at the conference:

1. Solemnly declare, in accordance with the will of the Government and people of the Kingdom of Laos, as expressed in the statement of neutrality by the Royal Government of Laos of July 9, 1962, that they recognize and will respect and observe in every way the sovereignty, independence, neutrality, unity and territorial integrity of the Kingdom of Laos.

2. Undertake, in particular, that

(a) they will not commit or participate in any way in any act which might directly or indirectly impair the sovereignty, independence, neutrality, unity and territorial integrity of the Kingdom of Laos;

(b) they will not resort to the use or threat of force or any other measures which might impair the peace of the Kingdom of Laos;

(c) they will refrain from all direct or indirect interference in the internal affairs of the Kingdom of Laos;

(d) they will not attach conditions of a political nature to any assistance which they may offer or which the Kingdom of Laos may seek;

(e) they will not bring the Kingdom of Laos in any way into any military alliance or any other agreement, whether military or otherwise, which is inconsistent with her neutrality, nor invite or encourage her to enter in any such alliance or to conclude any such agreement;

(f) they will respect the wish of the Kingdom of Laos not to recognize the protection of any alliance or military coalition, including SEATO;

(g) they will not introduce into the Kingdom of Laos foreign troops or military personnel in any form whatsoever, nor will they in any way facilitate or connive at the introduction of any foreign troops or military personnel;

(h) they will not establish nor will they in any way facilitate or connive at the establishment in the Kingdom of Laos of any foreign military base, foreign strong point or other foreign installation of any kind;

(i) they will not use the territory of the Kingdom of Laos for interference in the internal affairs of other countries;

(j) they will not use the territory of any country, including their own, for interference in the internal affairs of the Kingdom of Laos.

The Declaration also included the provision for consultations in the event of violation or threat of violation of the sovereignty, independence, neutrality, unity and territorial integrity of Laos, in order to consider measures which might prove necessary to ensure observance of these principles and the other provisions of the Declaration.* As is well known, in 1954 the United States rejected a similar clause included in the Final Declaration of that Geneva conference.

The Protocol to the Declaration

Principles propounded by the Indochinese Left were even more prevalent in the Protocol to the Declaration on the Neutrality of Laos, dealing with the withdrawal of foreign military personnel from Laos and the operations of the International Commission for Supervision and Control.

The Soviet draft of the Protocol of May 17, 1961 foresaw the withdrawal of foreign military units and foreign military personnel from Laos within thirty days and contained clauses on the prohibition of the introduction into Laos of foreign military personnel and armaments, similar to the 1954 Geneva agreements. But it proposed substantial changes concerning the terms of reference of the ICSC. It stated that the Commission "shall conduct its work strictly

*See Appendix 10.

within the limits of the Cease-Fire Agreement entered into
by the three political forces of Laos, and in close cooperation
with the Laotian authorities." Agreement of the government
of Laos was seen as essential for the functioning of the Commission. Further, "decisions of the International Commission on all questions shall be unanimous, except that decisions on purely procedural questions shall be adopted by a
majority vote."[5] This sounded different from the provisions
of 1954. At that time the sovereignty and superior authority
of the local government were not so pronounced. Also, most
Commission recommendations could then be accepted by a
majority vote, the only exception being "questions concerning violation, or threat of violations, which might lead to a
resumption of hostilities." In the last case decisions had to
be unanimous.

If the Soviet draft Protocol went a long way to restrict the
freedom of action of the ICSC, the French draft, presented
to the conference on June 6, 1961, went in the opposite
direction. It aimed to endow the Commission with vast powers so as to enable it to act independently of the Laotian
government, and even as a kind of dominant body—a state
within a state. The Commission was to establish "a sufficient
number of operation centers" for fixed and mobile teams free
to perform their functions even in the absence of one of the
Commission members. The draft went on to stipulate that
the Commission "shall as of right, have free and unrestricted
access by land, sea or air to all parts of Laos, and shall have
full freedom to inspect, at any time, all aerodromes, installations of establishments and all units, organizations and activities which are or might be of a military nature." Further,
"decisions relating to the operations of the Commission or
the inspection teams, and all procedural decisions, shall be
taken by majority vote."

The French draft even proposed the establishment of the
kind of supervising body used in occupied countries, to be

composed of heads of the diplomatic missions of signatories to the Geneva Accords. This body would meet at least twice a year and discuss the reports of the Commission and other problems, according "to the needs of the situation."[6] These were much wider powers than those agreed on in 1954, but even they did not satisfy the United States. On June 27, 1961, the United States submitted a supplement to the French proposal which made the primary status of the Commission over the Laotian Government even more explicit. One of the articles proposed the disclosure before the Commission of location, strength and armaments of the local parties. It demanded that within thirty days, in advance of the withdrawal of foreign units, the parties simultaneously inform the Commission of:

> (1) the location, organization, strength and equipment of their forces, regular and irregular;
> (2) the location, organization, strength, equipment and nationality of all foreign military and advisory personnel and foreign armed forces, regular and irregular, associated with their forces; and
> (3) the location and quantity by types of armaments, munitions or military equipment in their possession or under their control, whether with units or in dumps or held in reserve.[7]

This sounded rather like an unconditional surrender. It was exactly what the Neo Lao Haksat had anticipated and what the Vietnamese had told me three weeks earlier: the United States, having the advantages of superior logistics and shorter supply lines (from Thailand), aimed to use the Commission to immobilize Neo Lao Haksat forces and impose foreign control over an independent-minded government of Laos.

This was clearly unacceptable, and met with opposition from the majority of conference participants. On July 14,

1961, the Indian delegation presented a new draft attempting a more realistic approach. The two key articles in this draft provided that:

> The Government of Laos having themselves declared their neutrality, it follows that its preservation and the consequent exclusion of outside interference in their internal affairs is their concern, interest and obligation. The International Commission for Supervision and Control shall assist in the preservation of the neutrality of Laos, establishing such machinery as may be necessary in agreement with the Government of Laos and in accordance with this Agreement, [and]
> The International Commission for Supervision and Control shall decide major questions by agreement among its members.[8]

The final wording of the Protocol to the Declaration on the Neutrality of Laos unmistakably followed lines proposed by the Neo Lao Haksat, the Neutralists and Hanoi. Several times it explicitly underlined the primacy of the Laotian government and of the parties to the cease-fire agreement over the Commission. The Commission had to act "with the concurrence of the Royal Government of Laos" and exercise its functions

> in full cooperation with the Royal Government of Laos and within the framework of the Cease-Fire Agreement or cease-fire arrangements made by the three political forces in Laos, or the Royal Government of Laos. It is understood that the responsibility for the execution of the cease-fire shall rest with the three parties concerned and with the Royal Government of Laos after its formation.

The Commission would render assistance to the Government "at the request of the Royal Government of Laos and in full cooperation with it." All main decisions of the Commission relating to violations of articles concerning the withdrawal of foreign military personnel, the prohibition of introduction of armaments and the violation of the cease-fire, as well as "conclusions on major questions sent to the Co-Chairmen and all recommendations by the Commission shall be adopted unanimously." Only on procedural questions and questions relating to the initiation and carrying out of investigations could a majority vote be practiced.* This was a major change from the 1954 Geneva provisions, reflecting a new balance of power in Laos and in the international aspects of the Indochina problem.

Withdrawal of Foreign Troops

Stipulating withdrawal from Laos of "foreign regular and irregular troops, foreign paramilitary formations and foreign military personnel," the Protocol defined "foreign military personnel" as: "Members of foreign military missions, foreign military advisers, experts, instructors, consultants, technicians, observers and any other foreign military persons, including those serving any armed forces in Laos, and foreign civilians connected with supply, maintenance, storing and utilization of war materials."

By October 7, 1962, the deadline for completing the withdrawal of foreign forces, the United States had withdrawn under the control of the International Commission 666 of its military personnel and 403 Philippine technicians "engaged on a contract basis" by the U.S. Military Assistance Advisory Group (MAAG) in Laos. At the same time the Democratic Republic of Vietnam withdrew under commission control forty of its military personnel, a symbolic figure, assuring the Laotian government that "all the Vietnamese military personnel sent to Laos at the request of the Royal

*See Appendix 11.

Government have been withdrawn according to the clauses of the Geneva Agreements, 1962."[9]

The Commission did not receive any report concerning the withdrawal of Thai troops (estimated by the Neo Lao Haksat at 3,500 instructors, technicians, officers and soldiers in the ranks of the Nosavan army), or South Vietnamese or Kuomintang (another CIA beneficiary) military personnel.* There was speculation that no side had fully implemented the agreements, and the ICSC message to the Co-chairmen noted without comment that "Various radio broadcasts and newspaper reports are making strong charges about the continued presence of thousands of foreign forces of various nationalities in Laos."[10]

During the seventy-five-day withdrawal period the Neo Lao Haksat and Hanoi hesitated to completely withdraw DRV military personnel and cadres. They suspected the United States of retaining its military presence in Laos in disguise or by mercenary proxy, aiming at the same time to enfeeble the positions of the Neo Lao Haksat as much as possible. Also, the link with South Vietnam–the corridor of jungle paths leading from Na Phao at the Mu Gia Pass, along Highway 12, south to Muong Phine and Highway 9, and ending in South Vietnam near the 16th parallel—was a matter of concern. Souvanna Phouma spoke often about the issues involved, appealed repeatedly to the DRV, and asked Chinese and Soviet diplomatic representatives to intervene with Hanoi to implement the respective provisions of the Geneva accords.

It was not until the beginning of October that Hanoi made a final decision. Returning from Hanoi on October 5, 1962,

*The new U.S. ambassador in Laos, Leonard Unger, told Souvanna Phouma that the United States was unable to order withdrawal of Kuomintang troops active on the Lao-Thai-Burma-Chinese border, as Washington had no control over them. It was estimated that out of 3,500 Kuomintang troops active in this area, about 850 were stationed on Laotian soil.

the DRV chargé d'affaires, Thanh, brought a personal letter from Pham Van Dong to Prince Souvanna Phouma which included birthday wishes and assurances of full implementation of the clauses of the Geneva agreements. Thanh told me that Hanoi's decision had been made at a special session of the Political Bureau of the Vietnamese Workers' Party attended by department heads of all institutions having contacts with Laos. The decision was to withdraw all Vietnamese personnel, without exception, including those active on the North-South trails. In order to avoid any suspicion, technicians working as advisers in civilian institutions were also to leave. Ho Chi Minh, Pham Van Dong, Nguyen Chi Thanh, Pham Hung and others strongly supported this solution.

DRV leaders stressed that the implementation of the Geneva accords was of cardinal importance not only for Laos but for the whole region: difficulties that might arise from the withdrawal, including negative consequences for the Neo Lao Haksat and the links with the South, would be negligible compared with potential positive results. However, the decision was conditional on the behavior of the adversary. Any violation of the Geneva agreements by the United States and Nosavan would immediately be countered.

The decision was taken without consulting the Neo Lao Haksat or Peking.* Chinese Ambassador Liu Chun, who was full of reservations, confirmed this to me two weeks later. He said that he knew the Soviet Union had expressed satisfaction; but only future developments would tell whether such a great risk would achieve anything. Hanoi was conscious of the risks and sacrifices, and gave careful consideration to the links with South Vietnam. The liquidation of the Laos trails did not mean cessation of contact and support for the NLF

---

*DRV leaders knew that this would create hardships for the Pathet Lao; Kaysone and Nouhak were subsequently invited to Hanoi to consider what could be done to overcome the difficulties.

—Hanoi decided to direct aid through other channels. I got the impression that alternatives did not seem to be lacking. Thanh could not tell me where these alternative routes were, but it had always been a rule of Vietnamese strategy not to rely only on one alternative.

Thus, Hanoi again gave Washington the benefit of doubt, and though highly suspicious of U.S. intentions, left the door open to whatever positive chain reaction the Geneva agreements might initiate. Whatever movement there was on the Laotian trails was suspended in the following months. The only DRV presence left in Laos consisted of about three thousand workers employed in building and repairing roads as ordered by the former Souvanna Phouma government, and a group of about three hundred drivers and transport personnel employed in supply duties for the Neo Lao Haksat and the Neutralists. Technically, at least, they did not violate the provisions of the Geneva agreements.

U.S. Performance

Hanoi waited for a sign of good will from the United States, but the response was negative. Washington's "intelligence estimate" was "that the Communists continued to pursue their goal of gaining control of all of Laos, but that for the time being, at least, they intended to do so primarily through political means and generally within the terms of the Geneva agreements . . . But even though the Communists would probably rely mainly on political means, the North Vietnamese would undoubtedly insist on maintaining some military presence, small and inconspicuous, and would use the infiltration routes circumspectly . . ." "To meet this situation," Harriman strongly felt that "our military advisers should be withdrawn promptly, and thereafter there should be no violation of any kind by the United States, neither 'black' reconnaissance flights . . . nor cloak-and-dagger hanky-panky."[11]

In fact, "black" reconnaissance flights over Laos "related to the deployment of American troops in Thailand" continued uninterrupted, though this was not made public until May 1964.[12]* On August 14, a U.S. F-101 jet was shot down near Khang Khay and a Philippine pilot was captured. Also, U.S. military personnel stayed in Laos, most of them attached as "civilians" to the different branches of the U.S. embassy, mainly in United States Operations Missions (USOM) and the United States Information Service (USIS). In the report of a U.S. senatorial mission to Vietnam and Southeast Asia, dated February 25, 1963, Senator Mike Mansfield revealed that after the withdrawal deadline 250 American servicemen remained in Laos. "From a total of two American officials permanently stationed in all of Laos in 1953," the report said, "the number of U.S. personnel rose to 850 at its height in 1961, a total which has now declined to 250."†

More remarkable, William H. Sullivan, Deputy Assistant Secretary of East Asian and Pacific Affairs and former ambassador to Laos, testified on October 21, 1969, before the Symington Senate Subcommittee on U.S. Security Agreements and Commitments Abroad, that "because of the special provisions of the 1962 Geneva agreements" the United States felt it could not establish in Laos a Military Assistance Command (MAC) similar to those established in spring 1962 in South Vietnam and Thailand. "The net result was that because these men (the attachés) were in the embassy," they became subordinated to the ambassador. In a sense, the

*Col. Robert L. F. Tyrrell, U.S. air attaché in Vientiane, testified in Symington's Senate hearings on October 21, 1969, that a resident air attaché's office was established in Laos in October 1962.

†*Newsweek* of July 16, 1962, estimated that at the time of the conclusion of the Geneva agreements U.S. military personnel in Laos amounted to 1,500 advisers.

embassy was converted into a mini-MAC: "There is no organic military command present and functioning, on Lao soil or within the confines of Lao territory," Sullivan explained. "By virtue of the 1962 agreements and by virtue of the circumstances prevailing in Laos, these are matters that fall within the province of the ambassador and his policy directions." Actually, in accordance with President Kennedy's May 1961 instructions, the ambassador was empowered to take over a supervisory and coordinating role between different agencies functioning in Laos.

Further details were provided at the same hearings by Colonel Peter T. Russell, who presented himself as Deputy Chief Joint United States Military Advisory Group (JUSMAG), Thailand, and as such "a nonresident member of the U.S. country team in Vientiane." Russell stated:

> To carry out and supervise military assistance for Laos some special organizational and procedural arrangements were necessary. The Geneva agreements of 1962 required that all foreign troops—except a small French military training contingent—be withdrawn from Laos. (deleted) There was created therefore an organization known as Deputy Chief JUSMAG Thailand, as an integral part of the Thailand JUSMAG Headquarters. (deleted)
>
> Some instrumentality was necessary to maintain contact with Lao Armed Forces and to validate their military aid requirements. To this end, a special group was established in AID, the U.S. Agency for International Development in Laos. This group is called Requirement Office, or RO/USAID, and is staffed by retired military personnel holding Foreign Service Reserve positions.*
>
> The members of RO/USAID are in daily contact with respective technical service officers of the Lao General Staff.

*The RO/USAID, according to Ambassador Unger's letter to Souvanna Phouma dated October 12, 1962 (published in the Symington hearings), was established weeks after the conclusion of the Geneva agreements.

SENATOR SYMINGTON: You say that in view of the provisions of the Geneva agreement the existence of a U.S. military mission in Laos was impossible. In essence, that means we had to do all this on a covert basis, does it not?
    COL. RUSSELL: I believe that is a policy decision.
    SENATOR SYMINGTON: Your statement speaks for itself on it.
    COL. RUSSELL: Yes, sir.

Locating the main operational military units responsible for action in Laos on Thai territory across the Mekong violated another Geneva clause, in which the signatories undertook that "they will not use the territory of any country, including their own, for interference in the internal affairs of the Kingdom of Laos." Both the United States and Thailand thus became guilty of violating this provision.

Covert U.S. operations in Laos after the conclusion of the Geneva agreements were directed mainly by the CIA, which kept its traditional links to the rightist forces, infiltrated the Kong Le units, and continued to pay great attention to the development of the Meo army. The "civilian" company Air America, an offshoot of General Chennault's Cathay Air Transport, Taipeh, was one of the CIA's major tools. On C-46 and C-47 transport planes bearing Thai and Lao insignias, or without any insignia at all, Air America carried most of the supplies, military personnel and troops involved in ongoing operations. Air America had bases in Thailand, and freely used Lao airfields. To make this activity appear to conform to the Geneva provisions, overt military performance was transformed into covert operations, military personnel acting from station posts in Thailand and South Vietnam were labeled "nonresident" members of the U.S. country team in Laos, military supplies for Meo units were delivered under USAID-USOM "social welfare" projects for refugees, and the whole "cloak-and-dagger hanky-panky" got the respectable cover of Prime Minister Souvanna Phouma's agreement.

The Meo Clandestine Army

The very notion of "refugees" in relation to the Meo tribes was at that time pure invention. The Meos were not yet fleeing the war, as they were after the intensification of U.S. bombardments in 1968 and the retaliatory operations of the Pathet Lao. Though some dislocation of Meo units occurred, as after the Ban Padong battle, main Meo movements were part of their traditional nomadic way of life, based on a "slash and burn" agriculture which required constant relocation of villages to new land suitable for opium cultivation. This movement may well have been enhanced by the increasing demand for opium.

Air America activities linked to the Meo project met with sharp protests from the Neo Lao Haksat in the second half of 1962, and Air America planes were shot down. In a note to the Minister of Foreign Affairs on January 23, 1963, Phoumi Vongvichit wrote:

"The government of national union, which has the task of caring for the fate of Laotian citizens, refugees or not, never decided to confer this task on the American authorities or other foreign bodies . . . The American authorities who daily send their planes over Laotian territory without the consent of the government of national union and supply bandits with arms, ammunition, equipment and provisions in order to sow trouble among the peaceful population of Laos, have committed a grave interference in the internal affairs of Laos and a flagrant violation of the 1962 Geneva agreements."

Responding to these protests on January 28, 1963, the U.S. embassy in Vientiane published a "Memorandum on the

Refugee Problem in Laos," which revealed arrangements between U.S. authorities and the rightist group for continuing Air America activities: "Following an exchange of letters between the Prime Minister and the American ambassador a new agreement governing the program for assisting refugees was signed by the representatives of the Lao Royal Government and the U.S. Government." Such an agreement had in fact been concluded behind the back of the government of national union by Nosavan's close associate Keo Vipakone, the Secretary of State for Social Welfare, and signed on October 7, 1962, the deadline for the withdrawal of foreign military personnel from Laos. The U.S. memorandum stated that according to this agreement "an increase in assistance to refugees has been arranged in the form of an addition to the initial program of the Social Welfare Ministry ... Where air transport is necessary, USAID makes it available through contracts with private American firms, including Air America, Inc. Air supply to refugees is a complex and large-scale operation involving 14 aircraft making 1,000 flights per month, carrying about 1,500 tons of cargo."

On November 11, 1969, when asked by the Senate Subcommittee on U.S. Security Agreements Abroad if the United States "did have advisers to the Meo forces in Laos in October 1962, that were not withdrawn at that time?" the then ambassador to Laos Leonard Unger testified: "Well, as I say, we had no military. There were, of course, civilians in Laos, U.S. government civilians, who were there, but there was nothing—" Senator Symington interrupted here to ask another question:

SENATOR SYMINGTON: (Deleted)
AMBASSADOR UNGER: (Deleted) There was no restriction in the Geneva accords that had any effect on them.
MR. PAUL (Counsel): Were there any civilians performing paramilitary advisory functions for the Meo forces (deleted)

in Laos after the October deadline for withdrawal of military advisers?

AMBASSADOR UNGER: Well, I think you have heard in other testimony a description of programs going on today. (Deleted)

The Meo program, developed as a large-scale experiment in counterinsurgency and intelligence, was expected not only to play a role in Laos but also to penetrate North Vietnam and even China itself. One Air America plane was shot down (on January 5, 1963) at Ban Kha, near the Chinese border.

This program had a disruptive effect in Laos, and Laotians of every political tendency showed great concern for its effects. On September 20, 1962, Phoumi Vongvichit discussed the problem with Souvanna Phouma. He drew the Prime Minister's attention to the fact that U.S. agents were enlisting minority groups on an antigovernment basis, not only Meo but also Lao Theung (Kha) living on the Bolovens Plateau on the border of South Vietnam. Vongvichit showed that U.S. agents recruited the Meo by telling them that the ethnic Lao, the Lao Loum, wanted to dominate the country; that was why no representative of the Meo minority was included in the government of national union. The Meo were told to organize themselves and demand autonomy, and U.S. agents promised them arms, money and training to achieve this end. At the same time, U.S. agents told the Lao Theung that the Lao Loum were keeping them in ignorance to use them better as slaves (*Kha* means slave). In the process, both the Meo and the Lao Theung were trained to perform military and intelligence tasks. To strengthen its influence and widen its activity among the Meo, the CIA was importing to Laos agents recruited among Meo tribes in Thailand.

Souvanna Phouma admitted that Vongvichit was right; he himself had received similar information, including one detailed report about the introduction of Thai Meo units into the province of Sayaboury, on the Thai border. The Prince told Vongvichit that he had already complained about these activities to Unger, and intended to speak with the Meo leaders, Touby Lyfoung and Vang Pao. He was inclined to believe that the United States would cease these activities; anyhow the government had sufficient arms to face the challenge. Souvanna seemed not to have full knowledge of the range of CIA projects. When it came to concrete dealings with the U.S. embassy, he eventually gave in, step by step.

A week later, in another conversation with Vongvichit, Souvanna denied having given the United States permission to use Air America planes to deliver supplies to the Meo. All aid, the Prince said, was to go through government channels; only the government had the right to administer any assistance needed by the population. He had made only preliminary soundings with the U.S. government concerning application for U.S. aid; all serious demands would be presented beforehand for approval by the three parties in the government. But on October 9, 1962, two days after the deadline for the withdrawal of foreign military personnel, Souvanna privately admitted to me that he had consented to a continuation of U.S. deliveries to the Nosavan army: "One could not possibly cut them off from supplies," he said.

The activities of the CIA and other U.S. military agencies were not secret. In May 1962 the London *Times* printed extensive disclosures of CIA operations in Laos, and in a debate in the British House of Commons opposition leader Harold Wilson asked Prime Minister Macmillan to make a personal appeal to President Kennedy to make sure he "puts the CIA house in order." Lord Privy Seal Edward Heath could only say that "Neither I nor Her Majesty's Government have any responsibility for the activities of the CIA."

On August 8, 1962, I asked Leonard Unger, who had just **recently been** appointed U.S. ambassador, how he envisaged further developments in the face of CIA activities, especially how cooperation with the International Commission could be fruitful if the U.S. embassy itself seemed not to be aware of many CIA operations. Unger was not perturbed. He answered that these were things of the past. In the past there certainly had been a variety of activities by different U.S. agencies in Laos, the details of which he did not know. But now he felt sure he was in command of affairs, and nothing about any independent action by the CIA had reached his ears since his arrival in Laos. If something like that should happen, he would ask to be relieved of his post. I took this as an assurance that CIA activities had stopped. That was not the case; but Unger certainly meant one thing he said—nothing happened without his knowledge.

I raised the same problem that same day with the new British ambassador, Donald Hopson. He also tried to assure me that CIA operations were over, and he used diplomatic language similar to Unger's. According to his information, "Kennedy had mastered the situation." Nosavan's continued defiance was only an expression of weakness. Hopson was basically right—Kennedy himself announced the full subordination of the CIA. Asked during an NBC interview on September 9, 1963, if "the CIA tends to make its own policy," he answered, "No . . . the CIA coordinates its efforts with the State Department and the Department of Defense."

At the end of September Hopson admitted to me that U.S. air operations in Laos, previously in the hands of MAAG, had been taken over by USOM, which continued to supply the Meo. I then again raised the problem with Unger. He was a bit irritated. Whatever the United States did in Laos, he answered, was with the agreement of the government. I said that according to my information, confirmed by both Neo Lao Haksat and Neutralist ministers, the matter had never been considered at a government meeting. Unger responded coldly that he could not enter into the internal arrangements within the government; Souvanna Phouma's consent was the determining factor for him.

Souvanna Phouma's Role

Allegations that U.S. military doings were carried out with Souvanna Phouma's full knowledge were only half-truths. In most cases the Prince's consent came after rather than before the fact. Souvanna did in fact ask the United States to extend its aid in different fields, and to continue supplying Nosavan's army, but execution was then left to direct contacts between U.S. representatives and the Rightists, and in the process—uncontrolled by the government—a growing U.S. military presence was shielded by the separate rightist establishment. In the beginning, apparently, Souvanna himself had only a faint knowledge of the real dimension of U.S. operations. But when matters were partly discovered and branded by the Neo Lao Haksat as a breach of the Geneva agreements and a violation of the Plain of Jars June 1962 agreement, Souvanna disregarded the protests.

All this created tension within the government. Controversies grew from month to month, reaching a climax in the actual collapse of the government in spring 1963. Until the collapse the United States and the Rightists, using the government facade, continued their operations with few constraints. As a rule Souvanna Phouma's consent became available beforehand, and was taken for granted. Often he was not even consulted. The outside world was kept ignorant of these operations. As one reason for keeping the operations clandestine, Sullivan mentioned (in the Symington hearings) the need not to "necessitate cognizance by the Soviet Union of what we are doing" in order to avoid "official *démarches* either to us or to the Royal Lao Government, which they have not yet done." Official Soviet cognizance of U.S. operations in Laos (as opposed to press statements or letters sent

to the British Co-chairman of the Geneva conference), it
followed, could have embarrassed the United States, especially because, as Sullivan said, the Soviet Union had not
violated the 1962 agreements, and perhaps even more because such a move could destroy "the basic understanding"
on Laos still existing between the Soviet Union and the
United States. Sullivan called the Soviet Union "the primary
partner with us in attempting to establish an agreement in
Laos." A curious revelation.

The fact of the matter was that, as Harriman had foreseen,
after Geneva and the formal reconciliation in Laos, Souvanna Phouma changed fronts. "The Kennedy strategy,"
Schlesinger remarked, "ended the alliance between the Neutralists and the Pathet Lao."[13] Having used the Neo Lao
Haksat to regain the premiership in Vientiane, the Prince
reshuffled alliances in order once again to head the conservative forces, landing anew in the U.S. camp. This was not a
sudden reversal. The Prince proceeded slowly and carefully.
Even years later he insisted that U.S. authorities not disclose
the full extent of his cooperation—Sullivan mentioned this as
an additional reason why the United States kept military
operations in Laos covert. Souvanna wanted to maintain his
reputation as a neutralist, and the United States readily took
cover behind his "neutralist" facade.

Conversation in Washington

Souvanna Phouma's new orientation and U.S. intentions
in Laos became apparent immediately after the signing of the
Geneva agreements, in confidential conversations Souvanna
had in Washington on July 27, 1962. Against the advice of
the Neo Lao Haksat, the Prince had gone straight from
Geneva to the United States, where he had talked with President Kennedy, Secretary of State Dean Rusk, Secretary of
Defense Robert McNamara, Undersecretary of the Treasury

Henry H. Fowler, Presidential Advisor McGeorge Bundy, Assistant Director of the International Agency for Aid and Development Seymour J. Janow, and, as the Prince confided to me, the chief of the CIA. An impressive list, indicative of the importance the United States attached to Laos.

I later read the secret minutes of these talks. They reflect Souvanna's feelings and U.S. preoccupations four days after the signing of the Geneva agreement, and they cast much light on the aims and policies of both sides. While U.S. representatives pressed for Souvanna's redefinition along the old pro-Western anticommunist lines, the Prince still seemed torn by different and sometimes contradictory motives, the poles of what Souphanouvong termed Souvanna's "dual nature—patriotic and reactionary." While he wanted to bring peace to Laos, he felt socially allied with the West and conservative forces. Eventually he succumbed to U.S. pressures.

The talks referred to the role of the Laotian settlement in global U.S. strategy; to the U.S.-Soviet dialogue on Indochina; to U.S. policy in Laos, especially to prospects of alliance reversals among the three parties; and finally to the execution of the Geneva agreements.

The minutes I read opened with Kennedy's toast at the White House lunch. Several times Kennedy alluded to the existence of a U.S.-Soviet agreement on "the maintenance of an independent Laos" which went back to the Kennedy–Khrushchev meeting in Vienna. U.S. strategy seemed to count on Soviet disengagement while the United States sought a military solution in South Vietnam. Kennedy repeatedly stressed the aim of establishing a working cooperation between the United States and the Soviet Union—"powers whose interests in other parts may be in conflict"—but not once did he mention the People's Republic of China or the Democratic Republic of Vietnam. Did this indicate a tendency to play on a division in the socialist world? In a subsequent conversation with Souvanna, Rusk also saw U.S.

strategy linked to Soviet performance. He stressed the "great importance" the United States attached to the work of the Co-chairmen, and told the Prince of his strong conviction that "Khrushchev would execute the Geneva agreement."
Global strategy was apparently very much in the minds of U.S. leaders. "The agreement which has been signed in Geneva," the President said in his toast, "in a sense goes to and has its effect upon the sort of world peace that goes far beyond your borders and, in fact, involves the relations between many powers whose interests in other parts may be in conflict. So our concern, Prime Minister, for your future is very real, because it involves really the future of the United States." This echoed Kennedy's March 1961 statement on Laos. Confusion as to whom the United States was confronting in Indochina persisted: "The destiny of Laos ties up with the relations between the great powers at a very critical time in history," the President said.

Kennedy also spoke of the interrelationship between the Laos problem and "the security of the countries which are neighboring on your borders." His main concern was evidently for South Vietnam; the conflict in South Vietnam, again, was seen as a key world issue. Peace and security in this region, Kennedy told Souvanna, "are very much tied up with the success of your personal efforts . . . If you fail, if the accord at Geneva should turn out to be merely paper, then, of course, relations all over the world would become more difficult and the belief in negotiations would be subjected to a serious attack." There was some truth in this remark—another of Kennedy's self-fulfilling prophecies—but Kennedy hoped to evade U.S. responsibility by focusing on Souvanna's performance: "If I may say so, Mr. Prime Minister, you carry with you not only the well-being of your own country and people but also, I think [your efforts] will have an important influence on the peace of that part of the world."

Rusk's Counsels

Souvanna must have been impressed by the many compliments paid him. He surely liked the flattery, and he yielded quickly to the suggested equation between the interests of the United States and his personal aspirations. Reading the minutes of the personal discussions, however, I was struck by the fact that Souvanna did not seem to grasp immediately all the blunt proposals offered to him. He had been away from direct dealings with U.S. leaders too long, and seemed still to be too much involved in local Laotian controversies to be able to follow U.S. intentions. He did not always see their aim of quickly moving him away from existing alliances and placing him in an executive role in relation to U.S. policies. The conversations therefore did not lead to final conclusions in all cases. They served rather to air the issues and reestablish a general framework of cooperation.

His first private conversation was with Dean Rusk. Rusk opened by saying that the United States had no ambitions in Laos, and asked how the United States could be helpful in maintaining Laos's independence. Souvanna had a long list of urgent needs: schools, hospitals, power stations, cover for the Laotian currency. But Rusk quickly brought him back to sober politics: "The United States," he said, "understands well its obligations under the new Geneva agreements, under which no aid should be accompanied by any political conditions; but we have a law on aid which we must follow, and one should not interpret this as political conditions."*

The U.S. law listed many conditions, one of which was not to assist "communist forces." The problem was then to exclude the Neo Lao Haksat—who were part of the government of national union but who were judged to be commu-

*Apart from the texts of the lunch toasts, which were in English, the rest of the minutes were in French, and quotations given here are in my translation—M.T.

nists—from the benefits of U.S. aid. And what about the Neutralists? If they were to be included, they would have to break away from the Neo Lao Haksat. U.S. aid required the establishment of special channels well tuned to local politics. Rusk did not offer details, but Souvanna was given food for thought. Instead of fostering unity in Laos, the United States was out to divide the country even more deeply this time through political and financial pressure.

Souvanna quickly acted on Rusk's advice. At the beginning of September, he sent a letter through General Nosavan to the U.S. embassy in Vientiane asking "in compliance with the assurances of support which I have received from President Kennedy and other members of the U.S. Government during my stay in Washington D.C. in July 1962," for the continuation of supplies to the Nosavan army and other US-sponsored military and non-military projects.[14] The request was made without prior consultation with the Neo Lao Haksat, even though they directed the Ministry of Economy and Planning. Neither was the International Commission notified about any military supplies. The Prince's request, as disclosed by Colonel Russell, resulted in the establishment of the RO/USAID "instrumentality," subordinated to JUS-MAG Thailand.

Rusk inquired next about the "delicate question" of foreign military personnel. U.S. personnel, he said, could easily be identified, and were in Laos in "a relatively small number"; other foreign personnel were more difficult to identify. Souvanna Phouma answered that he himself "did not hide his anxiety about this issue," but had received assurances from Pham Van Dong that "Vietminh elements" would be withdrawn before the deadline, and that "no difficulties will be made internally or externally." Souvanna expressed the hope that the Geneva agreements would be implemented.

Another topic raised by Rusk was "the basic orientation of the Lao people." Rusk was especially concerned with the possible outcome of future elections. The 1958 performance, which gave a victory to the Left, had to be avoided: "If the noncommunists unite with the majority of the population, they will certainly gain strength. But if they remain divided in small parties, their force will disperse and their chances will be lost." Souvanna immediately understood this hint. He tried for a moment to reassure Rusk that the majority of the Neo Lao Haksat were not communists; but, turning to the crux of the problem, he said: "In the light of past experience I see the danger; this is why [in 1958] I united the Independents and Progressives into one party, the Rally of the Lao People . . . These facts are still relevant. One should not scatter forces; a single political party such as created by Prince Sihanouk would be sufficient. In case even one red point showed up, it would be discerned immediately." This was an unequivocal declaration of intent. Souvanna was ready to change fronts. Rusk was satisfied, and did not return to this problem.

The Secretary of State then asked Souvanna about Laos's future relations with neighboring countries, and if the United States could be of any help in this respect. The Prince apparently misunderstood Rusk, who perhaps hoped, after Souvanna's declaration of readiness to change internal alliances, to hear a similar statement about external alliances with U.S. allies. But, reacting impulsively, Souvanna jumped to complain about South Vietnam and Thailand.

Bangkok was the Prince's main concern: "Thailand has always wanted [to conquer] Laos. Looking at the map edited in 1893 by a French geographer, we see the real Laos. Today ten million Laotians live in Thailand . . . From the moment Laos achieved independence, and was no longer in French bondage, the Lao on the other side of the Mekong began to form a nationalist movement. The leaders of this movement were jailed and killed. Four ministers of Lao origin were killed under Phibul and Pridi. Thailand fears that this move-

ment will grow stronger. In 1954, thanks to the Geneva
agreements, the Laotians hoped for a period of peace. But the
Thais, particularly General Phao, sent Thai agents from
Bangkok to kill one of my ministers, the Minister of Defense
[Kou Voravong], a cousin of General Phoumi Nosavan. The
assassin was arrested but was not put to trial. We do not
demand or claim our territories. If we were to make demands, they would first concern South Vietnam and Cambodia. We have sufficient land for several millions . . ." Rusk
interrupted this passionate anti-Thai statement, but the
Prince came back to the same theme in his subsequent conversation with the President: "Concerning political aid, I
would appreciate it if you could explain to Thailand that it
should not interfere in Laotian affairs. As I have explained
to Mr. Rusk, misunderstandings have always existed between Thailand and Laos: let Thailand not interfere in our
internal affairs."

Kennedy's Preoccupations

Kennedy started his meeting with Souvanna with a statement assuring the Prince that the United States identified
itself with Souvanna's policies and not with the stand of the
previous government. Kennedy was preoccupied with three
problems: (a) the integration of the Laotian armed forces; (b)
the future elections, because "the communists are well organized and may exploit the division in the ranks of the
non-communists," and (c) the International Control Commission: "If the Commission acts in a way to open infiltration
to South Vietnam, if the Laos agreement should open the
corridor, this would create serious difficulties."

The Prince did not fully understand Kennedy's "integration" concern, and answered by assuring the President that
he really wanted the implementation of the agreements but
could not say anything concrete about the integration of

military forces, except that "evidently this would not be very easy." Only in later conversations did it dawn on Souvanna what the U.S. really meant by "integration"—the old concept of disbanding Pathet Lao forces. As expressed later by S. J. Janow of AID: "You understand well the serious problem in the United States of creating the impression that we are aiding a country in the communist block. We want to see Pathet Lao forces demobilized, and a small group of your forces integrated." The United States was sticking to Sullivan's proposal, defeated in Geneva, of "dissolving" the Pathet Lao. It was trying to enlist Souvanna Phouma to make the proposal work. But the Prince seemed to understand that things would not be easy.

Concerning elections, the Prince was more explicit. He repeated his assurances that "we are interested in uniting different parties," and developed a theory to prove the soundness of his plan: "The Western powers would not assent to a government led by the Neo Lao Haksat," and in the same way the East would not accept a government headed by Phoumi Nosavan; only elections favorable to the Neutralists could satisfy both East and West. But Kennedy continued to show apprehension about the Neo Lao Haksat: "We are perturbed that the demobilized elements of the Pathet Lao might in a year's time become involved in important political activities . . . Considering the nature of communists who want to extend their influence, why should they accept a neutral Laos, and not a communist Laos?"

Souvanna was inclined to see internal Laotian problems as extensions of external power plays, and answered: "They need peace. I discussed matters with Chou En Lai. The Chinese fear a U.S. presence in Laos. What they want is to protect their country by a buffer state dividing it from SEATO. Ho Chi Minh and Pham Van Dong said the same thing in 1956 and 1960. They need peace to consolidate their economies and internal systems. On the other hand, [they understand that] the West would not allow Laos to become a satellite of a socialist country."

This was perhaps a simplistic theory, but it reflected to some extent the interests of Peking and Hanoi. Souvanna seemed to plead for U.S. disengagement, too. But Kennedy insisted on the continuation of the U.S. military presence: "I suggest, in order to assure peace in Laos, that we maintain a certain degree of armed strength in neighboring countries." Was this a reference to the military build-up in South Vietnam and Thailand? It clearly violated the Geneva agreements prohibiting the use of other countries' territory to interfere in Laotian affairs, but Souvanna Phouma did not oppose the suggestion. Against his own government's declaration (in the Geneva agreements) not to recognize "the protection of any alliance or military coalition, including SEATO," Souvanna stated that he did not think that SEATO should be disbanded, "because SEATO makes the socialist bloc reflect." Again, Souvanna was wavering and undecided.

Souvanna preferred to speak about the work of the International Commission only in general terms. He was certainly aware that these were two conflicting conceptions of the Commission's role: to assist the Laotian government in the preservation of neutrality, against foreign interference; or to control the Laotian government itself, attempting even to influence the internal balance of forces. The Geneva agreements clearly leaned to the first understanding, but the United States was dissatisfied with this and hoped for a reversal in practice, where Souvanna could be very helpful. Souvanna said that he himself wanted "to use" the Commission both in internal and external affairs: "It is our duty to respect our obligations under the Geneva agreements. It is also our duty to turn to the ICC to assure that the agreements are respected. The ICC should serve as arbitrator between the three forces. I hope to be able to use the ICC especially in relation to external forces and the retreat of troops." The President did not return to this problem, but later raised the question of the "Vietminh withdrawal." Souvanna answered again that Pham Van Dong had assured him that Hanoi would "not engage in any activity which might create internal or external difficulties for Laos."*

"Demobilization" and "Infiltration"

Souvanna's meeting with McNamara was short. The Secretary of Defense was chiefly interested in "demobilization" and sealing off the infiltration routes through Laos. "We have given instructions to the Chief of the Military Mission [in Laos]," McNamara said, "to be ready to withdraw [U.S. military personnel] on condition that others do the same. In accordance with the Protocol to the Geneva agreement, Laos should not be used for infiltration from North to South Vietnam. The infiltration must stop. Political independence in Southeast Asia will not be achieved unless the infiltration is halted."† But "infiltration" became a catchword expressing essentially the hopelessness of coping with the insurgency in South Vietnam and its political fabric. "Infiltration," as Kennedy had said, became "the built-in excuse for failure and the built-in argument for escalation." It was well known that in those early stages of the conflict only individuals, cadres and very small units—all of them Southerners—moved along the Laotian trails. According to

*Shortly after his return to Laos, Souvanna told me that he had discussed the problem of South Vietnam with Kennedy, De Gaulle and Lord Home. The problem was, he said, to find a team to replace the government of Ngo Dinh Diem. The Americans themselves, according to the information he received, were already working to set up such a team. He did not divulge the source of his information, but he mentioned that he had met the chief of the CIA, who assured him of his full support.

†From the start the United States interpreted the Geneva agreements as conditional obligations only. All depended on events in South Vietnam, and the prospects were bad.

Rusk's testimony of February 18, 1966, it was only in 1965 that "the communists apparently exhausted their reservoir of Southerners who had gone North" after the 1954 Geneva agreements. And it was well known at that time that the NLF relied primarily on captured or locally provided weapons. But in any case, when speaking about withdrawal of U.S. military personnel from Laos, McNamara had in mind only the overt U.S. presence; the covert presence was at that moment being established and enlarged.

Before Souvanna was able to answer McNamara's question, a call from the White House interrupted the conversation. The "demobilization" issue was then taken up by Seymour Janow. When Souvanna heard Janow's interpretation of demobilization—the liquidation of Pathet Lao forces—he was somewhat startled. The Sananikone government had tried to "demobilize" the two Pathet Lao battalions in 1959, and the result had been a return to civil war. Now the Pathet Lao were much stronger. Thus the Prince answered Janow: "It is difficult at the moment not to accept the Pathet Lao forces into the national army. We agreed in Zurich and in Geneva on the need for integration. I hope that the American people will not object to support for the Lao army. Those forces must be fed. Demobilization can not be executed instantly. You should aid the Lao, the whole country, without discrimination."

Janow objected. The United States was eager to support Phoumi Nosavan's soldiers (now totaling about 70,000) and the Meo army, but not the 30,000 Pathet Lao and Neutralist soldiers. "It would be difficult for us to support an army of 100,000 if we could not have clear proof of integration and demobilization." The goal obviously was to disarm the Pathet Lao and most of the Neutralists. Janow also showed interest in other strategic projects: road and airfield building, Operation Fraternity (another CIA cover organization), aid and supplies for the Meo "refugees," maintenance of the armed forces and police. He concluded the conversation by expressing hope that the United States "would be able to continue the present activities in Laos."*

U.S. policy for Laos after the conclusion of the 1962 Geneva agreements seemed well formed. Though in its letter and spirit Geneva had confirmed the neutralization of Laos and the military-political gains of the Left, the United States still sought to return to old policies—to disarm the Neo Lao Haksat and maintain the armed strength of the Rightists, to mobilize the conservative elite and the rightist officer clan against the popular trends of democratic change. Bent on old strategical concepts and preoccupied with the struggle going on in Vietnam, the U.S. administration seemed not even to acknowledge the commitment to neutralize Laos. Unperturbed by the Geneva agreements, the CIA built up the clandestine Meo army, while the military converted Thailand into a warehouse for escalation. Matters began to center on the military contest in South Vietnam—in the Laotian context the connection being "infiltration."

Soviet Attitudes

The stubbornness of the Kennedy administration in pursuing the Indochina struggle stemmed mainly from misconcep-

*According to a USAID task force report, official U.S. aid to Laos, military and economic, from 1955 to June 1962 amounted to $442.2 million, divided as follows:

I.	Total AID assistance (in millions of dollars)		290.4
	A. Internal Security & Government Support		
	Military Budget Support	184.4	
	Civil Budget	18.2	
	Police Support	13.7	
	B. Economic Project Assistance	49.8	
	Unspecified	24.3	
II.	Total Military Assistance Program (MAP)		150.6
III.	Total Mutual Security Program (MSP)		441.0
IV.	PL 480		1.2
V.	Grand total		$442.2

tions about the nature of the struggle. The Indochinese Left was totally underrated, and the contest was seen mostly as a key battle in the global confrontation with expanding communism. Thus Washington paid more attention to Moscow and Peking than to Hanoi and the Neo Lao Haksat. In 1961–62 the Soviet Union, because it maintained the air-bridge to Laos, was actually seen as the chief adversary, and U.S. strategy paid great attention to Moscow's moves. Signs of Soviet reluctance to continue its Laotian involvement thus encouraged the U.S. leadership to aim for victory.

Soviet discouragement concerning Indochina first showed in the Kennedy–Khrushchev Vienna talks; further evidence followed during the Geneva conference; and after Geneva, the evidence was abundant, ranging from a demonstrative Soviet disengagement in Laos, through noises of disbelief in the capability of the Asian allies to withstand a massive U.S. assault, to repeated Soviet offers to the United States to proceed more quickly on an agreement on European problems. All this misled U.S. leadership and produced an eagerness for greater commitments in Indochina: Soviet withdrawal seemed to promise rapid victory.

Moscow meticulously implemented its resolution to disengage from Laos after the Geneva agreements. Shielding itself behind the accords, unmoved by evidence of continued U.S. political and military interference, the Soviet Union ceased supplying the Neo Lao Haksat and the Neutralist forces, dismantled the air-bridge to Laos, and except for low-cost symbolic aid projects, refused to negotiate with the government of national union any assistance agreements that could balance lavish U.S. investments. In political conversations with representatives of the Neo Lao Haksat, Soviet diplomats advised a strategy of restraint and concessions that in concrete conditions had little chance for success.

When Abramov returned to Vientiane from Moscow on August 12, 1962, he told me that Moscow saw the formation of the government of national union and the conclusion of

the Geneva agreements as great achievements of the policy
of peaceful coexistence and important links in the East-West
dialogue. Moscow hoped that the Laotian success would
pave the way for the reopening of the Berlin negotiations,
which Soviet Deputy Foreign Minister Kuzniecov was instructed to take up in Geneva with U.S. representatives.
Moscow attached importance to the correct implementation
of the Laotian experiment: the general aim was to turn the
Laotian settlement to profit in European affairs.

Prime responsibility for local developments, especially in
the internal affairs of Laos, was left to the local parties—the
Laotians, Vietnamese and Chinese. Moscow estimated that
this line had been proved to be beneficial. It made the Asian
parties more aware of the dangers of a military-political clash
with the United States, and in this way had hastened the
formation of the government of national union. Moscow also
felt that this line eased the atmosphere with China.

The Soviet Union was resolved to maintain this line,
and did not respond to proposals, mainly from Hanoi, for
another conference of socialist countries to work out new
guidelines for action in the changed situation and against
increased U.S. pressures. Both Peking and Hanoi made it
clear that in their present circumstances they were unable
to extend any large assistance to Laos and expected the
Soviet Union to take over the burden. But Moscow was
not ready to compete with the United States, and did not
respond.

Aid to Laos was a crucial problem. Immediately after the
installation of the government of national union, Nosavan
began to use U.S. funds to pressure the Neo Lao Haksat and
the Neutralists. Just the move to Vientiane demanded resources far beyond what had been needed in the Khang Khay
and Sam Neua retreat. The currency issued in Khang Khay
(printed in Moscow) had no value whatsoever in the Vientiane zone, and Nosavan skillfully took advantage of such

financial difficulties. He bought up wavering elements in the Neutralist ranks, and was even ready to pay advances and give loans to the Neo Lao Haksat, on condition that he receive exact pay-lists and data on the stationing of Pathet Lao units. In these circumstances, both the Neo Lao Haksat and Hanoi considered an equal input of financial aid to the government of national union from socialist countries as a most vital condition for maintaining political equilibrium. In a conversation with Tchivilev and myself on July 9, 1962, Souphanouvong stressed that the financial hardships of the Neo Lao Haksat and the Neutralists posed the most critical problem at the moment. He proposed to counterbalance U.S. subsidies to Nosavan with aid from socialist countries. Tchivilev himself was concerned but, as he confided to me, he had instructions from Moscow not to discuss any problems of aid.

On August 26, 1962, on the eve of his departure from Laos, Abramov again summed up the state of affairs in relation to the Asian allies. The Soviet Union, he told me, had dismantled the air-bridge to Laos and withdrawn its crews. The ten planes which constituted the air-bridge had already been turned over to the Democratic Republic of Vietnam. The Vietnamese had enough pilots to handle the planes, and the Soviet Union was aiding Hanoi in training additional crews. The real aim was to leave responsibility for further developments to the Asian parties; U.S. activities were completely omitted from this reasoning.

The Soviet Union was aware that the main issues now revolved around South Vietnam. Abramov referred to developments in South Vietnam, and emphasized that the execution of the Geneva agreements on Laos depended to a great extent on the corridor running through Laos. He was in fact propounding the U.S. line making "infiltration" an excuse for continuing the war. In point of fact, Hanoi decided five weeks later to close down the Laotian corridor; but this did not halt U.S. interference in Laos or the war in South Vietnam.

The Airlift Dismantled

The abrupt Soviet disengagement, and especially the decision to dismantle the airlift to Laos, met with disapproval not only from the Neo Lao Haksat and the DRV but also from the Chinese. Peking sent Moscow a special letter on the subject, and on September 3, 1962, Soviet Deputy Foreign Minister Kuzniecov handed a note to the Chinese embassy containing a long response substantiating the Soviet position. It began by saying that the Soviet Union agreed with the People's Republic of China that the situation in Laos was complex and serious, and that Nosavan, backed by the United States, Thailand and South Vietnam, was creating difficulties in the implementation of the Geneva agreement. One should have expected this, the note continued, as the reactionary forces in Laos and their allies could not be satisfied with the Geneva agreement, which served better the Laotian patriotic forces and the socialist camp. The note went on:

> In this situation the socialist countries and the national-democratic forces in Laos should take advantage of what is valuable and positive in the Geneva agreement to wage a political struggle against the Laotian reaction, and the United States standing behind it, in order to finally eliminate its positions in the country.
>
> It is important that all of us should attentively follow our adversaries' actions and actively denounce their attempts to violate the Geneva agreement. Our friends in Laos whose representatives are members of the coalition government have extensive opportunities to pose these violations of the Geneva agreements before the coalition government, and to demand an investigation of each violation by government machinery,

or, where necessary, by the Commission. Naturally, the government of the Soviet Union will in such cases give active support to the Laotian comrades, taking advantage particularly of its position as Co-chairman of the Geneva conference.

Such a line will either force the Nosavan group to implement the Geneva agreement, or it will unmask them as the violators of these accords. Essentially, this line can be executed only if the socialist countries and the national-democratic forces in Laos do not give rise to accusations that they themselves violate the agreement on Laos, or evade its implementation.

Therefore, when on July 22 the Laotian comrades asked to use Soviet transport planes stationed in Vietnam to ferry military supplies, we responded that on account of the enforcement of the Geneva agreement we would be unable to comply. In connection with this we would like to draw attention to the following passage of your letter: "Since mere technicalities can, as far as the outside world is concerned, transform this air transport into transport of a civilian nature, no difficulties will arise from the point of view of violation of the Geneva agreement."

But surely you will agree that the transport of military material to Laos on Soviet planes with Soviet crews could not go unperceived. It would immediately be used by our enemies as reason to destroy the agreement on Laos. First of all, the destruction of the Geneva agreement would seriously damage the interests of the national-democratic forces in Laos. And any of our steps which might violate the Geneva agreement would create difficulties for the socialist countries in other international problems, too. We would put in the hands of our enemies a great political trump; enabling them to say in their propaganda that socialist countries do not meet their obligations. For example, how would socialist proposals to guarantee a free city status for West Berlin look if socialist countries began to violate the only recently signed Geneva agreement? The great confidence in the socialist countries shown now by many nonaligned states in Asia, Africa and South America would be seriously undermined.

In order to transfer civilian supplies from the Democratic Republic of Vietnam to Laos, according to the request of Souvanna Phouma and Souphanouvong, we have agreed to leave our crews for two more months, intending to assist Laos with air transport of urgent civil materials during the rainy season. The transport of these materials is carried out openly, on the request of the coalition government, not allowing our adversaries to accuse us of violating the Geneva agreement. After this period the planes will be handed over to the Democratic Republic of Vietnam for its needs. Clearly, we do not assume, as it appears from your letter, that the Democratic Republic of Vietnam will carry out any ferrying in place of the Soviet Union.

We hope that with the end of the rainy season it will become possible to use local overland transport. Then it will be possible to use the six hundred trucks which the Soviet Union turned over to the national-patriotic Laotian forces. We have also turned over to Laos a large amount of road-building machinery, to keep the roads in good condition.

We have openly stated our point of view concerning Laos, and we hope that you will show understanding for it.

The note contained a lucid statement of the situation, but whatever theory it expounded could only be judged against the background of prevailing Laotian realities. The government of national union existed only on paper. Unity existed only in words. The government had appointed three committees to deal with the problems of the cease-fire, unification of administration, and army. But all three marked time. A cease-fire agreement was never reached, and the *de facto* partition of the country with separate armed forces persisted. All government departments remained, in fact, in the hands of the Nosavan administration. The Neo Lao Haksat as well as most Neutralist ministers were given only figurehead roles. Their power did not extend much further than their offices, where, in reality, they were immobilized. Nosavan issued a confidential circular letter to the government staff stating that they still remained subordinated to the old administration, which was paying their salaries. He even ordered the Vientiane radio not to broadcast the new government's political program, pronounced by Souvanna Phouma at the installation ceremony. Not only were Neo Lao Haksat and Neutralist ministers strangled financially, but they were left without security. Except for a few Neo Lao Haksat and Neutralist guards, Vientiane security was exclusively controlled by Nosavan, fully in the hands of the infamous Direction Nationale de Coordination.

Taking advantage of this situation, the United States reinforced the Rightists with funds and supplies, while the Neo Lao Haksat seemed about to be cut off from their most essential resources. Military supplies at the moment were perhaps of minor importance. The Neo Lao Haksat even proposed to Souvanna that new stuff reaching Hanoi from Czechoslovakia should be left there for the time being without introducing it to Laos; but at the same time the United States was building up Meo forces in the rear of Neo Lao Haksat and Neutralist positions. It was more than naïve to think that in such a situation protests within the government or activization of the International Commission (which also needed government authorization) could be effective. In any case, the Soviet Union itself, as Sullivan testified, never directly protested to the United States about violations of the Geneva agreements. And it refused to extend any substantial nonmilitary aid to the government of national union. Reading the Soviet note, the Chinese certainly must have wondered if Moscow had not carried out the whole Geneva exercise so carefully only because it wanted to barter it for a Berlin settlement.

Three weeks after the delivery of the Soviet note to Peking, the Soviet chargé d'affaires in Vientiane showed the text to Phoumi Vongvichit, at the moment the leading Neo Lao

Haksat personality in Vientiane. Phoumi was bitter and depressed by its content. He told me that the problem of supplies was a key issue. Because of lack of rice Neo Lao Haksat and Neutralist forces had already suffered desertions to the Rightists; forced withdrawals might be necessary from certain forward areas where supplies did not arrive at all. Of the six hundred lorries given to the Laotians by the Soviet Union, the Neo Lao Haksat only had sixteen in good shape. Souvanna himself had told Vongvichit that he had encountered difficulties in obtaining Soviet assistance. There was nothing to do, Souvanna meant, but to rely more on U.S. aid.

The post-Geneva setup worked to contradict the general aims of the Geneva agreements. Instead of converting Laos into a neutral buffer, which would stimulate national reconciliation, reduce tension in the area, and lead to the neutralization of Indochina, the agreements were used to veil increased outside pressures to divide the country, to intensify the war in South Vietnam, and to move toward an all-out Indochinese war.

The U.S. belief that Soviet disengagement would make victory easier was wrong, as was the Russian belief that it would bring its Asian allies around to its Euro-centered strategy. Nor did the hoped-for Berlin agreement materialize. Instead there was an acceleration of the dynamic of the Indochina conflict.

Chinese Appraisals

On September 24, 1962, I had a long conversation with the Chinese ambassador, Liu Chun, who had just returned from Peking. The Chinese saw Laos in the larger context of U.S. strategy in Asia. On the eastern wing (Taiwan, South Korea, the Philippines and Japan) the United States' prime effort was to maintain and strengthen its military positions; on the western wing (India and South Asia) it relied primarily on economic-political penetration; and the main edge of its military-political offensive was directed against Southeast Asia. This was its main front against the socialist countries. The knot of contradictions in this area—between imperialism and local nations, between the old and new imperialism, between imperialism and young states craving independence—meant that the political-military issues would remain unresolved for a long time.

In this context Laos became the place where all these tendencies intersected, where the knot of various interests became the most tangled. At the same time it was impossible to separate the Laotian problem from South Vietnam, where a severe military battle was raging. The United States had agreed to a cease-fire in Laos to gain time, to strengthen Nosavan's position, to try to win over Souvanna Phouma, and, above all, to isolate South Vietnam and concentrate on suppressing the armed struggle of the national liberation movement. Taking all this into consideration, the most important task for the progressive forces in Laos was to consolidate their military and political positions. All work in the coalition government and in Vientiane must be subordinated to the chief task of retaining and securing the liberated areas. Simultaneously, for tactical reasons, great weight should be attached to conciliating Souvanna Phouma and the neutral center.

According to the Chinese assessment, there were three possibilities for future development in Laos: (a) the preservation of the government of national union and implementation of the Geneva agreements; (b) a formal retention of the government of national union with a partial execution of the Geneva agreements, and a parallel maintenance of the three divided power centers, with continued contention, strife and clashes; and (c) the nonimplementation of the Geneva agreements and the program of the government of national union, its breakup, and a return to war. The first perspective was unreal and the second probable, but one had to be prepared for the third.

The Neo Lao Haksat and Hanoi generally shared Peking's appraisal.

Souphanouvong's Plea

The new Soviet ambassador to Laos, Sergei A. Afanassiev, who arrived in Vientiane in October 1962, told me of a conversation Souphanouvong had had with Khrushchev before he returned to Laos after medical treatment in the Soviet Union. Pointing to the Geneva agreements, Khrushchev expressed doubt that the United States would renew fighting in Laos. He therefore saw no reason for a reinforcement of the Neo Lao Haksat positions. The main task was political, and though Souvanna Phouma was ideologically remote from the Neo Lao Haksat, it should be possible to cooperate with him; the problem was to find ways to win him over. As an example of positive development in Southeast Asia Khrushchev mentioned Burma.

Souphanouvong was not convinced. He saw in Souvanna's conduct a growing lean to the West and the Right and a visible anticommunist emphasis. In this situation, backed by the United States, the conservative camp might attempt to regain lost positions by force. Renewed fighting was not impossible, and the Neo Lao Haksat therefore had to consolidate and strengthen their forces.

Khrushchev and Souphanouvong obviously spoke from different perspectives. The Neo Lao Haksat's experience did not create confidence in its foe's protestations. The Vientiane setup was far from stable, and from South Vietnam they felt the heat of war. Together with Hanoi, Neo Lao Haksat leaders developed their own contingency plans. Thus, after the assassination of Quinim Pholsena in April 1963, when the government of national union was virtually wrecked, they were able to fall back on their traditional bases in the countryside, in the mountains and villages of eastern and northern Laos.

Thus the Geneva agreements brought only a short lull to the fighting in Laos. The focus of the Indochina conflict moved to South Vietnam, and the issues of peace and war became dependent on battles there. This was clearly foreseen in Geneva. During the last days of the conference, Soviet Deputy Foreign Minister G. M. Pushkin tried to convince Harriman that the time was ripe for negotiations on South Vietnam, suggesting that a third force, similar to that in Laos, was emerging in Saigon. Harriman gave no concrete answer, but when taking leave of Pushkin he expressed the hope that they would meet again at a conference on South Vietnam. The Chinese Deputy Premier and Foreign Minister, Chen Yi, in his concluding remarks stated that "so long as the flames of war are kept alive in Southern Vietnam, peace in Laos cannot be regarded as consolidated." Hoping for negotiations, Chen Yi invited Harriman to visit Peking. Harriman promised to think it over and discuss it in Washington; but the invitation was not accepted. Instead, the answer was an upsurge of fighting in South Vietnam. The struggle in Laos in 1961–62 served only as a prelude to the Second Indochinese War.

Chapter 15

Concluding Remarks

Historical Context and Perspective

The two Indochina wars—the first conducted by France and the second by the United States—occupy a unique place in contemporary history. They correlate closely with the evolution of international relations after World War II and they can serve to bring into focus the main currents of political and social change in the last twenty-five years. They intertwined with the anticolonial revolution, the awakening of Asia and Africa, and the expansion of socialism. They have played a key role in East-West relations, as well as in the rift between the Soviet Union and the People's Republic of China, and in the decline of the Western alliance. They have shaped relations within the crucial power triangle consisting of the United States, the Soviet Union and China. Finally, they have compelled many nations—including the mighty United States—to undergo agonizing self-appraisals and to turn inward in search of new values. The Indochina wars have reflected the main trends, interactions and clashes on the East-West and North-South axes, as well as the turmoil of an age led astray by ideological fixation and the lure of technology.

To understand Indochina is also to understand the rhythm of contemporary history. Since so many Indochinese variables are embedded in and seem to affect current international relations, an understanding of the dynamics of the Indochinese situation is essential not only for an accurate appraisal of the past, but also for the shaping of a better future.

From a simple colonial contest in the aftermath of World War II, the Indochinese conflict developed into a crucial struggle among the great powers. What might be called the inner circle of the conflict revolved around issues of national liberation and independence; the outer circle involved great-power interests which acquired paramount importance in the course of events. Outside interference, in fact, kept the conflict alive. The infusion of cold war dogma and ideological rationalizations increased tensions immensely. Projected onto ideological ground, great-power rivalries sharpened and expanded. In the meantime, ideology blurred the image of reality. Muddling up ideology with great-power interests served to conceal the real issues, and added fuel to the fire. Solutions became more and more difficult to reach. Transformed into a clash among the three dominant world powers —each with conflicting interests, different strategies and immense resources—the conflict escalated continuously.

U.S. involvement in Indochina was rooted in an ideological misreading of postwar Asian realities. The Chinese revolution was seen as a creation of the Soviet Union, and the national liberation movements in Vietnam and Laos as projects of Moscow and Peking. John Foster Dulles approached the conflict as an exercise in brinkmanship, playing with the idea of "rolling back" the Chinese revolution through the Indochinese gates. His "moving north" strategy, however, became stuck in the mud of conservative, backward regimes in Saigon and Vientiane. At the same time, after the Korean experience, military leaders in Washington started to doubt the wisdom of involvement in a war on the Asian mainland. Under the slogan "never again," they resisted the prospect of getting bogged down "in a wrong war, at the wrong place and against a wrong enemy." This coincided with a recession of the cold war in the mid-fifties, after the 1954 Dien Bien Phu fever of "united action" in Indochina had subsided. But politically matters were kept on the boil. The residual preservation after the 1954 Geneva conference of South Vietnamese and Laotian bridgeheads hardened into a vested interest of U.S. policy; out of this came the pernicious fascination with "nation-building" and counterinsurgency.

The Kennedy administration inherited the Indochina commitment at a critical juncture in Soviet-Chinese relations: the faltering of the seemingly monolithic structure of the socialist camp. A timely recognition of this important new development might have opened the way to a dogma-free diplomacy which might have reached far beyond Indochina. These developments were not completely unexpected. Signs of ferment in the socialist world had come as early as the beginning of the cold war itself with the breakaway of Yugoslavia. However, not only the politicians but also the scholarly high priests at the White House were unable to see through the fog of cold war theology. They were still haunted by the specter of world communist conquest and—as the Bay of Pigs adventure indicated—the Kennedy administration continued to see as its mission the export of counterrevolution. Khrushchev's January 1961 speech on the dispute with China was completely misread; the whole political constellation in and around Indochina appeared as in a distorting mirror. Deluded by the liturgy of wars of national liberation, the White House mobilized for a fateful contest, which made both the inner and outer circles of the Indochina conflict turn rapidly toward "the top of the ladder of escalation." The United States' pursuit of a military victory in Indochina became Sisyphean effort. The only possibility for settlement lay in the political realm—both in the inner and outer circles of the conflict.

The Inner and Outer Circles

Such were the circumstances leading up to the Laotian conflict—the prelude to the Second Indochina War. Renewed pressures in the inner circle—in Laos and South Vietnam—were incorrectly taken in Washington as symptoms of outer-circle dynamics, of a new offensive by a united socialist camp. Acting on an imagined threat of expansion on the part of the Soviet Union and China, the U.S. became embroiled—despite careful planning and against all calculations—in the longest military conflict in its history. The Vietnamese and Laotians, acting independently and on purely nationalistic grounds, made the decision to resist U.S. interference. Neither the Soviet Union nor China was fully consulted. Events followed the pattern of the First Indochina War when, for reasons rooted in European policies, in 1946 the Soviet Union opposed waging war against France. In the early sixties the Soviet Union objected even more strongly to a military entanglement with the United States, and China seemed reluctant to repeat the Korean experience. But the Vietnamese and Laotians were concerned above all with their own national problems. They were not inclined to consider carefully enough the great power interests, and misjudged both the determination of the United States to proceed with military intervention and the readiness of the socialist countries to extend unlimited aid.

It now seems clear that Vietnamese and Laotian leaders did not expect the United States to move so deeply into a war on the Asian mainland. Nor did they foresee that the conflict, instead of uniting socialist ranks, would intensify the Soviet-Chinese discord. Thus they were dismayed both by the abrupt cessation of Soviet military aid in 1962 and by the subsequent cleavage between Moscow and Peking. In the meantime the deepening Soviet-Chinese rift encouraged the United States to escalate hostilities. The Soviet Union was finally obliged in 1965 to resume large-scale military aid to Vietnam; China became closely tied to the progress of the war; and the United States got trapped in the selfish interests of entrenched Saigon mandarins and generals. Thus set in motion, the conflict quickly escalated, with the inner circle frequently turning the wheel of the outer circle.

Thus has Indochina come to underline the ominous potentialities inherent in great-power triangular relationships, as well as the potentialities of local conflicts propelled by the great powers. To a far larger degree than anticipated, the inner circle of local concerns and national feelings is able to command great-power behavior. This is true not only of the independent-minded local actor, as in the Vietnamese and Laotian national movements, but also in the case of clear-cut imperialist/client relationships. The Nam Tha episode serves as a good example.

Contributing to the confusion were failures to differentiate clearly between the inner and outer circles. Washington often failed to discern the true actors and to take discriminating action. Throughout the conflict it operated on the assumption that it was fighting China and the Soviet Union rather than the Vietnamese and Laotian national movements. On the other hand, moves launched independently by the local actors tended ultimately to restrict the freedom of their great-power allies. In the process, misjudgments on both sides of the front contributed to acceleration of the conflict.

The Triangle

The Indochina conflict revealed the depth of U.S.-Soviet-Chinese rivalries. To illustrate the dynamics of this triangular relationship, it is worth briefly reconstructing the hawkish balance sheets of each of the powers, and pondering their appeal. The United States stopped escalation short of all-out war; China did not intervene directly, despite provocation; and the Soviet Union did not introduce offensive weapons which might have critically changed the nature of the fighting. Still, the process strengthened hawkish sentiments in all three capitals. How near was the U.S. to the use of tactical or even strategic nuclear weapons? How close were the Vietnamese to issuing a direct call for help from the Chinese? How strong were the elements that could have transformed the conflict into a world conflagration?

The United States, of course, was the boldest of the three. The Indochina engagement found support in five consecutive administrations. Part of this support grew out of ideological obfuscation, part out of interests developed by the military-industrial complex, part from the ambitions of a powerful military establishment. The hawks always knew enough to present a highly optimistic picture of the benefits to be derived from the conflict. The Indochinese engagement, it was argued, did more to halt the advance of communist and radical movements than any other strategy. It had a beneficial influence in Asia: it proved to be effective in containing China; it reassured U.S. allies, strengthened their economies, and bought time to consolidate the "falling dominoes." Concretely, it brought about an encouraging change in Indonesia and was instrumental in toppling neutralist Sihanouk in Cambodia; above all, it deepened the contradictions between Moscow and Peking, resulting in a decline of communism all over the world. Militarily, though not crowned by victory, it gave the United States a unique opportunity to get acquainted with people's war strategy and to master counterinsurgency—key weapons against contemporary revolutionary movements. Some went even further and insisted on continuing the struggle for, according to many hawks, a military solution was essential not only to secure the dominance of Western-oriented regimes in the strategically vulnerable area of Southeast Asia, but also to safeguard U.S. interests in Asia and in the worldwide political confrontation with socialist powers and revolutionary movements.

Though fearing a war on its borders, Peking mustered its own reasons for encouraging prolongation of the conflict. The Indochina struggle proved to be the best way to wear down U.S. political and military strength, to weaken the United States both externally and internally. Continuation of the conflict spelled further military and political humiliation for the United States, opening prospects for a dislodgement of American forces from the Asian mainland. At the same time Indochina impeded the U.S.-Soviet dialogue, enfeebled the Western alliance, and enhanced anti-American sentiment all over the world. Continuation of the struggle helped China gain precious time to strengthen her own defenses. In fact, Vietnam and Laos served as superb experimental ranges for testing and mastering the strategies of protracted war—which Chinese leaders envisaged as the most effective defense against a superior enemy. Finally, Peking might also have nurtured hope that an arduous Indochina experience would turn the United States away from its borders, saving it from an otherwise unavoidable confrontation with a formidable foe.

The Soviet Union, least directly endangered by the Indochina war, could have had its own interest in the perpetuation of the conflict. Moscow could only be pleased by continuing U.S. military and political defeats in Indochina. The conflict exacerbated U.S.-China relations and eased Chinese pressures on the Soviet-Chinese border. China naturally would not fight a war on two fronts, and therefore had to ease up on claims against the Soviet Union. On the other hand, U.S. preoccupation with Indochina opened new opportunities for Soviet military, political and diplomatic ventures in Europe, the Middle East and Asia. Militarily Moscow could only have welcomed the opportunity to test in Indochina some of its more sophisticated conventional weapons, especially antiaircraft defenses. Finally, Soviet assistance to Vietnam served to enhance Moscow's image in the Third World and in leftist Western circles, impaired by the rift with China and such moves as the occupation of Czechoslovakia.

These hawkish accounts could be extended into much greater detail. Read separately they appear to be valid strategies for power-hungry empires; when weighed against each other they tend to pale, and bring into relief the dynamics of conflict perpetuation. We may draw comfort from the fact that the Indochina conflict did not develop to its logical end, escalating into a world conflagration; but the perils, still imminent, cannot be ignored. The trends and correlations revealed in Indochina may continue into the future.

Certain power constellations tend to reveal particular dynamics. Surrounded by conflict areas and by other powers competing to acquire strength, the U.S.-Soviet-China triangle weighs heavily on central world issues of war and peace. At the beginning of the seventies this triangle seems to resemble the triangle that dominated European politics just prior to World War II: the Soviet Union, the Western powers, and Nazi Germany. Negotiations then went on along all the legs of the triangle, each power pair competing to channel war toward the third corner. War finally broke out in the least expected corner.

The World Security Imbalance

The Indochinese conflict has brought into sharp focus the security imbalance inherent in contemporary world politics. In recent decades traditional great-power rivalries have been tremendously invigorated by many new socio-political and behavioral phenomena engendered both by the technological revolution and ideological intoxication. Fascination with power, mixed with doctrinaire dogmatism, has proved highly explosive. It has produced on the one hand a distorted perception of world realities, and on the other a zeal and self-confidence in action which far exceed real knowledge and information. Violence has seemed both expedient and justified.

Naturally such a state of mind in a divided world has increased the communication gap between adherents of different political religions. Ideological semantics have created walls difficult to cross; ideological fanaticism has tended to undermine morals and international law. The patterns developed around the 1954 and 1962 Geneva agreements are a case in point: power elites, separated from the people but animated by missionary fervor, found it easy to deceive both domestic and international opinion, and diplomatic cheating at the conference table continued in "hanky-panky" violations of the agreements the day after their conclusion. The balance between means and ends became profoundly unsettled. In international relations reason, decency and humaneness were displaced by the arrogance of power and a cynical success-failure syndrome. The human aspect of the struggle was lost from sight, dislodged by a pursuit of victory by any means. Only in failure did soul-searching begin.

The Indochina contest presented a clash between the rich and the poor, the haves and the have-nots; between nations equipped with high technology and nations at the start of their industrial development. The Vietnamese and Laotian national movements were able to stand up to France and the United States to a considerable extent as a result of outside aid, but it was their human qualities and spiritual strength which were the decisive factors. Man and tenacity proved superior to technology and firepower. Bewildered by obsolete power conceptions, the United States and its allies failed to take into consideration the element of human motivation, of energies liberated by social and national awakening. They underestimated revolutionary potential and determination, as well as the readiness to sacrifice when life in oppression becomes unbearable. Indochina may serve as a warning against the continuation of the structural gap between the wealthy and the poor and hungry.

The Indochina conflict has had a highly destructive influence on international relations, becoming a major barrier to peace and understanding—no major international issue can possibly be solved before the end of this war. However, although loss of life, human suffering and destruction reached levels seldom seen in the history of warfare, the bitter experience of this generation-long conflict, if rightly appraised and reconsidered, could serve as a stepping stone along the path toward a new point in human relations.

Notes

Chapter 1 **Background on Laos**
1. *The New York Times,* March 24, 1961.
2. Dwight D. Eisenhower, *Waging Peace 1956–1961* (New York: Doubleday & Co., 1965), pp. 609–10.
3. *The New York Times,* March 24, 1961.
4. Theodore C. Sorensen, *Kennedy* (London: Hodder and Stoughton, 1965), p. 643.
5. Arthur M. Schlesinger, *A Thousand Days* (London: André Deutsch, 1965), p. 306.

Chapter 2 **Moscow, Washington, and Peking**
1. Roger Hilsman, *To Move a Nation* (New York: Dell Publishing Co., 1967), p. 414.
2. Charles de Gaulle, *Mémoires d'Espoir, Le renouveau 1958–1962* (Paris: Librairie Plon, 1970), p. 268.
3. *Department of State Bulletin,* April 13, 1964, pp. 564–70. Reprinted in *Background Information Relating to Southeast Asia and Vietnam,* 2nd revised ed., Committee on Foreign Relations, U.S. Senate (Washington, D.C.: U.S. Government Printing Office, March 1966), pp. 119–20.

Chapter 3 **Lost Opportunities**
1. Anthony Eden, *Full Circle* (London: Cassel, 1960), p. 113.
2. Quoted from a speech given May 13, 1965, before the Dallas Council on World Affairs.
3. Quoted from a speech given before the Overseas Press Club, New York City, on March 29, 1954.
4. Dwight D. Eisenhower, *Mandate for Change 1953–1956* (New York: Doubleday & Company, 1963), pp. 346–47.

5. *Ibid.,* p. 354.
6. Eden, *op. cit.,* pp. 112–13.
7. Jean Chauvel, "La conférence de Genève sur l'Indochine et la conjuncture actuelle," *Politique Étrangère,* Vol. 35 (1970), no. 4, p. 364.
8. Testimony by Lieutenant General James M. Gavin before the Committee on Foreign Relations, U.S. Senate, 91st Congress, 2nd Session, May 12, 1970 (Washington, D.C.: U.S. Government Printing Office, 1970), pp. 55–57. See also James M. Gavin, *Crisis Now* (New York: Vintage Books, 1968), pp. 46–50.
9. Eden, *op. cit.,* p. 139.
10. Eisenhower, *Mandate for Change,* p. 370.
11. Jean Lacouture and Philippe Devillers, *La fin d'une Guerre: Indochine 1954* (Paris: Editions du Seuil, 1960), p. 245. This footnote was omitted in the English edition.
12. *Ibid.,* pp. 344–45; and Eden, *op. cit.,* pp. 132–33.
13. Eden, *op. cit.,* p. 132.
14. *Third Interim Report on the Activities of the International Commission for Supervision and Control in Laos, July 1, 1955–May 16, 1957* (New Delhi: Government of India Press, 1958), pp. 74–75.
15. *Lao Presse,* April 25, 1957, p. C.
16. *Ibid.,* pp. D, E; and *Department of State Bulletin,* May 13, 1957, pp. 771–72.
17. *U.S. Reaffirms Support of Laotian Government,* mimeographed statement, April 25, 1957, p. 2.
18. *Third Interim Report,* pp. 10–11.
19. Hilsman, *op. cit.,* pp. 111–12.

Chapter 6 **Souvanna Phouma's Enigmatic Roles**
1. *The New York Times,* January 20, 1961.
2. Hilsman, *op. cit.,* p. 125.
3. Schlesinger, *op. cit.,* p. 303.

Chapter 7 **The Red Prince and His Guard**
1. See map in Lacouture and Devillers, *op. cit.,* p. 278.
2. Sisouk Na Champassak, *Tempête sur le Laos* (Paris: La Table Ronde, 1961), p. 102. My translation—M.T.

3. *Ibid.*, p. 205.

4. *Le peuple du Pathet Lao lutte pour la paix, l'indépendance, l'unité et la démocratie,* Service d'Information du Gouvernement de la Résistance du Pathet Lao, 1954, pp. 25–26.

5. Decornoy's articles appeared in *Le Monde,* July 3–8, 1968. They were reprinted in Nina S. Adams and Alfred W. McCoy, eds., *Laos: War and Revolution* (New York: Harper and Row, 1970), pp. 411–423.

Chapter 8   **The Political-Military Tangle**

1. Bernard B. Fall, "Reappraisal in Laos," *Current History* (January 1962), p. 10.

Chapter 10   **Politics in Vientiane**

1. Schlesinger, *op. cit.,* p. 305.

2. Appendix to ICSC report of November 2, 1961.

Chapter 11   **General Taylor's Presidential Review**

1. Sorensen, *op. cit.,* p. 653.

2. Schlesinger, *op. cit.,* p. 474.

3. *Ibid.,* pp. 474–75.

4. Hilsman, *op. cit.,* p. 42.

5. *Ibid.,* p. 422.

6. Schlesinger, *op. cit.,* p. 474.

7. Hilsman, *op. cit.,* p. 439.

8. Schlesinger, *op. cit.,* p. 475.

9. *Ibid.,* p. 476.

10. Hilsman, *op. cit.,* p. 424.

11. ICSC report of November 11, 1961, appendix.

12. ICSC report to the Co-chairmen No. 15, December 15, 1961.

13. ICSC report to the Co-chairmen No. 16, January 1, 1962, appendix.

Chapter 12   **The Enlistment of Thailand**

1. Hilsman, *op. cit.,* p. 124.

2. ICSC report No. 17, March 8, 1962.

3. *Ibid.*

4. ICSC report No. 18, June 2, 1962.

5. *Bangkok World,* April 1, 1962.

6. Hilsman, *op. cit.,* p. 139.

7. *Ibid.,* p. 139.

8. *Bangkok World,* April 1, 1962.

9. ICSC report No. 18, June 2, 1962, appendix.

10. Hilsman, *op. cit.,* pp. 141–42.

11. *Ibid.,* p. 314.

12. Sorensen, *op. cit.,* p. 647.

13. Statement made November 10, 1969, before the Committee on Foreign Relations Subcommittee on U.S. Security Agreements and Commitments Abroad.

14. ICSC report No. 18, June 2, 1962.

Chapter 13 **The Geneva Pattern**

1. Hilsman, *op. cit.,* pp. 147, 149.

2. *Ibid.*

3. *Ibid.,* pp. 149–50.

4. *Ibid.,* p. 150.

5. *Ibid.,* p. 153.

6. Arthur Lall, *How Communist China Negotiates* (New York: Columbia University Press, 1968), p. 180.

7. Secret minutes of Souvanna Phouma's talks with Kennedy.

Chapter 14 **The Screen of Neutrality**

1. Hilsman, *op. cit.,* p. 580.

2. International Conference on the Settlement of the Laotian Question, LAOS/DOC/4.

3. LAOS/DOC/7

4. See Indian draft, LAOS/DOC/23, submitted July 13, 1961.

5. LAOS/DOC/5.

6. LAOS/DOC/11.

7. LAOS/DOC/17 rev. 1.

8. LAOS/DOC/24.

9. ICSC report No. 20, October 22, 1962.

10. *Ibid.*

11. Hilsman, *op. cit.,* pp. 151–52.

12. Arthur J. Dommen, *Conflict in Laos* (New York, F. A. Praeger, 1967), p. 238.

13. Schlesinger, *op. cit.,* p. 453.

14. Excerpts of this letter were published in the 1969 Symington Senate hearings.

Appendix 1

Note on
the Pentagon Study

The Pentagon study, with its attached documentation, occupies a unique place in the historical examination of the Indochina conflict.[1] Both because of the analysis and the wealth of materials it contains, it is essential to any contemporary study on Indochina.

The story presented by the Pentagon analysts is in many ways uneven. Different chapters reflect differing approaches according to the individual author and materials available. As a whole, the emphasis is on military planning rather than the political process. That the study was carried out in the Department of Defense with no access to White House files and only limited availability of State Department cables and memoranda is reflected in its contents. The analysts' inward orientation lead them to largely disregard the many local and global actors in the conflict.

Laos is treated as a whole very marginally, perhaps in strict accord with the study's title: "United States–Vietnam Relations." But this makes the dynamics of the U.S. Indochina involvement less clear. The authors themselves admit that U.S. engagement in Vietnam during the Kennedy administration was largely conditioned by events in Laos. In his "Summary and Analysis" of the "Kennedy Commitments and Programs, 1961," Leslie H. Gelb, chairman of the study's task force, emphasizes that in spring 1961 "the changed policy [toward Vietnam] and the somewhat enlarged aid program that accompanied it, reflected the pressures created by the situation in neighbouring Laos."[2] Further: "There is a strong case to be made that even the Fall, post-Taylor Mission, decisions were essentially dominated by the impact of Laos. But in May

[1961] the situation was unambiguous. Laos, not anything happening in Vietnam, was the driving force."³

This judgment is repeated by the analyst: "Vietnam in 1961 was a peripheral crisis. Even within Southeast Asia it received far less of the Administration's and the world's attention than did Laos. The *New York Times Index* for 1961 has eight columns on Vietnam, twenty-six on Laos. Decisions about Vietnam were greatly influenced by what was happening elsewhere."⁴ U.S. contingency planning in 1961 for sending troops to South Vietnam went under the heading of "Laos Annex."⁵

It is disappointing, then, to find Laotian political developments receiving so little attention in the study. The whole background of the Laotian situation, including events between 1945 and 1962, is presented in two pages in a chapter on "Hanoi and the Insurgency in South Vietnam," subtitled "DRV Intervention in Laos."⁶ Based on intelligence and secondhand anticommunist sources, the story is tendentious, inaccurate and highly sketchy. In the chapter on Kennedy's commitments, "The Situation in Laos" is dealt with in a half-page discussion on the "peculiar problem of Laos, where the Western position was in the process of falling apart as Kennedy took office," concluding with a remark that "throughout 1961, we find the effects of the Laos situation spilling over onto Vietnam."⁷

The net result of overlooking Laotian political events is a reduced understanding of both the national and socio-political issues in Indochina, and of the developments which brought the United States to war. This omission has an essential bearing on the study's vague assessment of the Kennedy administration's role in Indochina.

Another deficiency of the Pentagon study concerns the erroneous notion of coordinated Hanoi-Moscow-Peking action in Indochina and the uncritical repetition of Kennedy's mistaken interpretation of Khrushchev's January 6, 1961, speech on "wars of national liberation" (Cf. my analysis on pages 19–27). But taking Kennedy's interpretation for granted, the study confirms the role Khrushchev's speech played in expanding U.S. commitments in Indochina.

The study contains two main references to the speech.

The first reference, in the concluding part of the chapter dealing with the Eisenhower commitments, stresses that "Khrushchev's remarks . . . shocked the President of the United States, John F. Kennedy." Citing from Schlesinger's *A Thousand Days,* the study recalls that Kennedy "took it as an authoritative exposition of Soviet intentions, discussed it with his staff, and read excerpts from it aloud to the National Security Council." It adds: "The President and his principal cabinet officers returned to this speech again and again in their explanations of Administration policy." The Pentagon author then offers a short analysis that upholds the Kennedy judgment, especially confusing Khrushchev's remarks on "the armed struggle of the Vietnamese people" against the French with the developing insurgency in South Vietnam.[8]

The second reference, at the beginning of the chapter dealing with Kennedy commitments, is included in a subsection entitled "Problems With the Soviets." It reads: "The new Administration, even before taking office, was inclined to believe that unconventional warfare was likely to be terrifically important in the 1960's. In January 1961, Khrushchev seconded that view with his speech pledging Soviet support to 'wars of national liberation.' Vietnam was where such war was actually going on. Indeed, since the war in Laos had moved far beyond the insurgency stage, Vietnam was the only place in the world where the Administration faced a well-developed Communist effort to topple a pro-Western government with an externally aided pro-communist insurgency. It was a challenge that could hardly be ignored."[9]

The study thus fully sustains Kennedy's misreading of Khrushchev's speech, perceiving the Soviet Union willing and ready, in a common effort with other communist countries, to confront the United States in Indochina. By contrasting the Laotian and Vietnamese scenes, the analyst reveals little understanding of Indochinese dynamics.

More important, the study reflects a mistaken perception of the roles played by the Soviet Union and China. Throughout, the study's dominant concern is with "Communist expansion" perceived as part of an international great-power contest. Even in cases where a distinction is made between the interests of Hanoi, Moscow and Peking, the final judgment leans to coordinated communist bloc strategy. Referring to the growing insurgency in South

Vietnam at the end of the fifties, the Pentagon analyst notes: "Whatever differences in strategy may have existed among Moscow, Peking and Hanoi, it appears that at each critical juncture Hanoi obtained concurrence in Moscow with an aggressive course of action."[10] This judgment follows official U.S. thinking. A National Intelligence Estimate dated October 5, 1961, on "Bloc Support of the Communist Effort Against the Government of Vietnam" stated: "Hanoi is the implementing agency for Bloc activity in South Vietnam, and the Hanoi authorities are allowed considerable local freedom in conducting Viet Cong guerrilla and subversive campaigns in Laos and South Vietnam as two points of a single broad political-military strategy."[11]

Despite deficiencies, however, the study allows deeper insight into many aspects of the Indochina conflict. It contains particularly valuable material on the crucial period of the 1954 Geneva conference, confirming strong U.S. opposition to a negotiated settlement, and persistent efforts to retain a military and political foothold in Indochina. The Geneva agreements themselves, in contrast to U.S. public protestations, were declared by the National Security Council "a major disaster for U.S. interests,"[12] and post-Geneva planning concentrated on foiling the implementation of their provisions. One of the Pentagon analysts concludes that the United States assumed "a direct role in the ultimate breakdown of the Geneva settlement."[13] The study, however, is silent on the 1954–1955 military plan to attack North Vietnam, as it has been revealed by Lieutenant General James M. Gavin.* Yet a State Department internal memo on the unilateral U.S. Geneva declaration records that "Dulles rejected the idea of American participation in a guarantee of the settlement because, as he put it, this would commit the United States to sustaining Communist domination of territory." In parentheses the statement adds that "this was presumably a reference to the Republican goal of 'liberating' the captive nations"—an allusion to the "roll-back" strategy.[14]

The documentation contain new details of the behind-the-scenes Western negotiations during the 1954 Geneva conference, the se-

*Some reference to this problem may perhaps have been included in a six-page chapter of the study deleted from the part devoted to the evolution and planning of SEATO. Book 1, IV.A.3, pp. 26–31.

cret Paris agreement before the conclusion of the Geneva accords,
and its implementation after Geneva (cf. my account on pages
34–40). The analyst quotes the June 30, 1954, seven-point "unpub-
licized agreement" between Churchill and Eisenhower, and traces
the way to the July 14, 1954, Anglo-American-French understanding.[15]

The documentation is revealing. In a personal message to French
Prime Minister Mendès-France dated July 10, 1954, Secretary of
State Dulles appealed to preserve "the united front of France,
Great Britain and the United States" which demands "a clear
agreement on joint position" based on the U.S.-British "seven-
point memorandum." He then outlines the seven points as a rejection of the neutralization of Laos, Cambodia and Vietnam; a
refusal to accept elections "so early and so ill-prepared and ill-
supervised as to risk the loss of the entire area to Communism";
and a decision to "pursue successfully" the struggle against Communism.[16] Responding to this message, Mendès-France assured
U.S. Ambassador Dillon that "France would not accept anything
at Conference that was unacceptable to United States."[17] In the
meantime, as stated in a July 13 memorandum by the Assistant
Secretary of Defense, the United States discussed the formation of
SEATO with the British and insisted that "the organization be
established immediately in order that we will be in a position to
deal with the probable adverse political and military repercussions
in the Associated States [Vietnam, Laos, Cambodia] that will result
from an unsatisfactory settlement of the Indochina conflict."[18]

A July 14, 1954, message from Paris contained in the documentation shows the texts of the tripartite agreement.* It consisted of
a six-point "Agreed French-United States Position Paper on Indochina," an addendum reproducing the seven-point U.S.-British
understanding, an exchange of letters between Mendès-France and
Dulles, and a letter to Mendès-France from British Foreign Secretary Anthony Eden. All these documents remained secret. The
core of the agreement rested on the seven-point Washington understanding. The French-U.S. position paper records: (1) that "the

*Part of the texts are deleted from the U.S. government edition of the
Pentagon study. Full texts are reproduced in the Senator Gravel edition
of *The Pentagon Papers* (Boston: Beacon Press, 1971), Vol. I, pp. 554–
557.

United States will not be asked or expected by France to respect terms which in its opinion differ materially" from the seven-point understanding; (2) that "the United States is prepared to seek, with other interested nations, a collective defense association designed to preserve, against direct and indirect aggression, the integrity of the non-Communist areas of Southeast Asia following any settlement"; and (3) "If there is no settlement, the United States and French Governments will consult together on the measures to be taken."

The Mendès-France–Dulles exchange sets forth the conditions for a U.S. return to the Geneva negotiating table. Mendès-France acknowledged that the United States is "not prepared to participate with the Communist countries in any settlement which might appear to retain for them the benefits of aggression or the domination of non-willing peoples," and emphasized that "only the unity of the Western democratic front, supported by the immense potential which we have in common, can bring about the very military and strategic unity which we should seek eventually to establish in that part of the world." Dulles replied by stressing that "in the light of what you say and after consultations with President Eisenhower, I am glad to be able to inform you that the President and I are asking the Undersecretary of State, General Walter Bedell Smith, to prepare to return at his earliest convenience to Geneva to share in the work of the conference on the basis of the understanding which we have arrived at." Finally, Eden in his letter to Mendès-France, with a copy to Dulles, took note of the agreement reached, pledging "to do my best to help you to achieve a settlement on the basis set out in this correspondence."*

*In a letter to the French journal *Démocratie Nouvelle* published in the January 1968 issue, together with my article on the "Secret Negotiations on Indochina Preceding the Geneva Agreements," Mendès-France tried to deny that a secret Western understanding was concluded on July 14, 1954 in Paris. In his letter Mendès-France stated: "I affirm that on this occasion [the July 14 Anglo-American–French meeting in Paris] no secret agreement between the said three governments was concluded. The only common document which was drawn up and edited was the communiqué to the press." In a sense, keeping to the diplomatic language, this was formally true: there was no common tripartite document, the secret agreement consisted of bilateral documents supplemented by a tripartite exchange of letters.

Following the Paris agreement, the Western delegations in Geneva kept in close contact, trying as much as possible to introduce elements of the "seven points" into the final settlement. They consciously labored to make the accords less precise and full of legalistic loopholes. In one of the messages sent to Washington from Geneva, dated July 16, U.S. representative Alexis Johnson reports that he called the attention of French representative Chauvel to "paragraph 3 of position paper on Indochina agreed in Paris" which dealt with the diplomatic formula (nonuse of force according to Articles 2, 4 and 5 of the UN Charter) the United States was prepared to use in expressing its "respect" for a settlement. Chauvel replied that "in light of paragraph 3 of position paper, French draft provided only for conference 'noting' armistice agreement."[19] "Noting" the armistice agreements, the formula in fact used in the Final Declaration of the Geneva conference, seems then to have been interpreted by the West as legally less binding.

Thus, Leslie H. Gelb and his analyst found it possible to conclude that "as matters turned out at the conference, the final terms of the settlement came close to meeting seven Anglo-American conditions."[20] This, however, was not Washington's understanding; the Geneva accords were judged a "disaster." The United States worked hard to break up the agreements; although France was certainly not eager to cede Indochina to the U.S. military, it finally gave in to U.S. pressures. Ultimately, the Paris agreements prevailed.

In his summary of the post-Geneva developments, Leslie H. Gelb writes:

The policy of the United States was initially directed toward a partnership with France, a joint sponsorship of Diem . . . Almost at once, however, U.S. policy began to respond to military urgency, and this in turn caused the U.S. to move beyond partnership to primacy . . . In late September 1954, the U.S. cut out the French as middle-men in all its assistance for Vietnam, and began to deal directly with Diem, his government and his armed forces . . . [On December 13, 1954] General Collins [ambassador on Special Mission in South

Vietnam] struck an agreement with General Ely [French High Commissioner] in Vietnam by which, despite serious misgivings in Paris, France agreed to turn over the training of the Vietnamese army to the U. S. and to withdraw French cadres . . . On February 12, 1955, the U.S. assumed responsibility for training Vietnamese forces, and the French disassociation began . . . In May 1955, France, the U.S. and Britain met in Paris . . . Secretary Dulles then proposed to the French that they continue to support Diem until a national assembly were elected. British support for Diem seems to have swayed Faure [the French Prime Minister], and he accepted Dulles' proposal. The tripartite meeting ended on a note of harmony, but the undertones were distinct: the days of joint U.S.-French policy were over; thereafter, the U.S. would act independently of France in Vietnam.[21]

The documents contain more detail. Following the establishment of SEATO on September 8, 1954, a French-U.S. conference convened in Washington in late September agreed to "support Diem in establishment and maintenance of a strong, anti-Communist nationalist Government."[22] This meant either a permanent partition of Vietnam or the conquest of the whole country by Diem. Then, on December 13, 1954, came the Collins-Ely agreement "on development and training of autonomous Vietnam armed forces" which transferred to General O'Daniel, the Chief of the U.S. Military Assistance Advisory Group (MAAG) in Saigon, "full responsibility for training under Ely's broad direction" of Diem's troops.[23] The text of this secret agreement is not included, but the very fact that Collins, as mentioned in the messages to Washington, refused to "accept any references to the Geneva accord," and that the final text was "based on our [U.S.] draft" may serve as evidence that the authors were well aware that they acted in violation of the accord.

The strategy was well designed. A month after the conclusion of the Geneva accords, on August 20, 1954, the National Security Council in a Statement of Policy (NSC 5429/2) decided that the U.S. should:

make every possible effort, not openly inconsistent with the
U.S. position as to the armistice agreements, to defeat Communist subversion and influence, to maintain and support
friendly non-Communist Governments in Cambodia and
Laos, to maintain a friendly non-Communist South Vietnam,
and to prevent a Communist victory through all-Vietnam
elections . . . Working through the French only insofar as
necessary, assist Cambodia, Laos and free Vietnam to maintain (1) military forces necessary for internal security and (2)
economic conditions conducive to the maintenance and
strength of non-Communist regimes . . . Conduct covert operations on a large and effective scale in support of the foregoing
policies.[24]

In a nutshell this was a restatement of the seven-point Washington and Paris agreements, with additional directives concerning
implementation. An artful device was used to foil the all-Vietnam
elections. On April 6, 1955, in a message to Saigon and Paris,
Dulles outlined his tactics:

We have been working on problem of election in Viet-Nam,
in great detail . . . We feel best solution is for us be in position
inform French [and] British our views prior [U.S.-French]
talks and believe it best we can put such forward as support
of policy of Free Viet-Nam rather than as unilateral U.S.
recommendations . . . The basic principle is that Free Viet-
Nam will insist to the Viet Minh that unless agreement is first
reached by the latter's acceptance of the safeguards spelled
out, that no further discussions are possible regarding the
type of elections, the issues to be voted or any other factors.
After we have Diem's general acceptance we can proceed
inform UK and France of this plan . . .[25]

Policy recommendations of the Department of Defense dated
April 13, 1955, put the problem bluntly: "Make every effort to
abolish or postpone indefinitely the election proposed for Viet-
Nam, under the Geneva Accords, for July 1956."[26] The previously

accepted thesis that the initiative was in Diem's hands appears as another historical myth. In fact, both France and Great Britain played the role assigned them in Dulles' scenario.

The Pentagon study contains some scattered documents which shed light on the developments in Laos that lead to the crisis at the end of the fifties. An August 12, 1959, Operations Coordinating Board Report on Southeast Asia prepared for the National Security Council recorded:

> Progress has been made in furthering United States objectives in Laos, particularly with reference to the strengthening of Lao political leadership, the improvement of Lao relations with other Southeast Asia countries, and in providing for the training of the Lao National Army. Since the grant of special powers in January to a new cabinet [of Phoui Sananikone], there are indications that the prestige and morale of the Communist Neo Lao Hak Xat have deteriorated, while those of the non-communist have improved . . . Resumption of communist guerrilla activities in July may reveal communist recognition of their inability to make progress by "soft" tactics in the face of the improving Lao Government position. However, the military situation remains unclear and there is no conclusive evidence as to the exact composition, size and objective of the attacking forces. Nevertheless, it is reasonable to assume that the attacks were at least supported by the North Vietnamese Communists and that their minimum objective is the reactivation of the International Control Commission . . . Strong British support of the Lao Government's opposition to communist efforts to reactivate the International Control Commission was another encouraging development . . . Discussions in Paris at the end of May resulted in a general reconciliation of French and American views on means of improving the effectiveness of the Lao National Army through American participation in training in a manner that the French Government can justify in the light of its responsibilities under the 1954 Geneva Accords. The Lao Government has accepted French-American proposals, and a joint training program has been initiated.[27]

The report seems to express satisfaction with the overthrow of the government of national union, renunciation of Laotian neutrality by the Phoui Sananikone government, suppression of political freedom and the imprisonment of the Neo Lao Haksat leaders; though no exact information was available, it attributed the renewed guerrilla activity to North Vietnamese interference. U.S. attention was mainly directed to the military build-up in Laos. But a Special National Intelligence Estimate (SNIE) dated September 18, 1959, seemed more sober:

> We believe that the Communist resumption of guerrilla warfare in Laos was primarily a reaction to a stronger anti-Communist posture by the Laotian Government and to recent U.S. initiatives in support of Laos . . . Most of the guerrillas in the northern provinces are ex-Pathet Lao soldiers, and Meo and Black Thai tribal people. Elements of the Pathet Lao which refused integration and escaped to North Vietnam are probably involved . . . Hanoi and Peiping have warned that any foreign military intervention in Laos would be considered as a threat to their national security. However, depending partly on the scale and nature of the military move, the Communist military reaction to the Western intervention, whether under UN, SEATO or U.S. auspices, initially would probably take the form of further covert North Vietnamese intervention rather than overt invasion . . . We estimate that both Communist China and the USSR wish to avoid serious risk of expanding the hostilities more broadly in the Far East or beyond. We believe, therefore, that the Communists would seek through various uses of diplomacy, propaganda, covert action and guerrilla warfare to cause the West to back down.[28]

The next reference to Laos policy is included in a National Security Council "Statement of Policy on U.S. Policy in Mainland Southeast Asia." (NSC 6012) dated July 25, 1960. It contains a repetition of previous considerations and recommendations:

The national security of the United States would be endangered by Communist domination of Mainland Southeast
Asia, whether achieved by overt aggression, subversion, or a
political and economic offensive . . . Implement as appropriate
covert operations designed to assist in the achievement of U.S.
objectives . . . Provide military assistance for the development
and support of Lao armed forces . . . Encourage Laos to
formulate and implement a broadly conceived security plan,
including both internal and external security, which encom-
passes the services of all branches of the Royal Government,
civil and military . . .[29]

This policy statement was approved by the President and directed for implementation "by all appropriate Executive departments and agencies of the U.S. government" a week before the
Kong Le coup. Nobody expected the new turn of events. The
Pentagon study is silent about official U.S. reaction. The "Chronological List of Documents" quotes only a Special National Intelligence Estimate dated December 6, 1960, assessing that the Laotian
situation will remain one of "confusion, drift, and disintegration
. . . Laos is heading towards civil war."[30] The five-page document
itself is deleted. The last of the Eisenhower Laos documents consists of a December 20, 1960, summary prepared for the 470th NSC
meeting. It states that the Boun Oum government, which conquered Vientiane a few days earlier, "faces critical problems." The
State Department was of the opinion that it was "too narrowly
based to be popular." The United States had to provide "payment
of military forces and civilian officials throughout the Kingdom for
a three-month period," but, the summary adds, from this sum one
could deduct "the amounts paid to Phoumi [Nosavan] forces by
CAS," the Saigon Office of the CIA—a confirmation that Phoumi's
forces were on the CIA payroll. As "matters of concern to the
U.S." the one-page summary goes on to mention "the necessity to
bolster Phoumi forces" and—characteristically—"the desirability
of forestalling efforts by Nehru and others to reconstitute the
ICC," the International Control Commission.[31]

Finally, the study contains a memorandum sent on September

29, 1967, by Secretary of Defense Clark Clifford to President Johnson recalling the January 19, 1961, Eisenhower–Kennedy conference on Laos.* Some excerpts:

> President Eisenhower . . . felt that the Communists had de-
> signs on all of Southeast Asia, and that it would be a tragedy
> to permit Laos to fall . . . He said that the evidence was clear
> that Communist China and North Vietnam were determined
> to destroy the independence of Laos. He also added that the
> Russians were sending in substantial supplies in support of
> the Pathet Lao in an effort to overturn the Government.
> President Eisenhower said it would be fatal for us to permit
> Communists to insert themselves in the Laotian government
> . . . President Eisenhower said with considerable emotion that
> Laos was the key to the entire area of Southeast Asia . . . He
> reiterated that we should make every effort to persuade mem-
> ber nations of SEATO or the ICC [sic!] to accept the burden
> with us to defend the freedom of Laos . . . President Eisen-
> hower stated it was imperative that Laos be defended. He said
> that the United States should accept this task with our allies,
> if we could persuade them, and alone if we could not. He
> added that "our unilateral intervention would be our last
> desperate hope" . . . President-elect Kennedy asked the
> question as to how long it would take to put an American
> division into Laos. Secretary [of Defense] Gates replied
> that it would take from twelve to seventeen days but that
> some of the time could be saved if American forces then
> in the Pacific could be utilized . . . President-elect
> Kennedy commented upon the seriousness of the situation
> in Laos and in Southeast Asia and asked if the situation
> seemed to be approaching a climax. General Eisenhower
> stated that the entire proceeding was extremely confused
> but that it was clear that this country was obligated to
> support the existing government of Laos . . .

*This document is deleted from the government edition of the Study but
is to be found in the Senator Gravel edition of *The Pentagon Papers, op.
cit.,* Vol. II, pp. 635–637.

Extremely confused indeed! Brinkmanship seemed to offer an escape, and "contingency planning" became a habit feeding escalation; while talk was of peace, the action was for war.

At the National Security Council meeting on February 1, 1961, President Kennedy ordered that "the Secretary of Defense, in consultation with other interested agencies, should examine means for placing more emphasis on the development of counter-guerrilla forces."[32] On April 26, 1961—days before the cease-fire in Laos and the opening of the Geneva conference—an interdepartmental task force consisting of representatives from the Departments of State and Defense, the CIA, the USIA and the Office of the President came forward with a "program of action" including:

> In Laos, infiltrate teams under light civilian cover to Southeast Laos to locate and attack Vietnamese Communist bases and lines of communications. These teams should be supported by assault units of 100 to 150 men for use on targets beyond capability of teams. Training of teams could be a combined operation by CIA and U.S. Army Special Forces. *These operations should continue despite a possible cease-fire in Laos.* [italics added][33]

Three days later, on April 29, the situation in Laos was discussed in a high-level conference with the participation of the Secretaries of State and Defense, Attorney General Robert Kennedy, McGeorge Bundy, Charles E. Bohlen and high military officers. The memorandum on this meeting records:

> The Attorney General asked where would be the best place to stand and fight in Southeast Asia, where to draw the line. McNamara said he thought we would take a stand in Thailand and South Vietnam . . . Mr. Steeves [Deputy Assistant Secretary of Defense] pointed out that we had always argued that we would not give up Laos and that it was on the pleas of our military that we had supported Phoumi [Nosavan] . . . Admiral Burke pointed out that each time you give ground it is harder to stand next time. If we give up Laos we

would have to put U.S. forces into Vietnam and Thailand
. . . The thing to do was to land now and hold as much as we
can . . . The Secretary [of State] said that he was less worried
about escalation than he was about infectious slackness. He
said he would not give a cent for what the Persians would
think of us if we did not defend Laos . . . General Decker said
we cannot win a conventional war in Southeast Asia; if we go
in, we should go in to win, and that means bombing Hanoi,
China, and maybe even using nuclear bombs . . . General Le
May added that he believed we should go to work on China
itself and let Chiang take Hainan Island . . . General Shoup
suggested that B-26's should be used before troops are landed
. . . Mr. Kennedy asked what the others would then do
. . . Mr. McNamara said you would have to use nuclear
weapons . . . Mr. Bowles said he thought the main question
to be faced was the fact that we were going to have to fight
the Chinese anyway in 2, 3, 5 or 10 years and that it was just
a question of where, when and how. He thought that a major
war would be difficult to avoid . . . Mr. McNamara said that
the situation was worsening by the hour and that if we were
going to commit ourselves, then we must do so sooner rather
than later. The Secretary then adjourned the meeting.[34]

In this atmosphere Vice-President Johnson left on his historic
mission to Southeast Asia, India and Pakistan. On his return,
on May 23, 1961, Johnson submitted to President Kennedy a
memorandum which included the following policy recommendations:

I cannot stress too strongly the extreme importance of following up this mission with other measures, other actions, and
other efforts . . . I took to Southeast Asia some basic convictions about the problems faced there. I have come away from
the mission . . . with many of those convictions sharpened and
deepened . . . The battle against Communism must be joined
in Southeast Asia with strength and determination . . . Vietnam and Thailand are the immediate—and most important

—trouble spots, critical to the U.S. . . . The basic decision in Southeast Asia is here . . . I recommend that we move forward promptly with a major effort to help these countries to defend themselves. I consider the key here is to get our best MAAG people to *control, plan, direct* and *exact* results from our military aid program. In Vietnam and Thailand, we must move forward together . . . In Thailand, the Thais and our own MAAG estimate probably as much is needed as in Vietnam . . . [Sarit] is and must be deeply concerned at the consequences to his country of a communist-controlled Laos. If Sarit is to stand firm against neutralism, he must have—soon—corcrete evidence to show his people of United States military and economic support . . . The fundamental decision required of the United States—and time of the greatest importance—is whether we are to attempt to meet the challenge of Communist expansion now in Southeast Asia by a major effort in support of the forces of freedom in the area or throw in the towel. The decision must be made in a full realization of the very heavy and continuing costs involved in terms of money, of effort and of United States prestige. *It must be made with knowledge that at some point we may be faced with the further decision of whether we commit major United States forces to the area* or cut our losses and withdraw should our other efforts fail . . . I recommend we proceed with a clear-cut and strong program of action.[italics added][35]

Out of these convictions and appraisals came the "Asian Doctrine."

In the meantime, "unconventional warfare" was feverishly developed and put in action. In a July 1961 memorandum to General Maxwell D. Taylor, President Kennedy's military adviser, General Lansdale furnished some information on progress in this area.* Laos figures prominently in this report. A South Vietnamese Special Forces-type unit called First Observation Group, with a

*The text of General Lansdale's memorandum was deleted from the government edition of the Pentagon Study, but is to be found in *The New York Times* Bantam edition of *The Pentagon Papers*, 1971, pp. 130–138.

strength of 340 (increased to a total of 805) was engaged in "limited operations in North Vietnam and some shallow penetrations into Laos." Thirteen teams of Thai "Police Aerial Resupply Units" (PARU), trained by the CIA in clandestine operations in restricted areas, were active with the CIA Meo guerrillas in Laos. The CIA-trained and equipped Meo clandestine force in Laos numbered 9,000 men. Also, the Lao National Directorate of Coordination, i.e., the Vientiane security forces, were under CIA control. Lansdale further noted the service of about 500 Filipino technicians "augmenting U.S. military logistics programs," and the CIA use of Filipino "Operation Brotherhood"—"to support counter-guerrilla action." Finally, Lansdale was full of praise for the "extensive air support in Laos during the current crisis" of the Taiwan Civil Air Transport (CAT), a CIA proprietary which "provided air logistical support under commerical cover to most CIA and other U.S. government agencies requirements."

Some weeks later, on August 29, 1961, a National Security Action Memorandum recorded the President's decision for: (1) "An immediate increase in mobile training teams in Laos to include advisers down to the level of the company, to a total U.S. strength in this area of 500, together with an attempt to get Thai agreement to supply an equal amount of Thais for the same purpose"; (2) "An immediate increase of 2,000 in the number of Meos being supported to bring the total to a level of 11,000"; and (3) "Authorization for photo-reconnaissance by Thai or sanitized aircraft over all of Laos."[36] Realities seemed to confirm fully, or even to exceed, Neo Lao Haksat intelligence estimates about U.S.-Thai-South Vietnamese covert military operations in Laos.

But in Washington pressures persisted, too, for overt massive military intervention, despite the cease-fire and negotiations in Geneva. On September 20, 1961, the Joint Chiefs of Staff sent to the Secretary of Defense a draft memorandum for the President "on military intervention in Laos."[37] The ten-page memorandum is quoted in the "Chronological List of Documents," but the document itself was deleted. The quotation states only that "The political objective of the intervention is to confront the Sino-Soviet Bloc with a military force of Asian and Western powers capable of stopping the Communist advance."[38] In another memorandum dated October 9, 1961, and dealing with plans to use SEATO forces in South Vietnam, the Joint Chiefs of Staff refer to the idea of intervention in Laos and emphasize: "What is needed is not the spreading out of our forces throughout Southeast Asia but rather a concentrated effort in Laos where a firm stand can be taken saving all or substantially all of Laos which would, at the same time, protect Thailand and protect the borders of South Vietnam."[39]

It is interesting to note that all this planning took place at a time when the United States was engaged on the political level in efforts to win over Souvanna Phouma. The same White House National Security Action Memorandum of August 29, 1961, which recorded the President's decisions for further covert action in Laos also noted that the President approved:

> an intensification of the diplomatic efforts to achieve agreement to the Paris proposals on the part of Souvanna, especially by direct conversation between Ambassador Harriman and Souvanna, with an emphasis not only upon the interlocking importance of the Paris proposals, but also upon U.S. support of Souvanna in the event that he accepts the Paris plan.[40]

But Laos negotiations served only to gain time for regional military planning. High on the agenda were designs for a "concentrated military effort" and for the placing of combat troops in Indochina. These were the real points of reference of the October 1961 Taylor-Rostow Presidential mission to Saigon. An internal memo by the Deputy Secretary of Defense dated October 11, 1961 recorded these terms as:

> to look into the feasibility from both political and military standpoints of the following: (a) the plan for military intervention discussed at this morning's meeting [with the President] on the basis of the Vietnam task force paper entitled "Concept for Intervention in Vietnam," (b) an alternative plan for stationing in Vietnam fewer U.S. combat forces than

those called for under the plan referred to in (a) above . . .
(c) other alternatives . . . i.e. stepping up U.S. assistance and
training of Vietnam units . . .[41]

No mention was made in these terms of political alternatives
except that as a cover the State Department

will push ahead with the following political actions: (a) protest to the ICC on the step-up in North Vietnamese support
of Viet Cong activities, (b) tabling at the UN a white paper
. . . concerning Communist violations of the Geneva Accords,
and (c) consultations with our SEATO allies, principally the
British and Australians, regarding SEATO actions in support
of the deteriorating situation in Vietnam.[42]

The only other document on Laos to be found in the Pentagon
study is a short National Security Action Memorandum signed on
May 29, 1962, by McGeorge Bundy stating that the President had
approved the record of a Presidential Meeting on Laos held on
May 24. At this meeting, "the President requested contingency
planning in the event of a breakdown of the cease-fire in Laos for
action in two major areas: occupation of the Laotian province of
Sayaboury by Thai forces with U.S. backup, and occupation of
Southern Laos with Thai, South Vietnamese and U.S. forces." The
memorandum adds: "The President also asked that the above planning be undertaken by the United States without discussion at this
time with the Thais or the Lao."[43] These Presidential orders came
barely two weeks after the Nam Tha drama. Despite the bitter
experience of this episode, the United States seemed to follow up
the Bangkok-Vientiane play, though cautious enough not to ac-
quaint them immediately with the new plans. No further details on
this planning are recorded.
     Though few, the references to Laos in the Pentagon study and
its attached documentation confirm the reading of events given in
this book. The dominant concern of Pentagon analysts seems to
revolve around the success-failure syndrome. Their attention is
directed mainly to the question: Why did the United States fail? It

is, however, terribly important—and more so in the light of the facts laid bare by the Pentagon study—to raise all the other issues imposed by the Indochina wars: the human aspects, the moral-political questions, and above all, the problems of war and peace related to survival in our atomic age.

Notes

1. *United States–Vietnam Relations 1945–1967,* Study Prepared by the Department of Defense (Washington: U.S. Government Printing Office, 1971), 12 volumes. All references relate to this edition of the Pentagon Papers.
2. Book 2, IV. B. 1, p. ii.
3. *Ibid.*
4. *Ibid.,* p. 2.
5. *Ibid.,* pp. 31–32.
6. *Ibid.,* IV.A.5, Tab 3, pp. 60–63.
7. *Ibid.,* IV.B.1, p. 6.
8. *Ibid.,* IV.A.5, Tab 3, p. 71.
9. *Ibid.,* IV.B.1, p. 6.
10. *Ibid.,* IV.A.5, Tab 3, p. 31.
11. Book 11, p. 292.
12. Book 1, III.D., p. 2.
13. Book 2, IV.A.5, p.1.
14. Book 10, p. 676.
15. Book 1, III.A.3, pp. 37–42.
16. Book 9, pp. 626–629.
17. *Ibid.,* p. 631.
18. *Ibid.,* p. 636.
19. *Ibid.,* p. 646.
20. Book 1, III.A, p. 2.
21. *Ibid.,* IV.A.3, pp. ii-v.
22. Book 10, p. 765 (State Department message of September 30, 1954, to London, Paris, Saigon, Phnom Penh and Vientiane).
23. *Ibid.,* pp. 811 and 814 (Saigon messages to Washington).
24. *Ibid.,* p. 737.
25. *Ibid.,* p. 892.

26. *Ibid.*, p. 926.
27. *Ibid.*, pp. 1228–1239.
28. *Ibid.*, pp. 1242–1247.
29. *Ibid.*, pp. 1282–1293.
30. *Ibid.*, V.B.3, p. LII.
31. *Ibid.*, p. 1347.
32. Book 11, p. 17.
33. *Ibid.*, p. 52.
34. *Ibid.*, pp. 63–66.
35. *Ibid.*, pp. 161–166.
36. *Ibid.*, pp. 247–248.
37. *Ibid.* V.B.4, p. VI.
38. *Ibid.*
39. *Ibid.*, p. 298.
40. *Ibid.*, p. 247.
41. *Ibid.*, pp. 322–323.
42. *Ibid.*, p. 323.
43. Book 12, p. 467.

Appendix 2

Chronology of Events
1963–1972

Spring 1963 Souvanna Phouma's deals with the Americans cause tension in the Plain of Jars-Xieng Khouang area. Increasing polarization between Neo Lao Haksat and part of Kong Le forces. Kong Le troops reinforced secretly in men and equipment by Air America planes. Split among Neutralists: Kong Le sides with the Rightists, while another wing, under Colonel Deuan Sounnalath, calling themselves "genuine neutralists," remain in alliance with the Neo Lao Haksat.

March 19 U.S.-Thai SLAT (Special Logistics Action Thailand) agreement to upgrade the Nakhon Phnom air base on the Lao border and improve strategic communication lines linking Thailand with Laos, in order to support "emergency" operations of the United States.

April 1 Assassination in Vientiane of Foreign Minister Quinim Pholsena, leader of the left-wing Neutralists. The assassin, a corporal in the Kong Le forces, is seized but never put to trial.

April 12 Assassination in Vientiane of Colonel Khanti Siphatong, a neutralist officer designated to be chief of the mixed police force in the capital.

April 14–18 NLH ministers, including Prince Souphanouvong, leave Vientiane and take refuge in NLH-controlled areas. A rump NLH representation remains in Vientiane.

April Following sporadic fighting, units under Kong Le are dislodged by Colonel Deuan and NLH forces from Xieng Khouang, Khang Khay and most of the Plain of Jars.

May 4 NLH leaders condition their return to Vientiane on new security arrangements: demilitarization and neutralization of the capital, and the formation of a mixed police force. Their requests are not met.

May 17–18   Renewed fighting on the Plain of Jars as a result of fresh reinforcements received by Kong Le from General Nosavan. Spearate reports sent to Co-chairmen by the Indian and Canadian delegations to the ICSC on the one hand and by the Polish delegation on the other. Co-chairmen split on appraisal of events.

June 25   French military base at Seno handed over to Nosavan forces.

Summer-fall   Deterioration of the military situation. Sporadic fighting on the Plain of Jars, in central and southern Laos. Abortive negotiations to revive the government of national union.

September 9   Nighttime armed assault on the seat of the NLH representation in Vientiane, aiming to destroy any vestige of the government of national union. ICSC intervention and protection allows the NLH representation to remain in the capital.

November-February 1964   Intermittent fighting in the area of Xieng Khouang and central Laos.

February 1964   Special U.S. Air Warfare Unit in Thailand starts training Lao and Thai pilots for air operations in Laos. Thai bases are used for reconnaissance flights over Laos.

March 14   Secret meeting in Dalat, South Vietnam, between Nosavan and the South Vietnamese junta leader General Nguyen Khanh. Nosavan later denies reports about an agreement for South Vietnamese military operations in Laos.

April 2   Hanoi warns Souvanna Phouma about possible consequences of South Vietnamese military involvement in Laos.

April 6–12   Second National Congress of NLH adopts a new ten-point program of action, calling for unity, execution of the 1962 Geneva agreements, neutrality, economic reforms, formation of a national army and a mixed police force, democratic liberties, respect for the Throne, equal rights for women, development of national culture, and resistance to U.S. intervention.

April 17–18   Meeting between Souvanna Phouma, Souphanouvong and Nosavan at the Plain of Jars. Nosavan rejects the demilitarization and neutralization of Luang Prabang as a precondition for the reactivation of the government of national union.

April 19   Rightist coup d'état in Vientiane followed by a reshuffling of the Souvanna Phouma government (elimination of progressive Neutralists) and the merger of the Souvanna Phouma and rightist factions. The coup is seen as a move inspired by the CIA and the Pentagon to link Laos with the South Vietnamese battlefield and get nearer to the DRV borders. The neutralist ministers excluded from the government move to areas controlled by the NLH and form the Alliance of the Lao Patriotic Neutralist Forces, with Khamsouk Keola as Chairman and Col. Deuan as Vice-Chairman.

April 22   Prince Norodom Sihanouk of Cambodia appeals for a new international conference on Laos, to deal also with the problems of Vietnam and Cambodia.

May 13–22   The appeal for a new international conference on Laos is supported by China, France and the Soviet Union, but rejected by the United States and Great Britain.

May 13   Official integration of the Kong Le and rightist forces. Kong Le's position reduced to the local command of his units.

May 16   Split in the ranks of the Kong Le units, defection of six out of eleven battalions to the ranks of Deuan. In the ensuing fighting Deuan's troops, supported by NLH forces, dislodge Kong Le's units from the Plain of Jars.

May 21   Disclosure of U.S. reconnaissance flights over the Plain of Jars and areas bordering DRV. High-altitude flights, which started beginning of 1964, were on May 17 stepped up to armed, low-altitude "reconnaissance" flights. A fleet of from twenty-five to forty T-28 fighter-bombers manned by Air America, Thai and Lao pilots under the control of U.S. Ambassador Leonard Unger initiates bombing raids against NLH positions.

June 1–2   Honolulu strategy conference including generals Taylor and Westmoreland, Admiral Felt, Rusk, McNamara, McCone and Lodge discusses air war against DRV. Following the conference McNamara orders augmentation of war stocks at Korat (in Thailand on the railway line to Laos). The United States and Thailand agree to engage in bilateral military contingency planning, and to upgrade the logistical complex and air deployments in Thailand. By the end of 1964 Thailand contains about 3,000 USAF personnel supporting approximately seventy-five aircraft.

June 6–7   Two U.S. jets on low reconnaissance flights shot down over the Plain of Jars.

June 11   Bombing raids on the NLH headquarters at Khang Khay. Chinese representation hit.

June 13   White House suspends information on U.S. engagement and plans in Southeast Asia.

July 19   General Khanh, head of the South Vietnamese junta, starts the "March North" campaign, while Air Marshal Nguyen Cao Ky reveals joint U.S.-South Vietnamese planning (since June) for ground and air assaults in Laos.

July   U.S.-supported Vientiane military offensive against NLH forces.

July 25   In a note to Britain the Soviet Union declares its intention to resign as Co-chairman of the Geneva conference.

August 2   In a note to the Soviet Union, China urges the Soviet government "Truly to shoulder the responsibilities" as Co-chairman of the Geneva conference.

August 1–2   Air incursions and bombing of DRV border areas by U.S. planes coming from the direction of Laos.

August 2–5   Tonkin Gulf incidents.

August 10   Tonkin Gulf resolution passed by U.S. Congress.

August 11   In a high-level policy memorandum concerning U.S. strategy toward the forthcoming Paris talks between Souvanna Phouma and Souphanouvong, William Bundy states that "we should wish to slow down any progress toward a conference and to hold Souvanna to the firmest possible position."

August 18   T-28 fighter bomber with Thai pilot shot down over DRV.

September 10   President Johnson approves "limited" South Vietnamese air and ground operations into "the corridor areas" of Laos, together with Vientiane air strikes and possible use of U.S. armed air reconnaissance.

September 21   Failure of Paris meeting between princes Souvanna Phouma, Souphanouvong and Boun Oum. Vague support for a new international conference on Laos but no agreement on a return to the 1962 status quo.

October 6   U.S. State and Defense Departments instruct U.S. embassy in Vientiane to start air strikes against "infiltration routes" in Laos. The strikes begin on October 14, with Souvanna Phouma's approval.

December 14 With Souvanna Phouma's approval U.S. jets start Operation Barrel Roll in the Laotian panhandle, attacking "targets of opportunity" sighted by the pilots.

October 1964-January 1965 Sporadic fighting resumed. U.S. air raids all along southern, central and northern Laos up to the DRV borders. Two U.S. jet fighters shot down on November 17 and 21, 1964, and two bombers on January 13, 1965.

January 31-February 3, 1965 Abortive coup d'état by General Nosavan ends in his flight to Thailand.

February U.S. starts massive air war against DRV. Official figures admit 4,548 air strikes in northern Laos during 1965. Figures on southern Laos not available.

July 18 Elections to Vientiane National Assembly without NLH participation. Suffrage indirect and restricted to about 20,000 officers, civil servants, merchants and other notables. New assembly approves a new right-wing reshuffling of Souvanna Phouma's government.

October 1 Pathet Lao forces renamed Lao People's Liberation Armed Forces.

October 13 National Political Union Conference with the participation of NLH and the Alliance of Lao Patriotic Neutralist Forces issues a manifesto calling for the defense of the 1962 Geneva agreements, for resistance against U.S. intervention, for a settlement of the Laotian problem by peaceful means, and for a peaceful, neutral, independent, democratic, united and prosperous Laos.

1965–1966 Periodic fighting does not basically change the 1961–62 cease-fire line. Gradually intensified U.S. bombing raids from bases in Thailand and South Vietnam. In December 1965 B-52 bombers based in Guam join operations. Official U.S. figures for 1966 mention 7,316 strikes in northern Laos.

January 24, 1966 South Vietnamese Chief of State Nguyen Van Thieu confirms that U.S. and South Vietnamese aircraft are regularly bombing the "Ho Chi Minh Trail" in Laos.

January 31-March 1 During thirty-seven-day temporary bombing halt in North Vietnam, U.S. increases air raids against Laos.

October U.S. Forward Air Controllers established in Laos.

October 21   Abortive coup d'état by the operational commander of the Lao Air Force, General Thao Ma. The general and his accomplices find refuge in Thailand.

November 15   Removal of General Kong Le from the command of his troops. Kong Le takes refuge in the Indonesian embassy and asks for permission to leave for Indonesia. He accuses the U.S. of interference and denies reports of being associated with Thao Ma. Charges later that Souvanna Phouma "betrayed the national cause" by bringing Laos under "American domination."

December 21   Nosavan sentenced in absentia by a military court in Vientiane to twenty years' imprisonment.

1967–1968   War in Laos subordinated to operations in South Vietnam and air war against DRV. Vast expansion of the CIA-Meo "clandestine army" led by Vang Pao. Increasing involvement of Thai and North Vietnamese troops. No substantial change in front lines.

January 1, 1967   New elections to the Vientiane National Assembly, without NLH participation. The assembly was dissolved in October 1966 because of internal quarrels. New assembly confirms Souvanna Phouma's policies.

April 20   U.S. Joint Chiefs of Staff demand a major increase of troops in Indochina for the extension of the war into Laos, Cambodia and possibly DRV.

December 25   U.S. radar site at Muong Phalane (central Laos), built for guidance of air war against DRV, captured by NLH forces.

January 14, 1968   NLH forces occupy Nam Bac, a fortified Vientiane position in the North, near the Phong Saly, Sam Neua and DRV borders.

March 11   NLH forces take Phou Pha Thi, most northerly U.S. radar site, seventeen miles from the DRV border. Built on a 5,860-foot peak in 1966 to help guide all-weather bombing operations against DRV, the station was manned by a dozen Americans and a detachment of Meo Special Forces.

October 25–31   Extraordinary NLH congress adopts a twelve-point political program calling for unity in the struggle against U.S. aggression, equality among various nationalities, respect for Buddhism, democratic rights and freedoms, equality between men and women, a democratic administration of national unity, strengthening of the popular armed forces, developing a sovereign economy and improving the people's living standard, developing national culture and education, social reforms in village and town, and a foreign policy of peace, independence and neutrality.

November Aircraft available after the halt of raids against DRV transferred to bombing operations in Laos. Air war escalates into saturation bombings, especially in northeastern and southern parts of Laos. According to U.S. sources, three to four hundred planes operate daily over Laos. The escalation follows a substantial increase in the number of bombing sorties over northern Laos during summer 1968, after the partial bombing halt over DRV in March 1968.

January-June 1969 Intensification of military operations. Following heavy U.S. bombings, Vang Pao forces enter (end of April) the ruined and deserted town of Xieng Khouang. Reoccupied by NLH forces on May 26. This marks the first U.S. and Vientiane effort to disrupt the cease-fire line of 1961–1962.

August 20—September 25 Supported by the "most intense American bombing ever seen in Laos," a combined Thai-Vang Pao force captures the Plain of Jars, Xieng Khouang and the Muong Soui area. Fighting also reported in southern Laos.

September 28 U.S. estimates aircraft losses in Laos since 1964 at 380 planes. NLH claims to have shot down or destroyed on the ground 1,170 planes.

December 15 After secret hearing by the Symington Subcommittee of the Senate Foreign Relations Committee into U.S. operations in Laos, the U.S. Senate adopts (72 to 17) a rider to the Defense Appropriations Bill barring funds for the support of U.S. combat troops in Laos and Thailand.

February 11–26, 1970 Despite intense U.S. bombing and B-52 raids, NLH forces supported by DRV troops using tanks and heavy artillery recapture the Plain of Jars and surroundings. Renewed attacks on NLH positions by Vang Pao-Thai Special Forces in September-October produces only small gains, many of which are lost in NLH counteroffensive in November-December 1970.

March 6 NLH five-point proposal for a political solution stipulates a halt to U.S. intervention, neutrality, democratic elections to set up a government of national union, forming of a provisional coalition government before elections, cease-fire and cessation of bombings.

March 18   Coup d'état in Cambodia: overthrow of Sihanouk's administration.

April 24–25   Summit conference of the Indochinese Peoples. Joint declaration by the NLF, DRV, NLH, and the Cambodian United Front headed by Sihanouk pledges reciprocal support in the struggle for liberation.

April 28   NLH forces capture the town of Attopeu in southern Laos.

April 30   Combined U.S.-South Vietnamese invasion of Cambodia.

May 11   Souvanna Phouma rejects the March 6 NLH proposals but declares readiness for negotiations. Initial contacts fail to bring the parties any nearer.

June 9   NLH forces take the town of Saravane in southern Laos. Sporadic fighting on the Bolovens Plateau (continues into 1971). South Vietnamese troops accompanied by U.S. advisers increase incursions into Laos in the area of the Ho Chi Minh Trail.

September 28   A Staff Report of the Edward Kennedy Subcommittee to Investigate Problems Connected With Refugees and Escapees states that the official number of refugees in Laos is approaching 300,000. Rate of refugee movements coincides with the level of U.S. bombings. 1971 figures estimate 800,000 homeless Laotians—one-third of the country's population.

October 9   Intensification of B-52 bombing raids in southern Laos (Ho Chi Minh Trails), continuing through the dry season into 1971. NLH alleges that in 1970 U.S. dropped 3,000 tons of bombs a day on Laos.

February 8—March 25, 1971   Operation "Lam Son 719": large-scale South Vietnamese offensive with U.S. air support along Highway 9 into Laos. South Vietnamese claim to have reached the crossroads of Tchepone, but withdraw soon under a heavy NLH-North Vietnamese counteroffensive. Official South Vietnamese casualty figures list 1,445 soldiers killed and 4,016 wounded. U.S. admits loss of 105 helicopters. NLH claims to have put out of action 15,400 enemy troops, captured 1,000, and destroyed 496 aircraft.

May NLH forces occupy the Bolovens Plateau.

May 12 New NLH peace proposals stipulate an unconditional, immediate bombing halt over the whole of Laos, followed by negotiations for the formation of a provisional coalition government, and the revival of the 1962 Geneva agreements.

May 17 Seven years of U.S. bombings in Laos. Air sorties rose from 100–300 per day in 1964–68, to 700–1000 in 1970–71.

May 31 Souvanna Phouma rejects the May 12 NLH offer, stating that he will accept a cessation of bombing only as part of a complete cease-fire and not as a precondition for it.

June 22 In a message to Souvanna Phouma, Souphanouvong proposes an immediate cease-fire including the cessation of bombing raids, followed by discussions to achieve national concord and peace.

July 5 Souvanna Phouma agrees to partial cessation of U.S. bombings only. Further exchange of views fails to produce constructive results.

July-August Preceded by heavy U.S. bombardments, a new Thai-Meo Special Forces offensive captures the Plain of Jars. Simultaneously, Special Forces take Saravane.

November 22 *New York Times* estimates total tonnage of bombs dropped by U.S. planes on Laos to have reached 1.9 million tons (total tonnage dropped in World War II was 2 million tons). NLH estimates 3 million tons of bombs dropped on Laos since 1964. 80 percent of aircraft involved in the raids based in Thailand.

December 6, 1971–January 11, 1972 NLH forces recapture entire Bolovens Plateau, and town of Saravane.

December 18–24 Despite strong resistance and U.S. air operations, NLH-DRV forces recapture the Plain of Jars and its surroundings.

Appendix 3

Laos: April 1971*

Summary and General Observations from

A STAFF REPORT

prepared for the use of the

Subcommittee on U.S. Security
Agreements and Commitments Abroad
of the
Committee on Foreign Relations
United States Senate

by James G. Lowenstein and Richard M. Moose
of the Subcommittee Staff

on a trip they had made to Laos from April 22
to May 4, 1971, on behalf of the Subcommittee

. . . Most observers in Laos say that from the military point of view the situation there is growing steadily worse and the initiative seems clearly to be in the hands of the enemy. There are apparently no plans for retaking and holding any of the two-thirds of the country no longer under government control but only a hope, not too firmly held in some quarters, that the one-third of Lao territory now under government control can continue to be held . . . U.S. air operations continue in both northern Laos and in the south against the Ho Chi Minh Trail . . . Since February 1970 we have

*Washington: U.S. Government Printing Office, August 3, 1971.

been using B-52's in northern Laos on a regular basis . . .

The war in Laos is run in most respects by the Embassy in Vientiane. In fact, this undertaking seems to consume a considerable portion of time of the senior officers in the Mission. The "Operations Meeting" at the Embassy—which lasts from 9 A.M. to approximately 10:30 daily, including Saturday, and at which the Ambassador presides—is devoted in large part to detailed briefings by the Army and Air Attachés and the CIA Station Chief which cover practically every military engagement of the preceding twenty-four hours . . .

The United States continues to train, arm and feed the Lao Army and Air Force and to train, advise, pay, support, and, to a great extent, organize the irregular military forces under the direction of the CIA. The combat element of these irregular forces is about as large as the combat element of the Royal Lao Army . . . The cost of these irregular forces has been increasing every year, in part because as more territory has fallen under Pathet Lao control it has become necessary to rely increasingly on air transport, and in part because of the rising cost of ammunition . . .

The number of Thai in Laos, at the time of our visit, was about (deleted). Since then, (deleted). We were told that these "irregular" volunteers, as they are characterized by Thai and American officials, are recruited for service in Laos from outside the regular Thai Army . . . The costs involved are channeled through the CIA, although U.S. officials told us that they thought some of the funds come from the Defense Department budget . . .

The Royal Lao Government continues to be almost totally dependent on the United States . . . The cost of U.S. military assistance to Laos has risen rapidly in the past few months with the fiscal year 1972 program doubling since January . . . The United States provides not only for all of Laos's defense needs but for day-to-day needs as well . . .

The Lao Government's budget for the current year is 18.3 billion kip, or, converted to dollars at the official rate of 500 kip to the dollar, $36.6 million. By contrast the partial total of estimated U.S. expenditures in Laos in fiscal year 1971 is $284.2 million, composed of an estimated $162.2 million in military assistance, $52 million in the AID program, and $(deleted) million spent by the

CIA exclusive of the Thai irregular costs. This partial total of estimated U.S. expenditures amounts to $141 per capita for the approximately 2 million Lao under government control compared with a per capita GNP estimated at $66. Not included in the above U.S. expenditure total are items such as the cost of Thai irregulars in Laos. The planned increase in fiscal year 1972 military assistance coupled with AID and CIA expenditures at this year's level would bring the total of these three programs up to $374 million . . .

U.S. activities in Laos show the interlocking relationship between all U.S. agencies in Laos and all U.S. activities and commands in Southeast Asia. Thus, (deleted). The sortie rate of U.S. tactical aircraft is kept at Udorn [Thailand], but this information does not include the rates for B-52's or Navy aircraft. These figures are kept by the Seventh Air Force in Saigon. Within Laos, the CIA trains and advises irregular forces, but until last week the AID had provided these forces with rice in Military Regions I and II, while the military assistance program, operated ostensibly under AID in Laos, provides food and equipment to the regular Lao Army . . .

Finally, there is an evident determination among U.S. officials in Laos to continue to prosecute the war with only gradually reduced secrecy. It is argued, with regard to air operations, that many of these planes are based in Thailand and are there pursuant to agreements with the Thai Government which stipulate that (deleted). As far as operations of the irregular forces are concerned, some say that the CIA is not used to prosecuting a war in public and does not see what purpose would be served by doing so. Underlying many of these arguments for maintaining secrecy is the feeling that much of what the United States is doing violates the Geneva agreements of 1962, and ancillary "understandings" thereto . . .

Appendix 4

Speech by
N. S. Khrushchev,
January 6, 1961:

THE PREVENTION OF A NEW WAR
IS THE QUESTION OF QUESTIONS*

Comrades, the [November 1960 Moscow] Meeting [of the eighty-one communist and workers' parties] centered its attention on the issues of war and peace. All of us at the Meeting saw clearly that prevention of a world-wide nuclear war was the most burning and vital problem facing mankind.

Lenin pointed out that since the First World War the issue of war and peace had become the basic question of the policy of all countries—a matter of life and death for tens of millions. Lenin's words sound even more forcefully today, when weapons of mass annihilation threaten unprecedented destruction and death to hundreds of millions of people. There is no task more pressing today than to avert such a catastrophe.

The Meeting charted ways and means of making still more effective use of the new possibilities of averting world war afforded by the emergence of the socialist camp and its increased might, by the new balance of forces in the world. The peoples trust that the Communists will use all the might of the socialist system and the

---

Communism—Peace and Happiness for The Peoples, Vol. 1 (January–September 1961) (Moscow: Foreign Languages Publishing House, 1963), pp. 37–45.

enhanced strength of the international working class to rid mankind of the horrors of war.

Marx, Engels and Lenin saw the historic mission of the working class and its communist vanguard not only in abolishing oppression, exploitation, poverty, and rightlessness, but also in delivering mankind from sanguinary wars.

Lenin instilled in our Party the spirit of uncompromising struggle against imperialism, for durable peace and friendship among all nations. These principles have always been, and are, the essence of our foreign policy. Our Party remembers Lenin's words to the effect that capitalism, even while disintegrating and dying, is still capable of causing mankind great misfortunes. Our Party, always vigilantly on guard against the danger emanating from imperialism, is educating the Soviet people accordingly and doing everything to prevent the enemy from ever taking us by surprise. We alert the peoples to the danger of war in order to heighten their vigilance and rouse them to action, to rally them to the struggle against world war.

The attitude of the Communist Party of the Soviet Union to questions of war and peace is known to all. It has been stated time and again in the resolutions of its congresses and in other Party documents.

Wars arose with the division of society into classes. This means that the ground for all wars will not be completely eliminated until society is no longer divided into hostile, antagonistic classes. The victory of the working class throughout the world and the triumph of socialism will destroy all the social and national causes of war and mankind will be able to rid itself of this dreadful scourge.

In the present conditions we must distinguish between the following kinds of war: world war, local war, and war of liberation or popular uprising. This is necessary in order to work out the proper tactics in regard to each.

Let us begin with the problem of *world wars*. The Communists are the most resolute opponents of world wars, as they are of wars between states in general. Only the imperialists need these wars in order to seize foreign territories and to enslave and plunder the peoples. Prior to the emergence of the world socialist camp, the working class was unable to exert any decisive influence on the decision of whether there should or should not be a world war. In those circumstances the finest representatives of the working class advanced the slogan of turning imperialist war into civil war, that is, of the working class and all working people using the situation created by the war to win power. A situation of that kind obtained during the First World War, and was used classically by the Bolshevik Party, by Lenin.

In our time the conditions are different. The world socialist camp with its powerful economy and armed forces is exerting an ever-growing influence on the questions of war and peace. To be sure, acute contradictions and antagonisms between the imperialist countries and the urge to profit at the expense of others, the weaker countries, still exist. However, the imperialists are compelled to keep in mind the Soviet Union and the entire socialist camp, and are afraid to start a war between themselves. They try to minimize their differences. They have formed military blocs and have drawn many capitalist countries into them. Although these blocs are torn by internal conflicts, their members are united, as they themselves say, by their hatred of communism and, naturally, by their common imperialist nature and aspirations.

In the present circumstances it is not war between the capitalist, imperialist countries that is most likely to occur, although this possibility should not be ruled out entirely. The imperialists are preparing war chiefly against the socialist countries, and above all against the Soviet Union, the most powerful of the socialist countries. They would like to sap our might and thereby restore the one-time dominance of monopoly capital.

The task is to raise insurmountable obstacles to the unleashing of war by the imperialists. Our possibilities for blocking the war-mongers are growing, and we can consequently prevent a world war. It stands to reason that we cannot as yet completely exclude the possibility of war, since imperialist countries continue to exist, but it is now much more difficult for the imperialists to start a war than was the case previously, before the powerful socialist camp came into existence. The imperialists can start a war, but they have to think of the consequences.

I have said before that the maniac Hitler, if he had had an inkling of how his sanguinary gamble would end and of his having to commit suicide, would have thought twice before starting the war against the Soviet Union. But at that time there were only two socialist countries—the Soviet Union and the Mongolian People's Republic. Yet we smashed the aggressors, and in doing so made use also of the contradictions existing between the imperialist states.

Today the situation is entirely different. At present the imperialist camp is confronted by the socialist countries, which are a mighty force. It would be wrong to underestimate the strength of the socialist camp, its influence on world developments and, consequently, on the question of war or peace. Now that there is a mighty socialist camp with powerful armed forces, the peoples can undoubtedly prevent war and thus ensure peaceful coexistence, provided they rally all their forces for active struggle against the bellicose imperialists.

Now about *local wars*. There is much talk in the imperialist camp today about local wars, and the imperialists are even making small-caliber atomic weapons for use in such wars. They have even concocted a special theory on local wars. Is this mere chance? Not at all. Some of the imperialist groups fear that a world war might end in the complete destruction of capitalism, and are laying their stakes on local wars.

There have been local wars in the past and they may break out again. But the chances of the imperialists' starting wars of even a local nature are dwindling. A small-scale imperialist war, no matter which of the imperialists starts it, may develop into a world thermonuclear missile war. We must, therefore, fight against world wars and against local wars.

The aggression of Britain, France and Israel against Egypt is an example of a local war started by the imperialists. They wanted to strangle Egypt and thereby intimidate the other Arab countries fighting for their independence, and also to scare the rest of the peoples of Asia and Africa. When we were in London, British statesmen, Mr. Eden included, spoke to us quite frankly about their desire to settle accounts with Egypt. We told them plainly: "If you start a war, you will lose it. We shall not be neutral." When that war broke out, the United Nations formally condemned it, but this did not disturb the aggressors; they went ahead with their dirty business and thought they would soon reach their goal. The Soviet

Union, and the socialist camp as a whole, came to the defense of Egypt. The stern warning which the Soviet Government issued to Eden and Guy Mollet stopped the war. Local war, the gamble in Egypt, failed ignominiously.

That was in 1956 when the balance of forces between the socialist and imperialist countries was not what it is now. We were not as powerful then as we are today. Moreover, the rulers of Britain, France and Israel expected to profit by the difficulties that had arisen in Hungary and Poland. Spokesmen of the imperialist countries whispered to us, "You have your difficulties in Hungary and we have ours in Egypt, so don't meddle in our affairs." But we told the whisperers where to get off. We refused to shut our eyes to their knavish acts. We intervened and frustrated their aggression.

There you have an example of how a local war started by the imperialists was thwarted through the intervention of the Soviet Union and the entire socialist camp.

I have already said that local wars may re-occur. It is our task, therefore, always to be on the alert, to summon to action the forces of the socialist camp, the people of all countries, all peace-loving forces, in order to prevent wars of aggression. If the people of all countries are united and roused, if they fight indefatigably and combine their forces both in each country and on an international scale, wars can be prevented.

Now about *national-liberation wars*. Recent examples of wars of this kind are the armed struggle waged by the people of Vietnam and the present war of the Algerian people, which is now in its seventh year.

These wars, which began as uprisings of colonial peoples against their oppressors, developed into guerrilla wars.

There will be liberation wars as long as imperialism exists, as long as colonialism exists. Wars of this kind are revolutionary wars. Such wars are not only admissible, but inevitable, for the colonialists do not freely bestow independence on the peoples. The peoples win freedom and independence only through struggle, including armed struggle.

Why was it that the U.S. imperialists, though eager to help the French colonialists in every way, did not venture to intervene directly in the war in Vietnam? They did not do so because they knew that if they gave France armed assistance, Vietnam would receive the same kind of assistance from China, the Soviet Union and the other socialist countries, and that the fighting could then develop into a world war. The outcome of the war is known—North Vietnam won.

A similar war is being waged today in Algeria. What kind of a war is it? It is an uprising of the Arab people of Algeria against the French colonialists. It has assumed the form of a guerrilla war. The U.S. and British imperialists are helping their French allies with arms. Moreover, they have allowed France, a member of NATO, to transfer troops from Europe to fight the Algerian people. The people of Algeria, too, get help from neighboring and other countries who appreciate their love of freedom. But this is a liberation war, a war of independence waged by the people. It is a sacred war. We recognize such wars; we have helped and shall continue to help peoples fighting for their freedom.

Or take Cuba. A war was fought there too. But it began as an uprising against a tyrannical regime backed by U.S. imperialism. Batista was a puppet of the United States, and the United States helped him actively. However, the U.S.A. did not directly intervene with its armed forces in the Cuban war. Led by Fidel Castro, the people of Cuba won.

Can such wars recur? Yes, they can. Are uprisings of this kind likely? Yes, they are. But they are wars in the nature of popular uprisings. Can conditions in other countries reach the point where the cup of popular patience overflows and the people take up arms? Yes, they can. What is the Marxist attitude to such uprisings? It is most favorable. These uprisings cannot be identified with wars between countries, with local wars, because the insurgent people fight for the right of self-determination, for their social and independent national development; these uprisings are directed against corrupt reactionary regimes, against the colonialists. The Communists support just wars of this kind wholeheartedly and without reservations, and march in the van of the peoples fighting for liberation.

Comrades, mankind has arrived at the stage in history when it is able to solve problems that were too much for previous generations to solve. This applies also to the most burning problem of all, that of preventing world war.

The working class, which today rules in a vast section of the world and in time will rule throughout the world, cannot let the forces doomed to destruction drag hundreds of millions into the grave with them. For a world war in the present conditions would be waged with missiles and nuclear weapons, that is, it would be the most destructive war in history.

Among the H-bombs already tested there are bombs several times more powerful than all the explosives used in the Second World War and, indeed, ever since mankind has existed. Scientists have estimated that the explosion of a single H-bomb in an industrial area could kill up to 1,500,000 people outright and cause the death of something like 400,000 more through subsequent radiation. Even a medium hydrogen bomb would be enough to wipe out a large city. According to British scientists, four megaton bombs, one each for London, Birmingham, Lancashire and Yorkshire, would wipe out at least 20 million people. According to data supplied to the Senate by U.S. experts, the anticipated casualties in the United States in twenty-four hours of nuclear war are estimated at 50 to 75 million people. The well-known American physicist, Linus Pauling, says that the areas likely to suffer powerful nuclear blows are inhabited by about a thousand million people and that 500 to 750 million people are likely to perish within sixty days of a nuclear blow. Nor would nuclear war spare the people in the countries not directly subjected to bombing; in particular, many millions would die of subsequent radiation.

We know that if the imperialist maniacs were to begin a world war, the peoples would wipe out capitalism. But we are resolutely opposed to war, chiefly because we are thinking of the destiny of mankind, its present and its future. We know that the first to suffer in the event of war would be the working people and their vanguard —the working class.

We remember how Lenin approached the question of the destiny of the working class. Just after the Revolution, when the first socialist country of the workers and peasants was in a ring of fire, he said, "If we save the working man, if we save the main productive force of society—the worker—we shall get everything back, but should we fail to save him, we are lost."

There exists in the world today not just one country of workers and peasants, but a whole system of socialist countries. It is our duty to safeguard peace and ensure the peaceful development of this grand creation of the international working class, and to protect the peoples of all countries from a new war of annihilation. The victory of socialism on a world scale, inevitable by virtue of the laws of history, is now near. Wars between countries are not needed for this victory.

A sober consideration of the inescapable consequences of a nuclear war is indispensable if we are to pursue, with due consistency, a policy of averting war and mobilizing the masses for this purpose. Because the very realization of what a nuclear war implies strengthens the resolve of the masses to fight against war. It is necessary, therefore, to warn the masses about the deadly consequences of a new world war and so arouse their righteous anger against those who are plotting this crime. The possibility of averting war is not a gift from above. Peace cannot be got by begging for it. It can be secured only by active purposeful struggle. That is why we have been waging this struggle, and will continue to do so.

The entire foreign policy of the Soviet Union is focused on strengthening peace. We have used and shall continue to use the growing might of our country not to threaten anyone, not to induce a war fever, but to pursue a steadfast policy of combating the war danger and averting world war.

We have always proceeded from the desire to maintain and extend friendly relations with all peoples for the benefit of peace, in keeping with the principles of peaceful coexistence.

Comrades, experience has demonstrated the soundness of the Leninist policy of the peaceful coexistence of countries with different social systems consistently pursued by the Soviet Union and other socialist countries. Our Party considers the policy of peaceful coexistence, which Lenin has willed us, to be the general line of its foreign policy. Peaceful coexistence is the highway in the relations between the socialist and capitalist countries.

Appendix 5

Final Declaration
of the 1954
Geneva Conference*

Final declaration, dated the 21st July, 1954, of the Geneva Conference on the problem of restoring peace in Indo-China, in which the representatives of Cambodia, the Democratic Republic of Viet-Nam, France, Laos, the People's Republic of China, the State of Viet-Nam, the Union of Soviet Socialist Republics, the United Kingdom, and the United States of America took part.

1. The Conference takes note of the agreements ending hostilities in Cambodia, Laos and Viet-Nam and organizing international control and the supervision of the execution of the provisions of these agreements.

2. The Conference expresses satisfaction at the ending of hostilities in Cambodia, Laos and Viet-Nam; the Conference expresses its conviction that the execution of the provisions set out in the present declaration and in the agreements on the cessation of hostilities will permit Cambodia, Laos and Viet-Nam henceforth to play their part, in full independence and sovereignty, in the peaceful community of nations.

3. The Conference takes note of the declarations made by the Governments of Cambodia and of Laos of their intention to adopt measures permitting all citizens to take their place in the national

* *Further documents relating to the discussion of Indo-China at the Geneva Conference, June 16–July 21, 1954*, Command Paper 9239 (London: HMSO, 1954).

community, in particular by participating in the next general elections, which, in conformity with the constitution of each of these countries, shall take place in the course of the year 1955, by secret ballot and in conditions of respect for fundamental freedoms.

4. The Conference takes note of the clauses in the agreement on the cessation of hostilities in Viet-Nam prohibiting the introduction into Viet-Nam of foreign troops and military personnel as well as of all kinds of arms and munitions. The Conference also takes note of the declarations made by the Governments of Cambodia and Laos of their resolution not to request foreign aid, whether in war material, in personnel or in instructors except for the purpose of the effective defence of their territory and, in the case of Laos, to the extent defined by the agreements on the cessation of hostilities in Laos.

5. The Conference takes note of the clauses in the agreement on the cessation of hostilities in Viet-Nam to the effect that no military base under the control of a foreign State may be established in the regrouping zones of the two parties, the latter having the obligation to see that the zones allotted to them shall not constitute part of any military alliance and shall not be utilized for the resumption of hostilities or in the service of an aggressive policy. The Conference also takes note of the declarations of the Governments of Cambodia and Laos to the effect that they will not join in any agreement with other States if this agreement includes the obligation to participate in a military alliance not in conformity with the principles of the Charter of the United Nations, or, in the case of Laos, with the principles of the agreement on the cessation of hostilities in Laos or, so long as their security is not threatened, the obligation to establish bases on Cambodian or Laotian territory for the military forces of foreign Powers.

6. The Conference recognizes that the essential purpose of the agreement relating to Viet-Nam is to settle military questions with a view to ending hostilities and that the military demarcation line is provisional and should not in any way be interpreted as constituting a political or territorial boundary. The Conference expresses its conviction that the execution of the provisions set out in the present declaration and in the agreement on the cessation of hostilities creates the necessary basis for the achievement in the

near future of a political settlement in Viet-Nam.

7. The Conference declares that, so far as Viet-Nam is concerned, the settlement of political problems, effected on the basis of respect for the principles of independence, unity and territorial integrity, shall permit the Viet-Namese people to enjoy the fundamental freedoms, guaranteed by democratic institutions established as a result of free general elections by secret ballot. In order to ensure that sufficient progress in the restoration of peace has been made and that all the necessary conditions obtain for free expression of the national will, general elections shall be held in July 1956, under the supervision of an international commission composed of representatives of the Member States of the International Supervisory Commission, referred to in the agreement on the cessation of hostilities. Consultations will be held on this subject between the competent representative authorities of the two zones from 20 July 1955 onwards.

8. The provisions of the agreements on the cessation of hostilities intended to ensure the protection of individuals and of property must be most strictly applied and must, in particular, allow everyone in Viet-Nam to decide freely in which zone he wishes to live.

9. The competent representative authorities of the Northern and Southern zones of Viet-Nam, as well as the authorities of Laos and Cambodia, must not permit any individual or collective reprisals against persons who have collaborated in any way with one of the parties during the war, or against members of such persons' families.

10. The Conference takes note of the declaration of the Government of the French Republic to the effect that it is ready to withdraw its troops from the territory of Cambodia, Laos and Viet-Nam, at the request of the governments concerned and within periods which shall be fixed by agreement between the parties except in the cases where, by agreement between the two parties, a certain number of French troops shall remain at specified points and for a specified time.

11. The Conference takes note of the declaration of the French Government to the effect that for the settlement of all the problems connected with the re-establishment and consolidation of peace in Cambodia, Laos and Viet-Nam, the French Government will pro-

ceed from the principle of respect for the independence and sovereignty, unity and territorial integrity of Cambodia, Laos and Viet-Nam.

12. In their relations with Cambodia, Laos and Viet-Nam, each member of the Geneva Conference undertakes to respect the sovereignty, the independence, the unity and the territorial integrity of the above-mentioned States, and to refrain from any interference in their internal affairs.

13. The members of the Conference agree to consult one another on any question which may be referred to them by the International Supervisory Commission in order to study such measures as may prove necessary to ensure that the agreements on the cessation of hostilities in Cambodia, Laos and Viet-Nam are respected.

Appendix 6

Two Declarations by
the Government of Laos*

Geneva, July 21, 1954

A. With reference to Article 3 of the Final Declaration:
The Royal Government of Laos

In the desire to ensure harmony and agreement among the peoples of the Kingdom,

Declares itself resolved to take the necessary measures to integrate all citizens, without discrimination, into the national community and to guarantee them the enjoyment of the rights and freedoms for which the Constitution of the Kingdom provides;

Affirms that all Laotian citizens may freely participate as electors or candidates in general elections by secret ballot;

Announces, furthermore, that it will promulgate measures to provide for special representation in the Royal Administration of the provinces of Phong Saly and Sam Neua during the interval between the cessation of hostilities and the general elections of the interests of Laotian nationals who did not support the Royal forces during hostilities.

B. With reference to Articles 4 and 5 of the Final Declaration:

The Royal Government of Laos is resolved never to pursue a policy of aggression and will never permit the territory of Laos to be used in furtherance of such a policy.

The Royal Government of Laos will never join in any agreement

*Further Documents Relating to the Discussion of Indo-China at the Geneva Conference, June 16–July 21, 1954, Command Paper 9239 (London: HMSO, 1954).

with other States if this agreement includes the obligation for the Royal Government of Laos to participate in a military alliance not in conformity with the principles of the Charter of the United Nations or with the principles of the agreement on the cessation of hostilities or, unless its security is threatened, the obligation to establish bases on Laotian territory for military forces of foreign powers.

The Royal Government of Laos is resolved to settle its international disputes by peaceful means so that international peace and security and justice are not endangered.

During the period between the cessation of hostilities in Viet Nam and the final settlement of that country's political problems, the Royal Government of Laos will not request foreign aid, whether in war material, in personnel or in instructors, except for the purpose of its effective territorial defence and to the extent defined by the agreement on the cessation of hostilities.

Appendix 7

From the
Vientiane Agreements

1. AGREEMENT OF THE JOINT POLITICAL COMMIT-
TEE ON THE QUESTION OF PEACE AND NEUTRALITY
(Unofficial English Translation)*
    The Joint Political Commision consisting of the Political Dele-
gation of the Royal Government and the Political Delegation of the
Pathet Lao Forces, which are composed of:

On the Royal Government side:
1. H. E. Ngon Sananikone,	Head of the Delegation
2. H. E. Nou Ing Rattanavong,	Member
3. H. E. Thong Soutthivongnorath,	Member
4. Mr. Thao Tane Choulamontri,	Member
5. Mr. Thao Van Tanouane,	Member
6. Mr. Inpeng Sourvathay,	Member
7. Mr. Amon Vimonphan,	Secretary

On the Pathet Lao Forces side:
1. Mr. Phoumi Vongvichit,	Head of the Delegation
2. Mr. Nouhak Phoumsavan,	Deputy Head of the Delegation
3. Mr. Singkapo Chounlamani,	Member
4. Mr. Thao Ma Khaykhamphithoun,	Member
5. Mr. Maha Khamphan Virachit,	Member
6. Mr. Apheui Chandavong,	Secretary

* *Third Interim Report on the Activities of the ICSC in Laos July 1, 1955–
May 16, 1957* (New Delhi: Government of India Press, 1958).

met at Vientiane from 25 September 1956 to seek appropriate
measures for implementation of the principles agreed upon by H.
H. Prince Souvanna Phouma, Prime Minister of the Royal Government, and H. H. Prince Souphanouvong, Representative of the
Pathet Lao Forces on 5 and 10 August 1956.

The first issue on which the two Parties deliberated was that of
peace and neutrality. In regard to this question, the Joint Declaration of 5 August 1956 said: "The two Parties are agreed on the
adoption of the foreign policy repeatedly stated by H. R. H. the
Crown Prince and H. H. Prince Souvanna Phouma and according
to which the Royal Government is resolved resolutely to follow the
path of peace and neutrality, to sincerely apply Pandit Nehru's five
principles of peaceful co-existence, to establish good relations with
all countries and in particular with neighbouring countries, to
desist from adhering to any military alliance, to allow no country
to establish military bases on the Lao territory apart from those
foreseen in the Geneva Agreement".

To realise the principles cited above, the Political Delegation of
the Royal Government and the Political Delegation of the Pathet
Lao Forces deliberated fully on the above agreed principles with
a spirit of friendliness and in an atmosphere of good mutual understanding. The two Parties acknowledge that following the signature of the two Joint Declarations of 5 and 10 August 1956, our
country sent a Royal Laotian Government's Delegation on a
courtesy visit to the People's Republic of China and to the Democratic Republic of Vietnam and achieved good results. The two
Parties unanimously acknowledge that the achievement of a policy
of peace and neutrality is of great importance and is closely connected with the destiny of our fatherland. The two Parties unanimously acknowledge that it is necessary to promote further the
achievement of the policy of peace and neutrality so that it actively
progresses in all the spheres, with all the countries of the world,
without any distinction of the different political regimes, in particular with neighbouring countries, and have agreed upon the following measures of implementation:

(1) Foster friendly relations and establish diplomatic relations
in accordance with the 5 principles of peaceful co-existence with
all countries irrespective of their political systems, so as to guaran-

tee the policy of peace and neutrality resolutely followed by our country.

In so far as it particularly concerns the immediate neighbouring countries who have already proposed to establish diplomatic relations with our country, we shall commence doing it right now and shall strive to achieve it as early as possible.

Besides, if other countries would wish to maintain good relations with our country, the latter would be glad to accept them also.

(2) Pending the establishment of diplomatic relations with the above-mentioned countries, steps shall be taken for mutual recognition, economic and cultural exchanges with the said countries, sending of delegations to make courtesy visits to those countries and at the same time welcome their delegations which will come to visit our country.

(3) At a time when we do not have as yet the possibilities of sending our ambassadors to the aforementioned countries, we shall nevertheless accept that those countries set up their embassies in our country.

(4) In order to improve the standard of living of our people and lay the foundation for an independent economy and culture for our country, we shall endeavour, right from 1957, to get the assistance of all countries which would have the good will to help unconditionally our country, that is to say on an equal footing in conditions of respect of the sovereignty of our country, without any political or economic string and without any control or supervision on the use of that aid.

(5) Our country is resolved not to adhere to any military alliance and not to permit any country to set up their military bases on Laotian territory, apart from those envisaged in the Geneva Agreement. At the same time, our country shall resolutely resist any interference whatever in the internal affairs of our country, so as to safeguard the national sovereignty and the independence.

(6) The present agreement will enter into force with effect from the date of its signature. After the signature of this agreement, the two Parties must diffuse it among the people through all the means of propaganda which they have at their disposal.

Done at Vientiane, the 2nd November 1956,
*Head of the Political
Delegation of the Royal
Government.*

(sd) H. E. NGON SANANIKONE

*Head of the Political
Delegation of the Pathet
Lao Forces.*

(sd) THAO PHOUMI VONGVICHIT

2. AGREEMENT BETWEEN THE POLITICAL DELEGA-
TION OF THE ROYAL GOVERNMENT AND THE POLITI-
CAL DELEGATION OF THE PATHET LAO FORCES
RELATING TO THE MEASURES FOR THE GUARANTEE
OF CIVIC RIGHTS OF NON-DISCRIMINATION AND OF
NON-REPRISAL FOR THE MEMBERS OF THE PATHET
LAO FORCES AND EX-PARTICIPANTS OF THE RESIS-
TANCE THROUGHOUT THE COUNTRY AND THE MEA-
SURES FOR THE INTEGRATION OF THE PATHET LAO
CADRES AND EX-PARTICIPANTS OF THE RESISTANCE
IN THE ADMINISTRATIVE AND TECHNICAL SERVICES
OF THE KINGDOM AT ALL LEVELS
(Unofficial English Translation)*
Pursuing the growing atmosphere of cordiality and good mutual
understanding; expediting the national reconciliation and solidar-
ity with a view to unifying and reconstructing the fatherland and
safeguarding the national sovereignty and independence, the Joint
Political Commission consisting of the Political Delegation of the
Royal Government and the Political Delegation of the Pathet Lao
Forces comprising of:

* *Third Interim Report on the Activities of the ICSC in Laos, July 1,
1955–May 16, 1957* (New Delhi: Government of India Press, 1958).

On the Royal Government side:

1. H. E. Ngon Sananikone.	Head of the Delegation
2. H. E. Nou Ing Rattanavong,	Member
3. H. E. Thong Soutthivongnorath,	"
4. Mr. Thao Tane Choulamontri,	"
5. Mr. Thao Van Tanouane,	"
6. Mr. Inpeng Sourvathay,	"
7. Mr. Amon Vimonphan,	Secretary

On the Pathet Lao Forces side:

1. Mr. Phoumi Vongvichit,	Head of the Delegation
2. Mr. Nouhak Phoumsavan,	Deputy Head of the Delegation
3. Mr. Singkapo Chounlamani,	Member
4. Mr. Thao Ma Khaykhamphitoun,	"
5. Mr. Maha Khamphan Virachit,	"
6. Mr. Apheui Chandavong,	Secretary

met at Vientiane from 6 November 1956 to 23rd December 1956 so as to seek the measures for implementing the principles, agreed upon by H.H. Prince Souvanna Phouma, Prime Minister of the Royal Government, and H.H. Prince Souphanouvong, Representative of the Pathet Lao Forces, in the Joint Declaration of 5 August 1956 stating in brief: "The two Parties agree that all the political organisations of the 'Pathet Lao', such as the Neo Lao Haksat Front, the organisations of the youth, women, peasants etc., can undertake their activities in the legal forms as the other political parties; that there be a guarantee of the civic rights for the 'Pathet Lao' and former participants of the resistance without discrimination; that Pathet Lao cadres and those of the former participants of the resistance be able to take part in the administrative and technical functions at all levels according to their qualifications and after agreement between the two Parties".

After having deliberated, in a thorough and detailed manner, on the aforementioned principles in spirit and in letter, the Political Delegation of the Royal Government and the Political Delegation of the Pathet Lao Forces are in agreement in acknowledging that the co-operation between the two Parties, so as to bring together

all the Laotians again in the National Community, is in itself a
co-operation on an equal footing, under satisfactory and honoura-
ble conditions for the two Parties aimed at strengthening the national solidarity, reconstructing jointly a prosperous fatherland,
and safeguarding the national sovereignty and independence.

The two Parties unanimously acknowledge that the members of
the Pathet Lao, the persons connected with the Pathet Lao Forces
and the ex-participants of the resistance throughout the country
have contributed largely to the fight for national independence,
that consequently the guarantee for civic rights, non-discrimination and non-reprisal *vis-à-vis* the members of the Pathet Lao
Forces, persons connected with the Pathet Lao Forces and ex-
participants of the resistance all over the country without any
distinction as to their being civilians, military personnel or cadres
of this service or that rank are quite in conformity with the spirit
and reason, since they will contribute to the national reconciliation
and the unification of the fatherland in conformity with the aspirations of the entire people.

Starting from this spirit of sincere co-operation, the two Parties
are unanimously in agreement to lay down as follows the measures
for the implementations of the principles enunciated above:

**Chapter I: Measures for guaranteeing the rights to exercise their
legal activities to the various political bodies of the Pathet Lao
Forces and of the ex-participants of the resistance throughout the
country.**

(1) The United National Front called 'Neo Lao Haksat' and the
organisations of youth, women, peasants and others which constitute the political bodies of the Pathet Lao Forces and ex-participants of the resistance shall have the right to exercise their legal
activities throughout the country like the other political parties as
it is stated in the Joint Declaration of 5 August 1956, by fulfilling
the necessary formalities prescribed by the Law of the Kingdom
with regard to political parties.

The Royal Government shall give the assurance that it will grant
all facilities to the Neo Lao Haksat and to the said organisations
for fulfilling all the formalities according to the regulations, for

setting up their offices and branches for publishing their newspapers, and for acquiring the legal capacity as it is stipulated in article 8 of the Law No. 48 of 13 January 1950 relating to associations.

Chapter II: Measures for guaranteeing civic rights, non-discrimination and non-reprisal for the members of the Pathet Lao Forces, persons connected with the Pathet Lao Forces and ex-participants of the resistance throughout the country.

(2) The Royal Government shall guarantee fully to all members of the Pathet Lao Forces, persons connected with the Pathet Lao Forces, and to the ex-participants of the Resistance throughout the country the use and exercise of all the rights which the Laotian citizens possess with regard to democratic freedoms such as individual freedom, freedom to speak, write and publish, freedom of movement, freedom of association and meetings, freedom of belief and electoral freedoms, envisaged in the Constitution of the Kingdom and in the Joint Declaration of 5 August 1956.

(3) The members of the Pathet Lao Forces, the persons connected with the Pathet Lao Forces and the ex-participants of the resistance throughout the country shall enjoy all the equal civic rights in the national community in the political as well as economic and legal aspects. All activities of discrimination, division and reprisals between Laotian citizens, without any distinction as to their being members of the Pathet Lao Forces, or persons connected with the Pathet Lao Forces, or ex-participants of the resistance throughout the country, shall be formally prohibited.

(4) In future, it shall be forbidden, under any pretext to indict before the Tribunal or before any body for administrative discipline about activities or assaults connected with the military, political or administrative activity indulged in, from 9 March 1945 to this day, by any civilian or military person belonging to the Royal Government or any civilian or military person, member of the Pathet Lao Forces or connected with the Pathet Lao Forces or ex-participants of the resistance throughout the country, to the exception of offences of common law.

(5) All acts assuming a character of discrimination, reprisal or prohibition opposed to the members of the Pathet Lao Forces,

persons connected with the Pathet Lao Forces and ex-participants of the resistance throughout the country, in the free exercise of democratic freedoms and their civic rights, as stipulated in points 2 and 3 above and all prosecution, arrest, slander relating to the subject matter embodied in point 4 above, shall be considered as violations of the present agreement and suits shall be filed before the Tribunal as acts of national division, acts of sabotage of the unity of the fatherland and as infringements of democratic freedoms and civic rights of the people.

If the aforementioned acts entail material damages, the culprits shall be liable, besides the penalties of imprisonment and fines, for the restitution and damages in conformity with the civil code in force in the Kingdom.

If the acts in question are directed against any person or involve human life, the culprits shall be tried according to the penal code in force in the Kingdom.

(6) The Royal side shall give the assurance that it will take into consideration the clauses of the present agreement to make of it a law for the guarantee of democratic freedoms for the people, for non-discrimination and non-reprisals against the members of the Pathet Lao Forces, persons connected with the Pathet Lao Forces and ex-participants of the resistance throughout the country.

Chapter III: Measures for the integration of the Pathet Lao cadres and ex-participants of the resistance all over the country in all the administrative and technical services of the Kingdom at all levels.

(7) The Pathet Lao cadres and ex-participants of the resistance shall be integrated in the administration and the various technical services of the Kingdom at all levels, without discrimination and on an equal footing, in all the spheres together with the officials at the various levels of the administrative and technical services in the Kingdom.

—As regards the administrative cadres and the cadres and personnel of various technical services, at different levels formed by the Pathet Lao Forces, the Royal Government will consider their period of service in the ranks of the resistance as period of service in the Royal administration, and will endeavour to integrate them with the functions, ranks and specialisations which the Pathet Lao Forces have entrusted them with, so that they be able to enjoy in all the spheres the same rights as the officials of the Royal Government of the same rank, except in certain individual cases where it might not be possible to integrate them in the said ranks and functions, and in which case the Royal Government will integrate them in other services with equivalent ranks and functions.

—As regards the Pathet Lao cadres who were formerly functionaries or mandarins (officials) of the Royal Government, their period of service in the ranks of the Resistance shall be taken into account as being the period of service in the Royal administration; they will benefit of promotions in the minimum time; and if by their merit in the resistance they have benefited of a promotion to a higher rank, or if they had to change their branch or specialisation, the maximum efforts shall be made so that they preserve the rank and function which they occupy at the moment. In certain individual cases where it would not be possible to maintain for them that rank and that function they shall have an equivalent rank and function.

(8) The diplomas (Brevets) and certificates delivered by the Pathet Lao Forces shall be considered as equivalent to the diplomas and certificates corresponding to those of the Royal Government. With regard to distinctions, decorations and medals conferred by the Pathet Lao Forces, these can be preserved at home throughout the Kingdom, so as to constitute a souvenir and a proof of merit towards the fatherland for those who hold them.

(9) The Delegation of the Pathet Lao Forces will send to the Joint Political Commission the list and curriculum vitae of the cadres of the Pathet Lao and ex-participants of the resistance throughout the country who shall be integrated in the administration and various technical services at all echelons, so as to facilitate the scrutiny for postings or appointments of these cadres individually.

(10) In order to facilitate the return to Vientiane and in the various provinces of the cadres of the Pathet Lao and ex-participants of the resistance all over the country, the Royal Government will take upon itself to help them in the field of supplies, security

and transport in the course of their journey in a suitable manner according to their functions and ranks.

(11) A Joint Administrative Sub-Committee, consisting of 2 representatives of each Party and depending on the Joint Political Commission, shall be created with the task of classifying the functions, ranks and specialisations for the cadres of the Pathet Lao and ex-participants of the resistance who have to be integrated in the administration and technical services at all echelons and to propose them for the decision of the Joint Political Commission. The Royal Government will base itself on the decisions of the Joint Political Commission with regard to the functions, ranks and specialisations of cadres of the Pathet Lao and ex-participants of the resistance to adopt decrees for the corresponding postings. This Sub-committee shall be wound up after the successful completion of its duties.

Chapter IV: Implementation of the Agreement.

(12) The present Agreement will enter into force with effect from the date of its signature. The two Parties undertake the obligation of giving it wide publicity through all the means of propaganda of which they dispose so as to make it known to the entire people and to issue orders to the agents, competent and responsible for all the ranks and services so that they implement rigorously, each in his sphere, the present agreement. At the same time, Joint Political teams shall be created with the task of going on the spot to publicise and make the people understand thoroughly all the signed agreements so as to maintain and further strengthen day by day the spirit of national reconciliation.

SIGNED AT VIENTIANE, 24 *December* 1956.

The Head of the Royal Government   *The Head of the Pathet Lao*
   Political Delegation.   *Political Delegation,*
Sd/- H. E. NGON SANANIKONE   Sd/- PHOUMI VONGVICHIT

Appendix 8

Joint Communiqué of the Three Princes on the Formation of a Government of National Union*

Zurich, June 22, 1961

As agreed between them on 18 June last, the three Princes, Souvanna Phouma, Boun Oum and Souphanouvong, being the high representatives of the three parties in Laos, met at Zurich on 19 June and thereafter to discuss the problem of achieving national concord by the formation of a Government of National Union. The three Princes discussed successively the political program of the provisional Government of National Union and its immediate tasks.

With regard to these two matters, the three Princes agreed as follows:

I. *Political Program*

The Kingdom of Laos is resolved to follow the path of peace and

* *International Conference on the Settlement of the Laotian Question,* Command Paper 1828 (London: HMSO, October 1962).

neutrality in conformity with the interests and aspirations of the Laotian people and with the Geneva Agreements of 1954, in order to build a peaceful, neutral, independent, democratic, unified and prosperous Laos. A provisional Government of National Union will be formed, which will give effect to this policy of peace and neutrality, by carrying out the following political program:

Domestic Policy:

(1) To implement the cease-fire agreement concluded between the three parties concerned in Laos and to see that peace is restored in the country.

(2) To give full effect to democratic freedoms for the benefit of the people and to abrogate all provisions contrary to such freedoms; to bring back into force the law on the democratic freedoms of citizens and the electoral law approved by the National Assembly in 1957.

(3) To preserve the unity, neutrality, independence and sovereignty of the nation.

(4) To ensure justice and peace for all citizens of the Kingdom with a view to appeasement and national concord without discrimination as to origin or political allegiance.

(5) To bring about the unification of the armed forces of the three parties in a single National Army in accordance with a program agreed between the parties.

(6) To develop agriculture, industry and crafts, to provide means of communication and transport, to promote culture and to concentrate attention on improving the standard of living of the people.

Foreign Policy:

(1) Resolutely to apply the five principles of peaceful coexistence in foreign relations, to establish friendly relations and to develop diplomatic relations with all countries, the neighboring countries first and foremost, on the basis of equality and the sovereignty of Laos.

(2) Not to join in any alliance or military coalition and not to allow the establishment of any foreign military base on Laotian territory, it being understood that a special study will be made of what is provided in the Geneva Agreements of 1954; not to allow any country to use Laotian territory for military purposes; and not

to recognize the protection of any alliance or military coalition.

(3) Not to allow any foreign interference in the internal affairs of Laos in any form whatsoever; to require the withdrawal from Laos of all foreign troops and military personnel; and not to allow any foreign troops or military personnel to be introduced into Laos.

(4) To accept direction and unconditional aid from all countries that wish to help Laos build up an independent and autonomous national economy on the basis of respect for Laotian sovereignty.

(5) To respect the treaties and agreements signed in conformity with the interests of the Laotian people and of the policy of peace and neutrality of the Kingdom, in particular the Geneva Agreements of 1954, and to abrogate all treaties and agreements which are contrary to those principles.

II. *Immediate Tasks*

The provisional Government of National Union will carry out the following immediate tasks:

(1) Formation of a Government delegation to take part in the International Conference on the settlement of the Laotian question.

(2) Implementation of the cease-fire and restoration of peace throughout the country.

(3) Fulfillment of the undertakings entered into on behalf of Laos at the International Conference on the settlement of the Laotian question and faithful execution of the agreements concluded between the three parties concerned in Laos.

(4) Release of all political prisoners and detainees.

(5) Holding of general elections to the National Assembly for the formation of the definitive Government.

(6) During the transitional period, the administrative organs set up during the hostilities will be provisionally left in being.

As regards the formation of the Government of National Union the three Princes agreed on the following principles:

(1) The Government of National Union will include representatives of the three parties and will be provisional.

(2) It will be formed in accordance with a special procedure by direct designation and nomination by His Majesty the King, without reference to the National Assembly.

Exchanges of views on this matter will be continued between the three Princes at further meetings, in order to achieve national reconciliation as soon as possible.

Done at Zurich, This Twenty-second Day of June 1961.

Signed:

PRINCE SOUVANNA PHOUMA

PRINCE BOUN OUM

PRINCE SOUPHANOUVONG

Appendix 9

Three Princes' Agreement on Formation of the Provisional Government of National Union*

In pursuance of the joint communiqués of Zurich, Hin Heup, Plaine des Jarres and Geneva, Their Highnesses Tiao Souvanna, Chao Boun Oum and Tiao Souphanouvong in the capacity of High Representatives of the three forces of the Kingdom of Laos, met on 7, 8 and 11 June 1962 at Plaine des Jarres to discuss the problem of the formation of Provisional Government of National Union.

The three Princes have agreed upon the following:

1. *FORM:*

   (a) The Provisional Government of National Union will be presided by Prince Souvanna Phouma.

   (b) Prince Souphanouvong and General Phoumi Nosavan will be Vice-Presidents of the Council in the Government.

   (c) The Provisional Governments of National Union will consist of 12 departments:

   1. Ministry of National Defense, War Veterans and Rural Affairs.

*Appendix to Report No. 19, June 27, 1962, from the ICSC in Laos to the Co-chairmen of the Geneva Conference.

     2.   Ministry of Home and Social Welfare.
     3.   Ministry of External Affairs.
     4.   Ministry of Finance.
     5.   Ministry of Information, Publicity and Tourism.
     6.   Ministry of National Education, Fine Arts, Sports and Youth.
     7.   Ministry of Justice.
     8.   Ministry of Public Health.
     9.   Ministry of Public Works and Transport.
    10. Ministry of Posts and Telecommunications.
    11. Ministry of Religious Affairs.
    12. Ministry of Economy and Planning.

(d) Seven Secretaries of State:

     1.   National Education, Sports, Youth and Fine Arts.
     2.   Finance.
     3.   Social Welfare.
     4.   Public Works and Transports.
     5.   Economy and Planning.
     6.   War Veterans.
     7.   Rural Affairs.

2. The allotment of portfolios between the parties will be made in the following manner:

(a) The Group of Prince Souvanna Phouma will hold 8 ministerial posts with three Secretaries of State:

Ministry of National Defense, War Veterans and Rural Affairs.
Ministry of Interior and Social Welfare.
Ministry of External Affairs.
Ministry of Justice.
Ministry of Public Works and Transport.
Ministry of Religious Affairs.
Ministry of Public Health.
Ministry of Posts and Telecommunications.
Secretary of State for Social Welfare.
Secretary of State for Rural Affairs.
Secretary of State for War Veterans.

Their selection will be made as follows:

Three Ministers and a Secretary of State will be chosen from among the neutralists residing outside Xieng Khouang.

The three Princes agreed to entrust the three important departments of National Defense, Interior and External Affairs to the personalities belonging to the party of Prince Souvanna Phouma. All decisions concerning these three departments will have to be sanctioned by unanimous agreement made by the three Heads of groups.

(b) The Neo Lao Haksat will have the following two ministerial posts and two Secretaries of State:

Ministry of Information, Publicity and Tourism.
Ministry of Economy and Planning.

Secretary of State for Economy and Planning.
Secretary of State for Public Works and Transports.

(c) The party of Prince Boun Oum will have two ministerial posts and two Secretaries of State:

Ministry of Finance.
Ministry of Education, Fine Arts and Sports & Youth.

Secretary of State for Finance.
Secretary of State for Education, Fine Arts and Sports & Youth.

3. *COMPOSITION:* (See composition given yesterday)

4. The three Princes agreed that the Provisional Government of National Union will be in conformity with the provisions stipulated in the joint communiqué of Zurich.

5. All decisions of the Provisional Government of National Union will be taken with an unanimous vote.

6. Prince Souvanna Phouma was entrusted by the three Princes to submit the formula of the Provisional Government of National Union to H.M. the King and solicit the subsequent royal Nomination.

Prince Souvanna Phouma will fix the venue and date of the first meeting of the Provisional Government of National Union thus formed, to choose a delegation of the Kingdom of Laos to the Geneva Conference.

The first meeting of the Provisional Government of National Union shall be held 10 days after the signing of the present agreement.

7. The present agreement shall come into force from the date of signing the Agreement.

Made at Plaine des Jarres on 12 June 1962.

PRINCE SOUPHANOUVONG   PRINCE SOUVANNA PHOUMA
PRINCE BOUN OUM

Appendix 10

Declaration on the Neutrality of Laos*

Geneva, July 23, 1962

The Governments of the Union of Burma, the Kingdom of Cambodia, Canada, the People's Republic of China, the Democratic Republic of Vietnam, the Republic of France, the Republic of India, the Polish People's Republic, the Republic of Vietnam, the Kingdom of Thailand, the Union of Soviet Socialist Republics, the United Kingdom of Great Britain and Northern Ireland and the United States of America, whose representatives took part in the International Conference on the Settlement of the Laotian Question, 1961–1962;

Welcoming the presentation of the statement of neutrality by the Royal Government of Laos of July 9, 1962, and taking note of this statement, which is, with the concurrence of the Royal Government of Laos, incorporated in the present Declaration as an integral part thereof, and the text of which is as follows:

The Royal Government of Laos, being resolved to follow the path of peace and neutrality in conformity with the interests and aspirations of the Laotian people, as well as the principles of the Joint Communiqué of Zurich dated June 22, 1961, and of the Geneva Agreements of 1954, in order to build a peaceful, neutral, independent, democratic, unified and prosperous Laos, solemnly declares that:

*Treaty Series No. 27 (1963), *Declaration and Protocol on the Neutrality of Laos, Geneva, July 23, 1962,* Cmnd. 2025 (London: HMSO, May 1963).

(1) It will resolutely apply the five principles of peaceful coexistence in foreign relations, and will develop friendly relations and establish diplomatic relations with all countries, the neighboring countries first and foremost, on the basis of equality and of respect for the independence and sovereignty of Laos;

(2) It is the will of the Laotian people to protect and ensure respect for the sovereignty, independence, neutrality, unity, and territorial integrity of Laos;

(3) It will not resort to the use or threat of force in any way which might impair the peace of other countries, and will not interfere in the internal affairs of other countries;

(4) It will not enter into any military alliance or into any agreement, whether military or otherwise, which is inconsistent with the neutrality of the Kingdom of Laos; it will not allow the establishment of any foreign military base on Laotian territory, nor allow any country to use Laotian territory for military purposes of interference in the internal affairs of other countries, nor recognize the protection of any alliance or military coalition, including SEATO;

(5) It will not allow any foreign interference in the internal affairs of the Kingdom of Laos in any form whatsoever;

(6) Subject to the provisions of Article 5 of the Protocol, it will require the withdrawal from Laos of all foreign troops and military personnel, and will not allow any foreign troops or military personnel to be introduced into Laos;

(7) It will accept direction and unconditional aid from all countries that wish to help the Kingdom of Laos build up an independent and autonomous national economy on the basis of respect for the sovereignty of Laos;

(8) It will respect the treaties and agreements signed in conformity with the interests of the Laotian people and of the policy of peace and neutrality of the Kingdom of Laos, in particular the Geneva Agreements of 1962, and will abrogate all treaties and agreements which are contrary to those principles.

This statement of neutrality by the Royal Government of Laos shall be promulgated constitutionally and shall have the force of law.

The Kingdom of Laos appeals to all the States participating in the International Conference on the Settlement of the Laotian Question, and to all other States, to recognize the sovereignty, independence, neutrality, unity and territorial integrity of Laos, to conform to these principles in all respects, and to refrain from any action inconsistent therewith.

Confirming the principles of respect for the sovereignty, independence, unity and territorial integrity of the Kingdom of Laos and non-interference in its internal affairs which are embodied in the Geneva Agreements of 1954;

Emphasizing the principle of respect for the neutrality of the Kingdom of Laos;

Agreeing that the above-mentioned principles constitute a basis for the peaceful settlement of the Laotian question;

Profoundly convinced that the independence and neutrality of the Kingdom of Laos will assist the peaceful democratic development of the Kingdom of Laos and the achievement of national accord and unity in that country, as well as the strengthening of peace and security in Southeast Asia;

1. Solemnly declare, in accordance with the will of the Government and people of the Kingdom of Laos, as expressed in the statement of neutrality by the Royal Government of Laos of July 9, 1962, that they recognize and will respect and observe in every way the sovereignty, independence, neutrality, unity and territorial integrity of the Kingdom of Laos.

2. Undertake, in particular that

(a) they will not commit or participate in any way in any act which might directly or indirectly impair the sovereignty, independence, neutrality, unity or territorial integrity of the Kingdom of Laos;

(b) they will not resort to the use or threat of force or any other measures which might impair the peace of the Kingdom of Laos;

(c) they will refrain from all direct or indirect interference in the internal affairs of the Kingdom of Laos;

(d) they will not attach conditions of a political nature to any assistance which they may offer or which the Kingdom of Laos may seek;

(e) they will not bring the Kingdom of Laos in any way into any military alliance or any other agreement, whether military or otherwise, which is inconsistent with her neutrality, nor invite or encourage her to enter into any such alliance or to conclude any such agreement;

(f) they will respect the wish of the Kingdom of Laos not to recognize the protection of any alliance or military coalition, including SEATO;

(g) they will not introduce into the Kingdom of Laos foreign troops or military personnel in any form whatsoever, nor will they in any way facilitate or connive at the introduction of any foreign troops or military personnel;

(h) they will not establish nor will they in any way facilitate or connive at the establishment in the Kingdom of Laos of any foreign military base, foreign strong point or other foreign military installation of any kind;

(i) they will not use the territory of the Kingdom of Laos for interference in the internal affairs of other countries;

(j) they will not use the territory of any country, including their own, for interference in the internal affairs of the Kingdom of Laos.

3. Appeal to all other States to recognize, respect and observe in every way the sovereignty, independence and neutrality, and also the unity and territorial integrity, of the Kingdom of Laos and to refrain from any action inconsistent with these principles or with other provisions of the present Declaration.

4. Undertake, in the event of a violation or threat of violation of the sovereignty, independence, neutrality, unity or territorial integrity of the Kingdom of Laos, to consult jointly with the Royal Government of Laos and among themselves in order to consider measures which might prove to be necessary to ensure the observance of these principles and the other provisions of the present Declaration.

5. The present Declaration shall enter into force on signature and together with the statement of neutrality of the Royal Government of Laos of July 9, 1962, shall be regarded as constituting an international agreement. The present Declaration shall be deposited in the archives of the Governments of the United Kingdom

and the Union of Soviet Socialist Republics, which shall furnish certified copies thereof to the other signatory States and to all the other States of the world.

In witness whereof, the undersigned Plenipotentiaries have signed the present Declaration.

Done in two copies in Geneva this twenty-third day of July one thousand nine hundred and sixty-two in the English, Chinese, French, Lao and Russian languages, each text being equally authoritative.

U THI HAN (Burma), NHIEK TIOULONG (Cambodia), H. C. GREEN (Canada), CHEN YI (China), UNG VAN KHIEM (Democratic Republic of Vietnam), M. COUVE DE MURVILLE (France), V. K. KRISHNA MENON (India), A. RAPACKI (Poland), VU VAN MAU (Republic of Vietnam), DIRECK JAYANAMA (Thailand), A. GROMYKO (Union of Soviet Socialist Republics), HOME (United Kingdom), DEAN RUSK (United States)

Appendix 11

Protocol to the Declaration on the Neutrality of Laos

The Governments of the Union of Burma, the Kingdom of Cambodia, Canada, the People's Republic of China, the Democratic Republic of Vietnam, the Republic of France, the Republic of India, the Kingdom of Laos, the Polish People's Republic, the Republic of Vietnam, the Kingdom of Thailand, the Union of Soviet Socialist Republics, the United Kingdom of Great Britain and Northern Ireland and the United States of America;

Having regard to the Declaration on the Neutrality of Laos of July 23, 1962;

Have agreed as follows:

Article 1. For the purposes of this Protocol

(a) the term "foreign military personnel" shall include members of foreign military missions, foreign military advisers, experts, instructors, consultants, technicians, observers and any other foreign military persons, including those serving in any armed forces in Laos, and foreign civilians connected with the supply, maintenance, storing and utilization of war materials;

(b) the term "the Commission" shall mean the International Commission for Supervision and Control in Laos set up by virtue of the Geneva Agreements of 1954 and composed of the representatives of Canada, India and Poland, with the representative of India as Chairman;

(c) the term "the Co-Chairmen" shall mean the Co-Chairmen of the International Conference for the Settlement of the Laotian Question, 1961–1962, and their successors in the

offices of Her Britannic Majesty's Principal Secretary of
State for Foreign Affairs and Minister for Foreign Affairs
of the Union of Soviet Socialist Republics respectively;
(d) the term "the members of the Conference" shall mean the
Governments of countries which took part in the International Conference for the Settlement of the Laotian Question, 1961–1962.

Article 2. All foreign regular and irregular troops, foreign
paramilitary formations and foreign military personnel shall be
withdrawn from Laos in the shortest time possible and in any case
the withdrawal shall be completed not later than thirty days after
the Commission has notified the Royal Government of Laos that
in accordance with Articles 3 and 10 of this Protocol its inspection
teams are present at all points of withdrawal from Laos. These
points shall be determined by the Royal Government of Laos in
accordance with Article 3 within thirty days after the entry into
force of this Protocol. The inspection teams shall be present at
these points and the Commission shall notify the Royal Government of Laos therof within fifteen days after the points have been
determined.

Article 3. The withdrawal of foreign regular and irregular
troops, foreign para-military formations and foreign military personnel shall take place only along such routes and through such
points as shall be determined by the Royal Government of Laos in
consultation with the Commission. The Commission shall be
notified in advance of the point and time of all such withdrawals.

Article 4. The introduction of foreign regular and irregular
troops, foreign para-military formations and foreign military personnel into Laos is prohibited.

Article 5. Note is taken that the French and Laotian Governments will conclude as soon as possible an arrangement to transfer
the French military installations in Laos to the Royal Government
of Laos.

If the Laotian Government considers it necessary, the French
Government may as an exception leave in Laos for a limited period
of time a precisely limited number of French military instructors
for the purpose of training the armed forces of Laos.

The French and Laotian Governments shall inform the members of the Conference, through the Co-Chairmen, of their agreement on the question of transfer of the French military installations in Laos and of the employment of French military instructors by the Laotian Government.

Article 6. The introduction into Laos of armaments, munitions and war material generally, except such quantities of conventional armaments as the Royal Government of Laos may consider necessary for the national defense of Laos, is prohibited.

Article 7. All foreign military persons and civilians captured or interned during the course of hostilities in Laos shall be released within thirty days after the entry into force of this Protocol and handed over by the Royal Government of Laos to the representatives of the Governments of the countries of which they are nationals in order that they may proceed to the destination of their choice.

Article 8. The Co-Chairmen shall periodically receive reports from the Commission. In addition the Commission shall immediately report to the Co-Chairmen any violations or threats of violations of this Protocol, all significant steps which it takes in pursuance of this Protocol, and also any other important information which may assist the Co-Chairmen in carrying out their functions. The Commission may at any time seek help from the Co-Chairmen in the performance of its duties, and the Co-Chairmen may at any time make recommendations to the Commission exercising general guidance.

The Co-Chairmen shall circulate the reports and any other important information from the Commission to the members of the Conference.

The Co-Chairmen shall exercise supervision over the observance of this Protocol and the Declaration of the Neutrality of Laos.

The Co-Chairmen will keep the members of the Conference constantly informed and when appropriate will consult with them.

Article 9. The Commission shall, with the concurrence of the Royal Government of Laos, supervise and control the cease-fire in Laos.

The Commission shall exercise these functions in full cooperation with the Royal Government of Laos and within the framework

of the Cease-Fire Agreement or cease-fire arrangements made by
the three political forces in Laos, or the Royal Government of
Laos. It is understood that responsibility for the execution of the
cease-fire shall rest with the three parties concerned and with the
Royal Government of Laos after its formation.

Article 10. The Commission shall supervise and control the
withdrawal of foreign regular and irregular troops, foreign para-
military formations and foreign military personnel. Inspection
teams sent by the Commission for these purposes shall be present
for the period of the withdrawal at all points of withdrawal from
Laos determined by the Royal Government of Laos in consultation
with the Commission in accordance with Article 3 of this Protocol.

Article 11. The Commission shall investigate cases where there
are reasonable grounds for considering that a violation of the provisions of Article 4 of this Protocol has occurred.

It is understood that in the exercise of this function the Commission is acting with the concurrence of the Royal Government of
Laos. It shall carry out its investigations in full cooperation with
the Royal Government of Laos and shall immediately inform the
Co-Chairmen of any violations or threats of violations of Article
4, and also of all significant steps which it takes in pursuance of
this Article in accordance with Article 8.

Article 12. The Commission shall assist the Royal Government
of Laos in cases where the Royal Government of Laos considers
that a violation of Article 6 of this Protocol may have taken place.
This assistance will be rendered at the request of the Royal Government of Laos and in full cooperation with it.

Article 13. The Commission shall exercise its functions under
this Protocol in close cooperation with the Royal Government of
Laos. It is understood that the Royal Government of Laos at all
levels will render the Commission all possible assistance in the
performance by the Commission of these functions and also will
take all necessary measures to ensure the security of the Commission and its inspection teams during their activities in Laos.

Article 14. The Commission functions as a single organ of the
International Conference for the Settlement of the Laotian Question, 1961–1962. The members of the Commission will work har-
moniously and in cooperation with each other with the aim of

solving all questions within the terms of reference of the Commission.

Decisions of the Commission on questions relating to violations of Articles 2, 3, 4, and 6 of this Protocol or of the cease-fire referred to in Article 9, conclusions on major questions sent to the Co-Chairmen and all recommendations by the Commission shall be adopted unanimously. On other questions, including procedural questions, and also questions relating to the initiation and carrying out of investigations (Article 15), decisions of the Commission shall be adopted by majority vote.

Artilce 15. In the exercise of its specific functions which are laid down in the relevant articles of this Protocol the Commission shall conduct investigations (directly or by sending inspection teams), when there are reasonable grounds for considering that a violation has occurred. These investigations shall be carried out at the request of the Royal Government of Laos or on the initiative of the Commission, which is acting with the concurrence of the Royal Government of Laos.

In the latter case decisions on initiating and carrying out such investigations shall be taken in the Commission by majority vote.

The Commission shall submit agreed reports on investigations in which differences which may emerge between members of the Commission on particular questions may be expressed.

The conclusions and recommendations of the Commission resulting from investigations shall be adopted unanimously.

Article 16. For the exercise of its functions the Commission shall, as necessary, set up inspection teams, on which the three member-states of the Commission shall be equally represented. Each member-state of the Commission shall ensure the presence of its own representatives both on the Commission and on the inspection teams, and shall promptly replace them in the event of their being unable to perform their duties.

It is understood that the dispatch of inspection teams to carry out various specific tasks takes place with the concurrence of the Royal Government of Laos. The points to which the Commission and its inspection teams go for the purpose of investigation and their length of stay at those points shall be determined in relation to the requirements of the particular investigation.

Article 17. The Commission shall have at its disposal the means of communication and transport required for the performance of its duties. These as a rule will be provided to the Commission by the Royal Government of Laos for payment on mutually acceptable terms, and those which the Royal Government of Laos cannot provide will be acquired by the Commission from other sources. It is understood that the means of communication and transport will be under the administrative control of the Commission.

Article 18. The costs of the operations of the Commission shall be borne by the members of the Conference in accordance with the provisions of this article.

(a)   The Governments of Canada, India and Poland shall pay the personal salaries and allowances of their nationals who are members of their delegations to the Commission and its subsidiary organs.

(b)   The primary responsibility for the provision of accommodation for the Commission and its subsidiary organs shall rest with the Royal Government of Laos, which shall also provide such other local services as may be appropriate. The Commission shall charge to the Fund referred to in subparagraph (c) below any local expenses not borne by the Royal Government of Laos.

(c)   All other capital or running expenses incurred by the Commission in the exercise of its functions shall be met from a Fund to which all the members of the Conference shall contribute in the following proportions:

The Governments of the People's Republic of China, France, the Union of Soviet Socialist Republics, the United Kingdom and the United States of America shall contribute 17.6 percent each.

The Governments of Burma, Cambodia, the Democratic Republic of Vietnam, Laos, the Republic of Vietnam and Thailand shall contribute 1.5 per cent each.

The Governments of Canada, India and Poland as members of the Commission shall contribute 1 per cent each.

Article 19. The Co-Chairmen shall at any time, if the Royal Government of Laos so requests, and in any case not later than three years after the entry into force of this Protocol, present a

Appendix 11

report with appropriate recommendations on the question of the termination of the Commission to the members of the Conference for their consideration. Before making such a report the Co-Chairmen shall hold consultations with the Royal Government of Laos and with the Commisssion.

Article 20. This Protocol shall enter into force on signature. It shall be deposited in the archives of the Governments of the United Kingdom and the Union of Soviet Socialist Republics, which shall furnish certified copies thereof to the other signatory States and to all other States of the world.

In witness whereof, the undersigned Plenipotentiaries have signed this Protocol.

Done in two copies in Geneva this twenty-third day of July one thousand and nine hundred and sixty-two in the English, Chinese, French, Lao and Russian languages, each text being equally authoritative.

U THI HAN (Burma), NHIEK TIOULONG (Cambodia), H. C. GREEN (Canada), CHEN YI (China), UNG VAN KHIEM (Democratic Republic of Vietnam), M. COUVE DE MURVILLE (France), V. K. KRISHNA MENON (India), A. RAPACKI (Poland), VU VAN MAU (Republic of Vietnam), DIRECK JAYANAMA (Thailand), A. GROMYKO (Union of Soviet Socialist Republics), HOME (United Kingdom), DEAN RUSK (United States), Q. PHOLSENA (Laos)

Index

About the Author

MAREK THEE was born in 1918 and studied journalism, international relations and contemporary history at the University of Warsaw and at the Higher Schools of Foreign Service and Social Science at Warsaw. In addition to his posts with the International Commission for Supervision and Control in Indochina in 1955, 1956–57 and 1961–63, he served as consular and press attaché at the Polish consulates in Jerusalem and Tel Aviv (1946–49) and was in charge of the General Consulate of Poland in Tel Aviv (1949–52). From 1953 to 1968 he was attached to the Polish Institute of International Affairs in Warsaw. He left Poland in 1968 and has since been working as research fellow at the International Peace Research Institute in Oslo, Norway.